I0883404

HERNANDO COLÓN'S NEW WORLD OF BOOKS

HERNANDO COLÓN'S NEW WORLD OF BOOKS

TOWARD A CARTOGRAPHY OF KNOWLEDGE

José María Pérez Fernández
Edward Wilson-Lee

Yale
UNIVERSITY PRESS

New Haven & London

Published with assistance from the foundation established in memory
of James Wesley Cooper of the Class of 1865, Yale College.

Copyright © 2021 by Yale University.
All rights reserved.
This book may not be reproduced, in whole or in part,
including illustrations, in any form (beyond that copying
permitted by Sections 107 and 108 of the U.S. Copyright Law
and except by reviewers for the public press), without
written permission from the publishers.

Hernando Colón's catalogue symbols
© Patrimonio Nacional. Used by permission.

Yale University Press books may be purchased in
quantity for educational, business, or promotional use.
For information, please e-mail sales.press@yale.edu
(U.S. office) or sales@yaleup.co.uk (U.K. office).

Set in MT Baskerville and MT Bulmer types
by Tseng Information Systems, Inc.
Printed in the United States of America.

Library of Congress Control Number: 2020935984
ISBN 978-0-300-23041-3 (hardcover : alk. paper)

A catalogue record for this book is available from the British Library.

This paper meets the requirements of
ANSI/NISO Z39.48-1992 (Permanence of Paper).

10 9 8 7 6 5 4 3 2 1

CONTENTS

Acknowledgments, vii

Introduction, 1

CHAPTER ONE
Life in the Library, 15

CHAPTER TWO
Trade Secrets, 55

CHAPTER THREE
Cartography, 97

CHAPTER FOUR
New World Order, 125

CHAPTER FIVE
After Hernando, 167

Appendixes: Primary Texts, 199

ONE: Juan Pérez's *Memoria*, 201
TWO: Hernando's Will, 227
THREE: Hernando's Proposal to King Ferdinand for a Voyage around the World, 238
FOUR: Hernando's Appointment as the Coordinator for the Elaboration of a New Version of the *Padrón Real*, 243
FIVE: Hernando's *Memorial al Emperador*, 245

Notes, 249
Bibliography, 293
Index, 315

ACKNOWLEDGMENTS

Attempting to cover the extraordinary geographic and intellectual scope of Hernando Colón's activities would of course be impossible without the assistance and collaboration of a wide range of institutions and individual experts, and one of the great pleasures of this project has been the opportunity afforded to work with people of extraordinary generosity and talent from across the globe and from every discipline. This project began its life in a workshop held at the Parker Library at Corpus Christi College Cambridge, and we are grateful to the host, Christopher de Hamel, and the participants for helping us to scope out this vast undertaking: Brian Cummings, Vittoria Feola, Andrew Hadfield, Ana Carolina Hosne, Tess Knighton, Alexander Marr, Miguel Martinez, David McKitterick, Andrew Pettegree, and Jason Scott-Warren. At subsequent conferences and in private consultations we have also benefited from the advice, input, and encouragement of a countless number, including Anne J. Cruz, Andrew Hadfield, Neil Rhodes, Rocío G. Sumillera, and Greg Walker, as well as many others.

During the course of research on the book, both authors benefited from the crucial support of a number of institutions: a Villa i Tatti Berenson

Fellowship, a European University Institute Visiting Fellowship, a Renaissance Society of America Patricia H. Labalme Fellowship (held at the Fondazione Cini), a Visiting Fellowship from Sidney Sussex College, Cambridge (for José María Pérez Fernández), and a British Academy Mid-Career Fellowship (for Edward Wilson-Lee).

As a book about libraries, this project involved doing research in some of the most extraordinary collections in the world, and we were constantly humbled by the generosity and expertise of those working there. First mention certainly deserves to go to the Biblioteca Capitular y Colombina and its director Dra. Nuria Casquete de Prado, as well as its team of extraordinary librarians. We are also grateful for the support of the rare books librarians at the University Library, Cambridge; Christine Grafinger and the librarians and archivists of the Biblioteca Vaticana and the Achivio Segreto Vaticano, as well as for the assistance of Kirsi Salonen and Patrick Zutshi in navigating these collections; the librarians at the Fondazione Cini; at the Biblioteca Capitular, Salamanca; at the Archivo General de Simancas; at the Archivo de Indias; at the Archivo Histórico Provincial de Sevilla; at the Biblioteca Marciana; and both David McKitterick and Nicolas Bell at the Wren Library in Trinity College, Cambridge. A late but very substantial debt has been incurred to Matthew Driscoll, Guy Lazure, Kıvılcım Yavuz, and the faculty of the Arnamagnæan Institute at the University of Copenhagen, who were kind enough to share with us their discovery of the scribal copy of Hernando's *Libro de los Epítomes* in their collection and to allow us to work with it toward the first published account of the discovery, given here.

We are immensely grateful for the support of the wonderful team at Yale University Press, including our editor Sarah Miller, Ash Lago, Susan Laity, and Eliza Childs: the time and the attention they have all invested in our text has unquestionably turned it into a much better book. We are hugely indebted also to the anonymous readers of the volume for their generous, thoughtful readings of the text at various stages during its articulation. Working on the printed book in its early life impresses upon one the extent to which these objects are very much the product of a group, and we thank all those who have contributed to the present book.

HERNANDO COLÓN'S
NEW WORLD OF BOOKS

INTRODUCTION

The image of Christopher Columbus defiantly opposing the willful, ignorant adherents of tradition and setting sail with little more than transcendent logic is one of the totemic moments in the story of Western modernity. It is a figure that was first sketched by his younger and illegitimate son, Hernando Colón, when many years after his father's death he wrote a biography of the man he idolized: "He believed that as all the water and the land in the universe formed a sphere, it could be circumnavigated from West to East, a man walking each way until they came toe to toe, the one facing the other on the opposite side of the world."[1] This image of Columbus as a simple man whose great conception would drive him toward a sublime and universal act, making the world at once both complete and enclosed, would loom large over Enlightenment claims of European superiority, Romantic ideas of individual genius, and post-industrial accounts of modernity. It has also been assailed, almost since its first expression, as only a truly totemic image ever is: with assertions that Columbus was not the first to make the voyage west across the uncrossable Ocean, with the slow and gradual revelation of those deep and fanatical investments in late medieval orthodoxies omitted from his son's account but central to Columbus's thinking, and with the evaporation of confidence, in the aftermath of the world wars, that European modernity was inspired, justified the means it used, or was even desirable.

Part of the history of this fallen idol, however, remains largely unknown—namely, how this totemic image was formed in the world of Columbus's son Hernando, who himself expressed a similar vision in a 1511 proposal to complete the circumnavigation of the globe planned by his father. Years after his father's death—but years before he would attribute these thoughts to Columbus in his groundbreaking biography—Hernando wrote to King Ferdinand that after "the performance of this voyage . . . all the generations and people of the world will benefit from it as a whole, because they will finally experience what our predecessors were in ignorance of: the roundness of the world, how it can everywhere be navigated and inhabited, and many other important secrets that will be revealed as a result of this voyage, the knowledge from which will result in great advantages to all peoples."[2] Ferdinand's response to the twenty-three-year-old Hernando's proposal was tepid, and the eventual Spanish voyage of circumnavigation would be led by Magellan rather than a member of the Columbus clan, although the findings and consequences of the expedition would later become Hernando's responsibility in his post as the head of the Spanish mapmaking factory, the Casa de Contratación. But the circumnavigation of the world was not the only possible world-changing act of completion, and Hernando would spend the rest of his life embarking time and again on projects that worked through unprecedented fullness toward a state of total control: accurate cosmographic and cartographic pictures of the world in miniature; a full account of every word in Latin; an enclosed garden of all plants; and, finally, the building of a universal library which was to contain every part of human knowledge—in his own formulation, "all the books, in all languages and disciplines, that can be found within Christendom and beyond"—and also an unparalleled collection of printed images and music in addition to its texts in manuscript and print. This project, like the circumnavigation that eluded his father, was intended to bind the totality of everything within a circumscribed space, and in doing so to confer upon Spain and Christendom a tool of immense power.

Hernando's universal library, like his father's plan for universal navigation, emerged from a broader cultural fascination with the universal, a fascination that blended Christian eschatology with Scholastic and humanistic thought not only to imagine universal history, conversion, peace, conquest, and empire but also to construct engines for their execution. The idea of universal knowledge, of a total language as a single method for global communication that would bring together the natural and the social spaces of creation, was already important in Augustine's vision of history and human communities. In *The City of God* he laments the problem of human communication caused by the post-Babelian diversity of languages and invokes the concept of a *world community* as "the third stage in the hierarchy of human associations: first we have the home, then the city, finally the globe."[3] As we shall see, this idea was taken up by a number of Hernando's contemporaries. One of his librarians was to frame a plan for the conversion of the world, starting in Muslim North Africa, using the latest humanistic techniques for language instruction and rhetorical persuasion; close to where Hernando founded his library in Seville, the Franciscan friar Jacobo de Testera was creating pictographic materials for evangelization to achieve the same ends with native Americans.[4]

Even before Hernando envisioned a universal repository of knowledge, others had embarked on similar projects to harness the power of print. In Nuremberg in 1493, the humanist polymath and book collector Hartmann Schedel teamed up with the printer Anton Koberger to produce the monumental *Liber Chronicarum*, a history of the world broadly based upon Augustine's interpretation of biblical chronography. The result was the most complex and sophisticated printed artifact in the early, incunabular age of print. It combined images and texts with great technical dexterity, and included maps, cityscapes, micro-biographies with portraits that recounted the deeds of famous individuals—both historical and mythical—and genealogies of all sorts, biblical and secular.[5] An encyclopedic timecapsule of sorts which incorporated Pliny's *Natural History* in its account of little-known Asian territories, Schedel's *Liber Chronicarum* had taken inspiration in turn from the universalism of Aeneas Silvius Piccolomini's *Historia rerum ubique gestarum* (composed ca. 1458–61), an ambitious but unfinished cosmographic and historical compendium that brought together contemporary reports of Europe and Asia with ancient sources, including Strabo, Ptolemy, and Pliny.[6] The deep influence of Piccolomini's *His-*

toria upon Columbus and his son are on display in the manuscript text and images incorporated into their copy. Both father and son resorted to this vision of divine chronography to put forward the idea of Columbus's providential mission. But the eschatological universalism of Piccolomini and Schedel was not just concerned with the global history of the Christian *longue durée:* both include not only recent news of hostile encounters between Ottomans and Christians for Mediterranean supremacy but also prognostications, omens, and monstrous births—the same kind of detail, considered ephemeral by some, that Hernando would put at the core of his universal library.[7]

Hernando was not even the first to imagine the universal in library form. By the late fourteenth century, Coluccio Salutati proposed something similar in his *De fato et fortuna:* "Let there be founded public libraries into which a copy of all books would be collected; let the most learned men be placed in charge of the libraries, who would revise the books with most diligent collation, and who would know how to remove all discord of their [textual] differences with the judgment of correct definition."[8] This tract—which was never printed, but which Hernando bought in manuscript on 4 February 1531—was one of the earliest calls for the creation of public libraries as part of the wider humanist agenda for the recovery of lost or rare texts, their fixation in authoritative copies devoid of scribal corruption, and their eventual distribution in the original and in translation. Salutati imagined, in effect, an end of textual history, in which the vicissitudes of transmission would be purged and we would enter an eternity of stable copy. Libraries became part of the material infrastructure central to the humanist agenda and promoted by, among a host of other authors, well-known names that included Lorenzo Valla, Erasmus, Juan Luis Vives, and Elio Antonio de Nebrija—all of whom engaged in the fixation of texts through careful work of editing and translating, all of them involved in the technologies and methods for the generation and distribution of information and knowledge.[9] Hernando's library was, in many important ways, a bibliographic materialization of their intellectual agendas, but it was also something more: his vision for the library sought to turn it into a universal repository of information in printed format, which, as we shall show, went far beyond the normative canon of orthodox humanism.

In his plan for public libraries, Salutati may have been inspired by

Petrarch, whose intention to start a public library in Venice with a founding donation of his own books never came to fruition. One of Petrarch's most eminent followers, Giovanni Boccaccio, was also fully aware of the need of libraries to press on with their program of textual archaeology. After his death he donated his books to the monastery of Santo Spirito, a place that was frequented by Salutati alongside a remarkable group of Florentine humanists. Among them was the book collector Niccolò Niccoli, and it was from his manuscripts that the first modern public library did materialize in Florence, in the convent of San Marco, for the use of "omnes cives studiosi."[10] It was created under the patronage of Cosimo de' Medici, il Vecchio, using the manuscripts bequeathed by Niccoli after his death in 1437, designed by the architect Michelozzo Michelozzi, and committed to the custody of twelve trustees, who included Florentine celebrities and potentates like Leonardo Bruni and Poggio Bracciolini.[11] To supplement Niccoli's collection, Cosimo commissioned Tomasso Parentucelli to draw up a *canone* of all the books that were needed for a perfect library. This list, which "was considered by contemporaries to be the first modern and complete instrument for the foundation of a library which accepted the pagan classics and more than one subject," shows an idea of the library in transition to later humanistic ideals: its contents are still mostly sacred rather than secular, and Greek and Hebrew works feature only in translation.[12] Despite the fact that Parentucelli's *canone* limited itself to around 250 books, it was considered to be "universal" in the sense that it contained works from every faculty, and it was repeatedly compared by contemporaries to the library at Alexandria.[13] When, in a surprise election in 1447, Parentucelli became Pope Nicholas V, he found himself with ample opportunity and means to recast the model he had created for Cosimo in even more ambitious form, and the beginnings of the modern Vatican library are traced to his period as pontiff.[14] Lorenzo Valla, dedicating his translation of Thucydides to Nicholas V, described the pope's program of sending forth an army of translators and scholars to gather Greek texts and then render them into Latin as both a form of military conquest and a type of trade, images also echoed by the bookseller and humanist biographer Vespasiano da Bisticci in his descriptions of the Vatican library.[15] This blending of global trade, universal empire, and comprehensive book collections was to reach its crescendo in Hernando's great library project.

The bid to create a great public library at Venice did eventually come to fruition, though the founding donation was not to be the books of Petrarch but rather the great Hellenic manuscript collection of Cardinal Bessarion. While the heroic scholarly narratives of a previous generation, which saw Bessarion's manuscripts as largely responsible for the reintroduction of Greek to western Europe, have had to be tempered and heavily qualified, it is certainly the case that the symbolic value of Bessarion's transfer of manuscripts to the West resonated widely among European courts, and their cultural, political, and religious agents.[16] And for all the limited scope of Bessarion's collection in comparison to later universal library projects, it strove in various ways to extend its influence outward across the globe, both playing a part in his attempt to bring about an ecumenical union between the eastern and western branches of Christianity as a precondition for the recovery of the Holy Land—and the millenarian triumph over all infidels—and (more materially) through the fact that Bessarion's catalogues were copied and distributed, allowing the contents of the library to act at a distance, a form of extension that was to be a key component of Hernando's library project.[17] Bessarion's library was also a forerunner to Hernando's in that its formation and function were closely related to the geopolitical tides created by the expanding Ottoman Empire, driving European powers in search of cartographic and economic technologies that would allow them to keep their heads above water. Some of the knowledge of classical Greek geometry, mathematics, and cosmography, which was so central to the Columbian projects, was transmitted through the manuscripts that Bessarion brought to Venice. In a letter dated in April 1438, Ambrogio Traversari wrote to his circles in Florence in great excitement about the codices he had seen among Bessarion's books, which included texts by Strabo and Ptolemy so far unknown, or at least very rare, in European libraries.[18] The great mathematician and astronomer Regiomontanus (Johannes Müller von Königsberg) accompanied Bessarion on some of his trips to gather rare Greek texts and also learned the language under him, equipping himself with the sort of techniques in textual and philological analysis required to revise Jacopo di Angelo's first Latin translation of Ptolemy's *Geography*.[19] Regiomontanus also provides a connection between the Mediterranean manuscripts of Bessarion's collection and the Hungarian Biblioteca Corviniana, the central European library put together under the sponsorship of King Matthias Corvinus, which toward the end of the fifteenth century was reputed to hold nearly five thousand volumes. Regiomontanus spent several years in Buda as part of the team of scholars that administered and conducted research at the Corviniana, a period during which he collected Greek texts, engaged in editorial tasks, and made astronomical observations while generating his own scholarship. The fact that after his prolific years in Italy and Hungary Regiomontanus decided to return to Germany and install a press in his own house underlines the prime importance he placed in the material infrastructure for the production and distribution of knowledge, seeing the need not just for sophisticated editions of mathematical and astronomical texts but also for a system through which to distribute them. Remarkable scholars like Regiomontanus and Elio Antonio de Nebrija—who as we shall see was also a very active editor of texts in a variety of disciplines—as well as collectors like Hernando, were all keenly aware that production of information, its recording, and its subsequent distribution required a complex framework of agents and technologies.

Through his books, as well as through personal contacts, Hernando was therefore acquainted with a panoply of models for the creation and use of libraries. Many of these projects dovetailed in turn with important developments in strategies for the distribution and dissemination of information, the redesign of knowledge, and the hierarchy of disciplines, as well as with scientific progress related to exploration, cartography, and cosmography. Over the course of his life Hernando formed connections to these universalizing projects in a plethora of ways. The trustees of the Biblioteca di San Marco in Florence, founded by Cosimo de' Medici using the books of Niccoli and the canon proposed by Parentucelli, also included Paolo dal Pozzo Toscanelli, the humanist cosmographer whose "narrow earth" theories were key to Columbus's plan and some of whose writings were copied by Columbus into his edition of Piccolomini's *Historia*. Also present at the court of the Reyes Católicos during Hernando's youth was one of the former Vatican librarians (*magister bibliothecae*), the then cardinal-bishop of Barcelona, Pere García, who had briefly held the post between 1492 and 1493.[20] The importance of great libraries was likewise a favorite theme of Peter Martyr d'Anghiera—the Italian humanist and tutor at the Spanish court, to which Hernando was transferred aged five after his father's triumphant First Voyage—who paid homage to Lorenzo de' Medici after his death in 1492 by wondering aloud who would now collect books on a comparable scale. Little could Peter Martyr imagine that the young son of Columbus, whom he would soon meet at the court of the Catholic monarchs, would outdo Lorenzo as a collector.

There was, however, a key difference between previous library projects and that on which Hernando was to embark—namely, the challenges and possibilities provided by the growth of print, which presented issues of scale that these previous libraries did not need to confront in their founding designs, and to which they were slow to adapt. The emergence of print led not only to an unprecedented number of available texts, aimed at a widening readership in a growing number of forms, but also to the possibilities of dispersion that came with economies of scale. While many of the humanists saw this as playing into their dream of an end to textual history—allowing stable, definitive texts like Valla's Thucydides, Erasmus's New Testament, and the Polyglot Bible to be present everywhere as textual gold standards—they largely envisioned this as a one-way process, with authoritative texts flowing outward but little or nothing returning along the same arteries to the institutions governing the analysis and distribution of knowledge. The nascent republic of letters was precisely that: a network of authoritative sources connected by private epistolary channels, and though these epistolary exchanges were sometimes published, it was with a view to exhibiting the processes of authority and not to invite public participation.

There were, however, certain fields—such as the exchange of geographic and economic information—in which the advantages of drawing from every available source were patently obvious, even if the information then needed to be subjected to a process of collation, filtration, and conversion into something useful and (what was more) something that elicited the trust and legitimacy habitually associated with authoritative information. These methods of absorption, tabulation, and collation offered a different route to the philological attempt to stabilize the world of knowledge one textual crux at a time, and one perhaps more suited to the rising tide of printed information. The exchange of economic information, which mingled data about the markets available and practical instructions for reaching them, flowed through long-established trade routes, routes along which the bulk of printed texts had little choice but to flow once they were added to the balance of trade. Recent scholarship has highlighted the central part of fifteenth-century mercantile culture in driving Columbus's voyages westward across the Atlantic—from the need to create new markets to compensate for the loss of eastern Mediterranean ports to the Ottomans, to the circulation of reports of lands to the west among Genoese and Venetian traders and the development of navigational technologies in service of ever more ambitious sea voyages. Hernando was to inherit this milieu along with his father's millenarian ambitions. Unlike many other book collectors of the day—but very much like the principal players in the print trade—Hernando was deeply connected to the circuits of international finance and trade and (what was more) did not view his books as part of the leisured withdrawal from this world of business, as an *otium* that opposed the *negotium* of the city.

In this volume we aim to provide for the first time a comprehensive account of Hernando's many projects—in cosmography, cartography, lexicography, and bibliography, bringing together plants and prints, demographic records, and sailors' reports and books—and to locate them all within the intellectual, technological, and social currents of their day. Some aspects of Hernando's work have been the subject of previous study—groundbreaking work on his image collection by Mark McDonald, for instance, or the thoroughgoing account of the catalogues by Tomás Marín Martínez—but they have largely been treated as separate undertakings, divided from each other by the material and disciplinary demarcations which (in truth) came after them, and which were largely a *result of* rather than a precondition for the kind of broad encounter which Hernando pioneered. Other parts of Hernando's project have come to light only during our research on the library and are receiving their first detailed examinations here. Perhaps most exciting among these is the scribal copy of Hernando's *Libro de los Epítomes,* which disappeared from view for almost five hundred years between Hernando's death and its identification in Copenhagen in 2019, and which preserves summaries of books from the library across more than two thousand pages, giving previously unthinkable insight into the library's holdings and how they were used (fig. 1).

Forty years ago, Elizabeth Eisenstein's bold argument for the centrality

FIG. 1. Fair copy of Hernando's *Libro de los Epítomes* (Copenhagen, Arnamagnæan Collection, AM 377 fol. Photo: Suzanne Reitz. Used with permission.)

of print in determining the course of European history—*The Printing Press as an Agent of Change*—put forward the notion that certain qualities of print inexorably led to the emergence of a culture of scientific rationalism which was seen as emerging in the Enlightenment. It was another totemic image that was almost immediately assailed from all sides: by those who saw it as unacceptable "technological determinism" and sought to restore the part of human agency to the emergence of Enlightenment ideals by undermining the claims to print's "revolutionary" effects, and by those who saw it as another teleological narrative for the inevitability of European dominance, pointing to the global context in which print and knowledge organization preceded any European advances. While the account of early print that has emerged over the ensuing years has highlighted the importance of local actors, few who have lived through the last two decades would be so skeptical of the ability of information technologies to effect immense changes upon the world in ways that quickly spiral beyond the control of those creating them or working with them at a local level. And while it is important to avoid triumphal accounts of European progress, it is nevertheless the case that European print does not have to have come first for it to present a distinctive case through the scale of its impact. Just as Columbus does not need to have been *first* to cross the Atlantic—the foremost effect of his voyages being to create a constant interchange between the east and west of the Atlantic—so the distinctive feature of European print is not its priority but the pervasiveness with which it became part of culture and society on the continent and in those parts of the world European nations subjected to their control. From these pervasive and consistent exchanges emerged certain ways of being—social, mechanical, and information technologies—that have had a profound if often invisible effect on how we see and interact with the world. It is the purpose of this account to trace those ways of being to their foundations and to document in the growth of Hernando's collections the underlying strategies for absorbing and organizing information that came to be foundational to the European world of knowledge during the age of print.

From his father and uncle, and the cultural environment of late fifteenth-century Europe, Hernando acquired a millenarian outlook that would be reinforced by the exceptional series of events he witnessed, or even experienced himself, starting with his father's triumphal return from the First Voyage across the ocean when Hernando was a child and his subsequent installation at court as a page, alongside the princely heir to a monarchy with a mission. His instruction at court familiarized him both with traditional Scholasticism, a tradition with which the royal tutor Fray Diego Deza was deeply imbued, and with Italianate humanism, to which the court was connected by Peter Martyr d'Anghiera and through the cultural influence exerted by Elio Antonio de Nebrija. Hernando's presence with his father on the Fourth Voyage was the definitive rite of passage that would expose him to the perils and the excitement of exploration. Hernando had a decidedly bookish and methodical mentality, but he was more than just an armchair explorer, for throughout his life he traveled to all the great urban centers of political, cultural, and economic power in Europe, a complement to his experience sailing around the new territories across the ocean, including modern Panama and Jamaica, where he spent a year stranded with his father. On these voyages he was always accompanied by crucial books and documents: there were astronomical tables and navigation charts that accompanied Columbus and Hernando on the

1502–4 expedition; on his second visit to Hispaniola he traveled with a chest filled with over two hundred books; and he made a series of book-shopping sprees around Europe during the rest of his life.

From bookish instructors at court, and from his own father and uncle, he acquired reading habits that he continued to use and develop throughout his life, as well as a variety of methods for gathering data from documents (printed as well as manuscript) and from the firsthand observation of the world. These habits included the use of alphanumeric tables for the interpretation and prediction of astronomical phenomena and for navigation and also, conversely, for the storage and codification of information. He exercised his skills in translating all these alphanumerical databases into other media, such as ekphrastic geographical descriptions and iconic cartography.

Hernando's activities and collections intersect with fundamental disciplines and practices that defined his world in three important areas: finance, cartography, and cataloguing techniques. His collection was erected upon a new and complex mercantile and financial infrastructure that ran on an unprecedentedly global scale, where goods and credit circulated not just between Europe, Africa, and the Levant, as they had already done for centuries, but now also across the Atlantic. Furthermore, the transportation methods and the financial instruments that furnished the communication networks of his times were not the only things Hernando borrowed for his library. The vast majority of his books record the date, place, price of purchase, and also the current exchange rate with Spanish *ducados,* turning them into exceptional repositories not just of textual information but also of financial and mercantile data. Hernando's notes therefore plotted a complex map with layers of data, including information about the European book world, the cultural hubs where knowledge was produced, the paths throughout which print circulated, and how in turn these currents stand in relation to the mercantile and financial networks of early sixteenth-century capitalism. This map is reconstructed here for the first time.

We do not aim to produce a merely materialist and financial account of Hernando's projects within their historical context; instead we argue that this aspect of his activities, and of his world in general, is an underexplored part of a wider world of measuring techniques, data recording, and information sharing, with shared practices even if put toward different ends. We shall consider how these methods worked within political and doctrinal contexts, in many cases being profoundly shaped by them. What turned Hernando's library into an epicenter of early modernity is precisely the way he combined the profit-driven practices of early financial capitalism with the political-religious project of the *Universitas Christiana,* the particular interests of his family with the Hispanic monarchy's millenarian sense of mission, and the universalism of early colonialism and its globalization of knowledge with a keen awareness of the importance of information and news reports produced and distributed in smaller formats. For the most part these last sources of information were totally disregarded by the great intellectual agents of his day, but his vision accommodated them with a sense of their true relevance.

During his period as *piloto mayor* at the Casa de Contratación Hernando had to coordinate the gathering of information and its conversion into maps to be employed by Spanish pilots—who were also trained at the Casa in navigation techniques, the interpretation of charts, and the proper methods for the collection of further information with a view to the creation of new maps or the improvement of those that were already in use, further refining Spanish cartographic resources. There is a common rationale underlying all of Hernando's projects, and the sophisticated new techniques under development for the accurate representation of the world were also employed in the classification and recording of knowledge and information in other realms and disciplines. For instance, the speed with which exploration was expanding, and the consequent maritime arms race among European powers, called for the development of efficient methods for navigation. This posed enormous challenges for mathematicians, astronomers, cartographers, and navigators, who worked under continuous pressure. These practical requirements therefore spurred research and the generation of knowledge in these disciplines and crafts, naturally contributing to the development of increasingly sophisticated systems for measurement and quantification and also tabulation and organization.

The representation of the earth and the cosmos by means of the techniques and symbolic languages developed for cartography and cosmography find an interesting parallel in Hernando's numerous catalogues of his collection. There is a close relation between the actuarial habits he embraced in his many activities, his tasks as a cartographic consultant and as coordinator at the Casa de Contratación, and the different parameters he used to devise catalogues that would allow proper navigation for readers among his vast collection. Using logging and cross-referencing systems borrowed from mercantile daybooks, Hernando recorded information on his collections in ways that aimed to make them sortable in a variety of ways—by author and title, by contents and subject matter, even by incipits, format, and design—just as actuarial information was often sortable by the type of transaction as well as by date, location, and associated names, and as Hernando's cosmographic data could be navigated by key descriptors (place names) as well as by geographic adjacency (using the maps derived from them). Each of these projects attempted to hew matters of sameness and difference ever more closely: extracting essential information that could at once guard against the duplication of items (books, geographic entries, transactions) while at the same time allowing these vast repositories of information to be sorted by means of hierarchies of difference (alphabetization, date of purchase, the use of sets), orders that could often be combined for ever-greater specificity. Yet while the abstraction and tabulation of this information was a necessary step to harnessing the immense powers of this information surge, it required a further transformation to make it useful to the haptic and intuitive minds of its users, resulting in the apparatuses of the balance sheet, the map, and the physical space of the library itself.

This book aims to break Hernando's world of information apart and then to reassemble it in much the same way he did and, in the process, to provide a radical account of information tools in the print age, which took root in complex historical circumstances that shaped them in ways that long outlived the world in which they originated.

CHAPTER ONE

LIFE IN THE LIBRARY

Since in all things my lord don Hernando Colón, who is in Heaven,
was so provident, he did not wish his library to be a dead library,
as the rest are, where, before finding a book, the user must look
up and down all the shelves and books, and read all the titles.
—Juan Pérez, *Memoria*[1]

Hernando's life is most accessible through the catalogues he made of the world around him and through contemporary descriptions of his collecting habits and practices. As is suggested in the quotation above, life for Hernando in a very real sense emerged out of acts of collecting and ordering. The disordered library was a "dead" library, and when he came to write the first biography of his revered father, he treated it as an ordered archive of Columbus's documents and placed the practices of collecting and ordering at the heart of his argument for Columbus's exceptionalism. The act of placing documents in order is central to all acts of life-writing, but Hernando's mind-set left him with a peculiar awareness that the archive itself is the only knowable thing, and that the subjects imagined through them were merely projections.

The birth of Hernando's collections came with the volumes he inherited from his father, many of which survive to this day, replete with Columbus's annotations. Although it was widely reported shortly after his death that the explorer had been a bookseller early in life—a suggestion Hernando was later to refute with great vigor—the books that can be securely identified with Columbus are few but were nonetheless crucial to his enterprise.[2] They included the cosmographical encyclopedia *Historia rerum ubique gestarum,* compiled by the Italian humanist Aeneas Silvius Piccolomini while he was serving as Pope Pius II, which Columbus owned in a Venetian edition of 1477, and Pliny's *Natural History* in Cristoforo Landino's Italian translation (Venice, 1489). From these Columbus gleaned the details of Aurea Chersonesus, the eastern edge of Asia, which he expected to find on his planned ocean crossing.[3] The "narrow earth" theory, to which Columbus subscribed when arguing that only a third of the world (and a mere 650 leagues) lay between western Europe and eastern Asia, drew heavily on the cosmography he found in his copy of Pierre d'Ailly's *Imago Mundi* (Louvain, 1480–83), in which Columbus's hand mingles in almost nine hundred annotations with those of his brother, Bartholomew, as well as with Hernando's own marginalia (figs. 2 and 3).[4] In further support of this "narrow earth" hypothesis, a letter from the Italian geographer Paolo del Pozzo Toscanelli—one of the twelve trustees of the Florentine Biblioteca di San Marco—has been copied into a blank page in the *Historia rerum,* either by Columbus or by Hernando, as well as a manuscript chronology of Jewish history (taken from Josephus), making these volumes little archives of Columbus's geographical and historical thought (figs. 4 and 5).[5]

To these three works Columbus added a fourth in 1497, after neither of his first two voyages provided conclusive proof that he had indeed reached Asia: an edition of Marco Polo's account of Cathay from the Netherlands, sent to him by a Bristol merchant named John Day.[6] Day's exchange with Columbus, trading print and cosmography along mercantile channels, is an early paradigm for the operations we analyze in detail in this book. The four volumes inherited from Columbus—Pliny, Marco Polo, the *Imago Mundi,* and the *Historia rerum*—place at the heart of Hernando's collection not only the classical and medieval worldview out of which the library was born but also some of the well-established trade routes along which information flowed, bringing to Spain documents from Venice, Bristol, and the Low Countries with news from several corners of the globe.

Hernando also inherited the bulk of his father's manuscript works.

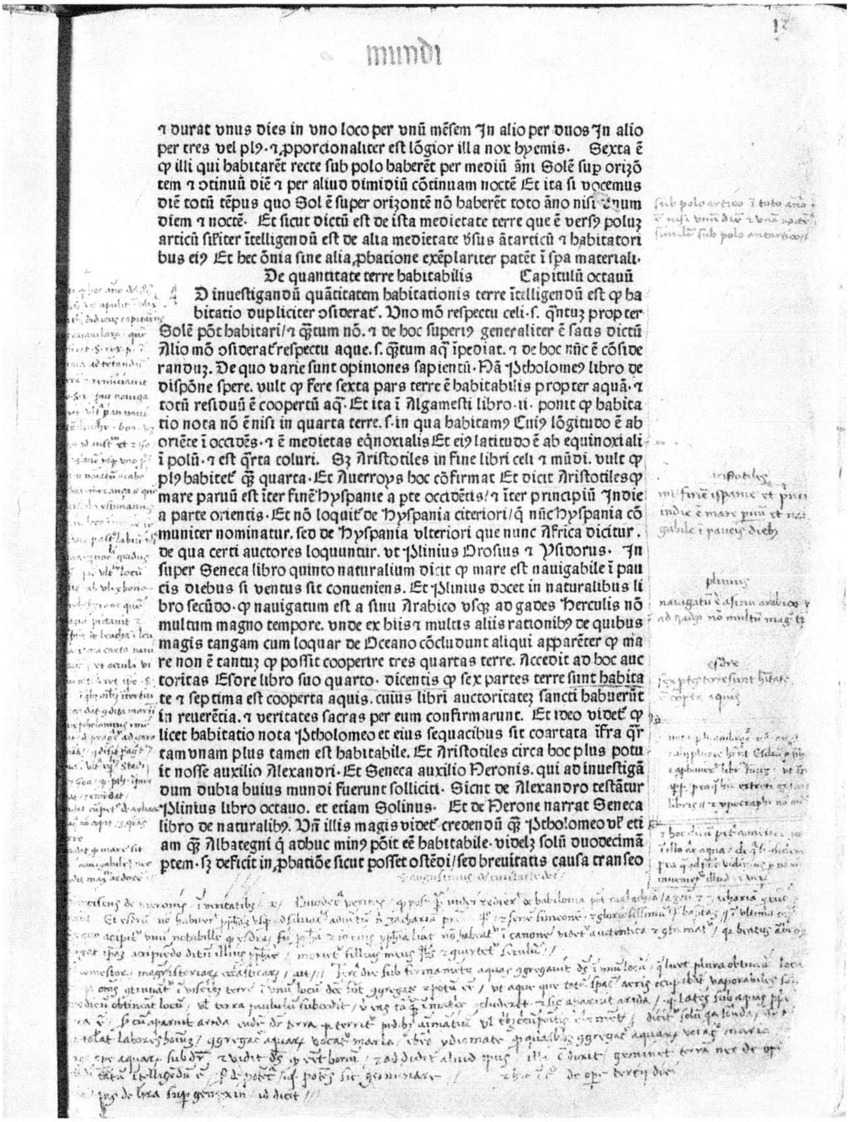
mundi

⁊ durat unus dies in uno loco per unũ mẽsem In alio per duos In alio per tres vel pl9·⁊ ꝓporcionaliter est lõgior illa nox hyemis· Sexta ẽ ꝙ illi qui habitarẽt recte sub polo haberẽt per mediũ ãni Solẽ sup orizõtem ⁊ ꝯtinuũ diẽ ⁊ per aliud dimidiũ cõtinuam noctẽ Et ita si vocemus diẽ totũ tẽpus quo Sol ẽ super orizontẽ nõ haberẽt toto ãno nisi ũnum diem ⁊ noctẽ· Et sicut dictũ est de ista medietate terre que ẽ vers9 poluꝫ articũ siſiter ĩtelligendũ est de alia medietate vsus ãtarticũ ⁊ habitatoribus ei9 Et hec õnia sine alia ꝓbatione exẽplariter patẽt ĩ spa materiali·

De quantitate terre habitabilis Capitulũ octauũ

Ad inuestigandũ quãtitatem habitationis terre ĩtelligendũ est ꝙ habitatio dupliciter ꝯsideratᷣ. Uno mõ respectu celi·s. qñtuꝫ propter Solẽ põt habitari/⁊ qñtum nõ. ⁊ de hoc superi9 generaliter ẽ satis dictũ Alio mõ ꝯsideratᷣ respectu aque. s. qñtum aqᷓ ĩpediat. ⁊ de hoc nũc ẽ cõsiderandũ. De quo varie sunt opiniones sapientũ· Nã Ptholome9 libro de dispõne spere. vult ꝙ fere sexta pars terre ẽ habitabilis propter aquã·⁊ totũ residuũ ẽ coopertũ aqᷓ· Et ita ĩ Almagesti libro·ii· ponit ꝙ habitatio nota nõ ẽnisi in quarta terre. s·in qua habitam9 Cui9 lõgitudo ẽ ab oriẽte ĩ occidẽs·⁊ ẽ medietas eqnoxialis Et ei9 latitudo ẽ ab equinoxiali ĩ polũ·⁊ est qrta coluri. Sꝫ Aristotiles in fine libri celi ⁊ mũdi. vult ꝙ pl9 habitetᷣ qᷓ quarta· Et Auerroys hoc cõfirmat Et dicit Aristotiles ꝙ mare paruũ est iter finẽ hyspanie a pte occidẽtis/⁊ ĩter principiũ Indie a parte orientis· Et nõ loquitᷣ de hyspania citeriori/qͣ nũc hyspania cõmuniter nominatur. sed de hyspania vlteriori que nunc Africa dicitur. de qua certi auctores loquuntur. vt Plinius Orosius ⁊ ysidorus· In super Seneca libro quinto naturalium dicit ꝙ mare est nauigabile ĩ paucis diebus si ventus sit conueniens. Et Plinius docet in naturalibus libro secũdo· ꝙ nauigatum est a sinu Arabico vsqꝫ ad gades herculis nõ multum magno tempore. vnde ex hiis ⁊ multis aliis rationib9 de quibus magis tangam cum loquar de Oceano cõcludunt aliqui apparẽter ꝙ mare non ẽ tantuꝫ ꝙ possit cooperire tres quartas terre. Accedit ad hoc auctoritas Esdre libro suo quarto· dicentis ꝙ sex partes terre sunt habitate ⁊ septima est cooperta aquis. cuius libri auctoritateꝫ sancti habuerũt in reuerẽtia. ⁊ veritates sacras per eum confirmarunt. Et ideo videtᷣ ꝙ licet habitatio nota Ptholomeo et eius sequacibus sit coartata ĩfra qrtam vnam plus tamen est habitabile. Et Aristotiles circa hoc plus potuit nosse auxilio Alexandri· Et Seneca auxilio Neronis. qui ad inuestigandum dubia huius mundi fuerunt solliciti· Sicut de Alexandro testatur Plinius libro octauo. et etiam Solinus· Et de Nerone narrat Seneca libro de naturalib9. Uñ illis magis videtᷣ credendũ qᷓ Ptholomeo vlᷓ etiam qᷓ Albategni q̃ adhuc min9 põit ẽẽ habitabile· videlꝫ solũ duodecimã ptem· sꝫ deficit in ꝓbatiõe sicut possẽt ostẽdi/sed breuitatis causa transeo

FIG. 2. Page from Hernando's copy of Pierre d'Ailly's *Imago Mundi* (fol. 13r), which he inherited from his father, with manuscript notes in his father's, his uncle's, and Hernando's own hand (© Cabildo Catedral de Sevilla)

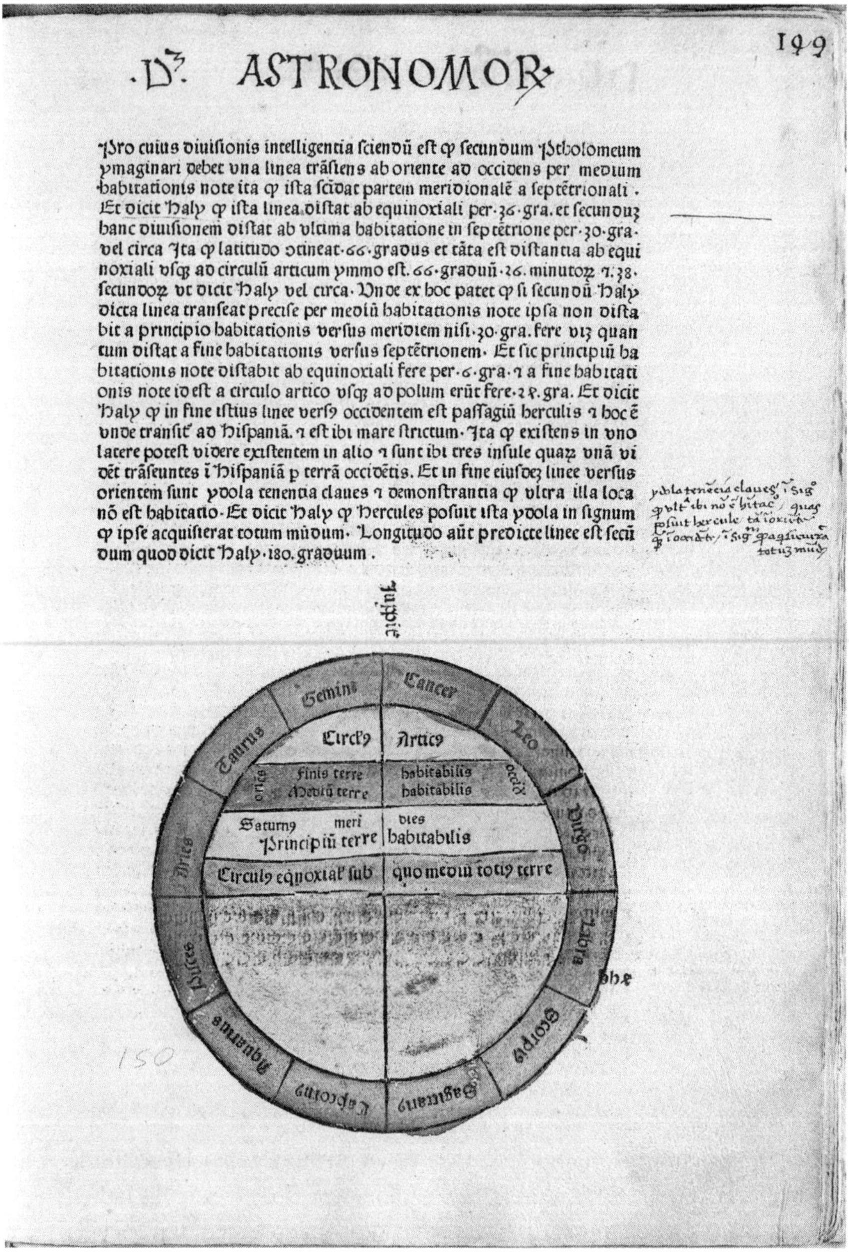

·D³· ASTRONOMOR·

199

Pro cuius diuisionis intelligentia sciendũ est q secundum Ptholomeum ymaginari debet vna linea trãsiens ab oriente ad occidens per medium habitationis note ita q ista scindat partem meridionalẽ a septẽtrionali. Et dicit Haly q ista linea distat ab equinoxiali per·36·gra. et secundũ hanc diuisionem distat ab vltima habitatione in septẽtrione per·30·gra· vel circa Jta q latitudo cõtineat·66·gradus et tãta est distantia ab equinoxiali vsq ad circulũ articum ymmo est.66·graduũ·26.minutoꝝ ꝛ.38· secundoꝝ vt dicit Haly vel circa. Vnde ex hoc patet q si secundũ Haly dicta linea transeat precise per mediũ habitationis note ipsa non distabit a principio habitationis versus meridiem nisi·30·gra. fere vꝫ quantum distat a fine habitationis versus septẽtrionem. Et sic principiũ habitationis note distabit ab equinoxiali fere per·6·gra·ꝛ a fine habitationis note id est a circulo artico vsq ad polum erũt fere·24.gra. Et dicit Haly q in fine istius linee versꝰ occidentem est passagiũ herculis ꝛ hoc ẽ vnde transit' ad Hispaniã. ꝛ est ibi mare strictum. Jta q existens in vno latere potest videre existentem in alio ꝛ sunt ibi tres insule quaꝝ vnã vidẽt trãseuntes ĩ Hispaniã p terrã occidẽtis. Et in fine eiusdeꝫ linee versus orientem sunt ydola tenentia claues ꝛ demonstrantia q vltra illa loca nõ est habitatio. Et dicit Haly q Hercules posuit ista ydola in signum q ipse acquisierat totum mũdum. Longitudo aũt predicte linee est secũdum quod dicit Haly·180. graduum.

FIG. 3. Another page from Hernando's copy of Pierre d'Ailly's *Imago Mundi* (fol. 199r), with manuscript notes (© Cabildo Catedral de Sevilla)

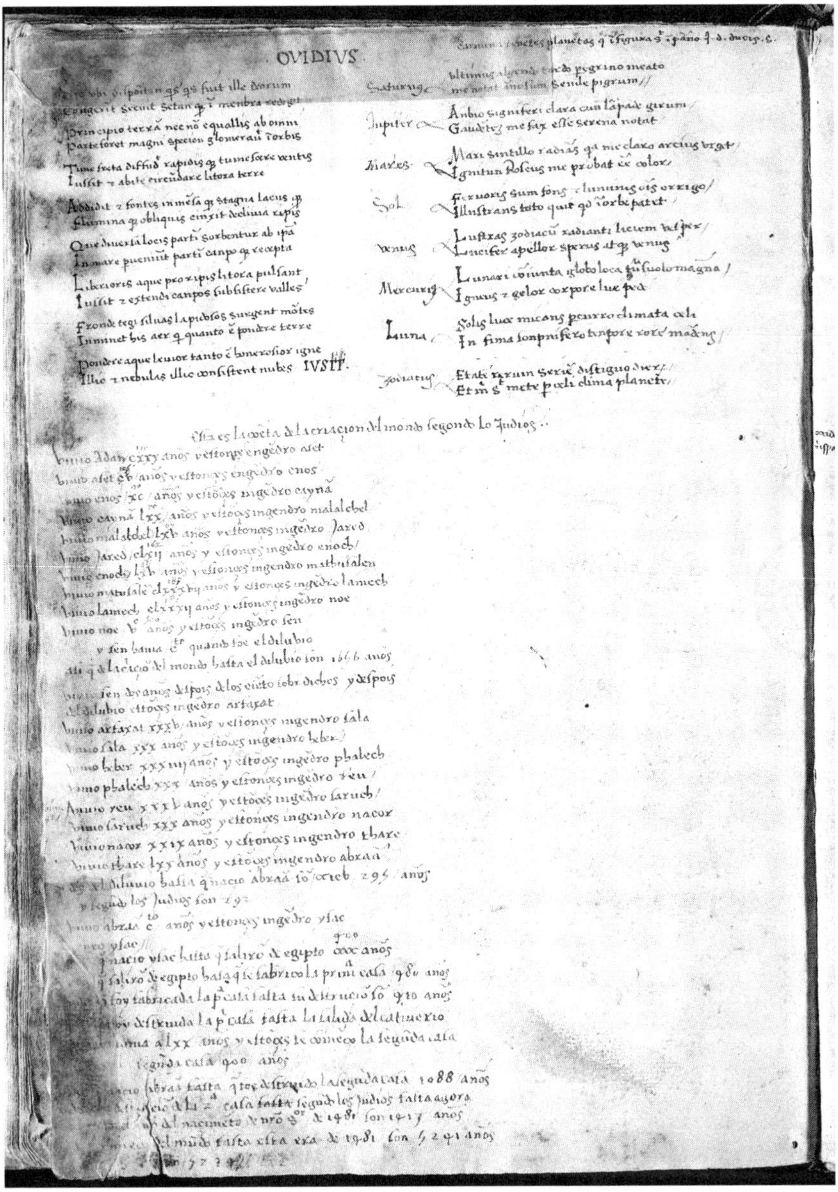

FIG. 4. Manuscript notes in Hernando's copy of Aeneas Silvius Piccolomini's *Historia rerum ubique gestarum,* inherited from his father, including a manuscript chronology of the history of the world since Genesis according to the Jews and a long quotation from Ovid's *Metamorphoses* (book 1, ll. 34–54) in which the Roman poet recounts the creation of the cosmos, with a brief catalogue of the planets with their main features (© Cabildo Catedral de Sevilla)

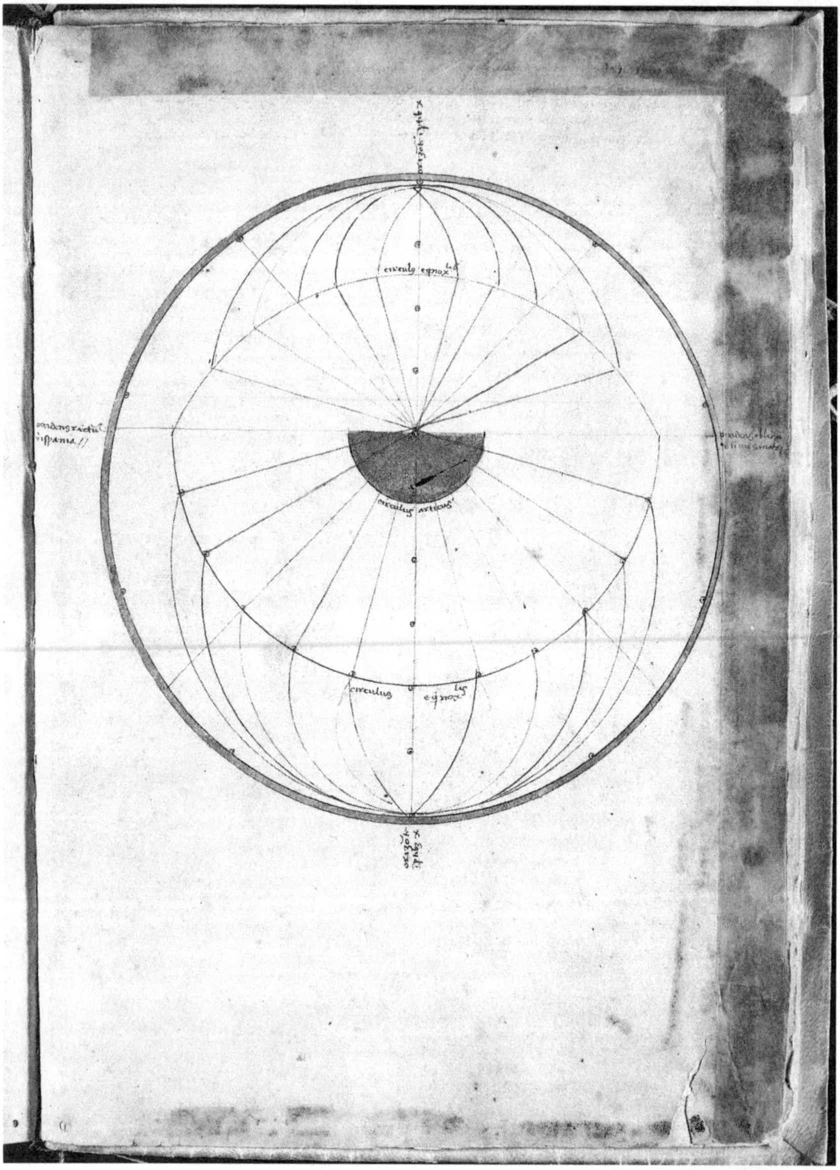

FIG. 5. Hand-drawn geometrical representation of a three-dimensional globe projected onto a planisphere in Hernando's copy of Piccolomini's *Historia rerum ubique gestarum* (© Cabildo Catedral de Sevilla)

Among these were certainly the logs of Columbus's voyages, meticulous records of the estimated distances traveled on each day of the voyages, at times interrupted by the long periods of fever-induced blindness to which Columbus was prone. Along with these nautical measurements, Columbus recorded in his logs zoological, botanic, environmental, geological, and ethnographic observations of peoples from the Caribbean islands and from the areas of the American mainland he visited: Paria in modern Venezuela on the Third Voyage of 1498, and the coast of modern Panama, which was explored on the Fourth Voyage of 1502–4. Columbus also commissioned reports from others, including the ethnography of the Taíno compiled by Fray Ramón Pané during the Second Voyage; our knowledge of this eradicated people, Columbus's first point of contact in the Caribbean, relies almost entirely on Hernando's copy of Pané's treatise.[7] To these elements of Hernando's Columbian archive, which survive largely intact, should be added the vast number of charts, maps, and documents that are mentioned in his inventories but are now lost: writings by the Sephardic astrologer Abraham Zacuto which were key to Columbus's measurements, nautical instruments and sea charts inherited by Columbus from his Portuguese father-in-law, and *mappaemundi* from the early period of Atlantic navigation.[8]

While Columbus's books, charts, and papers clearly form the original nucleus of Hernando's collection, he would have inherited them on the explorer's death in 1506, when he was almost eighteen years old. They were not, then, his first acquisitions chronologically. With Hernando's arrival at the court of the Reyes Católicos aged five, which suddenly removed him from the humble life he had lived with his unmarried mother in Córdoba, he acquired both the means and the need for books to further his education in the household of the infante Juan. While we lack the dated records for these early acquisitions, records Hernando was to keep meticulously in later life, we can reconstruct his early library with some confidence by taking precisely those books in the collection *lacking* dates of purchase, a set which aligns neatly with what we know of the infante's household.[9] The heavy contingent of Scholastic works in philosophy and theology may reflect the role of Fray Diego Deza, a Thomist from Salamanca, as the infante Juan's principal tutor, who as a strong and early supporter of Columbus may have been a shelter to young Hernando as he navigated the unfamiliar and inhospitable court. Among the indispensable texts must have been the expensive editions of Aristotle's *Opera* and Aquinas's *Summa Theologica,* both printed in Venice and purchased in Seville and costing 680 and 1,505 *maravedís,* respectively, representing almost a quarter of Hernando's yearly stipend as a page.[10] The Aristotle shows signs of schoolboyish annotations, with Hernando noting next to the prefatory biography the importance of patronage ("Aristotle had a lot of power because of Alexander, whom he always pressed to do good"). Hernando's notes also draw attention to Aristotle's association with books, marking passages that tell how Plato called Aristotle's house "the House of Readers" and how Aristotle's books were later acquired by Ptolemy.[11] Also a presence at court was Elio Antonio de Nebrija, a vigorous and controversial polymath whose *Introductiones Latinae,* commentary on Aulus Persius Flaccus, and *Introduction to the Cosmography of Pomponius Mela* are among Hernando's undated, probably early acquisitions. Nebrija's work on language and cosmography, which he saw as twin pillars of a projected Spanish Empire, was to be deeply influential on Hernando.[12] Hernando may have been guided in some purchases by another of the tutors in Juan's household, the Italian soldier, traveler, and man of letters Peter Martyr d'Anghiera, who was to provide a conduit between the New Learning and the New World voyages of exploration: not only were his letters to Pomponius Laeto (the doyen of Roman humanism) among the earliest to circulate reports of Columbus's discoveries in Italy, but Peter Martyr also quickly conceived for himself a role as premier historian of the New World, a task on which he spent much of the rest of his life, resulting in the monumental *Decades de Orbe Novo,* a work in progress whose second edition was curated by Nebrija.[13] Peter Martyr balanced the traditional education provided by Deza with a humanist academy—one anecdote recounts him leading his pupils through declamations of the poems of Juvenal—and Hernando's early collection seems to have been well stocked in the classical oratory and history most cherished by Italian humanists, including the works of Horace with commentaries by Cristoforo Landino (the translator of Pliny's *Historia naturalis*) and an early edition of the *Opera* of Lucian.[14] This group dating from before Hernando's mature cataloguing period, however, also suggests that from an early stage he was drawn toward many technical practices that were unlikely to be part of his courtly education: a wide range of medical volumes, including works of botany and pharmacology, and books on natural philosophy, astronomy, and cosmography.[15]

Though Columbus was absent for much of Hernando's childhood, a strong bond evidently formed between the two during the explorer's periods in Spain, as suggested by the series of documents which gives Hernando the same status as his (legitimate) elder brother Diego in the entail (*mayorazgo*) drawn up in 1498 and the documents transferring both sons to the suite of Queen Isabel in the same year, after the sudden death of the infante.[16] When Columbus returned in disgrace from his Third Voyage in 1500, facing accusations of mismanagement and increasing opposition at court to his control of New World affairs, he was driven by desperation and an increasingly millenarian vision to embark upon a new strategy to save his legacy. This was the moment at which the Columbian project began its transfer from father to son. The *Libro de las Profecías* (*Book of Prophecies*) is an archive in its most powerful, paradigmatic sense: both a collection of documents—authorities demonstrating the providential nature of Columbus's discoveries and predicting the apocalyptic events they would set in motion—and an instrument of political power (*árkhē*), which resonated with the political ambitions of the Hispanic monarchy toward a universal and millenarian empire. As Roberto Rusconi has shown, the *Book of Prophecies* gathers passages from the poetic and prophetic books of the Bible and, pairing them with visions of medieval mystics and "leaks" from North African Jewish communities, organizes them in three sections which collate Christian providential history with late medieval crusading and Atlantic expansion.[17] The manuscript is in a number of different hands, including an unidentified scribe probably of Italian origin, as well as sections completed by Gaspar de Gorricio (a Carthusian who served as Columbus's archivist and spiritual advisor during the last years of his life), by Columbus himself, and by Hernando, who was only twelve when the project began to take shape. Gorricio was instrumental in laying out a late medieval, modist framework—seeing different layers of literal, historical, spiritual, and prophetic meaning in each Bible verse—which justified the *auctoritates* being read as typologically prefiguring recent events. He also gathered references to be copied into the *Libro* and compiled an index of references to *insulae* ("islands") in the Bible, which was treated as a keyword to locate the sections relevant to Columbus's own island discoveries. While the long-standing belief that most of the *Libro* was copied out by Hernando has been rightly dismissed—his hand is easily identifiable as separate from the peculiar Italian humanist script in which much of it is written—there are nonetheless many passages which clearly are written by Hernando, mostly original verses in Castilian reflecting obliquely on the providential argument and his father's exceptionalism. A passage close to Columbus's heart, and quoted by him in several surviving letters, also illustrates the bridge formed between theology and humanism in this volume: not, this time, a scriptural citation but rather one from the chorus of Seneca's play *Medea* which predicts the breaking of the "chains of ocean" and the discovery of lands beyond Thule, and which Hernando has annotated as a prophecy of his father's discoveries in a later edition.[18] Columbus's own inscriptions in the *Libro* provide a remarkable insight into the place of this book in his world. Most notably, he used a blank space beneath the verses from *Medea* to record his observations from northern Jamaica of an eclipse on 29 February 1504, an astronomical marvel he used both to produce an accurate longitudinal measurement of the distance between Jamaica and Cádiz and (reportedly) to convince the local Taínos of his supernatural powers. The use of the *Libro* to note this observation, as well as his quotations from its *auctoritates* in letters written from Jamaica, where he and Hernando were marooned in 1503–4, confirm that he had the *Libro de las Profecías* with him on his fourth and final voyage to the New World. The *Libro* here appears as a sort of catalogue raisonné, an ordered and portable distillation of a distant cultural reservoir, allowing its holder to confront the exotic while holding on to the familiar, to make biblical prophecy, ethnography, and astronomical observation part of the same order. The project Columbus inaugurated was not only one of nautical logistics and imperial expansion but also an attempt to collate the records of Old World and New so as to provide a seamless account of the globe, an archive for the universal archon. Many of the features of this project, from the employment of an assistant to distill keywords from texts to the idea of a catalogic book which represented knowledge at a distance, were to reappear as central to Hernando's own universal library projects.

Our first detailed image of Hernando's collections comes from his second trip to the New World in 1509. Three years after his father's death, and seven years after he accompanied Columbus on the Fourth Voyage along the coast of modern Panama, Hernando was back in Santo Domingo in the entourage of his brother Diego, whose inheritance of his father's titles as governor of Hispaniola and Admiral of the Ocean Sea had recently been confirmed.[19] There is little reason to credit later accounts that Hernando was returning to the western Atlantic to further the establishment of Christianity through a program of church building; whatever the intention, he returned to Spain after little more than two months, possibly to continue his education (as Bartolomé de las Casas suggests) or, more likely, to fight the constant fires at court that threatened to destroy his father's legacy.[20] That Hernando had planned to settle in Hispaniola for a longer period is suggested by the inventory of his possessions there, which includes (as well as loose papers, charts, maps, and astronomical diagrams) the first known codicological collection in the New World—the first American library, of 238 volumes stored in four *arcas* (chests).[21] The smallest of these cases, made of walnut in Seville, held only 28 volumes and a bundle of medical recipes; the other three held 78, 73, and 57 volumes, with the last being marked with this cryptic symbol.

There is no reason to believe that the books were placed in the *arcas* especially for transportation; most fifteenth-century book collections, from the great library begun by Nicholas V at the Vatican to the university collection Hernando would have known at Salamanca, were stored at least partly in chests even at their permanent foundations, and Hernando's books must have moved with him often enough to encourage this arrangement. These chests were not specifically designed for books, however, and their multipurpose storage spaces encouraged the mingling of codices with loose papers, and also with non-paper objects, meaning that the book may have had no special categorical distinctness from other materials in the collection. Medieval monasteries kept their books in the same chests as the other institutional treasures—just as the Aztec apparently did with the precious and rare codices taken from them by Cortés—and it is unclear at what point we should envision Hernando's 1509 inventory of his possessions as no longer describing the contents of these chests. Were the loose-leaf medical recipes from one Doctor Torres, the *Book of Prophecies*, and the maps stored in these chests with the books—were the paintings, the string and putty, the hand tools and shot molds? The difficulty of drawing a boundary between books and non-book objects becomes even more pronounced when it is considered that many of the paper works had practical functions which might encourage their use away from the book repository, associating them more naturally with other tools: not only the maps, sheets of painting models, and sheets of music—which might have sat more naturally on navigational tables and been paired with other things he listed, such as the resin and sulphur used for painting or the strings for the *monachordio*—but the botanical and geometrical booklets, which might have more to do with apothecary jars and mapmaking than with theological treatises, which themselves might be kept more naturally with the "bread of Christ's feast" on the inventory. It was probably the case that, with only 238 titles, Hernando could remember each volume clearly, meaning that it was not yet necessary to conceive of a firmly separate class of "books," a notion that (counterintuitively) only emerges when there are so many books that they need to be set aside, divided, and organized as a class in order not to become unmanageable.

The year that Hernando returned from his second visit to the western Atlantic marked a point of maturity for both him and his collection. In 1509 he turned twenty-one, and also in this year he began to record the date of acquisition for his books (in addition to the price and place of purchase information he had recorded from the beginning), allowing us to reconstruct his whereabouts and collecting habits with greater and greater accuracy.[22] His book chronology seems to have followed a logical course of narrowing from broad and vague records of time to narrow and specific ones as the collection ballooned. The first notes on book acquisition record that he received a book as a gift *when he was traveling to the New World*, and the first records of year of purchase appear in 1509. By 1511 he was recording the month in addition to the year, and in the following decade he began to record individual days of the month as well.[23] The creation of categories here—proceeding from "years" to "months" and "days" of purchase—were clearly responding to challenges of scale, which should be borne in mind during our approach to Hernando's cosmographic, cartographic, and lexicographical projects, as well as to his accumulations for his library, where apparently conceptual divisions may have been responding also (or even principally) to the scale at which information was being produced by nautical reports, geographical censuses, and printing presses.

The volumes that came into Hernando's possession in the first half of 1511 have a consistency which suggests that he was still buying for immediate personal use and not yet attempting to make his collections reflect some broader conception of available knowledge, but it would be a mistake to think that this meant his collecting was unsystematic. Far from being opposed, the personal and the systematic seemed for Hernando to be intimately linked. Among the 1511 purchases there is, then, a heavy contingent of foundational reference books: language reference tools from Paris, including seminal Greek grammars by François Tissard and Manuel Chrysoloras (joining the key Greek lexicon by Crastonus which he already owned), Tissard's Hebrew grammar, Latin dictionaries and treatises on Latin versification, books of arithmetic and geometry, and Nebrija's treatise on weights and measures. Even many of the non-reference texts purchased during this period might be seen as companions to the references, such as Tissard's editions of Homer and Hesiod, which Hernando (whose Greek never seems to have been strong) would have had constant recourse to as his language tools.[24] Hernando's focus on classical languages was entirely in keeping with his efforts in this period to convince Ferdinand to revive Columbus's dream of a universal empire, something Hernando hoped to forward most directly through a proposed circumnavigation of the globe. Between the widely held conviction that classical tongues (and Hebrew in particular) had a foundational status that would lay the groundwork for universal communication, and the belief that geopolitical power was tied to the robustness of each nation's tongue, it was clear that language and empire were strongly linked in early modern European thought.

Hernando's departure for Rome in mid-1512 marked the beginning of a paradigm shift for his collecting and epistemic practices. The immediate reason for his being in Rome during much of the year between 1512 and 1516 was to act as his brother's proxy in a case in the Sacra Romana Rota—as demonstrated by a vast trove of newly discovered records from the trial—and there is little evidence for later assertions that he acted as an ambassador to the pope (or that he was attacked by pirates en route).[25]

It was a task for which Hernando would have been somewhat prepared, from the role he seems to have taken in the *Pleitos Colombinos,* an interminable series of law cases in Spain in which the family's rights over the New World as laid out in the 1492 Capitulaciones de Santa Fe were defended and mostly lost between 1493 and 1541.[26] Yet the records of the trial also show that Hernando's presence at the Vatican hearings was consistent but intermittent, and the long gaps between proceedings allowed him plenty of time to immerse himself in the cultural life of the World City.[27] His list of purchases in these early months aligns closely with a rare surviving list from the same period of those lecturing at the Studium Urbis, suggesting that Hernando was attending lectures at this prestigious institution, which was newly installed in premises next to Sant'Eustachio.[28] It was common practice in Italy—unlike in his native Spain—for older and elite members of society to attend public lectures, and Hernando was later to make the (almost certainly false) claim that his father had attended lectures at Pavia.[29] Yet Hernando clearly also recruited personal tutors, as there are a number of notes dated from this period that refer to him having a particular text expounded to him by "meo magistro," often accompanied by heavy glosses of the texts in question, which allow us to follow Hernando through his lessons. In December 1512 he was working with a tutor on Juvenal's *Satires,* and in 1515 we find similar notes in his copies of Suetonius's *Lives of the Twelve Caesars* and in an astronomical treatise by Silvestro da Prierio Mazzolini, with the tutors in question being identifiable with some confidence as Bartolomeo de Castro and Sebastianus de Veteranis. Hernando's links to Veteranis likely came through the Studium Urbis, where Veteranis was lecturing at this time, whereas Bartolomeo de Castro seems to have been part of the Spanish community in Rome. As Hernando's tutor he compiled a list of logical terms and another of Greek verbs and conjugations that survive in the Colombina collection, the latter including references to where each verb occurred in famous works, a lexicographical habit Hernando would soon adopt in his own dictionary.[30] Other glossing and summarizing exercises from the time, in the letters of Pliny the Younger and Lucretius's *De rerum natura,* do not record a specific tutor but may also have been linked to lectures at the Studium Urbis.[31] While some of these exercises were directed toward language learning, others—such as the "indice completissimo" he compiled to Suetonius in three columns over twenty pages, for which he provided folio numbers in this unpaginated volume—allow us to trace the emergence of Hernando's obsession with the tools of knowledge organization (fig. 6).[32] The compilation of indices was a common practice of the humanist classroom, though it is often linked to the desire for a copious and exact control of the classical tongues, as amusingly captured in Erasmus's parody of Christoforo Longolio (a lecturer at the Studium during Hernando's stay) as the pedant in *Ciceronianus* who compiles an index to Cicero to ensure all words not witnessed there are expunged from his vocabulary. The relative "fixity" of print made it possible to compile indices that were (in principle) usable across all copies of the same edition, and many humanists earned a living creating these tools, which could then be marketed to other humanist readers. Though few humanists followed Hernando in being more interested in the tools of organization than in the materials they organized, the sententiousness and exemplarity that was central to humanist thought and culture should be seen as tied up with, even emergent from, these print technologies.

Although there is plenty of evidence that Hernando entered into the classicizing obsessions of Roman humanism—purchasing guidebooks to the recent archaeological discoveries and closely annotating Flavio Biondo's treatises on antiquities—the horizons of his Roman experience were not bounded by the learned world of the Studium Urbis.[33] This period provides the first evidence that Hernando imagined his collecting activities as tending toward something other than the humanist library, which focused on a *canone* of central tomes and sought out the most authoritative witnesses in manuscript form. These libraries would have been familiar to Hernando through the original *canone,* drawn up by Tomasso Parentucelli in the mid-fifteenth century for the Medici in Florence before he became Pope Nicholas V, and through libraries like that of Angelo Colocci at his famous academy on the Quirinal, which also housed a gallery of antiquities, the remains of the Roman Accademia founded by Pomponius Laeto, and the premier Roman press for Greek-language works (the Ginnasio Mediceo, from which Hernando probably owned at least two works).[34] Hernando was just as conscientious in noting the cost, location,

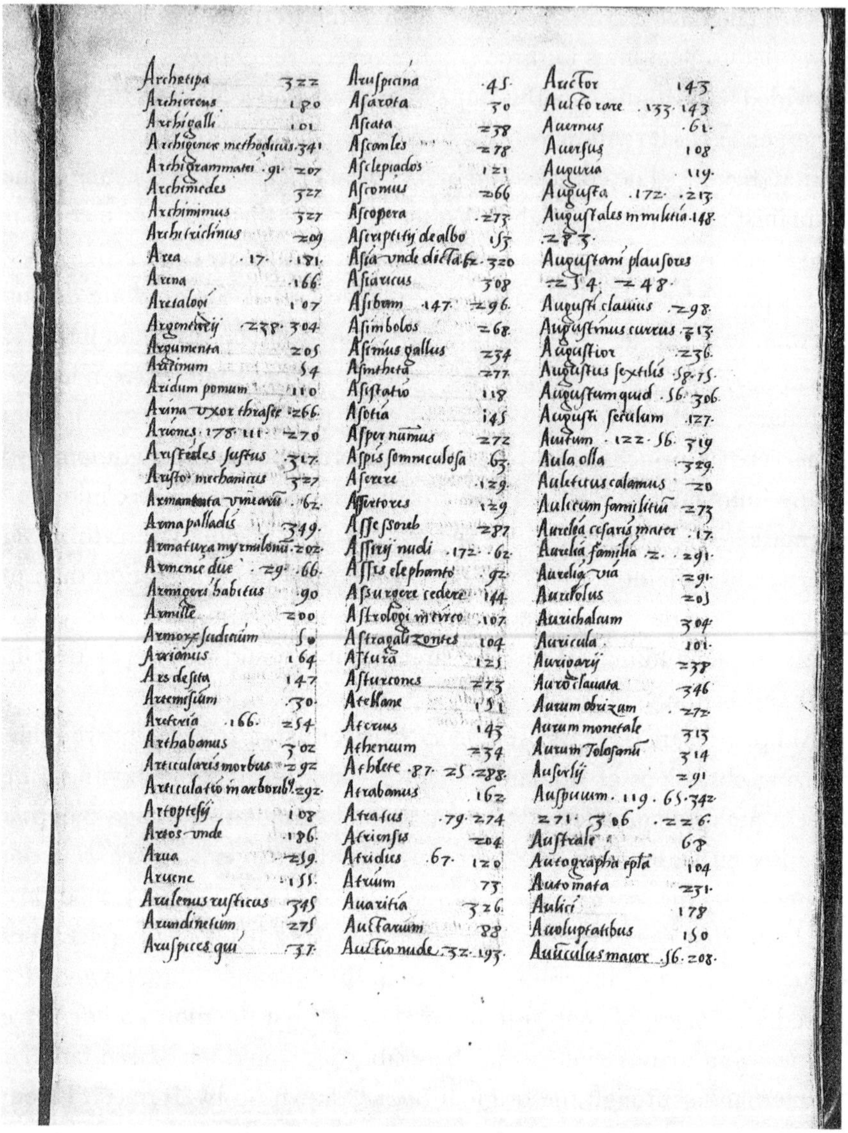

FIG. 6. Hernando's manuscript index in his copy of Suetonius (© Cabildo Catedral de Sevilla)

and date of purchase for the flimsy ephemeral works he began to acquire in large numbers—a negligible quirk, perhaps, and one that might seem to stem mostly from Hernando's obsessive need to list, if it were not for the fact that Hernando would eventually leave instructions that his librarians should acquire these *obrezillas* first and expensive tomes and manuscripts only afterward. Among the *tratados* that Hernando bought in these first months in Rome, identifiable by isolating purchases of only a few *quatrines,* were a book on falconry by "Agogo Mago" and several poetic pamphlets by Marco Rosiglia, of which Hernando's copies are the only ones that survive.[35] Hernando's purchases also show the immense chronological depth and geographical reach of early sixteenth-century Roman booksellers: in October 1512 he purchased (among many incunabula) a work by Martius Galeottus printed almost forty years before, as well as a large number of titles from the 1480s and 1490s; he also found works such as the five manuscripts dealing with the work of the eighth-century Jewish Persian astrologer Messahalla, which he bought in October 1512, and the first book printed in the Ethiopian language of Ge'ez, issued in 1513 as a collaboration between the Ethiopian community in Rome, the scholar Johannes Potken, and the printer Marcellus Silber, both German.[36] Hernando seems to have had a particular affection for the output of the Silbers' Roman workshop, buying 30 works printed by either the father Eucharius or the son Marcellus in 1512, a collection that would eventually reach 115 items.

Hernando would also have the chance while in Rome to explore one of the great institutional collections of the age, the Bibliotheca Palatina of the Vatican, so-called to distinguish it from the private library of the pope. The library had its beginnings in the pontificate of Nicholas V but was given its full form under Sixtus IV, who fixed its location and provided for two *custodes* who lived in the library and looked after the books. The librarianship itself was originally a sinecure that lapsed on the death of the pontiff, and in his youth Hernando may have known the librarian appointed by Alexander VI, a Borgia client called Pere García, who lived at the court of the Reyes Católicos as bishop of Barcelona and for whom the pope had passed over Angelo Poliziano, another figure whose works formed a key precedent for Hernando's projects. The library was organized during the time of Sixtus into four rooms: a Latin room, a Greek room, the *Secreta,* and the *Pontificia.* The latter two rooms, which held the documents produced by and about the Curia respectively, were reserved for Vatican personnel, while the Latin and Greek rooms were open to the public for two hours a day while the College of Cardinals was sitting.[37] Indeed, patrons of the library were able to borrow books from the Latin and Greek rooms, with names recorded in the Registri di Prestito—the Moroccan diplomat soon to be baptized as Leo Africanus even had volumes delivered to him during his captivity in the Castel Sant'Angelo.[38] If Hernando's name does not appear in these lists, it may be because the tomes were mostly lent to printers to use as control texts for printed editions—the main relationship between the library and the world of print, as it counted few printed volumes among its holdings.[39] Leo X, issuing a *motu propio* in 1513 which lamented the underfunding of the library, added a fifth room (the *parva secreta*) designed to house the overflow from the existing rooms. This extension, which housed its "volumi sciolti" in five chests and twelve cases beneath six desks, allowed a trickle of the miscellaneity of print into the Vatican, described in one catalogue as "libri sine nomme."[40] In 1481 this category included a mere 50 books, but this quickly grew to 150 and included (among other things) translations of Homer. It was around these "volumi sciolti" that Hernando was to reorient the world of his library.

We are fortunate to be able to immerse ourselves in the Vatican library thanks to the *Convivium Scientarum*, an epic verse catalogue of the library written in nearly two thousand lines of terza rima by Antonio de Tomeis in 1477.[41] As he progresses through the rooms of the library, de Tomeis inspects each bench and chest in turn, leaving a list of its contents and valuable descriptions of the library space:

Poi ch'eve operto, primo che mutato
me fossi, vidi seidici cassoni
pien pien de libri, ciascuno ordinato

sopre l'armarij eran li montoni
intorniati atorno a poco a poco,
tanti che nne farria cento sermoni.
(1723–28)

After opening [the door], and before
I turned around, I saw sixteen chests
Full of books, each of them ordered;

On top of the cupboards the piles
stood, all around the room,
Materials for a hundred sermons . . .

Di ferro, ugniun ben forte, li trovai
tuctu, ciascun di lor, incatenati
in quelli banchi, quanto li mirai,

Each one of them I found
with strong iron chains bound
to those benches, wherever I looked

e llí quactro custodi preparati
a guardia che ugniun mai se partissi
a che a cciaschun mostrarli fosser grati

and there four custodians ready
ensuring that none [of the books] disappeared
most willing to show them to all

di qual scientia veder si volessi
e a nisciuno mai fosse serrata
di qualsi a parte in tal luoco apparesse.
(1822–1830)

whichever discipline I pleased to see
although examined by none before
I could certainly find it in this place.

For all the praise lavished by de Tomeis on the *custodes*, it is evident that even in 1477 the scale of the library was becoming unmanageable, as the wanderer suggests when he collapses in homage to the *Commedia:*

Essendo al fin, sí straccho era, 'thronato,
di corporal fatiga e intellecto,
che mi pusi a sseder sença far fiato.
(1810–12)

I was, at the end, so exhausted and overwhelmed
In both body and in intellect too
That I had to sit down, breathless.

For all its ambition, the *Convivium* is not a practical catalogue of the collection, and readers were (as de Tomeis suggests) reliant in large part on the memories of the *custodes* to navigate the library. Such book lists as were made were often prompted by catastrophic events—such as the return to Rome from Avignon, which led to the 1443 inventory, and the 1533 list made after the Sack of Rome—and were intended as stock inventories rather than distillations of the collection. During Hernando's stay, however, steps were being made independently to compile fuller accounts of the collection, for instance, in the catalogues made by Fabio Vigli between 1508 and 1513 as part of a systematic survey of the great libraries of the day. Vigli's catalogue marks a notable advance in recording not simply the title of each codex but also its contents, together with remarks on volumes that particularly interested him: "In quinta Capsa Pontificie Bibliotheca Armenica anonyma. / Liber pulcherri[ma] lingua armenia: de armenicis characterib[us]: cui titulus latin[a?] in [?] pagina p[er]script[us] est: [epistolem?] tralate d[e] latino i[n] armeniu[m]."[42] These descriptions, which often cover a full side or more in the ledger summarizing the library's contents, resemble in some fashion the much more detailed and systematic surveys on which Hernando would later embark.

During the course of his life Hernando continued to intersect with other great library projects. About a decade later, in 1526, he crossed paths with one of the first curators of Bessarion's manuscript collection at the Venetian Biblioteca di San Marco when Andrea Navagero came to Spain as the ambassador from the Serenissima to the court of Charles V, a residence that occasioned many conversations with Spanish humanists, including a mythical encounter with the Spanish poet Juan Boscán in 1526, immediately after the wedding of Charles V to Isabella of Portugal.[43] Navagero provides a connection between the ideal manuscript libraries of early Petrarchist humanism that preceded Hernando's project and the more recent habits of book collection and information gathering by agents well situated in the age of print, who first coexisted with his own projects then continued to flourish after his death. Among the most remarkable of them were Giovanni Baptista Ramusio, who as Venetian chancellor was in frequent epistolary contact with Navagero during the latter's embassy in Spain, and the book collector Marín Sanudo, an obsessive hoarder of information through his diaries, some of whose books and manuscripts ended up as part of Hernando's collection. These international diplomatic and cultural networks were producing new varieties of travel literature, which Hernando amassed in several formats, including the many news pamphlets or *obrezillas* in his collection. This endless flow of reports from the new territories were eventually gathered into the next generation of encyclopedic projects, such as Ramusio's three-volume *Delle Navigationi et Viaggi,* the first global history of exploration and voyages.[44]

In his diaries Sanudo mentions another great Venetian book collector, Cardinal Domenico Grimani (ca. 1461–1523), whose library purportedly contained fifteen thousand books, and who enjoyed a well-deserved reputation as a sophisticated connoisseur. Erasmus, who made his acquaintance in Venice in 1509, considered him the most learned among the members of the Roman Curia.[45] Sanudo's entry in his diary with information about Grimani's library is dated 15 September 1523, the year of Grimani's death, and according to his testimony, part of Grimani's books were at the time in Rome. Hernando must in all likelihood have heard about this library during his youth when he spent long periods in Rome.[46] If the reports are to be believed, Grimani's library was one of the few collections of the age to rival Hernando's own, though almost no evidence survives regarding the size or contents of the collection.

Hernando's departure from Rome in 1516 was likely precipitated by a variety of momentous changes in his world: the ending of the case in the Sacra Rota, the accession of Charles to the Spanish throne after the death of Ferdinand in January, the recall of his brother Diego from Hispaniola to answer charges of malfeasance in his governorship, and the French victory at the Battle of Marignano, which once again tilted the balance of power in northern Italy (and, by extension, in Europe). The exodus of the papal court north to Florence, to come to terms with the young King Francis I, gave Hernando the opportunity to visit that city for the first (and only) time and to buy (among other things) the recently published bibliography of ecclesiastical writers by the great German bibliomaniac and library builder Johannes Trithemius, to whom Hernando paid the idiosyncratic tribute of noting the number of authors covered in his work (1,014) as well as the number listed under each letter of the alphabet (there are 103 under the letter *A*, 60 under the letter *B*, and so on).[47] Hernando returned to Spain with the hundreds of books he had acquired during his years in Italy and also a series of notational practices, which in the following years he deployed across a series of immense and ambitious projects. He continued to create indices and other paratexts to the books he bought, such as the edition of Pomponius Mela's *Cosmographia, siue de situ orbis,* which he bought in Madrid around November 1516, soon after his return from Rome, and which contains a manuscript index carefully arranged in tables.[48] A similar practice can be seen in his Venetian edition of Seneca's *Tragedies,* which he bought in March 1518 in Valladolid. Hernando immediately began to read it and, as his note in the volume details, to create over the next six years an index that covered the commentaries as well as the text itself, for which purpose he divided the plays into 1,800 numbered sections. In addition to this task, which was continued during his impending travels across

Europe, Hernando copied onto the flyleaf a life of Seneca as well as a section providing "arguments" for the ten tragedies.[49] Hernando's particular affection for this volume can be explained in part, perhaps, by the passage in the *Medea* which Columbus had felt predicted his discoveries, and next to which one can still partially make out, in Hernando's hand, this note: ". . . prophecia. . . . per patre[m] . . . cristoforo . . . almirante . . . anno 1492."[50] This drive to transform the use of a thing, by making systematic notes and arranging them as an apparatus, was not an isolated event. Hernando made other book indices, but he also in this period began to create an index of settlements on the Iberian Peninsula, assiduously noting the population of each hamlet, town, and city, recording its distance from surrounding settlements, and describing the routes between them.[51] A surviving set of instructions he created while producing this *vocabulario* of Spanish towns directs the rough notes made during information-gathering trips to be written on one side of paper only, allowing them to be cut up and repasted into a second volume, arranged alphabetically by initial letter, from which they would eventually be copied into a neat volume that would be alphabetized up to the fifth letter. This gathered and sorted information would eventually be used, Hernando writes, to make *tablas*—tables or maps—of Spain, divided up into a grid of squares "as on a chessboard." Just as the indices of books would allow the reader to gather *sententiae* on important topics, to form a consensus of authoritative thought, so the *vocabulario* of towns would create a new model of space, a countryside textured by myriad points of human habitation and fractured by the lines of communication between them. Any unsettled places that fell outside the index would, for all intents and purposes, simply disappear.[52]

This reform of written knowledge and of the landscape through the notational apparatus was followed by an even more foundational project, in which Hernando aimed to subject language itself to the same routine of ordered, systematic notes, forming an index of words that would allow its user to move forward with a definite understanding of language. Hernando's *Diccionario* or *Vocabulario Latino,* which he recorded beginning on Monday, 6 September 1518 at 8 a.m., set out to synthesize and systematize a number of existing, unsatisfactory lexicons of the Latin tongue, and was to reach 1,476 manuscript pages with an estimated 3,000 definitions before being abandoned, at an unknown date, in the middle of the second letter of the alphabet (at "bibo"). The generic titles these projects were later given by people other than Hernando—*Index, Cosmografía, Diccionario*—and the fact that they have become permanent fixtures of widely separated parts of our life (traveling, reading, language learning) should not obscure the fundamentally similar procedures Hernando was employing and the ends toward which these tools inexorably drove: the compilation of authoritative written lists of conceptual terms, towns, and words, and the corresponding creation of an exterior world of popular culture, temporary dwellings, and slang and their vagabonds, vagrants, and vagaries. Whatever the later history of these practices, Hernando's projects show a determination to strive for truly universal indices, noting settlements of as little as five people, indexing terms like "moonlight," and writing a definition of the word "Androgyny." It was, in a sense, the failure of unlimited projects like Hernando's that led to the narrowing filters of future lists.

The Columbus clan had feared that with the death of Ferdinand in 1516 the loss of a shared history would fatally damage their interests, but while Charles did order a review of the Columbus claims over the New World almost immediately upon accession, he seems to have found an affinity between Hernando's notational turn and his own desire to impose a new order on the complex polities he had inherited. From a royal decree of 1523 we learn that within a year of beginning his index of Spanish towns, Hernando was provided with royal letters patent that instructed local officials to cooperate with the census.[53] Hernando had, in his genius for information, devised a double-lock system which ensured the credibility of the information being gathered once he was no longer doing it in person: his emissaries not only were to gather the information from local "trusted people" but were to obtain a sworn attestation of the data before the local notary.[54] This fail-safe device, which sought to ensure that the information was not simply fabricated by either the emissaries or their local informants, would nevertheless be worthless if the said informants were to resist giving information altogether, presumably what prompted the royal charters provided by Charles. Once again, the apparent diversity of Hernando's cataloguing projects reveals itself as continuous when considered from the point of view of *technique,* in which realm he was constantly refining the tools to gather, collate, and archive information effectively.

Further evidence of the institutionalization of Hernando's projects came as he accompanied Charles north to his Habsburg territories, where the young king would be crowned King of the Romans, the first ritual step of his installation at the head of the Holy Roman Empire: at Worms in January 1521 Charles granted Hernando two thousand ducats for his services, most likely in part to underwrite the costs of the *vocabulario* of Spanish towns. Hernando shows no sign of desiring to convert these funds into a more secure or prominent standing at court: instead, he departed immediately on a tour through the major book-producing locations of Europe, spending these funds and more on what was growing into his central obsession—the acquisition and documentation of printed objects. Not staying to witness the Diet of Worms which would become famous for Luther's defiance, Hernando traveled through what Andrew Pettegree has called the "fertile crescent" of print, describing an arc from the Low Countries through southern Germany and Switzerland to northern Italy, where he reached his main destination at Venice in May.[55] By the time he left on 18 October, he had bought 1,637 volumes, an average of almost a dozen a day.

Our detailed knowledge of these purchases, and the certainty that he was not simply purchasing duplicate volumes later in his trip, comes from the earliest surviving catalogues of Hernando's collection, which can be dated to this period. Though it is hard to say when Hernando began his first systematic booklists, we can be certain that by 1521 he was hard at work on his first book register, sometimes called *Registrum A* or the *Índice de Autores Antiguo*. We know this because the shipment of Venetian books that Hernando had consigned to Octaviano de Grimaldo on 18 October 1521 was lost at sea, and so the list of them, which occupies the second (and only surviving) of the four volumes of the *Registrum A,* must have been made before that date. This list, extending from entry number 925 to entry number 2562, was retained by Hernando with the intention of methodically replacing each of the lost volumes and has, because of its traumatic history, become known by the poetic title of the *Memorial de los Libros Naufragados* (the "Memorandum" or "Catalogue of Shipwrecked Books"). There was one exception to this restoration project: by the time Hernando returned to Spain in 1522, opposition to Lutheranism had hardened and Reformist books were banned. Hernando never attempted to replace these controversial pamphlets from his lost consignment, although the recently rediscovered scribal copy of his *Libro de los Epítomes* shows that at least some titles related to Lutheran controversies continued to be read and summarized by those working in the library. They include Jan Briart's *Quaestio quodlibetica contra dispensationes* (Leipzig, 1519), which is epitomized as entry 1601 in the *Libro* (fols. 624v–625r, see fig. 7).[56]

The evidence from the *Registrum A* may suggest that the number of items in Hernando's library numbered 924 by the time he arrived in Venice in 1521, though since the first volume of the *Registrum A* is lost we cannot be certain of the logic of its arrangement. The surviving volume demonstrates, however, that by this date Hernando was already using a system that was to become central to his library-building practices, namely, a thorough accounting of books already owned that traveled with the purchaser through the book world and ensured that duplicate volumes were not purchased. Many of Hernando's cataloguing practices were driven by both the power and the danger of duplication. In order to guard against the purchase of duplicates, the detailed book register was accompanied by an alphabetical index, which preserves a fuller witness to the original registers than the *Registrum A* (although only listing authors' names alphabetically, accompanied by associated titles). Eventually, the alphabetic cataloguing system would feature entries not only on the authors of the volumes but also on titles and incipits, in an effort to outwit unscrupulous publishers who issued the same works with different titles and authorial attributions.

Hernando's interest in print was not restricted to the textual products of the industry: by some point in the late 1510s or early 1520s he was assiduously collecting printed images as well, and though his failure to date these purchases makes the growth of the collection harder to chart, by the end of his life it would be the largest collection of printed images in Europe.[57] The exigencies of cataloguing and storage, however, forced a separation between these images and the main body of the collection: as many (if not most) prints were unattributed and untitled, they resisted alphabetization in the same manner as Hernando's textual collection. Though in many cases the distinction between a printed image and a text would have been simple, there is undoubtedly also a zone of indistinction, bordered (for instance) by the ten-sheet, text-heavy *Triumph of Christ* (kept with the print collection) and the densely illustrated lives of saints, often made from one sheet folded into an octavo booklet and kept with the books. In some

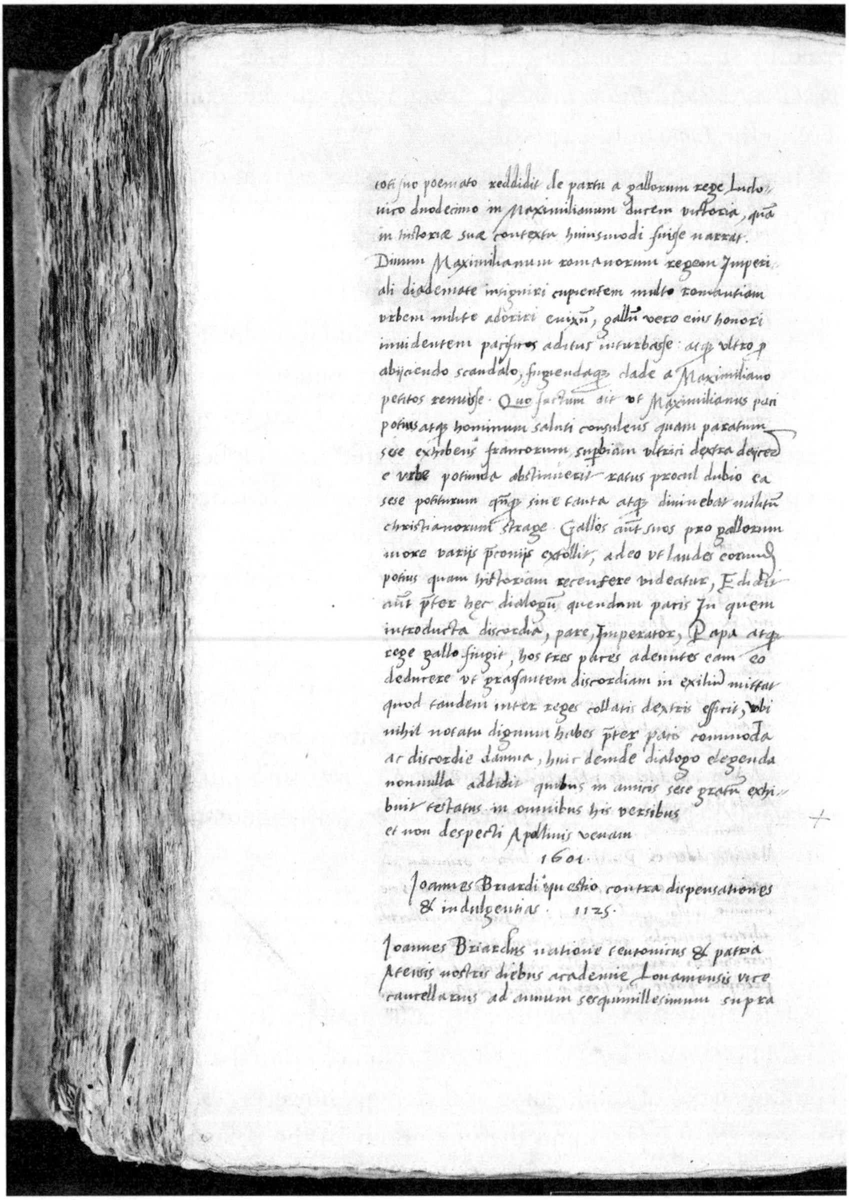

FIG. 7. Epitome 1601, Joannes Briardi (Jan Briart), *Quaestio quodlibetica contra dispensationes vel magis dissipationes commissariorum in genocio indulgentiarum,* in Hernando's fair copy of the *Libro de los Epítomes* (Copenhagen, Arnamagnæan Collection, AM 377 fol., fols. 624v–625r. Photo: Suzanne Reitz. Used with permission.)

sextum decimum quodlibeticam quandam questionem
in publico theologorum: et Pontificii Iuris professorum
coetu disputanti contra dispensationes ipse potius dis-
sipationes vocat commissariorum in negotio indulgen-
tiarum, Est autem questio huiusmodi An pia ad repa-
rationem aggerum contributio sit sufficiens causa re-
laxandi aut commutandi contribuentium vota Pro
cuius decisione obiectis hinc inde argumentis et premis-
sis nonnullis ad voti integritatem requisitis certis pro-
positionibus explicat, quando voti relaxatio sit conveni-
ens atque licita & quando illicita. In residuo concordat
auctoritatem psalmiste Psal. 54. dicis viri sangui-
num et dolosi non dimidiabunt dies suos, et Eze-
chielis 33. dicens Nolo mortem impii sed ut conver-
tatur et a via sua et vivat, ubi notat hominem
non posse preterire aut excedere statutum et diem
secundum divinam providentiam Cum tamen posse
falli in die statuto secundum causam naturales licet
non eque sepe atque falluntur in die quem simi-
lem sui ipsius a syderum sibi statuit, declarat
& Apostoli auctoritate prime ad Chorinth. 3°, ubi
dicit, Si quis videtur sapiens esse stultus fiat ut sit
sapiens, que obviare videtur ei quod dicitur pro-
verbiorum primo, ubi habet quod stulti sapientiam
atque disciplinam despiciunt, quorum quidem auctorita-
tum resolutionem non annoto ne videar libellum quem
hec collegi transcribere.

1602.

Joannes Trithemius de laudibus sancte Anne ~~Charon Opusculum tumultuarium~~. 1130

Jo. Trithemius natione germanus abbas Spanhensis
ordinis divi Benedicti preter alia quibus rem lite-
rariam ponit ad annum nonagesimum quartum

cases the "text" contained a higher proportion of image than the "print," as in the quarto booklet of the coronation of Ferdinand I of Hungary (kept with the books) and the seven-meter-long roll illustrating the genealogy of the House of Habsburg (kept with the prints).[58] It is highly possible that the main consideration was not the content or attributability of the printed sheet but the mode of storage. Hernando's inventory of 1509 makes no sharp distinction between books and loose sheets, with both being stored in chests (*arcas*), but as the collection grew Hernando devised the first ancestor of the modern wall-system library—bookshelves as we recognize them today—in order to provide a storage technique in which most items had a surface that was constantly visible and could be labeled. No such system was devised for the printed images, and they remained in chests. Although many of the short pamphlets were not, of course, individually bound—and would have been too thin to label if they had been—the fact that they were formed from *folded* sheets provided a spine along which they could be sewed into sammelband volumes containing many pamphlets. Hernando's surviving collection and catalogues seem to contain almost no broadsides or other prints on a single, unfolded sheet, despite the fact that his bibliographic cataloguing symbols had a specific sign for such print products, and their disappearance may be because unfolded sheets were kept with the (lost) print collection.[59] While the distinction between visual and textual cultures would later become petrified in European thought, for Hernando the difference may have hung on the seemingly incidental question of whether the printed sheet was designed to be folded or not. We should not, however, assume that the decision whether or not to fold was entirely insignificant, as the distinction between unfolded and folded sheets broadens when we consider the uses to which they were usually put: the unfolded sheet could be posted and seen by many people at once, allowing for simultaneous inspection by many viewers, whereas the folded sheet needed to be handled—its weight supported, its pages turned—and so its arc of spectatorship was often restricted to a single individual peering into its openings. Seen in this light, the "visual" and the "textual," the unfolded and the folded, map loosely but interestingly onto a distinction between the public and the private.

While the development of wall-mounted shelves of spine-labeled books may have turned the indistinguishable multitude of printed texts into a more manageable number of discrete items, it was nevertheless true that many of these volumes were miscellaneous collections of pamphlets bound together, and that even when the bound pages were conceived as a single work the title was of little help as a label. It was to become a complaint in the library, recorded by Hernando's last librarian Juan Pérez, that printers were fond of giving their books grandiose titles that did not reflect the contents.[60] In response to this, and the need to retain the use of titles (as a manageable labeling system) while not losing resolution on the information contained in the volumes, Hernando conceived a procedure in the early 1520s for developing a level of focus between the enigmatically brief title and the unmanageably copious text: his *Libro de los Epítomes*. This series of summaries of books in the library, often relying heavily on their existing paratextual tools (tables of contents, arguments), was designed (as his assistant Juan Pérez testifies) to allow the researcher to sample the contents of books and narrow their reading list before turning to the books themselves, and the newly discovered scribal copy of the *Epítomes* (which will be discussed further in chapter 4) suggests an intention to contextualize the works for readers by providing short biographical sketches of the authors. The *Libro de los Epítomes*, as well as preserving the contents of many books that are otherwise lost to posterity, is also a powerful demonstration of the primacy of paratexts in the culture of print: for Hernando's *sumistas*, and perhaps at times for the early modern reader more generally, the inundation of print forced them to economize their attention to individual texts and to *read the paratexts alone*, in isolation from the main body of the text. There was, in a sense, a hypertextual culture in which the currents were less to do with what was expressed at length in books and more to do with the distillations of those texts in book and chapter titles, tables of contents, marginal notes, and prefatory lives of the authors.

The life of the library moved into a new phase in 1526 through two innovations, and it is important that the apparent distance between these two is deceptive. On the one hand, Hernando decided, after a lifetime as an itinerant, to build a permanent home on the banks of the Guadalquivir in Seville; on the other, he began to work on systematic indexing of his books by subject matter. The Casa de Colón was originally known as the Casa de Goles from its location outside one of the main city gates, the Puerta de Goles, "Goles" being a name that referred to Hercules in the local idiom.

Among the many features that may have attracted Hernando to this location was its proximity to his father's tomb at the Cartuja de las Cuevas, its similarity to the extra-mural locations of classical and humanist villas, and the opportunities it allowed for the gardens central to humanist culture. Yet the main advantage to this riverside location, otherwise so inhospitable to a collection on paper, may have been the opportunity it offered as virgin terrain, as an abstract space in which to construct the perfect edifice to contain his collections. The plot was not, in fact, virgin, even if it was not built upon: the site had served Seville for some time as a *muladar,* or dung heap, though this execrable history was something of which Hernando was proud. Whatever the symbolic inheritance it gave to Hernando's project, it laid an easy and fertile ground for development, and there is evidence that he set about extensive landscaping for the house and garden.[61] The house itself, which was destroyed in the early seventeenth century, can be reconstructed in a fair amount of detail from contemporary documents and later descriptions: it was an oblong building of two stories, 198 feet by 78 feet—much like the humanist villas he would have seen on the Lungotevere promenade in Rome—and, like the Roman villas, was made up of cubed rooms on both floors (presumably giving it a fascia height of around 40 feet). The Italianate effect was in time enhanced by the addition of a neoclassical marble facade, commissioned in 1529 from Antonio Maria de Carona and Antonio Lanzio in Genoa.[62] It is unclear what portion of the Casa de Colón was set aside for Hernando's collections during his lifetime: from his will we know that he imagined fairly modest living quarters for those employed in the library, and that the inexorable expansion of the collection would eventually require all that space and more. While there is little to substantiate the later tale that the Casa de Goles was an "academy" of sorts during Hernando's lifetime, it is clear insofar as there was evidence for Hernando using parts of the Casa de Goles as "receiving" rooms during his lifetime, it was to receive not social callers (for whom he showed little predilection) but instead delegations of mariners for cartographic instruction, a practice perhaps better suited to a library than a parlor or "Great Room," and one which could easily have planted ideas that the house served as an academy.[63] Wherever in the house the books were, we know that they were originally divided into different rooms with some disciplinary identity—from the reference of Juan Pérez to a "sala de teología," in which the various *repertorios* were kept—and that Hernando had decided by the end of his life that this division should be removed in favor of a single, uninterrupted library room, a design he was reaching at much the same time that Michelangelo was designing the Laurentian Library in Florence.[64] Hernando would have seen in Rome, and perhaps elsewhere, the humanist fashion for libraries divided between Greek and Latin rooms, as it was believed classical libraries were, but the increasing preponderance of texts in languages other than Greek and Latin would soon have made this arrangement impracticable for Hernando's library. As the reference to a "sala de teología" suggests, the original division may have been along disciplinary lines, though of course this would immediately have created problems about where the walls should be: Was canon law part of the legal or the theological division? Were saints' lives theology or something else?[65] Part of the response to this difficulty may have been the *Libro de las Materias:* an attempt to create a subject index which stretched across the volumes of the library, so that someone looking for information on Jesus (in the example used by Juan Pérez) could find the many places where that figure was referred to, in works of Scripture and theology and poetry and history. As suggested by Juan Pérez's description of the *Libro de las Materias,* the first imagined use of this index was to allow someone creating a sermon to draw exempla from throughout the library, so that their homilies would rely on a vast body of authority. But Juan Pérez also imagines the index being used by someone preparing a humanist oration or even a work, perhaps of natural philosophy, on snakes. The *Libro de las Materias* was, in effect, a counterbalance to the necessary evil of divisions, of the bindings and walls which were required to support paper and buildings and to divide the library into manageable chunks, but which also created artificial boundaries between what was contained on the pages of the library: the *Libro de las Materias* created a network of connections between the words in the library that pays no attention to their authorship by particular people following particular conventions of writing.[66]

At the same time as building his library at the Casa de Goles and working around the limitations of the physical library by compiling his *Libro de las Materias,* Hernando was planting an immensely ambitious garden within the meander of the Guadalquivir that held his house. It would be a mistake to think of the garden only as a space of *otium* detached from the organizational projects inside the house. A document of 14 August 1528, laying out the terms of an agreement between Hernando and his gardeners—Alonso de Zamora and his wife Maria Rodriguez—shows the same rigorous attention to the gardens that Hernando later demonstrated in his perpetual instructions for the library, at once keenly sensitive to the qualities of the object being collected and to the need to make its utility accessible to the collector.[67] Hernando left precise instructions for watering the trees—there was a rotation such that each tree was watered every fifth day, with irrigation to encompass a two-foot radius around each tree to ensure the roots were sufficiently supplied. He also constructed, as he would later for his librarians, a system of rewards and punishments that tied the curators to their charge: Alonso and Maria were to live in the garden free of charge as long as their duties were properly attended to, but there would be penalties if any beasts were allowed to enter the garden or if any trees perished from inattention, particularly if those trees could not be replaced by ones of the same kind and size. Though the evidence about Hernando's garden is sparse and not always simple, a number of things can be inferred from what did survive: the garden seems to have been of immense size, with an estimate in the later sixteenth century of some five thousand trees, and, as suggested by the injunction to replace dying trees like for like, this copiousness aimed at variety rather than simply volume. Although it is hard to find solid evidence in the oral histories of Seville to trace several transplanted Latin American tree species to Hernando—including the ombú plant that still grows outside what once was the Columbus family mausoleum at the Cartuja de las Cuevas—some confirmation of the garden's global ambitions can be seen in Hernando's testamentary documents, where he states that the gardens were the finest he had seen in Europe and where he mentions a lost "Memoria de plantas y ortelanos," using the same term as was employed for various descriptions of the organization of the library.[68] Hernando's pride in his gardens may have derived, as it did with everything else he spoke of with satisfaction, from its scope and aspiration to completeness, and it seems highly likely that the global botanical network that was growing up in Seville at the time of Hernando's death got its start from the travelers who gathered around Hernando at the Casa de Contratación. The Sevillian doctor Nicolas Monardes (1493–1588), for instance, promulgated the central American *guayacam* plant as an herbal cure for syphilis, even though he had never traveled to the New World. In his transformation of late-medieval pharmacology into a global and systematic practice, Monardes owed a significant debt to knowledge appropriated from women and from non-Europeans: though it was rarely formally acknowledged, the tradition of using *guayacam* to treat syphilis came through one Antonio de Villasante from his Taíno wife (rechristened Catalina de Ayahibex). The extraordinary lengths to which Hernando went to include Maria Rodriguez on his garden contract suggests he recognized her horticultural talents and was interested in the couple only as a pair.[69] While the ordered botanical garden created a space for scientific plant observation, it was often merely a formalization of knowledge previously held by the world's women.

During the mass removal of the emperor's court to northern Italy in 1529, Hernando turned his attention from building and arranging the library to the question of how his repository was connected to the world. The fact that Hernando retraced the route he had taken in 1520–22, from northern Italy through Basel and up the Rhine through lower Germany into the Low Countries, confirms the dominance of geography in establishing the "fertile crescent of print," that small group of cities which, after an initial rapid expansion of print in the late fifteenth century, proved well enough connected (and resourced with capital) to survive the subsequent drought. As the market for printed products failed to grow at the same rapid pace as the industry, large numbers of presses in smaller towns failed, enabling a much smaller number of printing houses to monopolize the market during its slow maturation, overlaying long-established trade routes and financial networks with the new information channels. This period of concentration not only contributed to the increasingly urbane character of the public sphere, in which cities became the gatekeepers of national culture (as they long had been of trade), but also encouraged the porousness between mercantile and intellectual technologies that soon became evident in Hernando's knowledge-organization practices. In addition to collecting thousands of volumes in cities across northern Italy and the Rhineland, Hernando was in search of those with the necessary skills to make use of his collections. With this in mind, he ended his trip at the Collegium Trilingue in Louvain, where a decade before he had met

Erasmus and been presented with a copy of that author's *Antibarbarorum.* Though Erasmus was no longer an active presence at the college founded in his honor, the Erasmian emphasis on language as something that must be spoken and lived with was alive and well, and during his time there Hernando recruited the leading linguist Nicolas Clenardus (Cleynaerts) to join him in Seville and work on the library.

The relationship between these two men, documented in detail in Clenardus's letters, was founded in mutual convenience: despite plenty of evidence that Hernando tried his best to be a good Hellenist—owning from an early stage Crastonus's pioneering Greek dictionary and primers from François Tissard and Manuel Chrysoloras, and having a Greek lexicon compiled for him by his tutor in Rome—there is little evidence that he actually developed much fluency in Greek, let alone in Hebrew or other non-Romance tongues.[70] Clenardus had won fame in Paris and Louvain for his theatrical manner of teaching ancient tongues through conversation, and later he claimed that he could teach Greek or Latin to the dullest child in six months through his viva voce methods (which included, among other things, performances in Latin by two "Ethiopians," to prove that even "barbarians" could learn under his tutelage). He was attracted to Seville, as he recounted in a 1542 letter to Charles V, despite the otherwise mediocre terms being offered, by the promise of access to Arabic manuscripts in Spanish libraries. Clenardus recounts in his letters how he taught himself to sound out the Arabic characters by using proper nouns in the *Psalterium Hebraeum, Graecum, Arabicum, & Chaldaeum* (Genoa, 1516), but his progress as an Arabist was impeded at Louvain by the lack of access to texts and speakers of the language. The extent of Hernando's Arabic holdings at this time is uncertain—though his purchase of a manuscript guide to learning Arabic in 1516 might suggest some intention on his part to "Arabize"—but between Clenardus's interests, Hernando's universalist ambitions, and the increasing lust for Arabic manuscripts among Spanish book collectors such as Diego Hurtado de Mendoza, it seems likely that Hernando intended to expand in this area if he had not already begun to do so, given that his librarian Juan Pérez notes the use of the symbol "*ax.*" to denote Arabic books in the catalogues—a distinction only given to major languages, even if very few Arabic books survive or are found in the library catalogues.[71] Our reconstruction of the final shelf order of the library also suggests that significant space was set aside for Hebrew and Arabic books, meaning that Hernando anticipated large collections of these materials if he did not already have them. It also seems that there was at least some Arabic literacy among the library staff, as the "Alcoran en arabigo" mentioned in the *Abecedarium B* is marked as having been epitomized, though the epitome is sadly lost.[72] Clenardus's account of his encounter with Hernando features in his *Letter to Christians,* begun while he was in Fez around 1540–41 and left abruptly unfinished after his return to Granada, where he died in 1542. This *Letter* provides a link between Clenardus's linguistic enterprise—which envisioned a pedagogical crusade of Arabic-speaking Christian missionaries across north Africa—and Hernando's own millenarian and universal projects.[73]

The two other librarians recruited by Hernando during his 1529–31 tour of the continent may also give some idea of Hernando's ambitions for the library and the obstacles potentially facing him. The first was Johannes Vasaeus (Jan Waes), a fellow Dutchman whom Clenardus convinced to accompany him to Spain. Although Vasaeus was relatively young at the time, his later career as a historian of Spain and Portugal—eventually bearing fruit in a volume from the same *rerum memorandum* tradition as Piccolomini's *Historia rerum*—had its beginnings in his association with Hernando.[74] A number of the great library projects of the Renaissance, with which Hernando would have been undoubtedly familiar, brought new prominence to the long-standing association between libraries and historiography. They included the library collected by Johannes Trithemius at Würzburg, as the foundation of his projects in Germanic history and bibliography, and the emerging state library of Venice, where Pietro Bembo had been recruited in 1529 to serve jointly as ducal librarian and official historian of the Serenissima. In his intensifying campaign during the last decade of his life to gain official, imperial support for his library project, the prospect of using the collection for chronological and historiographical projects was a principal selling point, as suggested when (in his petition to Charles V) Hernando argues that one reason to build the library was "para que no se pierda la memoria de tan nobles varones como se desvelaron para nuestro bien segund de muchos esta ya perdida" (so that the memories of such noble men who worked for our benefit will not be lost, as many of them already have been).[75]

Hernando's other recruit, a Burgundian doctor of civil law called Johannes Hammonius (Jean Antoine), may suggest a further area of congestion in the library—the legal books, which numbered almost a thousand by the time of Hernando's death.[76] When later recalling the motivations behind the various epitomizing and cataloguing projects on which Hernando embarked, Juan Pérez, his last librarian, noted his master's frustration at the obstacle posed to intellectual endeavor by the sheer volume of works in each field and recorded Hernando's conviction that the knowledge in many fields (medicine and grammar, for instance) could be reduced by his distillatory methods to a single volume. In the same passage, however, doubt is cast on the reducibility of the law, for which Juan Pérez expects that "at most, say, four" volumes would be required. For all the time that Hernando had spent engaged in legal challenges to the Columbus fortune in the Sacra Rota in Rome and as part of the *Pleitos Colombinos* in Spain, it must have become increasingly clear that his lack of legal training would pose a significant obstacle to setting in order the hundreds of legal tomes already in the library. If a knowledge of legal books was primarily required to break the cataloguing jam in the library, it may also have offered new models for organizational processes: when Juan Pérez is describing the use of the *Libro de las Materias* for researching subjects across the shelves of the library, the closest analogy he can think of is one of the prominent law digests of the day, the "Bertachino."

Hernando may have felt himself unequal to undertaking universalizing legal and historiographical projects on his own, but his attentions were also during this period distracted elsewhere as he marshaled the resources of his library toward the more personal project of safeguarding the legacy of his father, whose celebrity and fortune were under siege in the early 1530s. Charles V, who had already sought to undermine the Columbus claim by acquiring the rights of the Pinzón clan to any American wealth arising from their part in the 1492 voyage, wrote on 25 October 1533 to Gonzalo Fernández de Oviedo, royal historian of the Americas, asking for further information on his claim that the New World had in fact been discovered and settled by the Spanish more than three thousand years before Columbus's crossing.[77] The following year, the *Sentencia de las Dueñas* deprived the Columbus dynasty of its remaining hereditary titles in and rights over the Americas, and Hernando's biography of his father, which was not available to a wider public until its 1571 publication in Venice in Italian translation, seems to have been written in response to this. A note by Hernando in his copy of the *Enneads* of Sabellicus records that he was reading this frequently cited source for the biography from 3 August to 21 December of 1534, and the *manicules* and annotations in that volume show Hernando's interest in precisely those parts of Sabellicus cited in the biography, both indications that he was likely working on the biography at this time.[78]

Hernando's biography of his father has primarily drawn attention because of its importance as a source for the Columbian voyages: given the loss of the original logbooks made by Columbus on these voyages and the limited transmission through other sources, such as Bartolomé de las Casas's digest of the logs for the First Voyage, Hernando's detailed accounts remain the major source for information on Columbus's part in the European encounter with the New World. Yet while more than a century of painstaking scholarship has concluded that Hernando's transmission of his father's logbooks is largely faithful, and provides the foundation for later historiography of the Americas by the likes of Bartolomé de las Casas, the eagerness of Columbian scholars to save this crucial source has often led them to downplay Hernando's part in shaping his father's biography (and the American historiography that follows from it). The major critical study of the biography by Antonio Rumeu de Armas attempts to hew the work precisely along these lines and, while establishing the account of the voyages as authentic using close and detailed criticism, argues impressionistically that the sections of the biography dealing with Columbus's life outside the voyages are not by Hernando at all, but rather are the work of a forger working under Hernando's name. Newly discovered marginalia offer a correction to this tendency in how the seminal sources on Columbus have been treated, and they offer a new way of understanding the coherence of these materials through the lens of Hernando's practices in the archive. The biography of Columbus, in a sense, is in itself an archive, in which Hernando follows a practice of ordered collation of Columbus's documents, bringing together the logbooks with official documents (such as the Capitulaciones de Santa Fe, copied out in full in the biography), treatises commissioned by Columbus (such as Ramon Pané's ethnographic descriptions of the Taíno), and the mixture of textual citation and personal recollection upon which he had to rely to refute undesirable versions of Columbus's early life, given the scarcity of other documentation available. In the act of life writing, Hernando himself became part of the archive, entering his own memories as items in the documentary record.

The partial reversal of the disastrous *Sentencia de las Dueñas* in 1536 gave Hernando breathing space to focus on his library projects, as well as financial resources in the form of funds he was granted as part of the settlement. His emerging clarity about the library can be seen in a series of documents drawn up in the last three years of his life, the first of which was a letter to Charles V asking for his support. While this *Memorial al Emperador* (translated in full in appendix 5) seems never to have been sent to Charles, it nevertheless represents the earliest blueprint of Hernando's eventual design. The document's primary purpose was to petition Charles to convert the lifetime pension of five hundred gold pesos granted to Hernando in the settlement into a perpetual grant to the library, to which (he tells the emperor) he intends to leave the entirety of his own estate. In order to convince Charles of the desirability of this foundation, Hernando put down in writing for the first time the grounds on which the library could claim extraordinary attention from the emperor, reduced to six principal points. The first of these was the unparalleled nature of the achievement, both in terms of its gathering of "all books in all languages and on all subjects which can be found within Christendom and without" and in terms of its aim not merely to "create a library of what can be found at this time" but to "ordain perpetually the searching out and collection of all new books." As in his proposal to circumnavigate the world, presented to Ferdinand in 1511, Hernando appealed both to the sovereign's desire for *fama* and to his obligation to *charitas:* Charles would be doing something "that no prince has been heard of doing until now," and he would be conferring great benefits upon the *Respublica Christiana.*

The second ground of Hernando's appeal was to ensure against the obliteration of culture: not only would the preservation and expansion of the library guarantee that "the memories of great men who worked for our benefit will not be lost, as many of them already have been," but it would also "result in greater certainty and harmony in matters touching religion and the governance of the state," allowing for lettered men to resort to this "refuge for whatever doubt arises." These concerns once again connect the library to the many other domains of Hernando's activity, from the biography of his father—which was a paradigm (at least in Hernando's mind) of preserving the deeds of great men from oblivion—to his work on geographical projects, both of his own creating and as an overseer of the work of the Casa de la Contratación. Hernando's efforts there were focused on harmonizing variant reports into an indisputable picture of the world, one which would provide a stable basis for Spain's empire to be known and controlled.

The remaining four grounds on which Hernando felt his library would be both instrumental and exceptional derived entirely from the way in which the library was being—or, in some cases, was expected to be—organized. These ideas will be discussed in the chapter on knowledge organization in the library, though it is worth noting here that, from the very earliest account of his library, Hernando considered his cataloguing systems as tools directed toward improving mastery of the world outside the library, not merely a means of making the collection work for its users. For each of his main cataloguing systems—the *Abecedarium,* the *Libro de las Ciencias,* the *Libro de los Epítomes,* and the *Libro de las Materias*—he articulated uses in terms of the effect they would have on the world not just of the book but of the reader, and he seems consistently to have maintained a dual focus on the organizational needs of his material collection and the ways these orders would work upon the world outside.

Hernando continued to develop, refine, and explain his vision for the library during the remaining few years of his life, providing detailed explanations of his ideas in two different copies of his will (excerpts in appendix 2). Even this, it seems, was not enough, and after his death on 12 July 1539 two further lengthy documents were produced, providing (occasionally conflicting) descriptions of Hernando's vision. One of these, the extraordinary *Memoria* of Juan Pérez (appendix 1), is a detailed description of the organization, daily functioning, and projected development of the library written by Hernando's senior assistant of many years' standing. The other is a series of codicils to Hernando's will by his executor Marcos Felipe, providing further documentation (including the petition to the emperor, which is copied into this notarized document as an addendum) as well as personal testimony communicated to him by Hernando.

Hernando's focus on ordering the library as death approached is a fitting emblem of how for him vitality and order were innately linked. Centuries before modern philosophy conceived of the *form of life,* Hernando crystallized the relationship between *life* and *order:* how each notion of order emerges out of a particular set of experiences, and how in turn our understanding of "a life" is in itself an act of ordering. The *Descripción,* the biography, the catalogues, the garden: these are different kinds of game, themselves given "life" by the order they create, which in turn can be used to understand Hernando's *form of life,* the particular kind of life he must have led so that these orders made sense. One can, as Wittgenstein points out, learn a game only by having mastered a certain number of previous games; each of Hernando's ordering games is related to the others by means of the underlying assumptions about the nature of games and their constituent parts, which allows for the difference between each game to be underwritten by an element of sameness. This sameness, however, is not semantic but rather material, that is, it proceeds out of the assumption that things are *useful* when they are *ordered,* from ship's tackle to books to geographical and financial data to plants. These ideas emerged in response to a series of practical challenges about how the material world of early modern Europe could best be known and used.

CHAPTER TWO

TRADE SECRETS

Shortly after his arrival in Rome in September 1512, Hernando paid three *quatrines blancos* for *Le selue damore*, which its Sienese publisher ostentatiously advertised on its title page as a novelty penned by none other than Lorenzo de' Medici.[1] In one of these poems (composed around 1486–92) Lorenzo catalogued the "myriad of . . . harmful and new innovations" (*mille . . . dannosi e novi ingegni*) of the current age, including the thirst for gold, measurement techniques for cartography (*misurare il mare e i liti a miglia*), the development of navigation methods, the recording of history, and the use of iron and horses as technologies for war—in contrast with the Golden Age, when no islands were known and the world appeared to end on the shore (*D'isole ancor non s'era il nome udito: / parea finissi il mondo ov'era lito*).[2] The irony of these unworldly lines being written by Lorenzo, a potentate whose wealth and power rested upon sophisticated banking practices and international trade, was set off by another of Hernando's purchases, Filippo Calandri's *De aritmethrica opusculum*, a handbook first published in 1492 and dedicated to Lorenzo, whose preface emphasizes that *la scientia arimethrica* [*sic*] is not just useful but absolutely necessary for trade, a business in which, he adds, Florence excels the rest. Calandri promised to shun mere theory (*lasceremo la speculation . . . a philosophanti*), to focus instead on a very pragmatic description of Florentine coins, weights, and measures (*exempli di monete, pesi e misura fiorentini*).[3]

The universalizing projects of Hernando and his father situated them in this paradoxical milieu, which shunned the technologies of fallen humanity while at the same time prizing them as central tools for working upon the world. Their respective projects—a new sailing route to the Indies and the eventual reconquest of Jerusalem for Columbus, an omnicomprehensive library as part of an imperial *Universitas Christiana* for Hernando—were founded on scriptural and classical narratives that decried the very methods and technologies facilitating their pursuit. These damned technologies included the invention of money and even the books which Hernando spent his life collecting, as made clear by Peter Martyr d'Anghiera, who portrayed the inhabitants of Hispaniola as proof that the golden age was not a myth, since they lived "naked, without weights, without measures, without mortiferous *money*, living in a golden age, free, without fraudulent judges, *books*, and content of their natural state."[4]

Hernando's vigorous attack on those who (following Andrés Bernáldez's *Crónica*) accused his father of being involved with the *mechanical* trades of bookselling and mapmaking before his 1492 crossing should be seen as part of a wider urge to subsume the material forces of history into various forms of agonistic narratives—heroic, millenarian, nationalistic, psychological—that would be interrupted by such practical considerations as how Columbus supported himself as a young man. In reality, all early modern voyages of exploration drew their impulses from the needs of trade, and the trade networks from which exploration sprang were in turn the same as those along which geographical and textual information flowed. While traditional accounts of the Renaissance centered on an influx of Greek learning from the East, it was in a sense the result of a *closing* channel of communication, not an opening one. Historians have over the past few decades restored the economic contexts of the age of discovery, showing how Venetian- and Genoese-sponsored voyages to the west and south of the Pillars of Hercules were driven by a need to replace markets lost in the eastern Mediterranean through Ottoman expansion. Columbus's maritime expertise derived from his mercantile work for the Centurione family, was later supported by Genoese financial networks, and was also shaped by the books and cartographical information that flowed through the same channels.[5] Columbus and his brother Bartholomew founded their projects upon the knowledge obtained by the exchange of confidential information—primarily cartographic data that were so valuable at the time that they frequently enjoyed the status of a state secret. Hernando's father used these networks to exchange intelligence as well as books, sometimes even using the same agent. The writings of Marco Polo, which were fundamental to Columbus's interpretation of the New World as part of Asia, came to him in the form of a book sent by Bristol merchant John Day, with whom he had come in contact during his days in the Centurione operation. In his letter to Columbus sent with this volume, Day included fresh information about John Cabot's 1497 expedition in search of the North Passage—which had returned just a few weeks earlier—and requested, in exchange, any information Columbus might have. Day was, in other words, trading in goods but also in news: he was an intelligencer and a mercantile mercenary of sorts—supplying in 1487 victuals and other goods for the Christian troops besieging Malaga—and one among the brigade of domestic and international merchants and financiers who helped sustain the more material and mundane foundations of the Hispanic monarchy's millenarian crusade. The letter and book Day sent to Columbus collapse the worlds of trade, information exchange, books, exploration, and empire—so often treated separately—into a single transaction.[6]

Yet the recent (and much-needed) demystification of the age of exploration has perhaps overlooked the extent to which the ability to react to these economic forces was itself heavily dependent on the tools developed in the late medieval and early modern periods to conceptualize this new world of finance and trade. These tools offered powerful methods for *rationalizing* and *coordinating* the world—in the literal sense of subjecting it to laws of *ratio* and reducing it to the same order—methods that Hernando would borrow when attempting to construct and map his collections. It is also important that the claims of these tools to rationalize, to provide an objective picture of the world, should not be taken at face value, stemming as many of them did from culturally specific contexts that warped and limited the ways in which they represented the world. Hernando's global vision, like that of his father, was shaped by the tools at his disposal to render accounts of the world, beginning with the very worldly techniques and tools he borrowed from financiers and merchants. Many of these relied on sophisticated symbolic systems for the representation and exchange of both value and knowledge, in a process which mirrored the verbal exchanges that wove the fabric of human societies—and, within a millenarian frame of mind, made them part of the fragmented, postlapsarian world, in counterpoint to the utopia of a common language for all humankind and a universal world community. In his travels around the transnational book markets, Hernando navigated a vast network through which circulated the goods, the information, and the currency and credit that constituted the lifeblood of not just the European body politic but also its cultural and economic counterparts. His visionary emphasis on *obrezillas,* printed matter in small format, was unique to his collection and driven in part by his connection to this mercantile and financial world. In the construction of his ideal universal library, an unprecedentedly comprehensive repository of knowledge, he aspired to collect not only the great texts and authors that furnished the traditional medieval curricula and its new humanist replacement, but also (and perhaps primarily) the more modest pamphlets spawned by print, which recorded the heterogeneous new world of news and information exchange aimed at a wider audience.

Trade, Finance, and the Exchange of Knowledge

The milieu from which Columbus's voyages emerged is perhaps best captured by the famous globe of Martin Behaim (ca. 1492), commissioned from this disciple of the mathematician and astronomer Regiomontanus by the Nuremberg community of merchants in 1490. This globe, which Lisa Jardine has called a "substantial piece of commercial and industrial espionage," draws heavily on information Behaim had gathered when he was part of the team of cartographers, mathematicians, and pilots who worked for John II of Portugal—the very same circles that included Columbus and his brother Bartholomew in the 1480s, before frustration led them to expand their search for patronage to England, France, and Spain.[7] In contrast with traditional portolan maps, a globe was a sphere whose measurement and representation required advanced skills in geometry and trigonometry—that is, the application of mathematics to the measurement of angles and triangles upon a curved surface. As Hernando himself would witness during the Juntas de Elvas-Badajoz, the accurate representation of the earth as a sphere and on a global scale posed fabulous challenges, not just in terms of distances and size but also in terms of the algebraic and geometrical skills required from cartographers. Trigonometry was fundamental for the representation of the earth and the cosmos, hence the proliferation of treatises on the sphere, many of which Hernando owned (including some penned by Regiomontanus, Behaim's teacher) and used for study during his time in Rome.

In addition to cartographic iconography, Behaim's globe featured detailed textual information about the holy grail of the age of exploration, the Spice Islands, describing in detail the trade route as well as the customs duties paid on products at each stage on their route from the Far East to European markets.[8] In the period before the circumnavigation of the globe, and in the absence of reliable measures of longitude, the arrangement of landmasses on the surface of the Behaim sphere was highly speculative, yet the linear measurements, of distances between specific locations (where these had actually been traveled) and of costs accrued during the voyage, were much more certain. This information was more accurately recorded in the portolan maps of the time, which represented travel in terms of distances along a straight line, as it would have been experienced by coasting ships maintaining a fairly even distance from the shoreline. Early modern planispheres attempted to transform a one-dimensional set of information—distances traveled, or costs accrued—into a two-dimensional picture of the world as it wrapped around the terrestrial globe. This heavy reliance on a linear method of accounting—reducing the world to vectors of distance to and from, profit and loss, items in and out of a collection—is amusingly illustrated by Columbus's intentional under-accounting of the distances they were sailing westward in 1492, an attempt to maintain calm among his crew but one that suggests their picture of the world was still largely the linear one used in the portolan maps. This foundational model will appear time and again in many of the practices in which Columbus and Hernando were involved and is crucial for understanding Hernando's world of knowledge.

However, Hernando's plans were developing even as the globe expanded and more territories came under the representational power of increasingly sophisticated measuring techniques. Navigation gained in accuracy and speed, which facilitated the opening of new markets and led to an intensification in the flow of information, in turn rendering these new cartographies ever more accurate. In order to represent and rationalize—in order to control—this flow of information, and all the goods, and all the capital that circulated throughout the new global networks, cartographers, sailors, merchants, and financiers called for more sophisticated systems that gradually developed from simple linear calculation into something more complex, involving the triangulation and cross-referencing of multiple streams of data and driving the development and spread of trigonometry, double-entry bookkeeping, and sophisticated financial instruments as symbolic methods for the representation of the globe and the cosmos, on the one hand, and for the rationalization and control of economic and financial activities, on the other.[9] Financial operations and currency exchange required complex operations that involved the calculation of difference and equivalence in value across distance and time and modes of symbolic representation to express this. As his library grew in size and scope, Hernando's catalogues started to combine simple linear systems with more sophisticated cross-referencing methods, by the simultaneous use of several catalogues that recorded different categories of information (*autores, ciencias, epítomes, materias;* see fig. 8).[10] A reader could thus easily navigate through the *mare magnum*—to borrow the name used by Francesco Marucelli for his universal bibliography—that was Hernando's global repository of knowledge. In short, without catalogues, or with simply linear catalogues that did not cross-reference the information that they recorded, the mere accumulation of books would have turned Hernando's massive library into a globe full of *terrae ignotae*, a *mappamundi* punctuated by a series of scattered, linear portolan maps, a return to a cartography of islands amidst uncharted regions teeming with fabulous beasts and monsters. Not that Hernando's plans were all brought to fruition: at the time of his death the many catalogues he devised—well beyond the four listed on his tombstone—were still incomplete. Like the library he had conceived, which was to be constantly expanded with new publications, the catalogues were also fated to be permanent works in progress. But his original ambition had always been to turn them into comprehensive records of all the materials in the custody of his universal library. In doing so, he employed methods that were of a piece with other similar strategies for information

© JUNTA DE ANDALUCIA
CONSEJERIA DE CULTURA

FIG. 8. Hernando's design for his tombstone, in his testament, which includes his four main catalogues (*autores, ciencias, epítomes, materias*) as part of the coat of arms (Archivo Histórico Provincial de Sevilla)

management, which involved what Ann Blair describes as the four crucial operations in early modern compilations: storing, sorting, selecting, and summarizing.[11] But beyond this method, Hernando's catalogues also reflected a general trend for the mathematization of knowledge and the development of more sophisticated systems for the production, storage, and exchange of data of all sorts, involving ever-increasing levels of abstraction when it came to the symbolic representation of information and value, of time and distance. The worlds of trade, finance, and the early exchange of news, on the one hand, and cosmography with its associated disciplines on the other, employed methods that shared not just similar habits but also common epistemological foundations as they underwent similar developments immediately before as well as during Hernando's lifetime.

Despite his attempts to establish himself and his family as members of the Spanish aristocracy after the successful voyage of 1492, Columbus's continued reliance on the worlds of trade and finance generally—and that of Genoa specifically—can be traced through the course of his later career. As he prepared to sail on his Fourth Voyage of 1502, on which Hernando was to accompany him, Columbus prepared a *Book of Privileges* that compiled the contractual agreements he had made with the Spanish crown, from the Capitulaciones de Santa Fe agreed on 17 April 1492 to the various confirmations and clarifications of these privileges he had secured in the intervening years.[12] This volume, prepared alongside the *Book of Prophecies,* paralleled the aspects of Columbus's dealings ordained by God with those agreed among men, but it also revealed the thin boundary separating these notarial and theological strains. Columbus's *Book of Privileges* was modeled on the *Book of Privileges of the Genoese Nation* (1491), a compilation of official documents commissioned by the Genoese merchants in Spain as a witness to their financial privileges and rights in the Hispanic kingdoms.[13] In a way, it was only natural for Columbus to resort to the inveterate contractual practices of his fellow Genoese merchants and financial agents, for as Margarita Zamora has pointed out, the language employed in these agreements reached between Columbus and the crown reproduced the same conventions found in notarial documents, most of which were of course devoted to commercial and financial exchanges.[14] Elvira Vilches has more recently underlined the combination of millenarianism and commercial-contractual language employed not just in the Capitulaciones de Santa Fe but also in Columbus's first letter to the monarchs announcing the discovery, where he committed himself, in seven years, to provide Isabel and Ferdinand with troops for the eventual conquest of Jerusalem—troops that Columbus promised as the return of the monarchs' initial investment in the first voyages of exploration established in the Capitulaciones.[15] Columbus produced four notarized copies of his *Book of Privileges:* one of them was to be deposited at the monastery of the Cartuja de las Cuevas in Seville, which served as a proto-archive of Columbian documents during the last years of Columbus's life; another copy was sent across the ocean to La Hispaniola. The last two copies were sent, by two different messengers for extra security, to Genoa. For further emphasis on their symbolic importance, these two copies were produced in expensive parchment, bound and boxed. One was to be held by Nicolò Oderigo (former Genoese ambassador to Spain), and the other would be deposited for safekeeping in the Casa di San Giorgio.[16] This institution, the oldest chartered bank in the world, had emerged from the consolidation of various *compere*—consortiums of creditors to the state—and, from its beginnings as a holder of public debt in the form of shareholder bonds, became the anchor for Genoese trade operations across Europe and the Mediterranean to the Black Sea, and (later) across the whole globe. The vaults of this bank and the systems and iconography of its ledgers provide one of the most unexpected and arresting prototypes for Hernando's library and its tools for organizing the information of the world.

In archiving his most treasured documents with the Casa di San Giorgio, Columbus was not merely maintaining links to his Genoese nation (a loyalty confirmed by his bequest to the state through the bank), he was also lodging his claim at the center of a vast network that would allow these claims to be drawn upon and enforced across the world. The critical mass generated by the creation of the Casa had prompted the development of sophisticated financial instruments, such as the *luoghi*—bond issues that allowed the bank to raise capital—and bills of exchange, which allowed money to be moved around Europe and eventually beyond.[17] Hernando used these Genoese financial networks to circulate virtual, paper currency and credit along the axis between Germany, Spain, and Hispaniola, which he subsequently converted into ready cash to pay for his gargantuan purchases of books between 1520 and 1522. Confidence in the Casa was sufficient that it came to act as the fiscal arm of the Genoese republic, through the institution of a tax farm that allowed the bank to collect taxes using its networks in exchange for a set fee to the state. These were not, however, simply market-driven expansions and formalizations of rational economic activity: instead, the Casa (and those who followed, like the Medici) were indebted to preexisting networks and practices that had been created by the papacy, starting in the eleventh century, to centralize church finance and enable funding to be raised on a large scale in order to fund the Crusades. Letters of credit had also been frequently employed by travelers and pilgrims for safe international money transfer—frequently facilitated by the Knights Templar—before merchants took up this and similar financial practices in the thirteenth century and turned them into more sophisticated methods for their own, more purely profit-driven purposes.[18] Doctrinal prohibitions against usury and the dramatic expansion of trade gradually led to more complex financial instruments. As the banks could not charge interest on the money they lent—owing to theological strictures as well as widespread unease at the "unnatural" growth of money from itself—a system was developed in which profits *technically* accrued from the use of variable exchange rates. As de Roover illustrates, "A London banker offered fewer sterlings for having to wait three months before receiving a ducat in Venice or a florin in Florence. For the same reason, the banker in Italy was unwilling to part with a ducat or a florin unless he received in London a greater quantity of sterling. Between two places, the exchange rate tended to be higher in the place which gave its currency to the other. The organization of the money market was such that it favored the lender to the detriment of the borrower."[19] The development of these and similar financial practices relied on operations that involved the numerical calculation of difference and equivalence along the axes of time and space, and required the coordinated exchange of reliable information among all the agents involved.[20] This operation, understood as one of commercial exchange rather than moneylending, seems to have satisfied the theologians.

The use of exchange rates as one of the foundations for the banking system required both a secure, rapid system for transmitting information about the *actual* exchange rate (so that the inflated rate charged as a substitute for interest could be set accordingly) and a way of instilling confidence that this system worked, so that capital could continue to be raised through bond issues. Confidence in the system therefore was founded upon the exchange of information among different agents who bestowed mutual trust upon each other. But its efficiency also relied on the use of standard symbolic systems and proper methods to represent and record value. After all, the *luoghi* (debt bonds) were fluctuating, virtual commodities that existed only as tables, figures, and names within the manuscript books that recorded the public debt.[21] Deposited, as Columbus did with his own *Book of Privileges,* at the central headquarters of the Casa di San Giorgio in Genoa, these symbolic records sanctioned the value and underwrote the credit of all the operations coordinated and backed by the Casa and its many Genoese associates. In other words, the material value of the precious metals, the goods, and the currency that circulated throughout those global markets managed by Ligurian agents ultimately lent credibility to the merely semiotic value recorded in the tabular and numerical arcana deposited in Genoa. In turn, the development of abstract monetary instruments—such as bills of exchange and letters of credit—displaced the traditional exchange of commodities and minted money in precious metals and ended up creating a virtual market of complex financial vehicles based on contractual arithmetic operations. In 1600 the *arbitrista* Martín González de Cellórigo attributed the recurrent economic crises that had afflicted Spain over the course of the preceding decades to the fact that wealth had circulated in quasi-immaterial formats, "up in the air, in papers and contracts . . . and letters of exchange." González de Cellórigo even rejected the sort of value that circulated in currency, silver, and gold, expressing his preference for tangible goods whose trade could generate actual wealth.[22]

The very financial technologies aimed at rationalizing currency exchange required further levels of abstraction, as in 1535 when the Genoese instituted an international currency exchange at Besançon (the market where annual accounts had been settled for some time), consisting of "a virtual basket of five gold coins issued by Venice, Genoa, Naples, Castile, and Milan called the *scudo di marco.*"[23] The *scudo di marco* was not an actual coin but a money of account, and the transactions denominated in this virtual currency were described as *cambio aereo*—ethereal exchange. Instead of establishing exchange rates upon a one-on-one relation between two different currencies and two different locations, the *scudo* aimed to create a more sophisticated, complex, and multilateral—albeit also centralized—foundation for the calculation of international exchange rates, combining the respective values of five different currencies. Its main function was that of a central and more predictable exchange medium which transformed currency trading from a myriad of local binary transactions to a common and more controllable market where bills were cashed at secure and preestablished rates thanks to a Genoese legal procedure, the *pacto di ricorsa.* To make matters even more disorientating, the fixed location of the currency market at Besançon soon disappeared, replaced by a floating and virtual market that materialized wherever it was convenient to the Genoese. The result was what Pezzolo and Tattara describe as "an offshore capital market which operated on an international scale," a forum for the arbitrage of international interest rates whose unprecedented level of financial sophistication and abstraction turned it into the first financial market completely independent of commercial activities.[24] The capacity of Genoese bankers to turn the flow of American gold and silver into such innovative and stable financial instruments and practices turned them into the main creditors of the Hispanic crown during the late sixteenth and the early seventeenth centuries. It was precisely these accounting methods, local anchors, and communication networks upon which Hernando would found his book-collecting system. The considerable variety of information that circulated throughout these networks was the lifeblood of financial activities, but it also furnished data employed for the elaboration of cartographic documents—iconic and ekphrastic—which were then employed by explorers and merchants.

The complexity of these transactions, and the crucial need for confidence, prompted the development of information-sharing tools, the so-called *quaderna di mercatura,* manuscript notebooks which passed from generation to generation. These documents were in turn closely related to the *lettere merchantesche,* letters in which financiers and merchants recorded and exchanged information that combined political news with dry economic figures and any other data that could affect business. Giorgio Doria has demonstrated in great detail how the comparatively disproportionate financial success of a small city-state like Genoa relied on an extremely efficient network that gathered and exchanged reliable information and granted it a formidable edge over the competition.[25] Also employed by other financial and trading centers in Italy, and elsewhere, *quaderni di mercatura* and *lettere merchantesche* recorded a large amount of very practical information, much of it involving quantification, measurement, and currency equivalence.[26] The earliest surviving *quaderni di mercatura* date from the thirteenth century (around 1270), and as the expansion and increase of finance and trade called for ever more sophisticated methods, these handbooks evolved accordingly into educational tools for a population of merchants, bankers, and clerks, who thus turned into extremely valuable human capital.

Girolamo Tagliente's *Libro d'abaco*—a copy of which survives among Hernando's books—combines training in complex mathematical operations involving the exchange of goods between different locations in different currencies (*ragione mercantile*) with basic skills in geometry for the very practical purpose of measuring land, buildings, and walls (*pertegare le terre con larte di la geometria et altre nobilissime ragione straordinarie*). Its third book lists a series of tables with the equivalence of weights and measures, as well as currency exchange rates between Venice, the rest of Italy, and other European trading centers (*la tariffa come respondeno li pesi et monede de molte terre del mondo con la inclita citta di Vinegia*). Its paratexts combine the mundane (for example, engravings that illustrate common, everyday mercantile activities) with the global-cosmographic: its title page displays Pythagoras and Ptolemy applying algebra and trigonometry to the measurement of an armillary sphere, and its title proclaims the global economic scope of Venice and the universal nature of its contents (figs. 9 and 10).[27] As with Hernando's library, then, the expansion of global power was seen to stem from the creation of an exchange mechanism that allows all the many measures of the globe to be under one, localized control.

As the need for up-to-date information became more urgent, instruments were developed—first and foremost the Medici *lettere di compagnia,* which integrated current information on exchange rates into the very bills of exchange themselves, closing the gap between the exchange of value and the exchange of information. The evident advantages that other kinds of information would provide to commodity traders soon led to these channels being used to send more varied and detailed reports on local economic and political conditions, in the form of newsletters that began to constitute the first regular news networks.[28]

LIBRO

Dabaco che insegna a fare ogni ra-
gione mercadãtile: ⁊ a ptegare le ter
re cõ larte di la geometria: ⁊ altre no
bilissime ragione straordinarie cõ la
Tariffa come respõdeno li pesi ⁊ mo
nede de molte terre del mõdo con la
inclita citta de Uinegia. El qual Lib
bro se chiama Thesauro vniuersale.

FIG. 9. Title page of Tagliente's *Libro d'abaco,* with Pythagoras and Ptolemy applying algebra and trigonometry to the measurement of an armillary sphere (© Cabildo Catedral de Sevilla)

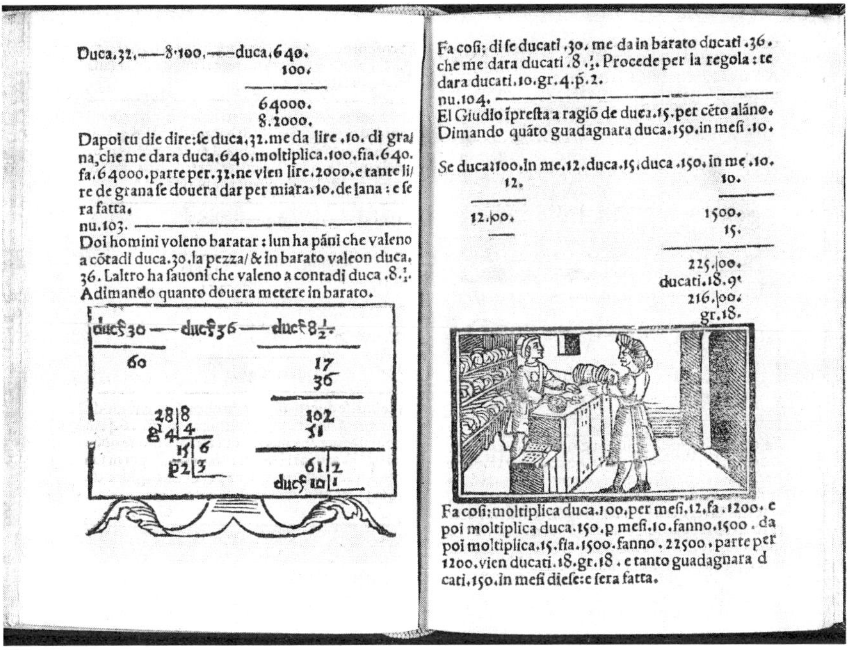

Duca.32.—8.100.—duca.640.
100.
64000.
8.2000.
Dapoi tu die dire: ſe duca.32.me da lire .10. di grana, che me dara duca.640. moltiplica.100.fia.640. fa.64000.parte per.32.ne vien lire.2000.e tante lire de grana ſe douera dar per miara.10.de lana: e ſera fatta.
nu.103.
Doi homini voleno baratar: lun ha pāni che valeno a cōtadi duca.30.la pezza/ & in barato valeon duca.36. Laltro ha ſauoni che valeno a contadi duca .8.½. Adimando quanto douera metere in barato.

Fa coſi; di ſe ducati .30. me da in barato ducati .36. che me dara ducati .8.½. Procede per la regola: te dara ducati.10.gr.4.p̃.2.
nu.104.
El Giudio īpreſta a ragiō de duca.15.per cēto alāno. Dimando quāto guadagnara duca.150.in meſi .10.
Se duca.100.in me.12.duca.15.duca .150.in me .10.

Fa coſi; moltiplica duca.100.per meſi.12.fa .1200. e poi moltiplica duca.150.p meſi.10.fanno.1500. da poi moltiplica.15.fia.1500.fanno.22500.parte per 1200.vien ducati.18.gr.18. e tanto guadagnara ducati.150.in meſi dieſe: e ſera fatta.

FIG. 10. Practical mathematical operations in Tagliente's *Libro d'abaco:* instructions on how to calculate the interest rate on a loan and, on the facing page, a problem that involves the selling and buying of everyday goods, illustrated with an engraving of a customer at a bakery exchanging coins for bread (© Cabildo Catedral de Sevilla)

When Hernando laid down in his testament, then, the system whereby funds would be distributed from his estate through Medina del Campo and Lyon to five cities along the "fertile crescent of print"—Rome, Venice, Nuremberg, Paris, and Antwerp—creating a deposit on which they could draw to send books back along the same routes to Lyon, Medina del Campo, and then on to Seville, he was attaching his library to a preexisting network with established practices designed to facilitate the smooth and dependable exchange of goods, currency, and information.[29] Whereas his father's projects had drawn on the maritime shipping routes and practices of late medieval trade, Hernando's network roughly overlaid the "Lotharingian Axis," the strip of land that went from the Netherlands and Flanders, western Rhineland, western Switzerland, down to the north of Italy, which had formed the "middle kingdom" carved out of Charlemagne's Europe.[30] Owing to the crucial inland shipping access provided by the

Rhine and the survival of free imperial cities, such as Basel and Strasbourg, along it, this axis had developed into the major mercantile artery of Europe—and, as a result, eventually also became the spine of the print trade. There is no small irony that the technologies of exchange, developed initially to facilitate pilgrimage to the Holy Land and to draw the capital of Europe to serve the millenarian ambitions of the Crusader popes, had—after a period of development as a tool of the market—returned to serve the millenarian ambitions of Columbus's voyages and Hernando's library. In a sense, the global nature of these ambitions—universal evangelization, global trade and credit networks, a library of all books from within Christendom and without—evolved as these networks grew to connect them to the world, a world that was known and interacted with only through the network. The reverse, however, was also increasingly true: the "world" was only that to which access was given through the network, making non-urban and peripheral groups—whose voices were not channeled through the urban markets and presses—increasingly alien, and making the stock-in-trade of the network (currency, financial instruments, news pamphlets, printed works) the primary means of perceiving the world.

The exponential rise in the number and complexity of transactions emergent from this network required in turn the development of tools for representing this world in ways that fostered confidence. The principal means of coordinating this information with predictable accuracy was the reduction to number, which could be subjected to various mathematical operations and orders. Double-entry bookkeeping, first documented in European records in the public accounts of the Genoese city stewards for the year 1340, allowed the incoming and outgoing materials in the network to be arranged along a number line, with vectors given as profit and loss, and enabled the relation of the individual to the network to be reduced to a series of figures, providing a simple *balance* which indicated the health of the institution.[31] In 1472 a document from the Fondaco de Tedeschi in Venice shows that Bavarian merchants were sending their youth to Italy to learn this art, among them Georg and Jacob Fugger.[32] The first formal treatment of this system to reach print was by Luca Pacioli, who in his 1494 *Summa de arithmetica, geometria, proportioni e proportionalità* sought to formulate for trade a language that gave it the same epistemological foundations that he saw in Euclid's *Elements* (which he later translated) and which in his 1503 *Divina Proportione* he would expand into a universal language based around the golden ratio, illustrating the geometric reducibility of polyhedra, letterforms, and even organic shapes like the human figure (drawn by his collaborator Leonardo da Vinci) and arguing that mathematics was the language whereby God had given the universe measure. Ciocci describes Pacioli's work as a monumental compilation of four subdisciplines in mathematics: arithmetic, algebra, accounting (*ragioneria*), and geometry; only Ptolemaic astronomy and trigonometry were beyond his scope.[33] Pacioli, who had worked in Venice as tutor to the children of a Jewish merchant, had been educated in the mathematical curriculum of its famous Scuola di Rialto, and was hence well placed to integrate the practical accountancy of the mercantile world and its training centers—the *scuole d'abaco* and their textbooks—with the more abstract world of Euclidean geometry, transferring the confidence generated by mathematical proofs into the world of trade. The *Summa* was published in a volume that also contained a *Libro de Mercantie*, which discussed several different systems of currency, weights, and measures employed in the Italian states in a manner reminiscent of the *quaderni di mercatura*.[34] Pacioli's treatment of double-entry bookkeeping in the "Treatise on Accounts and Documents" (*Tractatus de computis et scripturis*) spread the Italian mercantile practice further throughout Europe, where it became known as the *Venetian method*.[35] Hernando purchased both the *Summa* and the *Divina Proportione* on his arrival in Rome in 1512, and he may well have heard Pacioli lecture at the Studium Urbis, to which Hernando was connected by his tutor Sebastianus Veteranus and by a significant proportion of his book purchases.[36] According to Hernando's own testimony in his copy of Silvestrio di Prierio's *Commentaria in theoricas planetarum Georgii Purbachii* (Colombina 12-6-35), in 1515 he heard Sebastianus's lecture on Purbachius's trigonometry—one of the disciplines that dealt with the measurement and representation of the sphere and thus complemented the scope of Pacioli's work.[37]

The extension of these tools to nonquantitative phenomena was made when merchants began to provide serial or registry numbers for transactions in their "day books" (*giornali* or *tagebücher*), which allowed for complex records of dates, locations, and amounts to be accorded a single number, which could then be counted, ordered, and retrieved. It was likely during his time in Rome, or perhaps shortly after his return, that Hernando began registers for his books and prints—the *Registrum A* and the *Memoria de los Dibujos o Pinturas*—which provide a registry number for each entry, allowing further indices to be drawn up which ordered the information in different ways (alphabetically, by discipline, by subject matter, topographically within the library) without requiring the arduous task of transcribing the detailed information into each new index; instead, the registry number could be used to cross-refer the user back to the initial registry entry. The development of this technique was a crucial early step for Hernando's collection, given the fundamental problem of duplication once the collection expanded beyond the number of titles a single person could securely recall: the indices allowed him (or any holder of the catalogues) to use titles, authors, incipits, and features of illustrations to find existing entries similar to possible new purchases, and then to check against the full registry entry whether the two items were just similar or actually identical (just as indexed account books guarded against the same client running up multiple debts that were not tallied together). The infinite yet discrete nature of numbers—the fact that no two are the same no matter how high you count—provided a crucial framework onto which indiscrete worlds, where two things could appear to be the same, could be mapped.

During his peregrinations throughout Europe in search of books, Hernando had ample opportunity to familiarize himself with the workings of early modern trade networks. At a practical level, he relied for financing on complex loan arrangements on a global scale, given that most of the funds available to him—through his inheritance and, later, in terms of the direct grants from Charles—were not provided as ready funds but as warrants to be drawn on the treasury of Hispaniola. Hernando consistently exchanged these distant prospects for ready money from the European banking networks by either surrendering his right to collect from Hispaniola or promising to pay back at a higher rate at some point in the future. Like the silver that Genoese bankers turned into sophisticated financial instruments and considerable profits in Europe, Hernando's collection was founded upon the conversion of prospective American wealth into ready cash thanks to the loans and bills of exchange he negotiated with his Genoese associates. Charles V granted Hernando 2,000 ducats for his services during the Christmas season of 1520–21, and he further ordered Miguel de Pasamonte, the treasurer of Hispaniola, to pay Hernando a salary of 200,000 *maravedís* a year, funds that may have been of little immediate use to Hernando since he was then with the court in Worms. Given the financial networks of the time, however, this presented little problem, and before the grant had even been made official Hernando had given power to the Genoese bankers Nicolas and Juan Francisco de Grimaldo to receive the salary in Hispaniola, a transaction that would be made through the medium of a procurator, whose papers were signed in Seville only a few weeks later.[38] Hernando promptly set off for Venice, where in June 1521 he received from Octaviano de Grimaldo, another member of the family, a further 200 ducats to fund his lavish book purchases, a debt acknowledged by Hernando's representative in Seville as a total of 270 ducats in October 1523 and finally paid on 12 May 1526.[39] It was similarly to Octaviano de Grimaldo that Hernando consigned the 1,637 books he had bought during his six-month stay in Venice for transportation by sea back to Seville. Despite the tragic loss of those books in a shipwreck, it was clear that there was no other communications network through which his library could be connected to the world. When, in the following decade, he began to put in place both the financial and the logistical arrangements for his library, he again turned to these same networks, sending notarized copies of his grants from Charles to Genoese merchants for safekeeping (as his father did with the *Book of Privileges*) and constructing an apparatus for drawing the information of Europe to the library that cloned the financial infrastructure he had come to know.[40] Funds were to be disbursed by the Genoese merchants in Seville to one of their agents in Lyon, who in turn would distribute an initial sum of 100 ducats to five factors—located in Rome, Venice, Nuremberg, Antwerp, and Paris—with instructions to each to come to an arrangement "with the bookseller best known to them" that each April he would submit 12 *ducados'* worth of the newest books, at trade prices, sending them on to Lyon in his "packet," thence to join the convoy going to the May fair in Medina del Campo, where they would be exchanged for the next year's float of 100 *ducados* and then transported on to Seville with the traffic returning from the fair.[41] The universal library, as envisioned by Hernando, was connected to the world through the financial networks, making the world of information and the world of trade ghostly reflections of each other. Like the Genoese bankers whose financial operations sustained the Habsburgs during the sixteenth and seventeenth centuries, Hernando's collection aspired to be the repository that could lend intellectual credit to the imperial ambitions of the Hispanic monarchy.

The link between *translatio imperii* and *translatio studii* was firmly established in the period, fostering a belief that Spanish imperial ambitions would need strong cultural foundations, and theories of *translatio studii* developed in tandem with economic and linguistic ideas about how communities fit together. When Antonio de Nebrija wrote in his 1492 *Gramatica de la Lengua Castellana* that "siempre la lengua fue compañera del imperio" (language has always been the companion of empire), he did more than just conceive of it in an abstract sense of language distilling the grace—and exhibiting the spirit—of the nation. He was following in the wake of Lorenzo Valla, who in the middle of the fifteenth century had thought of Latin as the greatest legacy of the Roman Empire, a *sacramentum,* and proclaimed that "wherever the Roman Empire is, there rules the Roman language too."[42] Valla extolled Latin as standing above all other goods the Roman Empire gave to the peoples it conquered: it established and taught the liberal arts, provided excellent laws, and opened the path to *all knowledge,* so these peoples could no longer be thought of as barbarians.[43] Nebrija, Vives, and Erasmus—whose *Antibarbari* was conceived, like Vives's *Declamationes Sullanae,* as an instrument to cleanse and hone the use of Latin as a vehicle for knowledge—followed in the wake of Valla in thinking of language as a tool for civilization against the barbarians, a fundamental instrument for education and by extension for the necessary reform of the disciplines and of learning. But there was also a keen and inseparable sense of language as the vehicle and constitutive element of large and complex political communities, in all their diverse dimensions: administration, law, commerce, the arts, and religion. All these structures were inseparable from the community of speakers who wove them into existence and from the knowledge of the world that went with it.

Hernando's project was an extension of these humanist programs in several important respects. In the first place, if language was conceived as the companion of empire, then Hernando's library would go hand in hand with the *Universitas Christiana* as one of the main instruments for its civilizing mission as the legitimate heir of Rome's legacy. The library would also become a repository of religious and political capital that would cement the foundations of universal empire, since it would provide "sertidunbre y sosiego para en las cosas que tocan a la religion y a el govierno de la republica" (certainty and harmony on things regarding religion and the governance of the republic). It would further turn into a fundamental weapon in the establishment and defense of cultural supremacy—an instrument of empire, or even its symbolic embodiment, as Valla would have it: in the *Memorial al Emperador* Hernando reminds Charles V that his obligations include the combined use of arms and letters in the exercise of his imperial prerogative, "since it is your function, as prince and emperor, to favor and support the joint progress of arms and letters" (*pues a vuestra magestad como a principe y enperador conpete ayudar y fauorescer y ser aconpañado de las letras juntamente con las armas*).[44]

But beyond these lofty ambitions, the library also had a very pragmatic end for its common users as a vast reservoir of information and knowledge from which they could withdraw data by consulting its catalogues. In his *Memorial al Emperador* Hernando emphasizes this duality in his project, which has also been designed "para beneficio comud [*sic*] y para que aya refujio donde los letrados puedan recurrir en qualquier duda que se les ofresciere" (for the common good, and so that there is a place of safekeeping to which scholars can have recourse when they encounter anything that raises doubts). To this end he enumerates the different catalogues and describes their function as instruments to locate and retrieve information. This pragmatic aspect of the library as a tool for data storage and management (the *Memorial* also describes the tasks assigned to its librarians and clerks) links Hernando's imperial and millenarian outlook with the contractual mentality of his age, with the constellation of rational languages and measuring practices in which he was so conversant and which eventually furnished the methods he employed, first in collecting his books and then in their organization.

The pragmatic, use-oriented side of humanism also took an interest in the creation of civic communities that arose out of contractual relationships established in legal-discursive terms. As Maifreda points out, Jean Gerson's *De Contractibus* had already "listed among the characteristics of the new society the impossibility of escaping the contractual life of the marketplace—even for those who did not wish to become wealthy and dedicate themselves to commerce—without being cast out of civil life, and the corresponding introduction of the possibility of listing and measuring anything."[45] This triumph of contractual processes in civic life is inescapably linked to those measurement techniques which some viewed as part of fallen human nature, which allowed for common metrics by which people and goods could be related to each other. We have already seen how Lorenzo de' Medici and Peter Martyr voiced the common idea that prelapsarian life was run by natural-divine law, where contracts were not necessary since greed (that is, self-interest) did not exist and everything was held in common. History was not recorded, neither books nor navigation nor money had been invented, nor were the earth and its shores subject to measure. But now we live in history and under positive laws. In this market, says Prodi, "everything is weighed, numbered, and measured. The contract is defined as a *legitimate civic exchange,* that is, according to *civil law.*"[46] Language was understood in analogous terms, as a form of contractual exchange founded upon shared norms and social habits that ensure mutual credit and the accumulation of knowledge: Juan Luis Vives described it in his *De disciplinis* not just as the instrument of human society but also as "the treasury of erudition"—*aerarium est eruditionis, ac instrumentum societatis hominum.*[47] In his *De sermone* (which Hernando bought in Rome in June 1513), Giovanni Pontano proclaims that truthfulness or sincerity, established through conversation and discourse (*oratio ac sermo*), constitutes the link that keeps societies together (*uinculum retinendae societatis*). This is not the sort of *ueritas* to be found in disciplines like mathematics or the syllogisms of logic, he clarifies, but what he calls *ueracitate,* the sort of mutual credit to be established by common social habits (*moribus*) and reliable civic exchange. "I speak of that truth," he concludes, "that neither in conversation nor in discourse, nor even in habits ever proclaims anything pretended, deceitful, or made up."[48] If language was an instrument for the creation of creditable things and the social structures that grew up around them, one of Hernando's ambitions for his library was to turn it into a refinery and reserve for this knowledge economy—in Vives's terms, a universal and omnicomprehensive *treasury of erudition.*

Hernando's books are typical products of this fallen age, printed mirrors where history is recorded, where information and knowledge in all disciplines are codified and exchanged using ever more sophisticated measuring methods. His manuscript notes can be used to generate a map of European currency markets—since they record the same information shared by financiers to conduct their contractual business. From 1520, Hernando's purchase notes added to the records of date, price, and location further information on the exchange rate between the local currency and Spanish *ducados,* providing a detailed and dynamic map of early modern economies and exchange rates across Europe and aligning him with a mentality which sought to allot cultural phenomena a place within a measurable, standardized balance of trade. The addition of this notation coincided with the first of his extraordinary book-buying journeys through Europe, allowing us, in reconstructing his purchases, to take stock of the early modern book world as never before.

The Renaissance Bookshop: A Grand Tour

Hernando departed from the Galician port of La Coruña in June 1520, accompanying Charles V and his party north toward Aachen, where Charles would be crowned King of the Romans, the first part of the ritual of imperial investment. Yet though Hernando, as part of the court party, would have had access to the transactions at the highest levels of European diplomacy and display over the coming months—likely accompanying Charles to England for talks with Henry VIII, after which the kings of England, France, and Spain held rival pageants at Antwerp and the Field of the Cloth of Gold—there is little evidence that he concerned himself with affairs of state. His purchases from the bookstalls of Flanders, however, are well documented and show the beginnings of his superlative ambition. The haul of 4,300 purchases over the coming two years began in Ghent in July and August 1520, from which period slightly under 50 books survive. These volumes, for which Hernando was able to pay in Spanish *maravedís,* were overwhelmingly quartos (33, with 9 octavos and 3 folios), at a total cost of 1,606 *maravedís* (a little over 4 *ducados*), ranging from 2 *maravedís* for an oration on the Apostles' Creed to 200 for a folio volume of the *Revelations* of Saint Brigit of Sweden. Only a single volume was printed in Ghent itself, with the vast majority (30) published in Paris; there were 3 apiece from Cologne, Antwerp, and Basel, 2 from Strasbourg, and a single purchase from each of Nuremberg, Hagenau, Zwolle, Louvain, and

Deventer. Hernando's appetite for Parisian books may in part have been driven by the ongoing wars between France and Spain in northern Italy, which prevented French goods from reaching Spain directly. Although most of Hernando's purchases in Ghent were fairly recent printings, his purchase of a 1499 incunabulum gives a foretaste of the immense chronological range revealed by Hernando's purchase notes in the bookshops of Europe.[49] All 47 surviving titles purchased in these months were in Latin, and while there is no consistency among the widely varied subject matter (which covers sermons, theology, oratory, law, medicine, architecture, poetry, and language manuals), there is a marked pattern of interest in the great humanists and their printers, with Erasmus, More, Lorenzo Valla, Juan Luis Vives, Jodocus Badius, Froben, and Janus Panonius among these first purchases. The overall impression is of a bibliophile keen to acquire the latest publications of the intellectual celebrities of the age, though the sating of these appetites was highly dependent on access to the right channels of trade and information.

Hernando's movements after leaving Ghent cannot be gleaned from inscriptions in the surviving books, as most of the volumes he accrued along the road south to Venice were lost in the shipment he entrusted to Octaviano de Grimaldo in October 1521. The only books to survive from the time he left Worms to his departure from Venice are those that Hernando saw fit to carry with him on the return journey: the copy of the *Antibarbari* presented to him by Erasmus in Louvain on 7 October 1520 and a single volume, by Sebastian Brant, purchased during his Venetian stay. Instead, we are indebted to the surviving volume of the *Registrum A*—the *Memorial de los Libros Naufragados*—to trace his route through Brussels, Louvain, Cologne, Mainz, and Wittenburg, to Worms, where he spent Christmas, then via Speyer, Strasbourg, Selestat, and Basel to northern Italy, where he passed from Milan to Pavia, Genoa, Cremona, and Ferrara before arriving in Venice at the beginning of May 1521. The detailed and roughly chronological entries in *Registrum A* allow us to follow Hernando into the bookstores along this spine of Europe and to sense their connection to the continental networks of commerce and communication. The relative fragmentation of the Germanic states meant that Hernando had to pay in *reblaz* and *penins* in Spira, *laparts* in Strasbourg, and *creycers* and *raps* in Basel; after arrival in northern Italy the zones of exchange were somewhat wider. Hernando was able to pay in *quatrines* across Lombardy—Milan, Pavia, and Cremona—and this internal currency flow seemed to be matched by the movement of books, with items printed in each of these cities being equally available in the others. It is only when he reached Venice, however, that both the financial and print markets come to seem wholly international: in the days after his arrival Hernando was able to finance his shopping spree—buying 182 books on 22 May alone—in Spanish *maravedís,* suggesting that the booksellers were sufficiently connected to currency networks to be comfortable working in foreign coin; it may even have been a profitable form of speculation. Hernando moved to paying in the local currency—*sueldos* and *bezos* (that is, in soldi and half-soldi coins)—after securing his advance of 200 ducats from Octaviano de Grimaldo in early June, but he periodically returned to paying in *maravedís* after that, perhaps during periods when his local funds ran low (a penmanship exercise in the late-June section of the *Registrum* suggests that he had spent his 200 ducats by then and was writing to Octaviano de Grimaldo for more).[50] The scale of Hernando's purchases meant that soon the distinction between his trade and other forms of mercantile activity became blurred: by late June he had reached an agreement, at least with some booksellers, to pay for his books by the page rather than bothering to barter over the price of each individual volume: his negotiated rate of 112 *maravedís* and half a *blanca* (that is, 112.25 *maravedís*) per 100 pages meant that his 200 Grimaldi ducats would have translated into 59,840 pages. The entries from this point often included the number of pages in each volume, which could then be totted up and priced accordingly.

While a large proportion of the books purchased in Venice came from that city's prodigious printing houses—or those in nearby Ferrara and Bologna—there was also a wide range of titles from outside of Italy. Since his arrival in northern Italy, however, Hernando may have noticed that his efforts to identify each volume he purchased using publication data—the place and date of printing, and the name of the printer—were frustrated by the fact that a majority of the shorter works failed to include this information, prompting the frequent use of the expression "caret impressione" in the catalogue. Although the information may be absent simply because these works were not prestige objects, and therefore felt no need to boast of their provenance, the inevitable result was that there was a flood of cheap print which was not linked to a particular point of origin and could not be subjected to state controls over the flow of information. The many genres that made up this class of *obrezillas*—saints' lives, news pamphlets, erotic and bawdy *frottole*, prognostications, popular spiritual aids—constituted a public forum far more voluminous and harder to control than its elite counterpart in the republic of letters. If Hernando was to provide the nerve center for a Spanish universal monarchy, it was essential to be able to tap into this diffuse and powerful undercurrent.

Leaving Venice late in October, Hernando traveled toward Nuremberg, stopping to buy a few books in Trento in mid-November and presumably passing through Innsbruck and Augsburg, following the well-established corridor between Bavaria and the Veneto, and on which Hartman Schedel had drawn in creating his universal chronology, the *Liber Chronicarum,* which was one of Hernando's first purchases in Nuremberg. While the level of acquisition in Venice allows for the possibility that he gave thought to each volume he purchased, his rate of collection on the return journey to the Low Countries from October 1521 to March 1522 suggests that Hernando had moved toward a strategy of bulk buying with an aim of completeness: 700 books during a month in Nuremberg, 200 during a two-day stay in Frankfurt, and 1,000 during a few weeks in Mainz.[51] The 52 surviving titles from Frankfurt—about the right proportion, given the disappearance of around three-fourths of the library—include a 1 *pfenig* tract by Martin Luther (his *Tractatulus De his qui ad ecclesias co[n]fugiunt*), two music manuals, and a Latin-German dictionary arranged around the domestic spaces where the objects named would be found, compiled by the Erasmian Johannes Pinicianus—a lexicographic cartography of European private domestic spaces and artifacts, as a counterpart to the global geographic and material culture across the ocean itemized in dictionaries like the *Vocabula Barbara* that Nebrija compiled for his edition of Peter Martyr's *Decades de Orbe Novo*.[52] Lutheranism was strongly represented in Hernando's 1520–22 haul: in Spira he had purchased Luther's *Explanatio dominicae orationis* (February 1521), and a few days later in Strasbourg he had acquired a copy one of Luther's most important works, *De captivitate babylonica ecclesiae*.[53] Later that year, in Venice, he had bought ten other works by Luther. Although Wagner vigorously argues against any heterodox component in Hernando's faith and attributes his interest in Luther merely to his bibliomania, these purchases confirm a very relevant general pattern: Hernando was particularly interested in printed matter that dealt with current events and controversies—hence his emphasis on *obrezillas* and the design of a specific sign (which he calls *pro vel contra*) in his catalogues to flag a book "where some author defends another, or challenges him." In the redesign of knowledge that Hernando was mapping with his catalogues, controversies in print became an important genre that deserved a category of its own.[54] Even if he did not witness the tense encounter between Luther and Charles V in Worms, the storm generated by Reformist publications, and the controversies in which Erasmus was frequently engaged, were all borne witness to in the materials and tools of the library.

Rejoining the imperial party in the Netherlands, Hernando and his purchases from north of the Alps shared the return leg of the voyage, through England, where in little over a month he bought about a hundred titles from the booksellers around St Paul's. The scale of purchases in England was modest compared to his acquisitions elsewhere, but this was at least in part because of the radically transnational nature of the European book market, which had allowed Hernando to buy London-printed books in Seville and in Rome, and which meant that, while he did buy a few local texts by John Colet and Richard Pace, most of what he bought in London was from Venice, Paris, and Antwerp.[55] Despite the small scale of Hernando's haul, the fact that he found continental books in London that he had not found elsewhere on his thorough and meticulous trawl suggests that the London bookstores were very healthy indeed.

The Word on the Street: Hernando's *Obrezillas*

Although Hernando's purchases included a significant contingent of works by the great humanist authors and publishers, from an early stage he also showed a marked interest in collecting the most ephemeral works of the print marketplace, works which would form the core of his universal library. Humanists such as Juan Luis Vives, in the *Declamationes Sullanae*—which Hernando purchased in Ghent for 20 *maravedís* in August 1520—argued for a new curriculum founded on Latin prose inspired by classical Roman oratory, to make it more fit for handling the concerns of the sixteenth-century public forum (see fig. 11). Although this was an ambitious project for reforming the curriculum and hierarchy of knowledge based on "strategies for handling public affairs . . . [that were] thought and wrested *from the midst of life*" (emphasis ours), the sort of humanism represented by Vives usually imagined itself to be dealing only with the elites of the *docti* and the *doctissimi,* not the *indocti* or the *semidocti.*[56] In contrast, Hernando's collection contained from the beginning those ephemeral materials—chapbooks, leaflets, popular literature, collections of refrains, so-called *literatura de cordel,* and in general anything in a small, inexpensive format—that were excluded from the early modern republic of letters, and in his plans for the library made purchasing just such flimsy products of the print market a priority.[57] And far from these being permitted into the library with condescension, merely as a gesture toward completeness, they provided one of the central frameworks through which Hernando conceived his bibliographic creations.

It is clear that Hernando had a conscious and discrete notion of the *obrezilla,* the ephemeral work, as a category, not only in his direct instructions to future librarians to "always take care to buy all of the little pamphlets [*obrezillas pequeñas*] of whatever quality they might be," but also in the fact that his bibliographic hieroglyphs, designed to give the reader of his catalogues a lot of detail about any given book at a single glance, contained a specific set of markings for book length, branching off to the left of the main symbol (which denoted book size—folio, quarto, octavo, and so on).[58] Four of the seven distinct markings deal with books of fewer than twenty pages: the first is for broadsides (a single sheet), the second for *ultrapica* works of between one and five pages, a third for *tractatuli* of five to ten pages, and the fourth for *tractatulos* of ten to twenty pages. With only three categories for all the rest of the titles in the library (*liber parvus, liber mediocris,* and *liber magnus*), it is clear that Hernando anticipated the need for distinction among the vast number of small works in the library. Hernando's concern to make the size of the works (in all dimensions) in his library clear to anyone browsing the catalogues is a stunning demonstration of the existence of *géneros editoriales* or "publishing genres," an idea first posited by the book historian Víctor Infantes—that, for readers in the early decades of print, the typographical design and the *size* of the printed object they were holding suggested a vast amount about what its likely contents were and

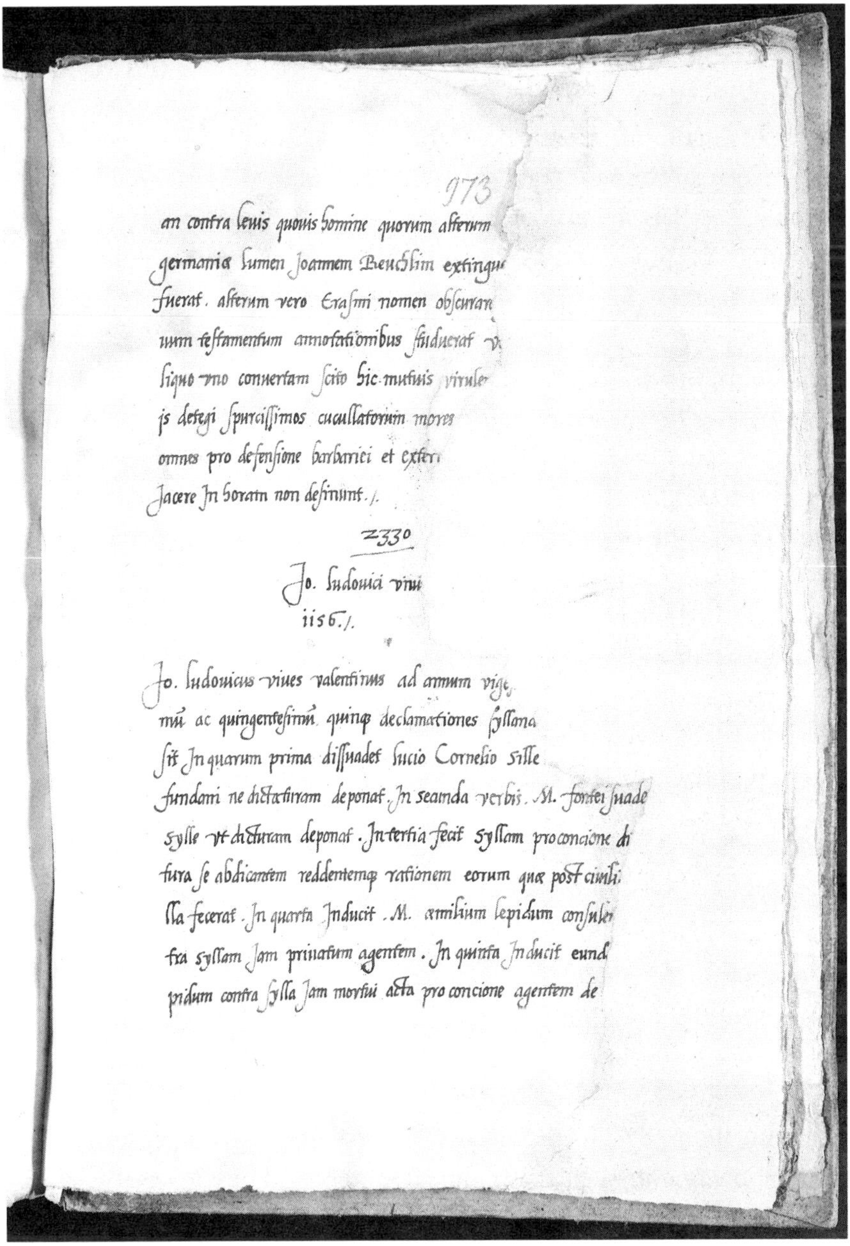

FIG. 11. Hernando's epitome 2330, of Juan Luis Vives's *Declamationes* in his fair copy of the *Libro de los Epítomes* (Copenhagen, Arnamagnæan Collection, AM 377 fol., fol. 973r. Photo: Suzanne Reitz. Used with permission.)

to whom it was addressed.[59] The inclusion in Hernando's library of these little works, then, made it a repository for many genres to which most early modern collections were effectively blind.

One of the most fascinating categories of such works—rejected entirely, for instance, in Gesner's "universal" bibliographic project, the *Pandectae*—were the popular calendars and prognostications that Hernando collected so avidly.[60] In June 1522, as the imperial party made its way back from the Netherlands to Spain, Hernando took advantage of a stop in London to buy the *Prognosticon futuri saeculi* by Saint Julian, a Visigothic theologian born in Toledo around 642.[61] For Hernando and his patrons in the Hispanic monarchy, self-appointed heirs to the legacy of their Visigothic forebears, Saint Julian and his ancient prognostications were part of a millenarian teleological narrative which had flourished during the Middle Ages, as suggested by the large number of manuscript witnesses to Julian's works.[62] These prognostications of the early and High Middle Ages, in turn, provided the pattern for the more recent versions that poured from the printing presses from an early stage, and which ranged from learned Latin treatises to vernacular works aimed at a broad audience. To this stage, in which the prognostication transitioned between a space for elite theology and a mirror of public opinion, belong Johannes Lichtenberger's *Prognosticon astrologium ab anno 1488 ad anno 1567*, which Hernando bought in Rome in 1515, and Paul of Middelburg's prognostication for 1484 to 1504, which Hernando owned in two editions. In both cases, Hernando's copies are the only surviving witnesses to these editions.[63]

For all that these prognostications were disdained by many humanists for their occult underpinning, they were in fact public instruments that expressed a large variety of social, political, cultural, economic, and religious concerns. Lichtenberger's *Prognosticon* is centered on an epochal conflict with Islam, but he also deals with other sorts of current events and international politics, such as political relations among the German aristocracy and Emperor Maximilian, and the diplomatic and military conflicts between current European powers—many of which focused on the struggle for hegemony in the Italian Peninsula. This blending of celestial forecasting and current events had been present from the beginning of Hernando's projects in the work of Pierre d'Ailly, whose *Imago Mundi* had interrogated the heavens with the rational certainties provided by the

Ptolemaic system as he also sought to solve and account for the Great Schism that afflicted the church during his lifetime, serving in turn as one of the sources for Lichtenberger. D'Ailly combined astrology, prophecy, and cosmography in a way that was to provide a mold for Hernando's interests and his knowledge-organization projects. Against this background of great works in the cosmographic and cosmological canons, many of these prognostications in small format emerged as weathervanes of public opinion. They were also conduits for the exchange of knowledge among the different linguistic and cultural communities across Europe that Hernando visited during his voyages—a forum for public opinion and a market for knowledge that functioned alongside and underneath mercantile, diplomatic, and humanist networks. Hernando's openness to this channel of communication set him apart from other "intelligencers" on the European scene.[64]

The particular interest of these pamphlets for Hernando is perhaps most strikingly demonstrated by the sammelband that today bears the shelf mark 12-1-13, which brings together a series of eleven prognostications for the year 1492. The collection is, of course, wholly in keeping both with the millenarian readings of Columbus's voyage from within his immediate circle and beyond and with Hernando's interest in the resources of cheap print; it also suggests that Hernando's knowledge-organization projects not only took account of these *obrezillas* (where others such as Gesner overlooked them), but they also may have played a central part in his bibliographic thinking. On the verso of a blank sheet at the end of this series of pamphlets is a manuscript list in Hernando's hand of prognostications relating to that crucial year, followed on the next verso by a series of symbols and registry numbers corresponding to the *Registrum B* numbers for these pamphlets (from 6378 to 6387, figs. 12 and 13). The symbols are not the same as the bibliographic hieroglyphs described by Juan Pérez; instead they appear to represent an earlier sign system, denoting the order in which the tracts should be placed in this volume. In other words, it seems that some of Hernando's earliest organizational experiments focused not on the order of books on the shelf, or the abstract order of titles in a catalogue, but rather the even smaller-scale consideration of the order in which pamphlets should be bound together.

In the Italian markets where Hernando's interest in *obrezillas* was formed,

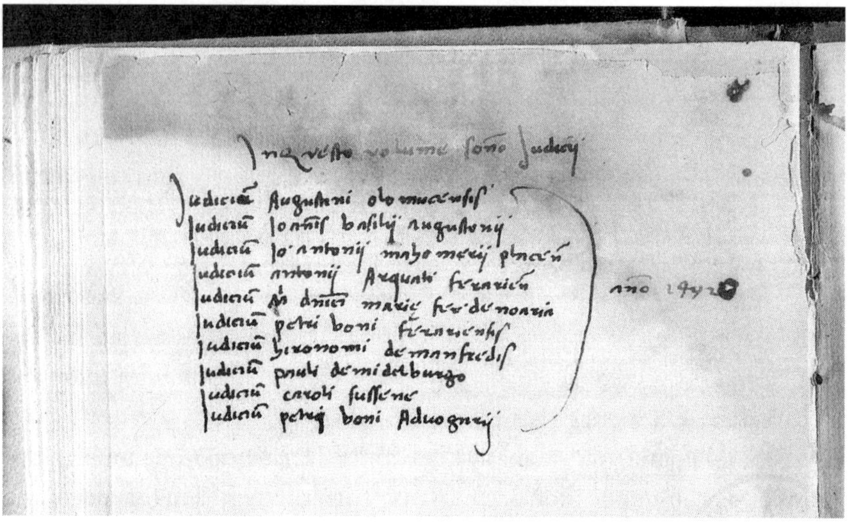

FIG. 12. Verso of a blank sheet at the end of sammelband 12-1-13, which brings together a series of ten prognostications for the year 1492, with a manuscript list in Hernando's hand of prognostications relating to that crucial year (© Cabildo Catedral de Sevilla)

these *pronostici* belonged in the same publishing category as *avvisi,* pamphlets which dealt not with the future but with the emerging present—*current events.*[65] Pamphlets like the *guerre in ottava rima*—which reported on the latest military and political news from the Italian wars—looked almost indistinguishable from the *prognosticons* and also from erotic romance fiction (also in *ottava rima*), not just sharing a size and typographic appearance but even reproducing the same title page designs. They were all, in short, part of a single publishing genre. So Hernando's sammelband 6-3-29 features not only an *Interpretatione di Daniel Propheta,* a prophetic-millenarian pamphlet mapping current events onto the ever-popular allegory of Nebuchadnezzar's dream, but also several erotic narratives, such as the *Ipolito et Dianora* and *La compagnia del Mantellaccio co laggiunta* (6-3-29[9]), all of which also bear strikingly similar title pages, and all of which were demonstrably bound together in Hernando's lifetime.[66] The sammelband of "Historias Toscanas" that sits next to this on the shelves of the modern Colombina (6-3-30) brings together a number of *guerre in ottava rima* and other works treating the military and political situation with a copy of *El diluio di Roma: che venne adi quindici di nouembre M.D.X.IIII* (purchased

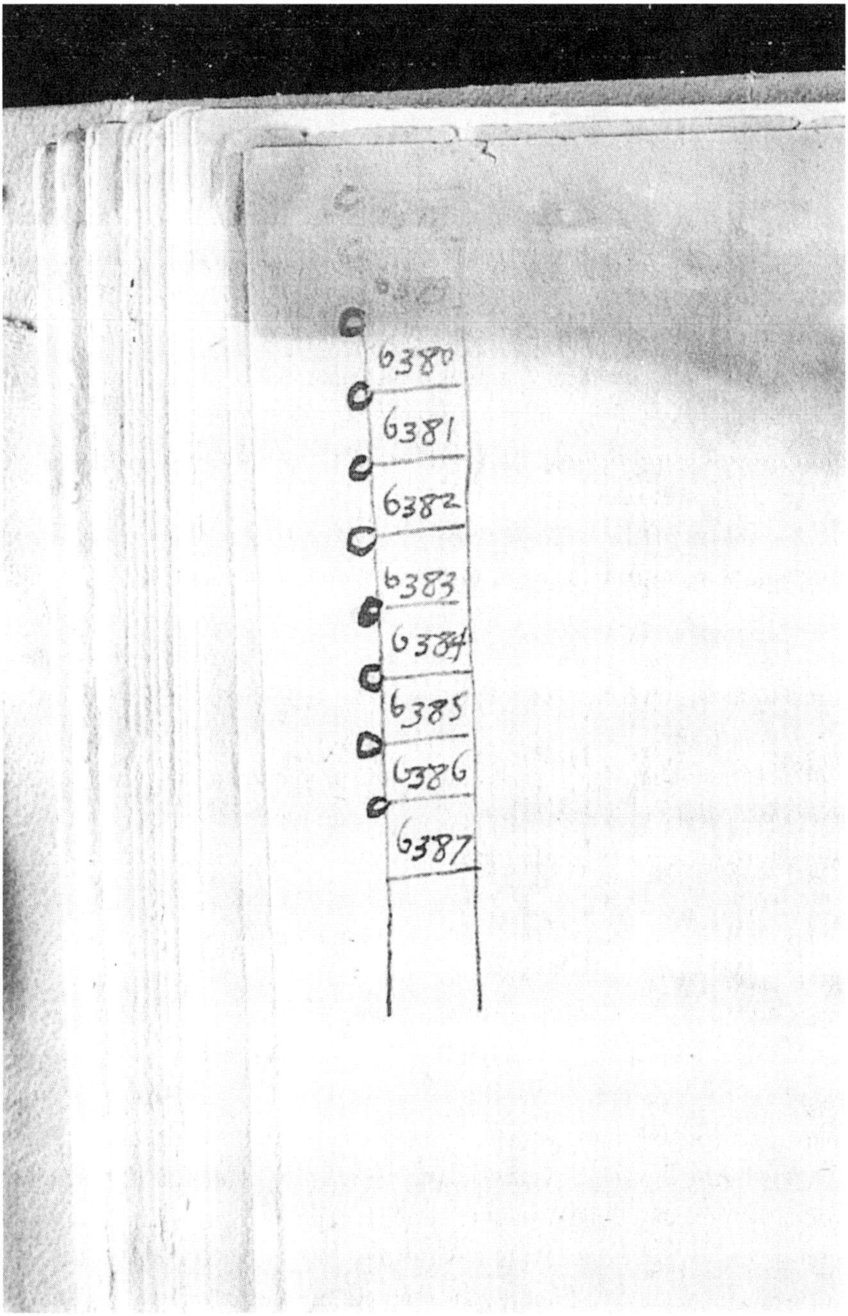

FIG. 13. Hernando's manuscript note in sammelband 12-1-13 with symbols and registry numbers corresponding to the *Registrum B* numbers (from 6378 to 6387) for the prognostications that he had bound into a single volume (© Cabildo Catedral de Sevilla)

in Rome in December 1515).[67] This report of a meteorological event from the year before blends the prophetic qualities attributed to such wonders with a journalistic account of a recent event, allowing for wider political and military news to be folded in. This sammelband also contains another of Hernando's characteristic manuscript indexes, showing that he fully intended for these tracts to be bound together: in his mind they represented a continuum of knowledge, from the latest information about the world to speculation regarding the future, and he intended to represent this continuity in the physical volumes of the library. It was, of course, information flowing through the same channels as the financial data used by the merchants, organized using similar systems of registration, and running the same gamut from the most current state of affairs to the grounds they provided for future speculation.

Much as many humanists would have liked to stay above the fray by ignoring this undistinguished multitude of *obrezillas,* many of the sammelbands in Hernando's collection demonstrate that these pamphlets were also forums in print, where key political, scientific, and theological questions were thrashed out. A good example can be seen in the pamphlets that deal with the flood forecast in Rome in 1524, which unleashed a torrent of publications debating the credibility of the prediction and its likely meaning. This public speculation provided a forum for discussing the schism in the church caused by Lutheranism, its causes, and the courses of action that would likely lead to its resolution or its worsening. Among the *obrezillas* Hernando owned on the topic are some of Tomasso Gianotti Rangoni's pamphlets, which were issued in both Italian and Latin versions (by the same publisher), adopting a dual address to the international learned community and to the Italian public.[68] As is so often the case, Hernando's copies of these pamphlets are the only ones that have survived, so it is perhaps unsurprising that, with very few exceptions like the work of Paola Zambelli, these prognostications have been underappreciated as a forum for early modern public debate.[69] The borderline between these pamphlet controversies and the kinds of advice to princes for which humanist oratory was particularly honed was porous. In another of his sammelbands, 8-2-33, Hernando gathered a series of pamphlets appealing to the Holy Roman emperors on a range of issues: appeals to Maximilian and Charles V from the intellectuals (*studiosum*) of Germany and the gentry, with lists of problems in the empire to be addressed; and Juan Ginés de Sepúlveda's appeal to the emperor to make peace with Christian nations so as to turn his attention to the Turkish threat.[70] But the volume also contains pamphlets on Lutheran controversies which blur the line between public debate and appeals to the sovereign.[71]

The role of print in fostering early news culture (and social currents such as Lutheranism that may have fed on this) is well attested to. But the fact that there was an emergent forum of print which predated Luther, which created networks for the circulation of news and fostered public debates in formats like diplomatic orations, prognostications, *romances noticieros,* and similar *obrezillas,* has attracted far less attention. Hernando's purchases all over Europe turned his collection in the Casa de Goles in Seville into a repository of documents that mapped these exchanges and recorded the forums created by these heterogeneous communities of authors, publishers, and readers. They all had in common a small and ephemeral format, easy to manufacture and distribute, which facilitated an early response to common concerns among their intended readerships. It did not occur to Vives that his ideal of knowledge produced "from the midst of life" and its common affairs would find in Hernando's *obrezillas* one of its most copious and powerful sources.[72]

Hernando's *obrezillas* also included a large number of popular recreational tracts, including Spanish *literatura de cordel* alongside a considerable number of its Italian counterpart, the *libretti.*[73] A wonderful example can be found in the modern volume 6–3–24, a sammelband with a number of pamphlets that illustrate the varieties of popular Italian poetry that were in circulation at the time: its contents cover a spectrum from recreational poetry, to political and military news in ballad form, to patriotic propaganda in *ottava* and *terza rima.* It includes, for instance, the only surviving copy of a rare edition of Boccaccio's *Nimphale Fiesolano,* composed in *ottava rima,* the *Lamento de Italia* in *terza rima,* dedicated to Pope Julius II, and a twenty-leaf patriotic tirade about the greatness of Venice, its leaders, and its deeds (6-3-24[2]).[74] The sammelband also features several works by Perossino della Rotonda, a prolific author of balladic news, among them his *Lamento de Bartolomeo Dalviano*—one of the unique copies preserved in Hernando's collection—which deals with a major political and military player in the Italian Wars.[75] But the sammelband's concerns are not confined to European affairs: reports in *ottava rima* about the military clash in Syria between Bayezid III's army and the Egyptian sultan Qaitbay, and on Bayezid's embassies to the Vatican and the princes of Europe around 1489–90, turn it into a form of global news review. And, if we were in danger of forgetting that Columbus's voyages were conceived as part of this global news, the sammelband also contains the sole surviving copy of an Italian version, in *ottava rima* by Giuliano Dati, of Columbus's first letter with news of the territories across the ocean.

Hernando's thirst for cheap print continued unabated throughout his life, and by the 1530s the infrastructure and culture of information exchange had developed sufficiently to allow something recognizable as a modern news network to emerge. These connections are strikingly illustrated, for instance, by Hernando's sammelband 13-2-16, which gathers together pamphlets on the *Jornada de Túnez,* Charles V's 1535 expedition against Tunisia, launched from Barcelona in the month of June. The campaign ended with the reconquest of Tunisia from Barbarossa, who had taken hold of this important outpost in 1534, disrupting European trade in the Mediterranean and bringing the Ottoman threat to the very doorstep of southern Europe. As part of the pan-European anxiety over Ottoman encroachment, the *Jornada* was big news, and these *obrezillas* were published very soon after the events they reported: *L'assault de L'Empereur a Barberosse* was written on 25 June of 1535, a mere ten days after Charles's troops set sail from Sardinia, and Hernando bought the tract in Lyon a month later—and in so doing preserved the only surviving copy of this report.[76] The same day he bought this, Hernando also bought a related news pamphlet penned by Francesco da Ferrara on the same subject (*La grant armee de L'Empereur lequel sen va combatre contre le Turc. Barberousse et tous infidelles*);[77] a few months later he purchased a letter about this campaign (*La copie dune lettre mandee de Thunes de la prinse de la gollete au Seigneur do[n] Gaspard de Mendoza gentilhomme de Lempereur*).[78] The snapshot of Hernando's book buying in Lyon provided by these pamphlets, which must have been displayed unbound with their title pages announcing the latest events, gives a striking impression of a newsstand coming into being.

These nascent communications networks were not, however, restricted to the communication of political and military news and the exchange of ideas during religious controversies: they also provided for a rapid transmission of technical expertise and knowledge, further evidence that too stark a division should not be drawn between the worlds of proto-journalism, theological controversy, and scientific debate. A good example of the intertwining of these concerns can be seen in Hernando's many pamphlets on the Fifth Lateran Council, which took place during Hernando's intermittent residence in Rome (1512–16).[79] Although the Lateran Council was ostensibly convened to deal with matters of church government, it was called in large part as a response to the Council of Pisa, which met in the Italian city in 1511 at the behest of Louis XII of France and in open defiance of Pope Julius II, meaning that it was, in effect, war by other means: another maneuver in the endless series of conflicts in northern Italy which formed a main subject of Hernando's "news" pamphlets. But the Lateran Council was also centrally concerned with the establishment of an accurate liturgical calendar, which meant harmonizing official church chronometry with updated advances in astronomical observations. Hernando must have been aware of the Spanish role in these debates, including the report commissioned from the University of Salamanca and sent to the Lateran Council in 1515; he also bought the findings of the council on calendrical matters—*De correctione kalendarii propositiones XIII*—almost immediately after its publication in July 1516, and he had his mathematical tutor (one "Maestro Pedro de Salamanca") send him from Rome another pamphlet from this debate, Andreas de Pace's *In nouum modum corrigendi kalendarium,* while he was back in Spain in 1517.[80] De Pace's pamphlet is contained in a sammelband that brings together four different works on calendar reform, all published between 1513 and 1516 and purchased soon afterward, which together constitute both a textbook on the most current astronomical thought and a report on the proceedings of the council in this matter.[81] In another sammelband (12-1-19), Hernando's copy of Sebastianus Veteranus's *Disputatio de eccentricis et epiciclis* (a gift from the author himself) is bound with Savonarola's diatribe against astrologers, again fusing technical advances with the debates over epistemological authority to which they gave rise.[82] The same writers whose works were central to these debates—Peuerbach; Regiomontanus; Nicolas de Cusa (see, for instance, 8-6-12); Johannes Stoeffler, whose *Calendarium romanum magnum* Hernando bought at Nuremberg in 1521—were, by contrast, also key to the efforts of merchants and cartographers to establish accurate measurements of astronomical time for wholly practical reasons.[83] These pamphlets make clear the inseparable nature of current events, their interpretation within a political and millenarian context, and the establishment of methods for the accurate measurement of time and space, which together provide the raw materials for the institutions that Hernando was to found back in Seville, both in the mapmaking factory at the Casa de Contratación—designed to absorb astronomical measurements of longitude and latitude and fashion them into tools for the expansion of the Hispanic universal empire—and his library, which would set no limits on the kind of information it would digest.[84]

It is also significant that it is precisely among these *obrezillas* concerned with prognostication, political strife, and astronomical measurement that we find some of Hernando's earliest experiments with knowledge distillation and organization. His manuscript sammelband 5-3-25 contains not only prognostications in Latin and Italian but also the *Sumaria plurium iuditiorum anni MDXV*, a manuscript summary of these prognostications by Hernando or one of his assistants.[85] The sense that these distillations and collations of prognostic tracts provided an early form of what would later take shape in Hernando's *Libro de los Epítomes* is confirmed by the fact that this collection also contains the *Compendia diversorum librorum* and the *Fragmenta librorum ex nota Ferdinandi Colonis*, which are some of the few surviving drafts that witness the process by which Hernando and his assistants compiled the epitomes and sketched out the plan for organizing the library. The link for Hernando between prognostication and knowledge organization does not appear to have been an isolated phenomenon: one of the manuscripts that he purchased from his fellow information-hoarder Marin Sanudo, during the sale of part of Sanudo's library in 1531, was the *Iuditium ab anno 1515 ad annum 1524*, in which Sanudo had summarized the predictions of various almanacs for almost the exact years when Hernando was also distilling prognostications and beginning to think about expanding these methods to his library as a whole.[86]

One of the books Hernando was summarizing in this sammelband, as he attempted to collect and collate the prognostications contained in these ephemeral tracts, was the *Introductio ad Sapientiam* by Juan Luis Vives, a proposal for reforming the curriculum in order to produce an elite readership consuming a strictly controlled canon of texts, which would result in a new type of elegant yet terse and clear sort of language based upon the usage of the best authors. Vives was later to expand on this in the *De disciplinis*, which Hernando bought on 29 July 1531, only a few days after it was published.[87] Here Vives included a catalogue for an ideal library as well as a defense of learning and a restatement of the utopian, humanist ideal of a universal language taken "from the midst of life" and everyday communicative exchange, capable at once of dealing with the particular affairs of the forum and the abstract life of the mind. This universal language would facilitate common, global communication and, eventually, the augmentation of knowledge. As a global currency that circulated in print format, knowledge could then be eventually deposited within an omnicomprehensive library of the scope and dimensions conceived by Hernando in his blueprint for the Librería Fernandina.[88] Perhaps closer to Hernando's thought was Angelo Poliziano, whose *Panepistemon* shared with Vives's orthodox humanism the epistemological framework of the liberal arts and an emphasis on the immediacy of experience, but who also includes in his classification of knowledge the "mean and manual" disciplines and arts which "life requires." In his search for new methods Poliziano proposed to anatomize Aristotle's *Ethics* as a physician would do with the study of the human body; once it had been broken down into its different components, he would resort to the use of tables and mathematical calculations (*tabulariorum calculos*) in order to classify them. The entry on *Astronomia* in the *Loci Communes*, Hernando's commonplace book, includes a manuscript tree diagram with Poliziano's classification of doctrines (fig. 14).[89]

It is easy to see, in this context, how Hernando's plan for a universal library was an expression of the same ambitions in a slightly different form. Hernando's collection contained the books that Vives recommended for his ideal library; but it also included other materials that Vives would have rejected—such as romance or chivalric fiction, as well as his beloved *obrezillas*—in large part because Hernando's library was founded on an inductive rather than a deductive model. The ordering of knowledge, and the world, that emanates from Hernando's collection is distinctly comprehensive, above all when compared with the focus of orthodox humanism. By prioritizing these new formats and their heterogeneous contents, Hernando's collection was creating a repository of knowledge

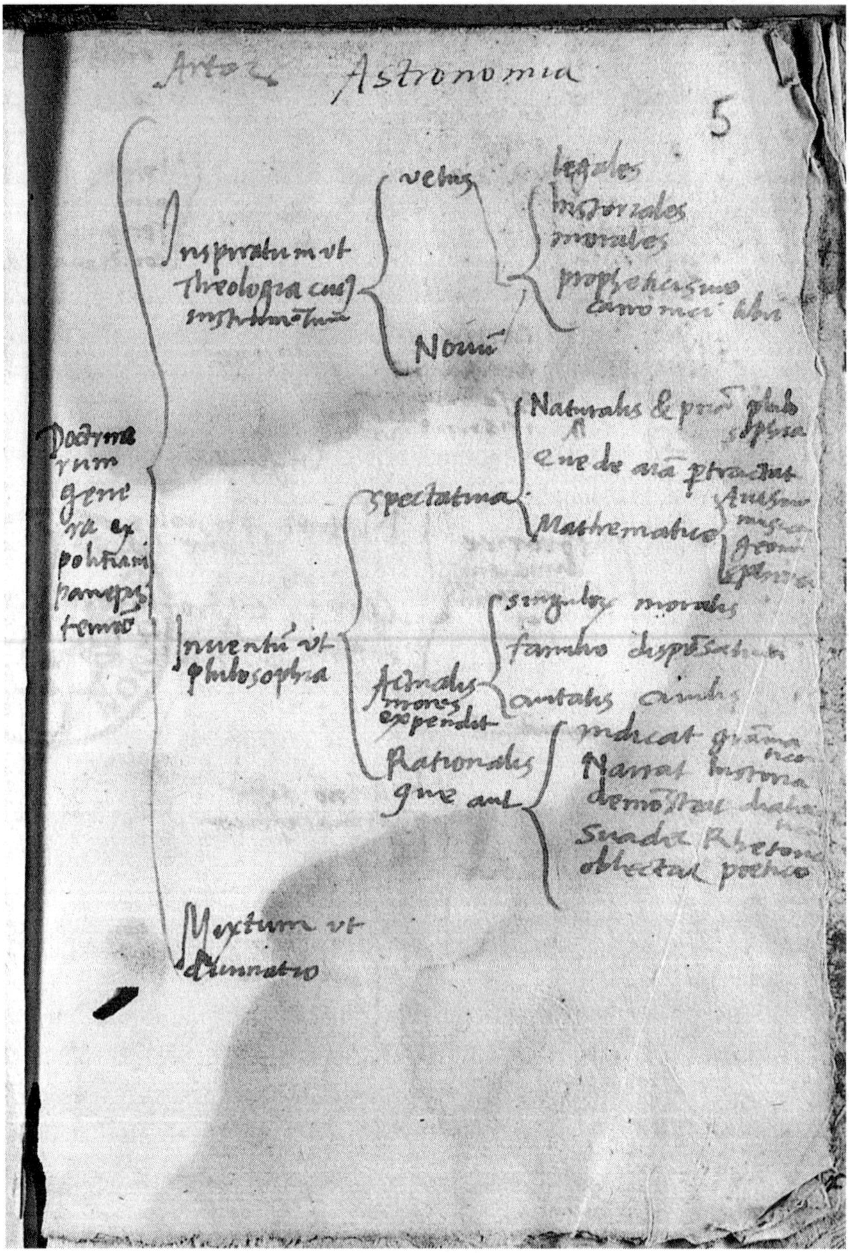

FIG. 14. Hernando's entry on *Astronomia* in the *Loci Communes* (7-2-60, fol. 5r), his commonplace book, which includes a branching diagram with Poliziano's classification of doctrines (*Doctrinarum genera ex Politiani Panepistemon*) (© Cabildo Catedral de Sevilla)

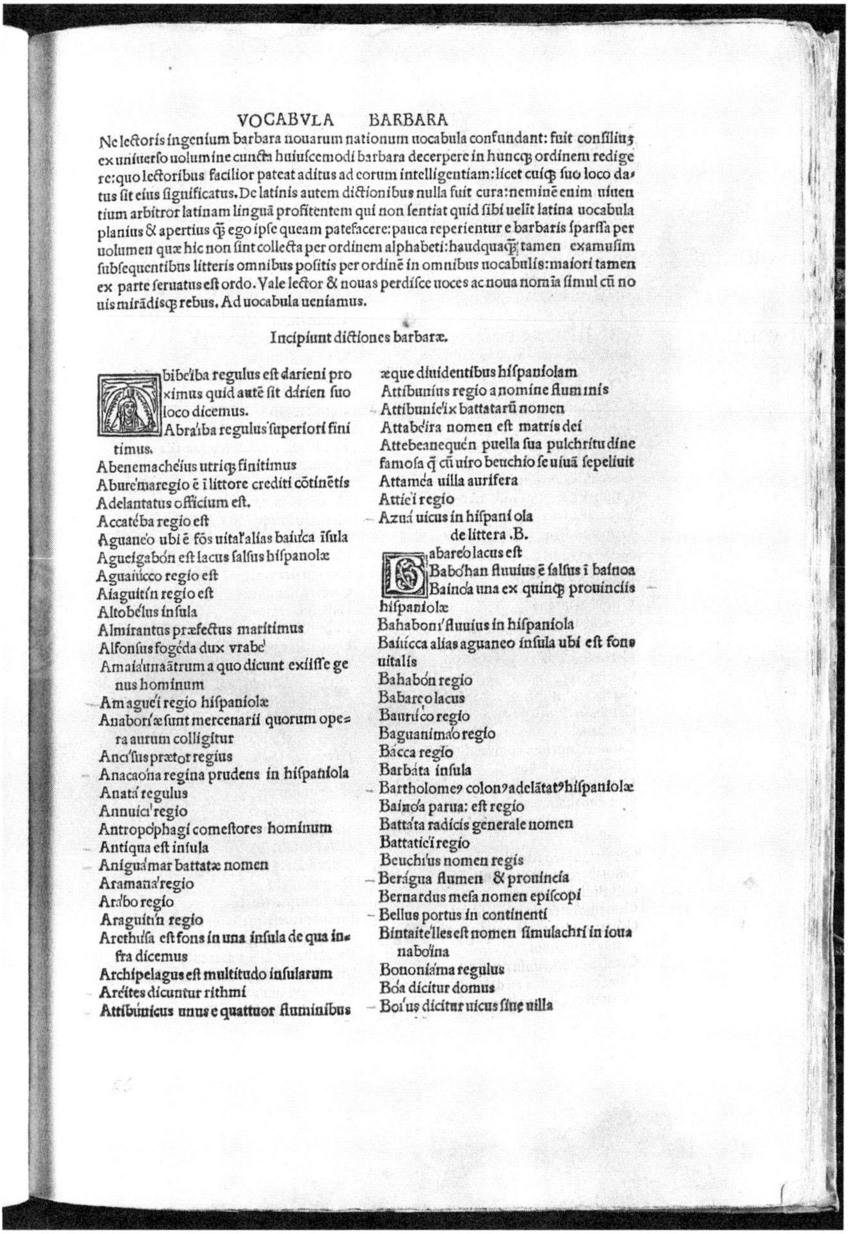

VOCABVLA BARBARA

Ne lectoris ingenium barbara nouarum nationum uocabula confundant: fuit consiliu꞉ ex uniuerſo uolumine cuncta huiuſcemodi barbara decerpere in huncq꞉ ordinem redigere: quo lectoribus facilior pateat aditus ad eorum intelligentiam: licet cuiq꞉ ſuo loco datus ſit eius ſignificatus. De latinis autem dictionibus nulla fuit cura: neminē enim uiuentium arbitror latinam linguā profitentem qui non ſentiat quid ſibi uelit latina uocabula planius & apertius q꞉ ego ipſe queam patefacere: pauca reperientur e barbaris ſparſſa per uolumen quæ hic non ſint collecta per ordinem alphabeti: haudquaq꞉ tamen examuſim ſubſequentibus litteris omnibus poſitis per ordinē in omnibus uocabulis: maiori tamen ex parte ſeruatus eſt ordo. Vale lector & nouas perdiſce uoces ac noua nomīa ſimul cū nouis mirādisq꞉ rebus. Ad uocabula ueniamus.

Incipiunt dictiones barbaræ.

Abibéiba regulus eſt darieni proximus quid autē ſit dárien ſuo loco dicemus.
Abraíba regulus ſuperiori finitimus.
Abenemachéius utriq꞉ finitimus
Aburémaregio ē ī littore crediti cōtinētis
Adelantatus officium eſt.
Accatéba regio eſt
Aguanéo ubi ē fōs uital'alias baiúca īſula
Agueigabón eſt lacus ſalſus hiſpanolæ
Aguaiúcco regio eſt
Aiaguitín regio eſt
Altobélus inſula
Almirantus præfectus maritimus
Alfonſus fogéda dux vrabe'
Amaiáuna ātrum a quo dicunt exiiſſe genus hominum
Amaguéi regio hiſpaniolæ
Anaboríæ ſunt mercenarii quorum opera aurum colligitur
Ancíſus prætor regius
Anacaóna regina prudens in hiſpaniola
Anatá regulus
Annuíci regio
Antropóphagi comeſtores hominum
Antiqua eſt inſula
Aniguámar battatæ nomen
Aramaná regio
Arábo regio
Araguitín regio
Arethúſa eſt fons in una inſula de qua infra dicemus
Archipelagus eſt multitudo inſularum
Areítes dicuntur rithmi
Attibúnicus unus e quattuor fluminibus æque diuidentibus hiſpaniolam
Attibunius regio a nomine fluminis
Attibuniéix battatarū nomen
Attabéira nomen eſt matris dei
Attebeanequén puella ſua pulchritudine famoſa q̄ cū uiro beuchio ſe uiuā ſepeliuit
Attaméa uilla aurifera
Attiéi regio
Azuá uicus in hiſpani ola

de littera .B.

Babareó lacus eſt
Babóhan fluuius ē ſalſus ī bainoa
Bainóa una ex quinq꞉ prouinciis hiſpaniolæ
Bahaboní fluuius in hiſpaniola
Baiúcca alias aguaneo inſula ubi eſt fons uitalis
Bahabón regio
Babareo lacus
Baurúco regio
Baguanimáo regio
Bácca regio
Barbáta inſula
Bartholomeꝰ colonꝰ adelātatꝰ hiſpaniolæ
Bainóa parua: eſt regio
Battáta radicis generale nomen
Battatíci regio
Beuchíus nomen regis
Berágua flumen & prouincia
Bernardus meſa nomen epiſcopi
Bellus portus in continenti
Bintaitélles eſt nomen ſimulachri in iouanabóina
Bononiáma regulus
Bóa dicitur domus
Boíus dicitur uicus ſine uilla

FIG. 15. Nebrija's *Vocabula Barbara* in his 1516 edition of Peter Martyr's *Decades de Orbe Novo,* the first lexicon of Americanisms ever printed (© Cabildo Catedral de Sevilla)

that de facto redefined its hierarchy from the bottom up. His library aspires to become—to borrow a phrase from a book published by Jerónimo de Chaves in 1544—a chronographic *reportorio de los tiempos,* past, present, and future, a textual repository that would trace the cartography of vast global spaces, such as the *Vocabula Barbara* with Americanisms that Nebrija crafted for his edition of Peter Martyr's *De Orbe Novo* (see fig. 15), but also of more modest, domestic spaces, like those carved out in the lexicographic catalogues of Johannes Pinicianus's dictionary. It would take many years until bibliographers, librarians, and collectors paid any attention whatsoever to this sort of format. Hernando's catalogues, an unfinished work in progress, are among some of the best expressions of an early modern world in flux, in the transition from the end of the fifteenth century to the early decades of the sixteenth century, a world where the empirical emphasis on common life and experience coexisted with the abstract use of alphanumerical codes for the classification of disciplines and the quantification of knowledge.

CHAPTER THREE

CARTOGRAPHY

"This map shows the *entire earth,*" remarks the Carthusian monk in one of Erasmus's *Colloquies,* "over which I wander in thought more enjoyably and safely than one who sails to the new islands."[1] Renaissance Europe's encounter with the new global horizons was made accessible to a wider public—even those cloistered away like Erasmus's monk—by means of maps, which generated among these audiences the perception of an unprecedented totality in a single place. Erasmus later revealed that this monk represented his own experience, saying in propria persona, "I'm convinced I travel around the world more safely on a map, and observe not a little more in histories, than I would by roaming all over lands and seas for twenty years like Ulysses."[2] Beyond its more practical applications—to serve, like archives and libraries, as repositories of valuable data coveted by competing powers in search of new wealth and trade routes—cartography also mediated between the imagination of European audiences and a new world not seen firsthand but which they could now grasp thanks to the technologies employed in the production and distribution of ekphrastic and iconographic cosmography.

The new spaces that were being cleared for inquisitive (and acquisitive) early modern European eyes were shaped not only by how the data informing them were quantified, classified, and visualized but also by the systems designed to reconcile heterogeneous streams of information. Cartographic information could be codified in natural language, that is, descriptive or ekphrastic cartography, and also in other, more specialized rational and symbolic systems, such as geometry and algebra, which required advanced skills to keep pace with the growing amount of data being stored and managed. The function of the map as a distillation of heterogeneous information, presenting to the spectator the product of a complex process of collation that was afterward hidden from view, was one of which Hernando and other mapmakers were wholly conscious. By the end of the 1520s the volume of cartographic information generated by exploration had created a problem for the Hispanic monarchy, which on 6 October 1526 enjoined Hernando to coordinate a team of experts charged with turning the ceaseless flow of data into a single universal navigation chart—the *Padrón Real*—and a "mapamundi o esfera redonda."[3]

One of the chief cartographers on this team, Alonso de Chaves, left a record of their practices in a manuscript treatise entitled *Espejo de navegantes* (ca. 1537), an eclectic handbook combining very practical knowledge with more abstract and theoretical notions of classical cosmography.[4] A map, he reflected in one of the more philosophical passages, is a site for the symbolic duplication of the world: "In its absence, the image of the world is represented, and in its design, its writing, and its painting, it renders for our understanding the same design, similitude or position that the world has with itself."[5] In this combination of *traza, escritura y pintura*—design, writing, and painting—maps are more efficient than merely ekphrastic accounts, for the latter are linear, whereas the information encoded in a map is presented simultaneously and therefore is far easier to grasp than any superabundance of words: "And thus, by this instrument, with fewer means and in a smaller space, *we comprehend all we could never do with large volumes of books and writings*. And this instrument, the sages of antiquity found, was the most convenient and profitable for navigation, and also *to represent before us in a brief figure what cannot be understood with many words*."[6] The disappearance, however, of Chaves's *Carta Moderna* (1536)—like that of the majority of the maps of this period—means that what remains to us is the verbal repository of information that lay beneath it, including a table, or an index, to navigate through its contents, revealing a system of classification very similar to Hernando's catalogues.[7] Hernando's work on cartographic projects is of a piece with his interest in recording and measuring systems. These systems combined the epistemological and technical concerns drawn from such classical authors as Ptolemy and Euclid with the scrutiny, redaction, and translation of their texts by the philological humanism of Lorenzo Valla, Erasmus, Juan Luis Vives, and Elio Antonio de Nebrija. The mathematization of knowledge developed in parallel with a renewed appreciation of the importance of language as an instrument for society and for the reform of the disciplines, and it constitutes the background against which Hernando's projects and methods unfolded—above all those he developed for his catalogues.

All the World Around

Before Hernando became a catalographer and a cartographic consultant, he had an intense stint as a hands-on navigator on Columbus's fourth and last voyage (1502–4), which acquainted him with some of the established methods and practices he would later refine. His detailed knowledge of the technical aspects of navigation are made clear in (among other places) his biography of his father, where he painstakingly describes the logic of his father's decisions and the innovations that arose in the face of new challenges. Columbus's seacraft included careful observation of weather patterns and astronomical measurements with the astrolabe, the compass, and other instruments, combined with the use of alphanumeric tables. These measurements and the data they provided were carefully recorded in navigation charts based on preexisting portolans, which were used to trace the path they had sailed and to establish the route forward. Alongside all these calculations, which required sophisticated technical expertise, Hernando recorded his father and his uncle Bartholomew in the act of identifying lands unknown to them. In doing this Columbus combined expert use of the ad hoc portolans crafted during his previous voyages with existing sources of information on distant lands—including Pliny, Marco Polo, Piccolomini's *Historia*, and Pierre d'Ailly's *Imago Mundi*—along with prophetic materials to bridge the distance between what was being seen and what was required to make the expeditions meaningful to European minds. It was a process that required the conflation of firsthand observation with close reading and textual interpretation. Hernando must have become vividly aware of the need for reliable methods to record and classify these geographical observations, which involved merging data from lived experience with what could be derived from maps, books, and other documentary sources, with a view to incorporating them within larger historical patterns that could later be reproduced in cartographic form.

Perhaps the most detailed example of this process comes from Columbus's letters on the Third Voyage, in which he musters the authority of Scripture, alongside a varied collection of authors, pagan and Christian, from Ptolemy and Strabo to Saint Ambrose, Venerable Bede, and Scotus—many of the same sources used in the *Book of Prophecies*—to demonstrate that he has found Eden in the mouth of the Orinoco. "I hold it for certain truth," he proclaims, "that *the place I mentioned is the Terrestrial Paradise,* and *I found my case on good reasons and upon the aforementioned authorities.*"[8] Hernando continued in this tradition by producing (in the wake of his own second visit to the New World in 1509) a series of documents that illustrate similar views about exploration and empire—and hint at the cosmographic foundations of his collection. In one of the few of these documents to have survived, the *Declaración del derecho que la Real Corona de Castilla tiene a la conquista de Persia, Arabia, e India, e de Calicut e Malaca* Hernando mentions another, more foundational, one, which he calls *Colón de Concordia.*[9] This *Colón de Concordia* predates Hernando's involvement in cosmographic activities at the Casa de Contratación by at least ten years, and its contents appear to have been very similar to the *Book of Prophecies,* with which it shares a decidedly millenarian tone. The work, noted Hernando, was divided into three books, "in the first of which is shown that in our times the world would be navigated in all its different regions, from East to West, and the form that this would take; in the second it says that the Gospel would be distributed and received all through the world, and in our own time; and in the third I proved that the universal empire must come to the Spanish crown."[10] Like the cosmography of his father, the worldview expressed here is founded on the *authority* and *reason* of scholars (*por razón y autoridad de doctores*), *prophecies,* and *Scripture* (*con profecías y autoridades de la Sagrada Escritura*).

This foundation can be seen in Hernando's proposal for a voyage around the world, dated on 19 July 1511 in Seville, though here scriptural authority blends with technical proficiency in a fashion that was characteristic of Columbus and which would later be refashioned by Hernando for his own ends. In this plan, a copy of which is preserved in the New York Public Library, Hernando reminds King Ferdinand that his father was the first to propose a circumnavigation of the world and acknowledges that Columbus's writings underpin his own ambition to continue with this mission. The weight of his argument to persuade the monarch rests on a double foundation: the expertise and sailing experience he acquired with his father and uncle and the knowledge he obtained from their books—as well as other books and documents that Hernando himself gathered afterward: "And besides discovering all these territories, my father the Admiral very often proposed to carry out this voyage around the world; and as I expressed (with all due respect) my feelings about the matter, based upon the experience I gained by navigating with my father, what I learned from his own teachings, from the many books and documents that he left me, and what I have culled from other sources."[11]

Hernando's life rummaging among the international book markets should also be seen as a search for texts that could be used for the interpretation of this new global world, continuing the process of collating existing knowledge with new reports in pursuit of clearer pictures of the world. Hernando's universal library is part of Europe's attempt to take stock of what was known so far, with a view to confronting the formidable challenge that lay ahead in making sense of these new *others* and the way in which they altered the received teleological patterns of Christian chronography. His books mustered the full spectrum of different disciplines, generic conventions, and symbolic systems in order to accomplish this task.

The proposed circumnavigation of 1511 was the last of Hernando's projects in which physical exploration would take the leading part. Although he traveled extensively within Europe on book-buying tours for the rest of his life, and reached out through cartographic emissaries across the Iberian peninsula and throughout the world, in his later life these voyages served the ends of information-gathering rather than being ends in themselves. In doing so, however, Hernando was merely aligning himself with long-established practices which saw travel as a way of extending local control over the global, a relationship mediated by the many forms of cosmography but perhaps principally through the portal of the map, which offered the alluring prospect of making the unimaginable scales and incomprehensible strangeness of global travel available in an immanent and controlled experience. Making the global accessible locally, however, also meant adapting data to local understandings, and in late medieval Europe this meant conforming to Christian notions of the shape of time.

Representations of Time and Space: Cosmography and Chronography

Three distinct intellectual traditions underpinned Renaissance cosmography: (1) Aristotelian natural philosophy as formulated in his *Physics*, which contributed the framework for an understanding of natural phenomena, including axiomatic notions like motion, causation, place, and time; (2) Euclidean geometry and Ptolemaic geography, which provided the tools for the mathematical representation of the universe; and finally (3) Pomponius Mela's and Pliny's works, which served as models to incorporate the human, animal, and plant kingdoms into this universe.[12] These authors and their texts provided the lexicon and the methods through which all the phenomena in the cosmos and nature, including all things human, would be reconciled within the scope of cosmography—from the materiality of the human body to the organization of human societies. Cartographic science did not simply mediate between the new abstract rationalist grids of Ptolemaic mapping techniques based on Euclidean geometry, on the one hand, and the traditional portolan maps based on rhumbs, the pole star, the magnetic compass, and the "rule of marteloio," on the other. It also coexisted with religious millenarian components and the lingering authority of accounts of these regions based largely upon the imaginative response to terrae incognitae. The need to reconcile these contentions produced not just new vocabularies for describing the world but also systems of cartographic iconography, which combined science with myth, trigonometry with fable, and transformed sequential narratives into the synoptic language of images.

Much like in Hernando's library, where cheap prognostications were made part of the same order as elite programs of scholarship and theology, early modern cartography blended the fantastical with the geometrical to a much greater extent than cartographers of the day admitted.[13] While the mathematical Ptolemaic method was often adduced as superior in its rationality to narrative ekphrastic models, it was often immediately sidelined after being reverentially invoked at the beginning of cartographical treatises. The author in question then proceeded to accumulate reams of pages with geographical descriptions in the Strabonian fashion, resulting in the long continuance of chronographic prose and reports of marvels within purportedly Ptolomaic tracts. These reports in turn informed imaginative culture of the period, with chivalric and romance fiction using descriptions of the mysterious and exotic East not unlike the accounts to be found in the equally popular Mandeville or in Pliny. This circle was closed when the fictional and imaginary patterns of chivalric and romance fiction were employed to describe new realities for which Europeans had no other ready vocabulary—as in Bernal Díaz del Castillo's account of his 1519 expedition to Mexico, or in the Magellan expedition's use of the name "Patagonia" (from the celebrated Amadis cycle) to describe the land of giants they found below the equator.[14]

The overlap between discursive and cartographic modes of representation of times and spaces was present from the very beginning of Hernando's collection, as suggested by a manuscript note dated to 1485 in Columbus's copy of Aeneas Silvius Piccolomini's *Historia rerum ubique gestarum* (Venice, 1477): "The King of Portugal, in the year of our Lord 1485 sent to Guinea Master Joseph [Vizinho] his physician and astrologer to measure the height of the sun in the whole of Guinea, which he did thoroughly and reported [the results] to the most serene king, I being present."[15] The note gestures toward new navigation techniques that took into account the curvature of the earth and used the height of the sun to establish latitude—in contrast with portolans, which recorded two-dimensional flat spaces and worked upon simple measures of distance and direction. Besides confirming that Columbus and his brother Bartholomew honed their navigational skills under the Portuguese—in the same milieu that generated the Behaim globe—the procedure described by the note involves the advanced application of the numerical and geometrical languages of mathematics and astronomy, and it relates these to the text by Piccolomini in which the note was made, which aspired to become, as its title proclaims, a comprehensive chronographic account recorded in discursive format. Although left unfinished, it managed to provide a description of Asia (the main focus of interest for the Columbuses) with more recent news on the clashes between the Ottoman Empire and Christian Europe. This copy of Piccolomini's *Historia* was one of the treasured books inherited by Hernando, whose father and uncle had turned it into an archive of manuscript notes, maps, and drawings that reveal the nature of their interests. Held within the volume are manuscript quotations from Augustine's *The City of God* that formulate Christian teleology, a geometrical representation of a three-dimensional globe projected onto a planisphere, and a copy of the letter and the map sent to the Portuguese Fernan Martins by the Italian cosmographer Paolo dal Pozzo Toscanelli with his description of a new western route to the Indies (see figs. 4 and 5). But the volume also contains temporal as well as geographic schemas, including testimonies of Jewish chronography in a fragment from book 8 of Josephus's *De antiquitate,* a manuscript chronology of history since Genesis according to the Jews, and a long quotation from Ovid's *Metamorphoses* (book I.34–54), where the Roman poet recounts the creation of the cosmos, with a brief catalogue of all the planets with their main features.[16] This seemingly eclectic collection in fact reflects the inseparability of Christian chronography from geographical thought at the time. In the traditional hierarchy of knowledge, history, as the discipline that dealt with the axis of time, had always enjoyed a superior status with respect to cartography, whose concern was space. Whereas the physical spaces of the earth were subject to change—as Ptolemy had suggested, and Hernando himself also acknowledged in his project for a voyage around the world—Christian time was an epistemological constant, the fundamental axis upon which the fragments of individual and social phenomena unfold and must be interpreted—in Augustinian terms, as syllables, words, and musical notes in the sequential disclosure of God's master plan.[17] This fundamental binary of Columbus's little archive, which required spatial data obtained by observation to be reconciled with ideological frameworks describing the arc of history, was to continue to be central to Hernando's encounter with the world.

Even the mathematical, geometrical models of Ptolemy could be vessels for ideology, since this mathematical grid could be easily put forth as the projection upon the globe of the heavenly harmonies and proportions of the cosmos as understood by the church. It also contributed to reinforcing the model of divinely sanctioned political power and social structure, which now acquired a rational and geometrical framework that displayed its vision of the world with elegant clarity.[18] This appropriation of Ptolemy smoothed out the particular "accidents" of the earth to fit them within a universal grid, in the same way in which the corruptions of society could be reconciled within a model of theologically sanctioned political power. This is why, after the disastrous schism in the church, Pierre d'Ailly went in search of answers within the mathematical patterns of Ptolemaic cosmography as keys to God's plan, combining Ptolemy with a millenarian, providential reading to provide heuristic tools for a proper understanding of the earthly chaos that had been unleashed by human dissent. This millennial narrative inheres in most, if not all, medieval *mappaemundi*, and as such, they are not merely synchronic maps but also diachronic icons that represent the history of the world from its creation in conceptual, narrative, and visual terms—*traza, escritura y pintura.* They conflate, in other words, cosmography with chronography.

The combination of traditional medieval maps and the authority of classical cosmographers founded upon Ptolemy is already evident in Andrea Bianco's 1436 atlas. In three different layers, Bianco's map includes: (1) a portolan chart, meant for practical navigation, exploration, and trade; (2) a map modeled on Ptolemaic geometrical and mathematical patterns; and (3) a traditional medieval map, with its strong Christian narrative component in terms of the well-established pattern of Creation, Fall, and Redemption, including, notably, the location of Paradise. That Columbus was still relying on this pattern of medieval *mappaemundi* and teleological chronography while he also employed Ptolemaic patterns, geometry, and algebra is demonstrated by the fact that he found no contradiction between his use of Zacuto's tables and his conviction that he had spotted Eden at the mouth of the Orinoco River. The map elaborated by Henricus Martellus a few decades later (ca. 1489–90) used Ptolemaic projections to codify textual information taken from Marco Polo in combination with the reports provided by Portuguese sailors and cosmographers like José Vizinho, a collation of materials similar to Bianco's that nonetheless disguises the narrative sources within the rationalist grid.[19] While he was in the service of the king of Portugal, Bartholomew Columbus was among the cartographers who coordinated the information collected for the elaboration of this map; his position was more or less identical to that assumed by Hernando a few decades later at the Casa de Contratación, with responsibilities for culling data from pilots with a view to updating charts.[20] What we are seeing, then, in Columbus's annotations to Marco Polo, and Hernando's own annotations (even in volumes like the *Utopia,* where he records information about the tides around that island), are data-gathering exercises preliminary to the creation of maps—maps that would themselves come to shape the early modern world.[21]

The proximity of book collecting, scholarship, and cosmography had deep roots that long predated Hernando. The vast amount of information furnished to Hernando by another of the founding volumes in his collection, Pliny's *Natural History,* had itself been distilled from that author's well-furnished library, using his prolific imagination, to serve the vast geographic scope of Roman power—for Pliny, like Hernando, relied on the reports sent throughout a network of informers from the farthest corners of the empire. Pliny's volume (like Hernando's library and the library-in-miniature of his catalogues) is a monumental compilation of sources, sources systematically listed in the table of authors and works of his book 1, where he underlines the importance of good libraries ("we ought to make not merely books, but valuable collections"). This table is no less than the catalogue of Pliny's ideal library, his own role being confined to the extraction and arrangement of these materials for the use of readers.[22] The result was an unprecedented compilation of information that would be used as an encyclopedic resource for centuries to come. When serving King Ferdinand at court and (more importantly) Emperor Charles V at the Casa de Contratación, Hernando was privileged with a similar position at the very heart of a vast and complex nexus of political and financial power that thrived on the information and wealth circulating throughout its global networks, networks he harnessed to obtain cosmographic information for the universal navigation chart and resources to enlarge his universal library. The continuity of Hernando's work in the Casa de Contratación and in his library project, however, must be seen in the light of the early modern decoupling of the library and the administrative archive after a long symbiosis that left significant structural legacies in each of them.

Manuscripts, Maps, and Libraries

The history of libraries shows that book collectors and translators have often followed close behind conquering armies and their entourage of wealthy magnates, scholars, and artisans with skills to produce the artifacts used to store and distribute knowledge, from clay tablets and papyri to parchment and printed paper.[23] Ptolemy and his work were the products of the legendary library and academy in Hellenistic Alexandria, where other important mathematicians and cosmographers, including Eratosthenes, also conducted cosmographic investigations and where literary scholars, including Callimachus, prepared bibliographical catalogues and fixed with them a canon of classical Greek literature that would endure for more than two millennia.[24]

The more recent story of Ptolemy's rediscovery in Western Christendom demonstrates the enduring connection between libraries and technical practice. The first translator of Ptolemy's *Cosmographia* into Latin was Jacopo di Angelo (ca. 1360–ca. 1410/11), a disciple of the Byzantine scholar Manuel Chrysoloras (1355–1415) who had first arrived in western Europe as a diplomatic envoy from Emperor Manuel II Palaeologus and later brought back a considerable number of Greek manuscripts. Chrysoloras translated Homer and Plato and also gathered around him a distinguished group of disciples who would become expert Hellenists: with their editions, translations, and commentaries, they helped spread classical Greek literature, historiography, philosophy, and science throughout the rest of Europe, leaving a legacy of students, including Leonardo Bruni, the Florentine chancellor Coluccio Salutati, and the book collector Palla Strozzi. It appears that Chrysoloras himself first took up the task of rendering Ptolemy into Latin, a project finally completed by Jacopo di Angelo da Scarperia in 1409 with a dedication to Pope Alexander V.[25] This translation was fundamental to the work of Pierre d'Ailly (author of Columbus's handbook) and of Paolo dal Pozzo Toscanelli, the physician, translator, library trustee, and astronomer for the Medici bank whose writings were so central to Columbus's plans for circumnavigation. The Ptolemy also importantly influenced Antonio Vespucci—uncle to Amerigo, the cartographer who would become the first pilot major at the Sevillian Casa de la Contratación—and of course Hernando himself, who inherited a copy of the Ptolemy from his father.[26]

The nexus between cartographers and libraries extended to include astronomers, as was perhaps inevitable in an age when the observation of the heavens put the earth very much at the center of things. Regiomontanus, the redactor of Ptolemy's *Cosmography,* whose relationship with Cardinal Bessarion and the Biblioteca Corviniana is a counterpart to the Toscanelli-Chrysoloras connection, drew many of the leading astronomical currents of the day into the library, which served as a space of both textual collation and technical innovation. After coinciding with Georgius Purbachius at the University of Vienna, Regiomontanus continued his translation of the Ptolemaic *Almagest,* which (though unfinished) was printed in 1496 as *Epytoma Ioannis de monte regio in almagestum ptolemei.* Hernando bought a copy of this edition (n.d.) in Salamanca (in whose university Regiomontanus was in common use), to which in 1521 he added a copy of Georgius Purbachius's *Quadratum geometricum.*[27] As well as feeding into the cartography of Martin Behaim, who trained under Regiomontanus and was central to the designs of Columbus, the work of Purbachius and Regiomontanus was studied by Hernando under Veteranus in Rome.[28] Hernando was certainly drawing on the work of these figures when he produced his opinion on current astronomical science for the Juntas de Elvas-Badajoz. He may also have been inspired by Regiomontanus's letter to Bessarion, printed in the edition that Hernando owned, in which the librarian of the Biblioteca Corviniana outlined how Ptolemy had used the meteroscope for celestial calculations of latitude and longitude, just as Hernando would use the space of his own library to instruct Spanish mariners in the use of navigational instruments.[29]

The unprecedented amount of information being amassed in global travel posed an enormous challenge, for it required not just a proper administrative infrastructure but, above all, efficient methods to turn all these data into something meaningful and useful. The response to this in the pioneering nations of Spain and Portugal was the creation of distinctive institutions for the processing of loose-leaf reports, engines to collate this heterogeneous material before it could reach the library and overwhelm it, sending it on only when it had been digested into a form deemed publishable in book and map form. The Portuguese Casa da Mina and the Spanish Casa de Contratación have been described as Europe's first scientific institutions, pioneering hubs of knowledge created by early modern European states to manage the complex logistics required by their imperial ambitions.[30] Before utopian projects like Bacon's *New Atlantis* (composed in 1624) and others that fantasized about scientific communities (parodied afterward in Jonathan Swift's *Academy of Lagado* in 1726), the Portuguese and the Hispanic crowns found themselves in urgent need of pragmatic and functional centers for the administration, research, and production of knowledge and communication technologies in order to channel and control the enormous amount of information that came under their ken. As sophisticated administrative centers, their functions included the development and production of standard navigation instruments alongside the keeping of accounts; the control of precious metals and financial flows; and the training, examination, and licensing of qualified personnel.[31] Although they were officially sponsored by their respective monarchies, in terms of the actual agents who provided information and produced their maps these two institutions were essentially transnational and relied on international networks of exchange for their staff and the implementation of their functions. The Florentine Amerigo Vespucci was appointed as the first *piloto mayor* of the Hispanic Casa de Contratación when it was established in 1503, and he also became the first head of its cosmographical department five years later. The same order that created this department and office in 1508 also enjoined all pilots to send back information from their respective voyages. In short, the Casa de Contratación was an advanced administrative center for the management of communication and trade. Unsurprisingly then, these institutions turned to information managers for their administrative personnel, as when Hernando was appointed to work with the Casa in 1518, and this trend continued in the next generation with the recruitment of the polymath Pedro Mexía to redesign the *Padrón Real,* an overlap that demonstrates the porous boundaries between history, encyclopedism, cosmography, and cartography.[32]

The Casa de Contratación was, then, an adjunct to Hernando's own project for a universal repository of knowledge, and the functions of the two were increasingly understood to be mutually dependent. Seville thus became more than just a cosmographic meridian—as Alonso de Chaves proposed in his *Espejo de navegantes.* With its institutions and its communities of sailors, merchants, cartographers, and bureaucrats the city became a powerful knowledge hub and research center, thriving on the reports and maps it received from the four corners of the globe as its economy flourished with the incoming flow of overseas goods and precious metals—whose value Genoese bankers then translated into sophisticated financial instruments. All of this required common standards for the representation of the world in cartographic and also in financial terms, a precondition for establishing and efficiently controlling the paths of transport and communication for these products, the arteries through which the lifeblood of the imperial body politic circulated.

Hernando's *Cosmografía* and Nebrija's Cartographic Humanism

The practice of entrusting the reconciliation of data streams to experts in information management was not without its critics, especially among those who saw it as a usurpation of the prerogative of mariners. A good example of this is the criticisms leveled at Hernando's cartographic assistant Alonso de Chaves, who was accused by his opponents at the Casa de Contratación of lacking actual sailing experience: Chaves, they said, might have spent long hours at his books, tables, and figures, but he had never set foot on a ship. Pilots resented the blind faith of some cosmographers in the abstract patterns provided by the Greek authorities. The situation worsened as exploration gained momentum, as the pilots engaged in actual navigation sent back a ceaseless and increasing stream of empirical information that frequently contradicted the tenets of cosmographers like Ptolemy and Sacrobosco. Hernando, by contrast, offered proof against accusations of inexperience given his heritage and navigational background, and with his pioneering project for the reconciliation of observational data and geometrical modeling, the *Cosmografía de España* launched in 1517.

Hernando had acknowledged the debate between mariners and cartographers and its paradoxes as early as his 1511 proposal for a circumnavigation of the world, in which he struggled to account for the mismatch between abstract models and empirical data. In his attempt to preserve the authority of classical authors, he presented a radical proposal. He exonerated the ancient cosmographers of any errors by attributing the contradiction between classical theory and current incoming data to the fact that the oceans, the islands, and the territories are always in constant change: "They should not always use the ancient cosmographers as their guide, because they acknowledge themselves the diversity and mutation of the territories, the islands and the seas, for they are never continuously the same, as proved by many authorities and also by experience."[33] This vision of a world in constant flux, however, reinforced the need for reliable methods for its measurement, quantification, and representation—and also constant data gathering to keep up with the fluid environment. By 1517, Hernando had absorbed the latest Italian developments for accruing and reconciling information into geometrical models within the space of the library, during his years of study at the academies of Rome. He was about to coincide with the great Spanish authority on rhetoric and linguistic norms, someone who had thought extensively about how these could be combined with the numerical patterns employed in the measurement and quantification of time, the cosmos, and the earth. Elio Antonio de Nebrija's work and his activities provided a background for the combination of rhetorical and scientific humanism which later evolved within Hernando's projects and his collection.

Nebrija's contribution to the humanist project of establishing language as a stable foundation for epistemology was part of a wider project of quantitative and metric standardization.[34] When Hernando met him in 1517, the seventy-six-year-old Nebrija was a venerable scholar and an emeritus chair at the recently created University of Alcalá. Almost two decades before, in 1498, Nebrija had published a little handbook—almost an *obrezilla*—titled *In cosmographiae libros introductorium multo quam antea castigatius*, Hernando's copy of which has not survived.[35] Nebrija's intention—to clarify the field and hone its tools—is perhaps most clearly captured toward the end of its fourteen leaves, where he includes a lexicon with terms used by cosmographers ("De vocabulis quibus Cosmographi vtuntur," fols. 13v–15v). Nebrija's lexicographical enthusiasm had already yielded a Latin-Spanish and a Spanish-Latin lexicon—in emulation of which Hernando took up his own project of a Latin vocabulary (see figs. 16 and 17).[36] Now, however, Nebrija was turning his hand to fixing the vocabulary that underpinned the culture of measurement and cartography, a first step toward an agreed and standardized procedure for representing the world in words and images. In this pamphlet appear for the first time in Spain many of the

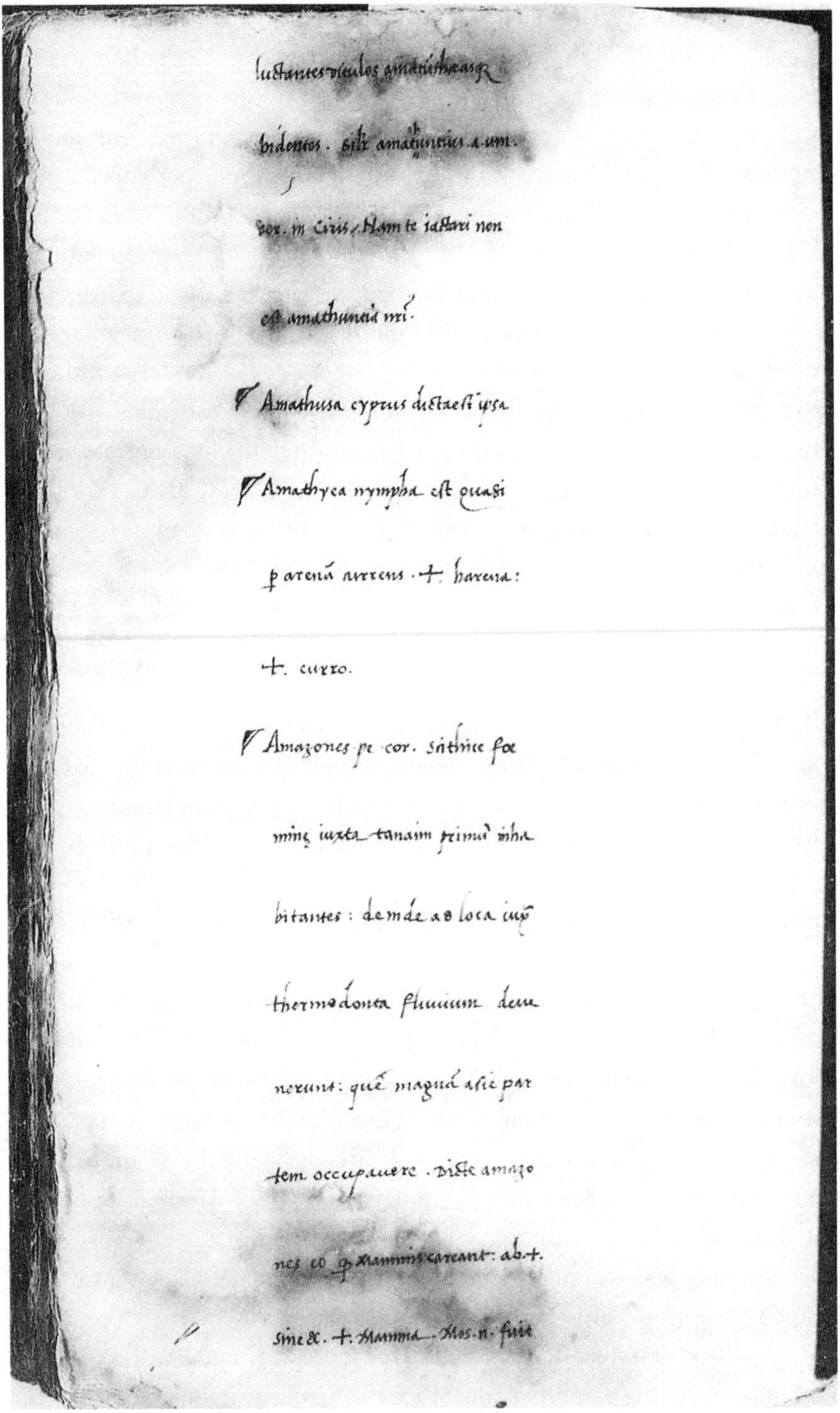

FIG. 16. A page from Hernando's unfinished Latin vocabulary with the definition of "amazons" (Amazones) (© Cabildo Catedral de Sevilla)

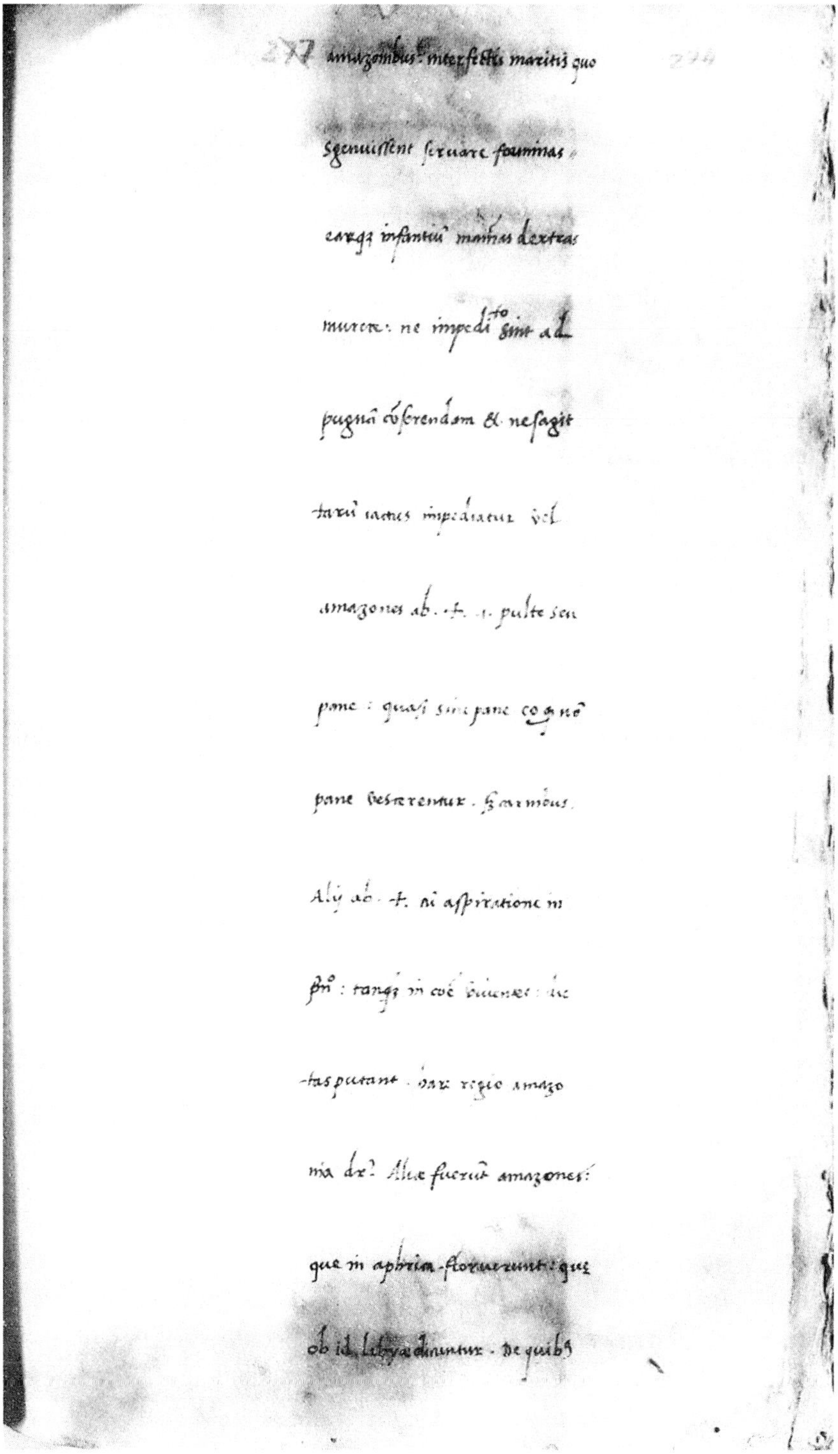

FIG. 17. Another page from Hernando's unfinished Latin vocabulary, also with a definition of "amazons" (© Cabildo Catedral de Sevilla)

words—"graticule," for instance, to describe the abstract grid upon which Ptolemaic coordinates were to be plotted—that described the central tools of the coming technological revolution.

Nebrija's *Cosmography* of 1498 rests upon the current authorities in the discipline, and he directs his readers to the usual names in the Greek canon: Ptolemy, Mela, and Strabo, establishing lexicographic, epistemological, and metrical standards. Another central, though unnamed, source for Nebrija's booklet was Abraham Zacuto, whose personal acquaintance he had made when both were part of the entourage of the *maestre* of Alcántara, Don Juan de Zúñiga. The Strabonian tradition of ekphrastic cartography stands in a very revealing contrast with Abraham Zacuto's *Almanach Perpetuum*.[37] Zacuto's numerical tables were used to calculate latitudes by direct observation of the meridian altitudes of the sun, and it circulated profusely in translation from the original Hebrew (*Hajibbur hagadol*), first in Jose Vizinho's Portuguese version, then in the Latin *Almanach Perpetuum* used by Columbus, who also knew through Vizinho of the practical use Portugal was making of this system along the African coast.[38] Hernando himself took a keen interest in Zacuto: among the two hundred unnamed titles that he and his brother Diego carried with them to La Hispaniola in 1509, Zacuto's tables were singled out by name.[39] Additional proof that Hernando used the tables is provided by his manuscript note toward the end of his copy, in which he describes a method to calculate on which day of the week each month begins (fig. 18). Zacuto had, then, played a pivotal role in providing data that enabled the Columbian voyages, but through Nebrija, he was also to provide some of the theoretical framework for reconciling streams of information within the space of the library and archive.

In his *Cosmography* Nebrija is particularly interested in the problem of establishing homogeneous units for measuring distance and time—dealt with primarily in chapter 9, "De diuersitate horarum diei ex declinatione ab eqnoctiali." The work devotes chapters to the units of measure used by cosmographers ("De mensuris qbus cosmographi utunt[ur]. cap.vj") and to the representation of the earth in a planispheric format following the Ptolemaic model ("Descriptio terre in plano ex ptolemeo. cap.vii"). These ideas were also the subject of Nebrija's lectures at the University of Salamanca during these years, subsequently systematized into a series of *relectiones*, and posthumously published in Alcalá by Miguel de Eguía in

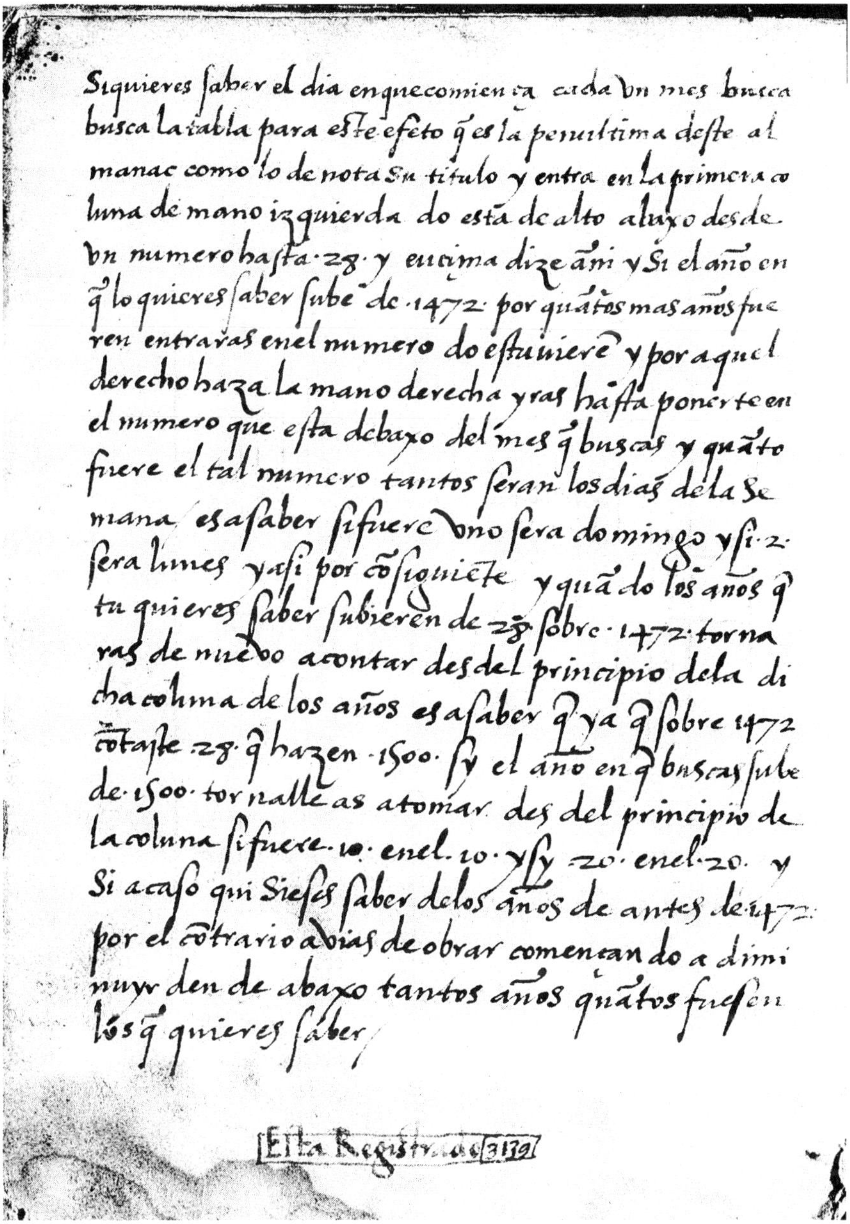

Siquieres saber el dia enque comiença cada vn mes busca
busca la tabla para este efeto q̄ es la penultima deste al
manac como lo de nota su titulo y entra en la primera co
luna de mano izquierda do está de alto abaxo desde
vn numero hasta ·28· y encima dize ānj y si el año en
q̄ lo quieres saber sube de ·1472· por quātos mas años fue
ren entraras enel numero do estuuiere y por aquel
derecho haza la mano derecha yras hasta ponerte en
el numero que esta debaxo del mes q̄ buscas y quāto
fuere el tal numero tantos seran los dias dela se
mana es a saber si fuere vno sera domingo y si ·2·
sera lunes y asi por cōsiguiēte y quādo los años q̄
tu quieres saber subieren de ·28· sobre ·1472· torna
ras de nuevo a contar desdel principio dela di
cha coluna de los años es a saber q̄ ya q̄ sobre 1472
cōtaste ·28· q̄ hazen ·1500· si el año en q̄ buscas sube
de ·1500· tornalle as a tomar desdel principio de
la coluna si fuere ·10· enel ·10· y sy ·20· enel ·20· y
si acaso quisieses saber delos años de antes de ·1472·
por el cōtrario avias de obrar començando a dimi
nuyr dende abaxo tantos años quātos fuesen
los q̄ quieres saber

Esta Registrado 3139

FIG. 18. Hernando's manuscript note toward the end of his copy of Abraham Zacuto's *Almanach Perpetuum,* in which he describes a method to calculate on which day of the week each month will begin (© Cabildo Catedral de Sevilla)

1527.[40] After dealing in these with *De mensuris, De ponderibus,* and *De numeris* (distance, weight, and number), Nebrija turned his attention to the measurement of time in 1516 with his *Tabla de la diversidad de los días y las horas,* which he presented to Hernando during the latter's visit to the University of Alcalá de Henares in 1517.[41] This work took as its focus a central question in cosmography, namely, the difference in time zones and in general the measurement of time: a sine qua non when it came to solving the fundamental problem of the exact calculation of longitude, which could not be achieved without the sort of technology required to measure the passage of time accurately on a sailing vessel.[42]

Nebrija's handbook is a typical product of humanist cosmography as he must have imbibed it—like the rest of his thinking—during his Italian phase.[43] His opening chapter discusses a series of basic principles about the earth and the cosmos, founded upon "ratione geometrica." He then invokes Greek authorities (*greci cosmon ab ornatu stellarum dixere*) and comes up with a list of authors that combines ancient natural philosophers with historians, grammarians, and poets (Pliny, Varro, Ovid, among others). In his *Cosmography* Nebrija puts as much emphasis on vocabulary as he does on units of measure: for instance, in chapter 6 ("De mensuris quibus cosmographi utunt") he approaches this topic as a lexicographer and a grammarian, trying to establish the equivalences between different cosmographic units of measure in different languages (above all in Latin and Greek, in this case). Again, his main intent is to achieve the kind of normalization which, founded upon "ratio" and linguistically efficient principles, would facilitate the accurate formulation and communication of cosmographic knowledge. His approach to the question of time zones proves much the same: the problem proposes itself as one of collation, of weighing the contesting authorities and attempting to synthesize them with the observed world—as represented by Zacuto's tables—in a marriage of the discursive and the numerical.[44] If cosmography was a representation of the world and the cosmos in their absence, as Hernando's collaborator Alonso de Chaves would have it, language, with its modular units and norms—that is, its orthography, punctuation, grammar, lexicon, and syntax—was in its own turn a verbal mirror of knowledge and human communities, a mirror which Nebrija had already limned during his lexicographical work.[45] Nebrija was concerned throughout the course of his entire career with the standards required for the normalization, classification, manufacture, and distribution of information and knowledge in all its different disciplines and formats, and in this he was a crucial inspiration for Hernando's own projects.

Shortly after being presented with Nebrija's *Tabla*, Hernando followed Nebrija's example with his own Latin vocabulary, as well as with his project for a *Cosmografía de España*. It is perhaps significant that the *Cosmografía* is described first—and in some detail—by Juan Pérez in his account of Hernando's projects, and it is evident that its core ideas were to persist, albeit somewhat transformed, as Hernando turned later in life to focus primarily on his library and its catalogues.[46] The opening of Juan Pérez's description establishes the classic millenarian-mercantile axes of Hernando's Columbian thought: the *Cosmografía* was intended, through the accuracy of its recording, to make Castile equal not only to the centers of late medieval Christianity (Rome, Jerusalem, and Babylon), but also to the centers of early modern trade (Paris and Antwerp), all places cited as having been the subject of similar censuses. Though this may have had deep roots in the census of Judaea that sent Mary toward Bethlehem—which indicated for some a profound connection between moments of millenarian and administrative climax—Hernando's methods were entirely modern and derived from techniques he had absorbed through his many experiences. The use of cartographic emissaries, gathering both figures (measures of distance, populations) and words (descriptions of countryside, records of lordship) using a set form, created a funnel to bring both numerical and descriptive data back to a central database. They combined use of professional cartographers, local authorities, and public notaries (a kind of triple lock) borrowed from the financial credit systems to create networks capable of acting as trustworthy channels of communications across great distances. The processing of these data after they had been gathered brought together the world of books and that of maps, creating an alphabetical index to give each settlement a distinct identity and a unique place in the list, while allowing for multiple different reports on that settlement to be fed in, iterating toward more accurate measurements of distance, fuller descriptions of terrain, and allowances for fluctuations in population. This heterogeneous torrent of information would then be laid out within the synoptic and rationalized space of the grid—using celestial measures of latitude, from tables such as Zacuto's, to fix the map at key points—which in turn allowed the map to be reproduced accurately and efficiently using the resulting grid coordinates, a matrix for the "printing" of infinite numbers of virtually identical representations of the peninsula. This, then, was an engine for distilling, organizing, and redistributing a representation of the world, an engine that Hernando would later conceive as reaching across the whole world, with a universal library at its heart. The creation of global maps, however, was a slightly different matter to a project for a peninsular one, given the hidden spaces, contending polities, and enormous distances involved in global mapping, as Hernando was shortly to discover.

Cosmography and Empire: Las Juntas de Elvas-Badajoz

Soon after his return from his trip around Europe between 1520 and 1522, Hernando was confronted with the need to put all these techniques for the quantification, measurement, and representation of the world at the service of the political agenda of the Hispanic monarchy, first at the Juntas de Elvas-Badajoz and later in the elaboration of a universal navigation chart and globe. The Juntas de Elvas-Badajoz is an excellent example of the dynamics involved in the relations between cosmography and politics and of the way these realms shaped each other. One of the main issues discussed during the Juntas was trade rights with the Moluccas, which required establishing a counter-meridian that would prolong the line originally drawn in the Treaty of Tordesillas, in 1494, to separate the Portuguese and Castilian zones of influence. Sanctioned by the authority of the pope, Tordesillas had resolved the dispute of the 1490s, but the voyage around the world recently begun by Magellan and completed by Elcano had rendered this treaty, and its accompanying map, obsolete. The meridian agreed on in Tordesillas was a straight line, moving from north to south on a two-dimensional map; now cosmographers needed to turn it into a vertical girdle around the sphere of the earth.

The technical preconditions for a proper settlement of the dispute with Portugal involved large-scale calculations to ascertain as accurately as possible the actual circumference of the earth, for upon this depended the efficient conversion of degrees into leagues. Without the calculation of the length of a degree it was impossible to accurately partition the globe into a Ptolemaic spherical grid. The technology required for another fundamental problem—measuring exact longitude at sea—would not be available for centuries. In sum, it was very difficult to locate the Moluccas with the required precision on a global *mappamundi*—which rendered the scientific settlement of the main political issue during the Juntas de Elvas-Badajoz an impossible task, as Hernando himself acknowledged in the report he put together after the meeting: "In conclusion . . . in no way will those who wish to play for time be able to be persuaded, and so I say that there can be no verdict in this case at present: it would be necessary to have an agreed test of the length of degrees, and once we had this, vessels and crews would have to be sent on each of the said routes (or better ones that they may find) to measure longitude, and thus be able to define and establish the beginning and the end of the demarcation in question, and the lands which are contained in each part or hemisphere."[47] As Hernando made clear in his briefing before the conference, it was not simply technological and metrical shortcomings with which they would have to contend, they were also up against the weight of public opinion. Hernando himself was faithful to Columbus's interpretation of the Tordesillas treaty, which allowed the Portuguese only as much of the world east of the Tordesillas line as had been reached by their voyages up to 1494 (slightly short of the Cape of Good Hope). The public, however, having been informed by the prognostications, travel reports, and news pamphlets that connected the worlds of elite geopolitics and astronomy to popular conception, had become convinced of another interpretation of the treaty, an interpretation that it would bc hard to unstick.

> D. Hernando Colón says that the first chapter of the treaty agreed between the Catholic Monarchs, who are in heaven, and the king Don Juan of Portugal, sets out a certain division of seas and land, of which, because of the lack of information and understanding among common folk, has led to a general belief that they had divided the world between themselves, and this led to the further popular opinion that they divided the world in half between them; so much so that this opinion was even held by the people that your Majesty sent to negotiate on this subject, who were under such a deeply rooted impression that they firmly believe that this is actually the case; and even though they have seen and read the said treaty many times, this is not

> enough and whenever they have to act on this matter they take this illusion for truth, especially when they see that this opinion was never contradicted there at court by the members of your Majesty's Council of Castille.[48]

Here Hernando certainly puts emphasis on how the circulation of inaccurate information has misled public opinion, how it has affected the reputation of the crown, and the difficulties involved in uprooting these perceptions. This episode throws some light upon another reason for Hernando's interest in *obrezillas:* though the news spread by these small pamphlets was not necessarily all true, reliable, or politically convenient, it nevertheless had an impact on the *pública fama,* the opinion of the *vulgo.* Like the shifting measurements of the world, the gathering of these *obrezillas* was necessary to ascertain not just what was known but also what was thought in the world, to allow policy to be drawn up in full knowledge of the opposition it would meet.

The failure at the Juntas de Elvas-Badajoz, owing to the disagreements between pilots and cosmographers, the varying legal interpretations of the treaty, and the problems posed by "la variedad que ay en los mapamundis y cartas de navegar," led to the order from the emperor for the elaboration of a new universal chart for practical navigational purposes and a globe, which would also reinforce the public legitimation of the territorial claims of the Hispanic empire.[49] Transportation and trade may have required functional maps that could guide pilots through safe navigable routes, but the sovereignty of the Hispanic crown over the new territories was of paramount importance in terms of diplomatic and geopolitical status, hence the need for a comprehensive, indeed universal, model which only cosmographers could provide.

Sebastian Cabot—*piloto mayor* at the time of the conference—was sent on a new information-gathering expedition to the Moluccas, sailing west in April 1526, and as a result Hernando was put in charge of mapmaking activities at the Casa de Contratación. The two main cosmographers under his supervision and coordination for the elaboration of the *Carta General de Navegar* were Alonso de Chaves and Diego Ribero. Hernando's 1526 letter of office from the emperor highlights how one of the main functions of institutions like the Casa da Mina and the Casa de Contratación consisted precisely in gathering and coordinating data in different formats—words and images, "informaçión así por escripto como por palabra y pinturas"—required for the production of maps.[50] It involved the double challenge of standardizing first the collection of data, and then the principles and categories for their classification. The maps and the methods founded on Ptolemaic patterns had been under constant revision in textual terms since Jacopo d'Angelo's translation—including Regiomontanus's important textual criticism applied to the collation of original and translation—and also in terms of the cartographic illustrations that accompanied the different editions of the *Geography,* which were under constant renovation as new information cropped up about new territories in addition to more accurate data about already known areas. Ptolemy had acknowledged that cartography relied for its results on the information provided by correspondents and agents, who should ideally be trained in the sort of scientific criteria that would make their observations and reports useful for those who gathered the empirical data. To this end, pilots were to be trained in the basic principles of cosmography and astronomy, so that the information they collected would be standardized and thus compatible with the patterns within which it would be integrated once it reached the cosmographers at the Casa de Contratación.[51] With the assistance of Ribero and Chaves, Hernando established a more demanding curriculum for the education of the new pilots—many of whose predecessors were illiterate. They now had to go through more rigorous tests and examinations if they wanted to obtain their license.

The earliest surviving result of the team at the Casa de Contratación is the so-called Weimar chart of 1527, which was followed in 1529 by the Diego Ribero map now at the Vatican. These two are among the few remaining primary sources that illustrate the methods and techniques employed by the experts under Hernando's watch.[52] Ribero's map was the first to introduce updated technical and cosmographic information: he decorated his *mappamundi* with quadrants, astrolabes, and also texts providing the rules of navigation and information about various countries. It is, therefore, a complex semiotic artifact that codifies information in several different symbolic systems, as it also flaunts the tools and the technology employed in its elaboration. One of its purposes, as a diplomatic gift, was of course the public display of the technological mastery of the cosmographers and fleet working for Emperor Charles V, a complement to his vast dominions, an empire with legal foundations, as the map's title proclaims, in the international diplomatic agreement signed in Tordesillas in 1494. Diplomacy, cartography, navigation, and their tools all feature here as the handmaidens of empire.

This flurry of activity and the resulting string of maps was followed, about nine or ten years later, by the *real cédula* of 20 May 1535, which urged Hernando to send the Council of Indies and the Casa de Contratación the navigation chart that he had been enjoined to elaborate in March of 1526.[53] This document makes clear that the Weimar chart and the Diego Ribero map of 1529 were considered provisional in terms of their cartographic conclusions, for all their finished appearance as presentation maps. Whereas this *real cédula* of 1535 has been used by several scholars to demonstrate that Hernando failed to fulfill the emperor's command, Cerezo Martínez holds that the Weimar chart of 1527 and Ribero's *mappaemundi* are proof of Hernando's endeavors as the coordinator of cartographers at the Casa de Contratación, and proof therefore that he had actually delivered, at least, a provisional version that was used not just by the pilots but also for vital diplomatic purposes, above all in the case of the Ribero map. Cerezo concludes that a satisfactory and definitive version was not yet available almost ten years later due to disagreements between the pilots and the cosmographers and should not be blamed on Hernando's shortcomings.[54] There is the fact, besides, that there was no end to new information arriving from pilots and sailors, which turned the elaboration of a universal chart into a continuous work in progress—something incompatible with the concept of an ideal, quasi-Platonic, universal cartographic gold standard, which would require absolute stability in the thing being measured. Like Hernando's catalogues for his universal library, a universal, omnicomprehensive chart required a notion of knowledge more like calculus than geometry: fluid, evolving, and shifting rather than fixed and universal.

If Hernando failed to achieve what the emperor wanted, it was not for lack of trying. Hernando had been attuned since an early age, when his father's discoveries had been broadcast through Europe in the form of printed letters in Spanish and in translation, to the notion that information could spread through cheap print, and his surviving collections are witness to how he sought out and stored such texts more assiduously than anyone else of the age. The only surviving copy of Dati's Italian translation of Columbus's first letter reporting the voyage of 1492, in *ottava rima,* is preserved among Hernando's *obrezillas.* Hernando also owned Vespucci's *Mundus Novus,* a Latin translation of the Italian letter sent to Lorenzo di Pierfrancesco de' Medici with a report of a voyage to America in 1501–2, which was published as an eight-page quarto in its 1504 Aubsburg edition, and Vespucci's *De ora antartica per regem Portugalliae pridem inventa* (Argentoratum, 1505) as a twelve-page quarto. The cartographic resources of the *obrezillas* also extended to his prognostications, which contained celestial observations as well as reports from distant places. A substantial portion of Hernando's *obrezillas* was made up of almanacs, ephemerides, horoscopes, reports of astronomical events, extraordinary occurrences in the heavens, and nature in general, which were then interpreted as carriers of divine messages. Hernando owned 260 astrological prognostications dating from the fifteenth and sixteenth centuries, making his the single greatest known repository of public astronomy of the early modern age.[55] These local observations were integrated within the wider schemes of Hernando's universal map of knowledge in much the same way that portolans and pilots' reports fed into the cartographic projects, combining with broader schematics of the world's meaning to provide granular detail for how it took shape at the level of individual experience.

Beyond its use for political or economic purposes, a map is a tool for the cognitive apprehension and appropriation of the world, particularly so in this period when the craft of mapmaking became an *art* whose Ptolemaic grid (in the words of Portuondo) "conditioned Europe for new and seemingly empty spaces to be imagined as real." In this, the map strongly resembles an encyclopedia, or a library. It is a technology designed to cull first, and then harmonize, information from the scattered fragments of a world that we, of necessity, perceive disconnectedly and in flux. Its method produces an artifact that performs the illusion of a universal, comprehensive, and static order. In their ambition to be accurate representations of the world, maps were narrative artifacts, and the same can be said for libraries: Hernando's collection aspired to be a complex and heterogeneous, but also impossibly comprehensive, textual mirror of the world, nature, and the cosmos—as Chaves put it, an "imagen del mundo por ausencia suya." If, as Jacob proclaims, "terrestrial space, as a reality that can be seen and imagined, does not exist before or apart from its map," then also *human learning, its values and societies* did not exist outside the accumulated discursive layers and fragments that collectors like Hernando were trying to gather in their libraries.[56] In that respect, each library, with its own organizing principles and its own functions and aims, creates the knowledge and even the society from which it derives. In defining the items to be collected, and those to be left out, a collector and his librarians give us a blueprint of their worldview and the sort of knowledge delineated by their books, a profile that bears fruit in the catalogue—itself a map of the macro-map that is the library.[57]

Catalogues, like maps, present important challenges when it comes to developing technologies and alphabets for the representation of the universal in a single spot, in a finite format at scale. Cartography and cataloguing techniques share similar epistemological principles involving the relation between space, knowledge, and power and in the way in which they are designed and represented. These are, as Foucault puts it, "the forms of implantation, delimitation and demarcation of objects, the modes of tabulation, the organization of domains."[58] These forms include of course not just cartography and catalogues of all sorts but also disciplines and practices like architecture and urban design—systems, in general, and technologies for the symbolic organization of knowledge and power relations in spatial and temporal terms. It is a metaphor that English language use has already naturalized, because we speak of "realms"—originally a kingdom or polity, a territory or a region—to describe the cognitive scope of specific disciplines of knowledge. Hernando's knowledge of cartography carried over into the realms of the library and the regions of the catalogue.

CHAPTER FOUR

NEW WORLD ORDER

The volume known as MS 652 in the Real Biblioteca in Madrid is usually referred to as a miscellany because it brings together within its covers printed pamphlets (*On the Art of Drinking, On the Origin of Jurisdictions,* on the Italian attempts to map the North Sea) with various manuscript tracts, including a colloquy on the use of longitudinal degrees on Spanish maps, a tract on the *Juego de Pelota,* a case for the Spanish crown to claim the provinces of Arabia and Persia, and the most extensive description of early modern library practices in existence. This bewildering variety of texts seems to share an origin in the milieu of Hernando Colón—the *Colloquio* on longitude was likely written by Hernando and the *Declaración* on Arabia certainly was, while the *Memoria* by Hernando's last librarian, Juan Pérez, is dedicated to describing the *obras y libros* (works and books) of his patron.[1] The fact that Pérez's tract was written after Hernando's death in an attempt to record the founder's wishes for his library may explain why none of these tracts bears Hernando's characteristic notes and none is entered in his catalogues: it is, perhaps, a final gathering up of loose ends, and one fittingly representative of Hernando's widely ranging occupations. Yet our exploration of Hernando's life and library suggests we should be cautious about accepting simply circumstantial links between his apparently disparate interests, and that passing over seemingly disparate things with the dismissive label of *miscellany* risks overlooking the shared foundations that underlie these practices.

Though it is uncertain how long Juan Pérez had worked in the library by the time of Hernando's death, Hernando's will makes clear that he entirely trusted his assistant to faithfully transmit his wishes for the library, noting in his closing remarks that Juan Pérez should be left to "order and oversee" (*regir e governar*) matters regarding the library.[2] It was a trust evidently well placed, as Juan Pérez's *Memoria de las Obras y Libros de don Hernando Colón* provides a scrupulous account of Hernando's vision in minute detail, structured around the thirty-nine manuscript volumes which made up the sixteen *repertorios* devised by Hernando.[3] These volumes were kept together in a section of the *Sala de Teología*—a tantalizing glimpse at the original organization of the library into subject rooms, unattested elsewhere and replaced in the final library scheme—each with its own label, describing its nature and its use, affixed above it. They were also color coded, with bindings of red, white, black, and embossed leather.[4] Though previous scholarship has tended to label these volumes as *registra* or *repertorios* (and while we have for the sake of convenience referred to them as "catalogues"), Juan Pérez is purposefully indeterminate when writing about them, doggedly using only the terms "obras" and "libros," terms which hold back from classifying the nature of the projects contained within them. This reticence is understandable, as his description brings together not only the ways of navigating the books in the library but also a map of the image collection, Hernando's lexicographical project, and his attempt in the *Descripción* to document every human habitation in Spain, as well as the links between these projects and the manner in which this engine would be connected to the rest of the globe, both to draw information in and to redistribute it to the world.

Juan Pérez's *Memoria,* then, describes these central tools of the library in the following order, giving for each a physical description and an account of its genealogy, structure, and intended use (table 1).

The order in which Juan Pérez describes them is somewhat confusing, though the major Spanish account of the works sticks to this scheme, suggesting that the *Memoria* progresses from registers that distill didactic or

TABLE 1

Hernando's *Repertorios*

Martínez's Numbering	Common Names	Bindings
1 & 2	The *Cosmografía, Itinerario,* or *Descripción* of Spain	8 quarto vols.
3	The *Dibujos o Pinturas* (images)	3 quarto vols.
4 & 5	The *Libro de los Epítomes*	2 quarto vols. & 1 folio vol.
6 & 7	The *Libro de las Materias* (subject matters)	8 quarto vols.
8	*Tabla de Autores y Ciencias* or *Annotaciones*	>10,000 slips of paper
9	The Índice General Alfabético or *Abecedarium B*	2 folio vols.
10	The Índice Numeral or *Registrum B*	1 folio vol.
11	*Índice de Autores y Obras*	6 quarto vols.
12	The old book of *Autores y Ciencias*	1 quarto vol.
13	*Vocabulario* or *Diccionario Latino*	1 folio vol.
14	*Memorial de los Libros Naufragados* or *Registrum A*	1 folio vol.
15	*Índice muy generales*	2 folio vols.
16	The Índice Alfabético Antiguo or *Abecedarium A*	3 folio vols.

ideological content to those with a purely practical function.[5] The *Cosmografia*, the catalogue of pictures, and the *Vocabulario Latino*, however, don't fit into this scheme, and it also relies on a distinction between the practical and the ideological which, as the foregoing chapters of this book have sought to show, is unsustainable. Instead, Juan Pérez seems to be prompted in his ordering by a range of biographical, material, and structural considerations—when Hernando started a project, where its records sat on the shelves, and how central they were to his thinking—in a way that forefronts the radical indistinction between the practical and ideological. So, while our account of Hernando's modes of ordering relies heavily for its detail on the excellent and thorough work of Marín Martínez, we have opted for a simplified account of these volumes, based on a rough chronology, to shed light on the organizational innovations to which Hernando was driven by new challenges, combining the methods he was acquiring from actuarial and cartographical processes.

The work of Hernando's for which there is the earliest concrete evidence—and the one that Juan Pérez describes first—is the *Descripción*. While Juan Pérez suggests Hernando's intention was to "create a cosmography of Spain, and in it to describe all the peculiarities and memorable things that are in it," it seems that when he began the project Hernando's ambitions were slightly more modest. The first records after the incipit ("Lunes III de Agosto de 1517/Començe el ytinerario") consist only of distances and routes between towns, to which by increments were added estimates of population size, records of local lordships, descriptions of the countryside through which the cosmographer passed, and, eventually, notes on local peculiarities (agricultural practices, legends, devotional cults, wildlife) and history (including notable events such as rebellions). There was a long-term ambition to use the measurements to create maps of Spain, though it seems that these may never have come to fruition. This design may have been frustrated, in part, by the mysterious "jealousy" which caused the project to be halted by royal fiat in June 1523, but the project as described by Juan Pérez displays the crucial foundations laid for future projects during this immensely ambitious early venture.[6] His patron was prompted, Juan Pérez records, by the fact that "those who have never been to Rome, Jerusalem, Babylon, Paris, or Antwerp can know about them, even better than those who had, as the peculiarities of these places are better displayed in a drawing." Only for Castile, he asserts, is this kind of record lacking. Hernando's assertions here not only gesture to the seminal projects of humanists, including Leon Battista Alberti, Flavio Biondo, and a slew of Renaissance artists and architects—who sought to quantify, record, document, and reconstruct the physical structures of ancient Rome—but also look forward to Alonso de Chaves's assertions that "by this instrument [the map], with fewer means and in a smaller space, *we comprehend all we could never do with large volumes of books and writings*."[7] There was, then, from an early stage a radical link in Hernando's mind between making something—here the geography of Castile—available to those removed from it in space or time and the prominence of that thing within the scheme of global history: Hernando's *Cosmography* would, in its coordination of Castile, make the kingdom the equal of Rome, Jerusalem, Babylon, Paris, and Antwerp. As we have seen, this counterintuitive operation—in which the worth of a thing was directly proportionate to how accurately it had been measured, recorded, and transmitted—follows the model of financial networks, in which detailed, accurate, and trustworthy information allowed the possessor to act with authority at a distance. Trust was central to this proposition, as it allowed the agent to interact with the representation (of a currency market, of a geographical location) as if physically present to it, and Juan Pérez goes to some length to record the process by which the cosmographic information was guaranteed, with cosmographers being dispatched to every town in Spain to make eyewitness records and their records in turn notarized "before trustworthy witnesses."[8]

These cosmographical notes survive today in two parts, with 678 folios still resident with Hernando's surviving collection in the Biblioteca Colombina (10-1-10), and a further 65 folios which have become separated and are now held at the Biblioteca Nacional.[9] These pages are closely written in black and red ink in a number of sixteenth-century hands, with about 100 folios (largely at the beginning) in Hernando's own writing, and with the rest completed by his emissaries, some of whose names may be recorded in various penmanship exercises scattered through the pages. The entries vary from a few lines to a few pages, with an average of three entries per page, and each entry is given a number around which a box has been drawn, which seems to have been added after initial notes were made. These numbers allow an original order of the folios to be reconstructed, as their present form is slightly disordered. The rough nature of these field notes provides a fascinating insight into the contexts of information gathering which would likely have been invisible in any polished product, from the drawings of rabbit warrens outside Santo Domingo de la Calzada to Hernando's own jottings on subject divisions—a list of "philosophia, gramática . . ." that appears at the top of the *Cosmografía* pages in the Biblioteca Nacional—a striking affirmation of how Hernando's thoughts about his library developed in tandem with his cosmographical exercises.

As an intermediate stage between the local cosmographic observations and the creation of detailed maps of Spain, Hernando intended to create a *vocabulario,* an alphabetical register of the habitations recorded in the *Cosmografía,* the surviving part of which (Colombina 10-1-11) makes up the rest of the volumes described by Juan Pérez in this first part of the *Memoria.*[10] Juan Pérez speaks of seven further quarto volumes containing this alphabetical register from *A* to *C,* but what survives in the Biblioteca Colombina today is a single folio volume of 545 leaves, containing entries from *D* to *N.*[11] The technique of alphabetization, while hardly unique, was evidently new enough for Hernando to spell it out for his assistants in the *Cosmografía:*

> All the proper nouns should be written on a sheet, listing those which start with *a* on one sheet, and those which start with other letters on other pages. These sheets should be written only on one side. Then all the names that begin with a letter will be cut and distributed or arranged in alphabetical order, as in a vocabulary, up to the fifth letter, and even beyond when necessary. And then they will be copied in a book so that between one entry and the next there should be a two-finger space left blank. This is to include new names in those blank spaces in the same alphabetical order. Once there are written in this manner as many places and proper nouns as there are in Spain, they will be transcribed onto a book in that same order, but not with just one name on each sheet, but everything written in these notebooks will be recorded in this book, with all the information about Avila under "Avila" and any other information in its proper place, not in a continuous manner but rather in one part of the sheet information about the history of the place, and in another place information about its lord or owner, another will include information about its villages or parishes, and thus until each place [entry] is completed. And every entry, and every sort of information

> will be numbered, and they must annotate how many times this information has been recorded, either just once, or twice, or even more, since the more frequently something is recorded, the more likely this information is to be accurate and true, certainly more so than information that has not been so frequently recorded.[12]

These instructions were followed closely in the register by 545 folios divided into two columns. While about half (250) of these remain blank—leaving space, as Hernando wished, for in-filling as the project went along—the rest have names at the top of one or two of the columns, though only about 200 of the folios are filled in, mostly in Hernando's own hand.[13] Approximately 280 towns from the cosmographical notes have been transferred to this *vocabulario,* leaving it overwhelmingly uncompleted. Yet despite its rudimentary form at the stage of its abandonment, a few crucial features of this project have already begun to emerge: the desire to use multiple reports of the same thing to iterate toward an account that was more certain and truthful (*más cierto . . . más verdadero*); the recognition of the need for extreme accuracy (here alphabetization to the fifth letter and beyond) to prevent confusion between similar-seeming things; and the very presence of the alphabetical register, which anticipates the use of this information in a bureaucratic scenario, where a settlement and its statistics might need to be quickly located by someone in possession only of its name. These names, of course, might be almost identical to the names of other places far removed from them, a situation more likely to arise as the local history of toponymy was integrated into national- and international-scale systems. The *vocabulario* and the projected maps, then, would provide both local and global, as well as spatial and tabular, ways of visualizing geographic information, allowing those consulting it to alternate between these in pursuit of a reconciled understanding of how each location fit into a wider framework.[14]

These techniques can be seen at work once again in the project that Hernando began a little over a year after the *Cosmografía,* when on 6 September 1518 he recorded his first entry into his *Diccionario* or *Vocabulario Latino.* It is the largest of Hernando's works, at 738 folio pages containing approximately three thousand entries, beginning with *A* and ending with *Bibo.* Here the centrality of organizational techniques is made even clearer, for in this project Hernando was not claiming to undertake something unprecedented; instead, as Juan Pérez notes, it was Hernando's intention to create a dictionary by "extracting from all others the substance and the best parts of them." This method of collation, which iterates toward definitions within the conventional realm of language that are "más cierto" and perhaps even "más verdadero," is probably the first witness to the distillatory technique through which Hernando would later envision the library reduced to four books of law, one of medicine, one of grammar, and so forth. Certain of Hernando's sources for the *Diccionario* have been identified by the initials placed next to these in the margins, and these include Nebrija's *Dictionarium sive vocabularium*, the *Grammatice ars* of Palemon, and Nicolas Perotto's *Cornucopia*, to which can be added Ambrosius Calepino's *Dictionarium*.[15] But Hernando's quest to fix the definitions of words with the greatest possible confidence went further than simply collating previous dictionaries: as Juan Pérez notes, Hernando not only recorded "todos los sinificados que una dicción tiene" (all the definitions that a word possessed) but also "qué autores lo usan y [en] qué partes, trayendo allí autoridades" (which authors use them and where, adducing authorities there), leaving wide blank margins in order that further authorities could be added to lexicographical entries as they were discovered. As Martínez notes in his account of the *Diccionario*, the authorities are many and varied—Latin, Greek, Christian, and humanistic—marked out by their initials or abbreviations: "*Pli., Cic., Neb., Ovi.*"[16] As with the data for his *Cosmografía* and the *Padrón Real*, Hernando made up for the impossibility of absolutely stable description (of longitude, distance, or meaning) by substituting a position successively refined by alignment with new information. Importantly, the possibility of this system throwing up anomalous discrepancies was almost as important as its ability to provide trustworthy data: whereas anomalous compass data had allowed the Columbus circle to deduce the phenomenon of magnetic variation, the variation of lexicographical definitions between great authorities would lead inevitably to a conception of language as historical, organic, and conventional. Even more than "las tierras y las yslas y los mares" in cosmography, language also witnessed much "diuersidad y mutaçion" (variety and change).[17]

Hernando's unparalleled activities to gather and organize printed images have largely resisted attempts to fix them chronologically. We know less about the images than other parts of the collection in part because they have disappeared entirely, along with any purchase information that may have been recorded. And, unlike with the cosmographic and book registers, Hernando chose not to record dates in the 3,204 entries of the *Memoria de los Dibujos o Pinturas*. The survival of this volume which lists and organizes the prints, however, has allowed the collection to be reconstructed in some detail by a British Museum team led by Mark McDonald, and their conclusion that Hernando's image collecting began in earnest during his 1520–22 voyage through Europe seems reasonable.[18] It makes sense to discuss the *Memoria de los Dibujos* here because in creating it Hernando employed certain practices that had been used in the *Cosmografía* and the *Diccionario*, yet he also confronted new challenges requiring innovative solutions.

The title traditionally used for this book—*Memoria de los Dibujos o Pinturas*—is derived from Juan Pérez's assertion that Hernando wished to "collect all the drawings [*dibujos*], paintings [*pinturas*], and images [*imagenes*] that could be found." It is, however, a rather misleading label, as the images recorded in the list are without exception *printed* images. While Juan Pérez's vague description has led some scholars to conjecture that paintings owned by Hernando (such as the paintings by "Viñola" in the 1509 inventory of Hernando's possessions) or even his own drawings (mentioned in the same list) might have been stored in the same chests (*arcas*) mentioned by Juan Pérez as containing the prints, it is clear that this would not have been an appropriate arrangement for storing painted boards or canvases, and there is no evidence in the *Memoria de los Dibujos* for the presence of these types of material. Instead, Juan Pérez's intriguing formulation—*dibujos pinturas o imágenes*—seems largely to be prompted by the fact that he does not have a descriptor corresponding to the modern term "print" for a woodcut or engraving and so must resort to approximation. There is a further reason why paintings and drawings could not form part of the collection documented in these 560 folios. It is designed specifically, as Juan Pérez suggests, to prevent duplicate purchases: "My lord don Hernando also planned to collect there all the drawings, paintings or images he could find, . . . and it was necessary to order them to keep a record of those that had been bought so that the same painting was not bought twice."[19]

The need to avoid duplication, of course, only arises with the idea of a duplicate—something differing in no substantial sense from one or more like objects. For all the important qualifications by print historians that copies of the "same" book or print exhibit (sometimes significant) variations, it is clear that printed items (images and texts) constituted in the minds of Hernando and many of his contemporaries a category of "duplicates" or "copies," having a radically *shared* identity that was not true of drawings, paintings, or unofficial manuscripts. This was in part a function of *mechanization*—of the production of the book or text using a machine that could not choose to make its products differently—but not exclusively so: the category might also be productively aligned with duplicated documents, notarized copies of official documents which were considered to share the identity of the original in various important senses (legal, ecclesiastical, financial). This is clear both from Hernando's testimony at the Junta de Elvas-Badajoz and in his biography of his father, where he uses the duplicated nature of printed tracts and of notarized treaties and grants to create networks of accreditation for his claims. Hernando's many cataloguing projects have a fundamental link to this notion of duplication: not only is the act of ordering provoked by the need to prevent duplicates from entering the collection—a fear that Juan Pérez repeatedly cites as a driving force for Hernando's designs, and one which Hernando elsewhere confronted in the duplication of cosmographic observations—but the collection itself increasingly functions as a synecdoche of the world, bringing together those things that are understood to exist elsewhere in duplicate. The fundamental difference from the *cabinet de curiosité*—which aims to bring together things valued for their uniqueness—may help to explain why Hernando chose to collect many more cheap woodcut prints than costlier engravings, just as his will instructs that his library should collect ephemeral printed pamphlets *first,* before moving on to expensive printed tomes and only last to manuscripts: these objects are treasured precisely because of their ubiquity, of how they make the collection more representative rather than more unique. This characteristic will be fundamental to understanding the nature and order of the library collection.

The need to identify each print distinctly presented a further problem: as the vast majority of prints were unsigned and untitled, there was no way of simply alphabetizing an associated name or label. It was, in essence, a problem that required Hernando to translate data in one form (visual) into others (verbal, alphanumeric) in order to classify them, a reversal of the operation used in the Casa de Contratación, where measurements and verbal reports were translated into a visual representation. The organizational system Hernando devised for his picture catalogue relied on a series of visual identifiers, beginning with a division into six categories on the basis of subject matter:

humans
animals
inanimate objects
knots (geometric designs)
landscapes (including maps and city views)
foliage (organic designs)

Within these categories the prints are further subdivided on the basis of the size of paper used for the print—sexidecimo, octavo, quarto, *medio pliego,* folio, *marca real,* and *"rotula"*—and, within the "human" category (which takes up 478 of the 560 catalogue folios), by the sex and number of people represented, whether they are saints or secular, and whether they are clothed or nude. The categories given above are a hierarchical order, whereby if a print contains one human it goes in the "human" category (even if it contains animals or inanimate objects), and if a print contains one man it goes with "men" (even if it contains many women). For instance, the catalogue describes Albrecht Dürer's 1496 print *The Men's Bath House* (inventory number 2145) as a "pliego sized sheet of 7 naked men," giving its location as *humans* > *folio-sized prints* > *men* > *seven men* > *secular* > *naked.* As many of these categories would still contain a large number of prints, the *Memoria* then describes features of the image likely to be unique to that depiction—so, with Dürer's *Bath House,* we are told that the print depicts

> six naked men in a square, one plays a pipe with both hands, we cannot see the left thumb, the other plays a violin, we cannot see the left or right

> thumb, next to him is another who is drinking from a mug with the right, we cannot see the left [hand], below are two men in half length, of one we cannot see the left or the other's right or left, below is a vase and a pear, there is a city, a fort, trees, all of the men are in a hut close to a beam,

While this part of the collection has perhaps received the fullest exposition through the work of McDonald and his collaborators, it is worth noting that this *Memoria* contains a number of significant advances that would be integrated into Hernando's other organizational schemes. The imposition of categories—here the notion of a "main subject" and the division into humans, animals, and so on—anticipates a similar procedure that would be followed in the library, in the subject-based *Tabla de Autores y Ciencias,* and in the order of the books on the shelves. Yet the organizational scheme of the *Memoria de los Dibujos* also witnesses the creation of hierarchies, noticeable here in their arbitrariness but less visible in the organization of books: the categorical subordination of animals to humans, women to men, secular subjects to saints, and so forth channels the items of the library toward those parts that are considered most important, frustrating attempts to isolate, say, depictions of animals or women, which will have been removed elsewhere if they also depicted humans or men. In a similar fashion, arranging books on shelves would involve decisions about centrality and importance of subject matter, decisions that would inevitably hide subjects considered more peripheral or less important. The *Memoria* also recognizes the importance of using accidental qualities (rather than essential ones) to register a distinct object. There would be no point, for instance, in noting the presence of keys in a print of Saint Peter, as this would occur on *every* print; it is more useful, then, to note some aspect of the depiction entirely incidental to the subject, which was therefore unlikely to be shared by other depictions of the same subject. Finally, Hernando's habit of recording artist's monograms or trademarks, such as the "AD" of Dürer or the dove of Giovanni Battista Palomba, may have fed into his thinking about pictograms as a more efficient way of communicating than description, an idea that would eventually take shape in his creation of a series of bibliographic symbols—biblioglyphs—for his library.

Stacks of Information

Unlike the cosmographical and image registers, which were largely without known precedent, and the dictionary, in which Hernando merely followed an established practice of alphabetization, there were a variety of existing models for organizing book collections on which Hernando could draw for his library, even if no existing library mirrored his plans or offered solutions to every problem. Hernando would likely have been familiar with certain salient features of library organization, some of which he adopted but more often from which he significantly deviated.

As in so many areas of early modern life, the classical world cast a long shadow over Renaissance libraries, though this legacy was complicated by the extreme paucity of information on classical libraries. This paradox, of the crucial importance of models largely lost, is captured in Pedro Mexía's *Silva de Varia Lección* (Seville, 1540), the first publication to celebrate Hernando's achievement in creating his library. Mexía reproduces his history of libraries in large part from Isidore's *Etymologies*, beginning with ancient Jewish collections that held the books of their law, noting the burning of these libraries by the Chaldeans and reconstruction by the prophet Esdras [*sic*]. Next in line is the library of Pisistratus at Athens, remembered by the narrative of its successive lootings and removals, by Xerxes to Persia and then by Nicanor back to Greece.[20] The paradigm of ancient libraries, of course, was the Ptolemaic library at Alexandria, estimated by Mexía and others to have contained seven hundred thousand books "sought out from all the peoples and nations in all the world, in all languages and scripts," and a learned librarian for each subject—one for poetry, one for history, and so on. The disappearance of the library at Alexandria—destroyed, according to the belief of Mexía and his contemporaries, during Caesar's siege of the city in 48–47 BC—facilitated its transfer into myth, as suggested by Mexía's increasing Isidore's estimate of *seventy* thousand books at Alexandria by an order of magnitude. Hernando may have found particular inspiration in the figure of Eratosthenes, who served as librarian at Alexandria while also achieving significant advances in methods for calculating the circumference of the world—a combination Hernando mirrored in his own life. In February 1522 Hernando bought in Cologne a copy of Mattia Palmerio's Latin translation of the *Letter of Aristeas*, a Greek

Hellenistic text that recounts the origins of the Library of Alexandria.[21] This work must have spurred Hernando on in his project and encouraged him to emulate Ptolemy's librarian, Demetrius of Phalerum, who had "received large grants of public money with a view to his collecting, if possible, all the books in the world; and by purchases and transcriptions he to the best of his ability carried the king's purpose into execution."[22] The *Letter of Aristeas* is also known for its account of the origins of the Septuagint, the seminal Greek translation of the Pentateuch, a further link between universal libraries and authority. Mexía follows Isidore and others in citing Aristotle as the first founder of a private library, and Rome as the first creator of public libraries.[23] Those ancient libraries that were not destroyed by fire were believed to be dispersed by the Goths and Vandals, with the texts (according to Mexía) being reunited and reconstructed at last by the great Renaissance book hunters. Mexía ends his account with a description of Hernando's library as the greatest of the modern world, in language that echoes his description of the Alexandrian library. Yet apart from eye-watering estimates of the size of ancient libraries, almost nothing was known of the nature of their holdings or their organization (even if Renaissance librarians were unwittingly influenced by the catalogues of Alexandria, through their use of the medieval encyclopedia known as the *Suda,* which was in part derived from the *Pinakes* of the Ptolemaic library).[24]

In contrast to the example of classical libraries, which were venerated even though almost unknown, more accessible models went largely ignored by early modern library design. The great Umayyad library at Córdoba, which made Hernando's birth city a center of Arabic and Greek learning and was reputed to have as many as four hundred thousand items, was unknown to early modern historians of libraries, and the libraries of medieval Byzantium, such as the library witnessed by the Spanish traveler Pero Tafur in 1437 just before the conquest of Constantinople by the Ottomans, were known only in the vaguest terms. The first models which Hernando knew in detail, then, were likely collegiate and cathedral libraries, such as the Biblioteca Capitular in Seville or the one at Salamanca which was built between 1484 and 1488 to accommodate the books donated by Bishop Gonzalo de Vivero.[25] Until then, like most medieval book collections, the Salamanca cathedral books were kept in chests with the other treasures of the foundation; the new edifice provided a discrete location for books, furnished (as was becoming standard) with benches designed to hold them. Though early inventories do not show any clear signs of the collection being ordered, by the 1520s there were loose divisions between the law books and books of theology and arts, and by 1533 the library of 750 volumes was arranged on twenty-four benches in two rows of twelve, with loose gatherings: on the fifth bench were works of the church fathers, on the seventh was a collection of national laws, on the ninth natural history, on the eleventh sermons—much like, for instance, the Biblioteca Malatestiana Hernando may have visited in Cesena or the Biblioteca Laurenziana, which Michelangelo was designing for the Medici collection in Florence. It is clear, however, that the organization of the library was still not predicated around the order of books, as the subject groupings are quite loose and many of the benches had no particular subject or order uniting their books.

Hernando's move to Rome in 1512 would have familiarized him with libraries of very different scales and ambitions, including the Medici collection—brought to Rome in 1508 by Cardinal Giovanni de' Medici—and the Vatican library. These two shared a common origin in the figure of Tomasso Parentucelli, whose *canone* was drawn up as a foundational design for the library of Cosimo de' Medici.[26] The *canone* ordered its books in a hierarchy from the divine to the worldly, beginning with the Bible and its commentators, followed by patristic and Scholastic works, then Greek philosophy, Arabic philosophy, mathematics, and finally classical letters. Early copies of Parentucelli's *canone,* and the many library catalogues derived from it, have no need for the methods Hernando developed to guard against duplication, as these are *exclusive* collections of commissioned or carefully acquired manuscripts, designed to exclude everything not on an authoritative list, encouraging the librarian to in-fill anything that is missing but not to add. It stands in contrast to Hernando's *inclusive* accession model, in which everything should be bought for the library unless it was already there. The *canone* and other lists derived from it are also authoritative in a double sense—both composed of authorities and intending to confer authority upon the possessor—and therefore must by necessity be restricted to a size and structure that will not be beyond the capacity of the individual to understand.

Parentucelli's ascension to the papal throne as Nicholas V gave him an opportunity to develop his thinking on perfect libraries: he set about expanding the existing Vatican collection along similar lines, increasing the collection of around 340 books inherited from his predecessor Eugenius IV to around 1,200 through a mixture of purchase and copying (though contemporary praise exaggerated this number, as in Vespasiano da Bisticci's remark that Nicholas "congregò grandissima quantità di libri in ogni facultà, così greci come latini, in numero di volumi cinquemila").[27] The library of Nicholas V was kept in seven large cupboards, each housing around one hundred books, with four given over to biblical and theological books among which some order was maintained, and the three others containing law, mathematics, philosophy, and the *studia humanitatis* in a rather haphazard arrangement.[28] Although the growth of the library was halted during the time of Nicholas's successor, Calixtus III—who reputedly exclaimed, of Parentucelli's library, "just see what the property of God's church has been wasted on!"—its development resumed under Sixtus IV, when it was moved to its permanent location beside the Sistine Chapel and divided among four rooms.[29] The Vatican collection at the turn of the sixteenth century was still largely an antiquarian collection with very few printed or vernacular texts, with the *Commedia* being the only vernacular work allowed in the library. It was curated by two *custodes*, who seem to have lived at the library, and a librarian, an appointment that at the time of Sixtus was largely honorary, lapsing on the death of each pope and awarded for the most part to a holder who operated in absentia.

Our knowledge of the library's organization is complicated by the slightly patchy way in which the library was catalogued. As has been noted, the primary sources of information are inventories taken in response to upheavals, such as the 1443 list made when the library returned to Rome from Avignon, and the 1533 list to take stock of the damage inflicted by the Sack of Rome. In addition to these, there are some nonofficial lists, such as Antonio de Tomeis's epic poem-catalogue the *Conviviarum Scientarum* and Fabio Vigli's survey of great library collections undertaken between 1508 and 1513. While de Tomeis provides valuable information about the counting practices of the librarians and Vigli leaves interesting descriptions of the contents of some manuscripts—similar in some ways to Hernando's later distilling projects—these projects are rather nonsystematic and idiosyncratic and also not representative of how the library was navigated by its custodians and most readers. The inventory of 1481 (contained in Vat. Lat. 3947/3952) provides a more useful topographical guide to the library, with lists of books divided into room (Latin, Greek, *parva secreta*) and then by desk, prefaced by a complete alphabetical index.

Hernando may also have been influenced by another form of visual catalogue that had recently been installed in the Vatican. Raphael's rooms in the Stanza della Segnatura were originally designed for the library of Julius II—about 220 volumes, whose titles survive in a manuscript inventory at the Vatican Archives.[30] Raphael was appointed almost simultaneously with Tommaso Inghirami's installation as chief librarian, and according to Joost-Gaugier both may have collaborated in the design of the frescoes. The result constitutes a fabulous visual display of the redesign of knowledge that had taken place over the preceding decades, thanks to the labor of recovery conducted by quattrocento Italian humanism aided by Greek emigrés. Executed between 1508 and 1511—and therefore very close in time to Hernando's first visits to Rome—these walls stand in sharp contrast in both visual and epistemological terms with the iconographic program displayed more than a hundred years earlier in *The Triumph of Thomas Aquinas*, Andrea di Bonaiuto's fresco in the *Capellone degli Spagnoli* at Santa Maria Novella in Florence (ca. 1367), which presents a very different set of allegorical figures and a totally different hierarchy in the disciplines of knowledge, with Aquinas and theology at the top.[31] In contrast, *The School of Athens* in the Stanza della Segnatura amounts to the iconic appropriation of the cultural and intellectual capital of classical Greek and Hellenistic philosophers and scientists, whose works and reputation had come under the patronage of the Ptolemies—the dynasty founded by Ptolemy I Socer, the members of which saw themselves as the political and cultural heirs of Alexander the Great. All these authors and their works had then been systematically mapped by the librarians of Alexandria in the catalogues of its legendary library and its Musaeum, who in turn were inspired (according to a tradition recorded in Strabo) by Aristotle, the first builder of libraries.[32]

Aristotle and Plato stand side by side as the central figures in the *School of Athens*, and among the numerous philosophers and scientists who surround them, each of whom represents a discipline or branch of knowledge, is a group that allegorizes cosmographic science. Euclid appears with students who attentively watch the geometrical drawings he is drafting with his compass upon a tablet on the floor. One of the students directs his gaze from the tablet up to two other figures who hold spheres in their hands, representing cosmography and cartography. In contrast with other scholars, who identify him as Zoroaster, Joost-Gaugier identifies the bearded man holding a starry sphere in his hand as Strabo—who thus faces Ptolemy, with his back to the viewer. The former holds a cosmic globe whereas the latter holds a terrestrial sphere, thus representing complementary subdivisions of the discipline involved in the knowledge of the world and the cosmos, as well as an expression of the harmony and proportion existing between them. Strabo and Ptolemy are surrounded by the instrumental disciplines that constitute the foundations of cosmography and cartography. To the left we see Euclidean geometry, which deconstructs the spaces of the earth and the cosmos into a series of modular structures, to the right, two men symbolize the skills required for the visual representation of these spaces and their structures. Joost-Gaugier identifies them as the painters Protogenes and Apelles—who is here represented by Raphael, in a self-portrait. On the facing wall, we see a representation of the Christian narrative of the Fall and Redemption, founded on the superior knowledge provided by Scripture. The combination of secular and theological disciplines, which in Andrea di Bonaiuto's fourteenth-century fresco fell under the sole authority of Aquinas, appears now as two separate realms, one opposite the other. A third wall in the stanza represents Mount Parnassus, where Apollo is surrounded by the Muses and presides over the great poets in the canon—Homer, Virgil, and Dante prominent among them.

Just as the new accounting practices and new cartography sought to coordinate and represent complex sets of multidimensional information on flat spaces, so Raphael drew upon Euclidean geometry in the service of linear perspective, providing the walls of the Stanza della Segnatura with the visual illusion of depth. The alphanumeric grids used for the projection of three-dimensional bodies and objects upon the two-dimensional plane of a wall or a canvas proposed by Piero della Francesca in *De prospectiva pingendi* were closely related to Ptolemaic cosmographic projections, providing alphanumeric mapping techniques not only for Platonic solids and natural spaces, but also for the human body. Significantly, Raphael's self-portrait as Apelles places him not on Mount Parnassus but rather among the cartographers, as one of the many mappers of the known world.

Library without Limits

Our earliest glimpse of Hernando's book collecting and organizing practices arises from a disaster that preserved evidence about the first years of the library: the *Registrum A* or *Memorial de los Libros Naufragados,* the second and only surviving volume of an original four-volume catalogue of the library. It ends with these words: "Note that all the books listed here, from number 925 up to here, are those I left in Venice to Mr Octaviano de Grimaldo so he would ship them, and they perished at sea."[33] The 1,637 titles represented by these entries, purchased by Hernando between his departure from the imperial retinue in January 1521 to when he departed from Venice in October that year, follow a rough chronological order, so we can estimate that Hernando's library before his 1520–22 European tour was made up of somewhat less than a thousand books (logged in the lost first volume of the original four), and that by the end of this trip he had purchased around 5,800 books (the original collection, the 1,637 left in Venice, and the surviving books logged in volumes 3 and 4 of the original register, which were later transferred to a new registry system). The entries in the *Registrum A* display many of the characteristics that were to become central to knowledge organization in Hernando's library: a layout like the mercantile giornali, including the use of registry numbers to provide a concise unique identifier for ease of cross-referencing and tabulation; the noting not only of author and title data but also contents, incipits, and explicits (as in the digests of legal precedents), in order to check whether a similar title is actually identical or a variation; and a rudimentary form of subject classification noted in the margin next to each entry, including: "Theology, Astrology, Humanities, Grammar, History, Alchemy, Logic, Philosophy, Cosmography, Law, Medicine, Geomancy, Mathematics, Music, Poetry, Tuscan Verse, French Verse, Greek, Chaldean, Tuscan, Various" (fig. 19).[34]

The subject classifications were, at this stage, both too broad and insufficiently consistent to form the basis for an organization of the books by subject matter, but it is important to recognize that from an early stage

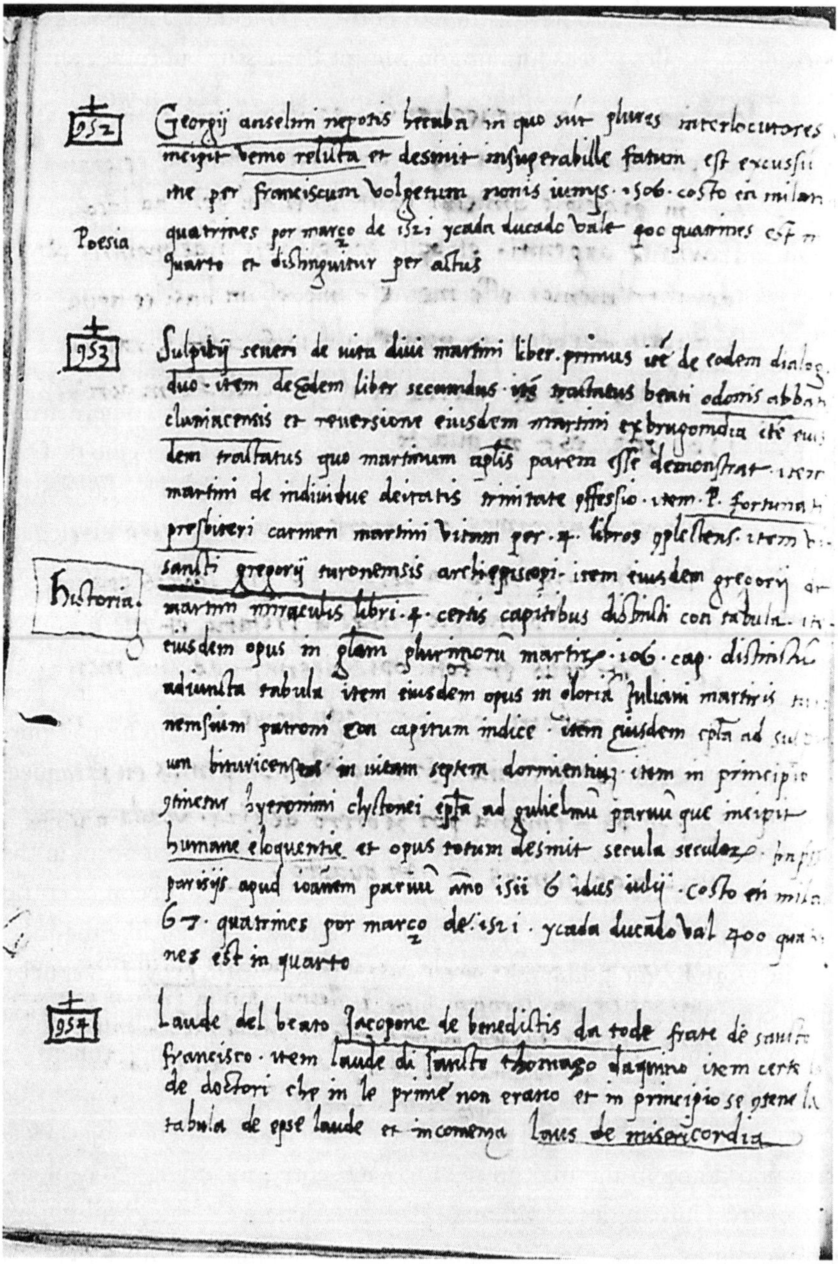

952 Georgij anselmi nepotis hecuba in quo sunt plures interlocutores incipit Demo reluta et desinit insuperabile fatum est excussi me per franciscum bolgetum nonis iunys 1506 costo en milan quatrines por marco de 1521 y cada ducado vale 400 quatrines est in quarto et distinguitur per actus

Poesia

953 Sulpitij seueri de uita diui martini liber primus item de eodem dialog duo item de eodem liber secundus item tractatus beati odonis abbatis cluniacensis et reuersione eiusdem martini ex burgundia item eiusdem tractatus quo martinum apostolis parem esse demonstrat item martini de indiuidue deitatis trinitate confessio item P. fortunati presbiteri carmen martini vitam per 4 libros complectens item sancti gregorij turonensis archiepiscopi item eiusdem gregorij de martini miraculis libri 4 certis capitibus distincti con tabula item eiusdem opus in gloriam plurimorum martirum 106 cap. distinctum adiuncta tabula item eiusdem opus in gloria Juliani martiris ...nensium patroni con capitum indice item eiusdem epistola ad sulpitium bituricensem in uitam septem dormientium item in principio continetur hyeronimi clyftonei epistola ad guilelmum paruum que incipit humane eloquentie et opus totum desinit secula seculorum. Impressum parisijs apud ioannem paruum anno 1511 6 idus iulij costo en milan 67 quatrines por marco de 1521 y cada ducado val 400 quatrines est in quarto

Historia

954 Laude del beato Jacopone de benedictis da tode frate de sancto francisco item laude di sancto thomaso daquino item certe laude de doctori che in le prime non erano et in principio se contene la tabula de epse laude et incomenza Jesus de misericordia

FIG. 19. Hernando's *Memorial de los Libros Naufragados* (© Cabildo Catedral de Sevilla)

tuta lopera finisse perdona al peccatore et e composto per capituli. 133.
est impressum venetiys per bernardinu benaliu bergomensem ano. 1512.
Coplas die 5 mensis decembris. costo en milan. 55. quatrines por março de. 1521.
y cada ducado val 400 quatrines est in quarto duaru columnaru et
est in carminibus tuscanis / este libro torne yo a mercar pero no
creo q esta ⁊ qdo como el desta estampa de venecia /

955 Vita sancti [illegible] per bernardu cornagia careualensem monachu edita
et incipit [illegible] prisci ite in principio ponetur eiusdem auctoris epta ad
Poesia augustinu sansonu et totu opus desinit qui sedet in te caret impressione
est in quarto costo en milan 8 quatrines por março de. 1521. y cada duca
do vale 400 quatrines et in fine otinetur quedam deprecatio ad virginem
que incipit o rosa que nescis

956 Legenda de santa margarita. que incipit ognuno intenda et finit con
grande alegreza. impressum in milano per alexandro pelizono adi 23 de
Coplas febraro costo en milan. 3. quatrines por março de 1521 y cada ducado
vale 400 quatrines est in quarto ⁊ figuris ac duabus columnis et in
carminibus toscanis.

957 Rime de bernardo belinzona fiorentino con profatione di prete
francisco tantio ne la sequente opa a ludovico maria sforcia duca di bari
et incipit cognosciamo et totum opus incipit o divo lampo et desinit
Coplas viua il moro impresso in milano per meistro philipo de mantegatiys ano
1493 adi 15 de iulio et in fine se contene la tabula de epsa opera costo
en milan 68 quatrines por março de 1521. y cada ducado vale 400
quatrines est in quarto et in carminibus tuscanis

958 Diariu ioanis cuspiniani de congressu cesaris maximiani et triu regu
hungarie boemie et polonie in viena panonie mense iuly ano 1515 in pri
cipio otinetur eiusdem ioanis epta ad iacobu villinger que incipit

Hernando was thinking about categorization, about levels of focus that would be neither excessively broad nor excessively precise to act as an aid for navigation. In order to facilitate this Hernando created an alphabetical index to this original register (the *Abcedarium A,* or *Índice Alfabético Antiguo*), which survives as Colombina 10-1-8 and in a seventeenth-century copy in the Biblioteca Nacional de España (MS 7232). This alphabetic register does not contain the complete purchase information and detailed description of the book registers, but it at least provides a snapshot of what Hernando's library contained by the early 1520s, the discarding of the three other volumes of the original registers having deprived us of further information. It also suggests, like the alphabetical lists of towns in the *Cosmografía,* that the envisioned user of these catalogues was distant from the books being described, part of an administrative machine capable of functioning at a distance and in abstraction from the material things being ordered.

At some point subsequent to his return to Spain in 1522—certainly before he left Spain again in 1529, but likely much earlier—Hernando decided to cut his losses and start a new main book register, transferring entries from three of the original volumes into the *Índice Numeral* or *Registrum B* (Colombina 10-1-4), which constitutes the most detailed surviving catalogue of Hernando's library. He retained the second volume of the original register—the so-called *Memorial de los Libros Naufragados*—with the intention of painstakingly replacing each of these lost volumes, a task attested to by the fact that many entries in the *Memorial* have numbers from the new register noted next to them, checking off the ones that have been replaced and entered into the new system. The new register, however, was even more ambitious, noting detailed publication information (name of printer, format, date and place of publication) and establishing these publication data as the gold standard for the identification of specific editions of works. Though this has become reflexive bibliographic practice, it is worth noting that this practice which aimed at reducing duplication and providing edition-specific information also provided a strong drive toward topographic and personal identities for printed texts, giving texts local identities (with which other localities might align, or against which they might set themselves) and making particular printers liable for their products. It was this catalogue which—despite the fact that the work required to complete the entries meant that it had only been completed for 4,231 books by the time of Hernando's death—became a prized document among nineteenth-century antiquarians, providing a glimpse of lost or otherwise unattested editions, especially after Archer M. Huntington paid for publication of a facsimile edition in 1905. While Hernando's own philosophy of texts was a predictably idealist one—his instructions for the library direct that the collection should hold only the latest edition and dispense with old ones, anticipating an iteration toward the perfect form of each text—it nevertheless provided a treasure trove for the bibliographic history that was written in the nineteenth century and beyond, with its interest in the differences between editions as witness to the fluctuating and unstable authority of the text.

Hernando accompanied this immense undertaking with another alphabetic catalogue—the *Abcedarium B* or *Índice General Alfabético* (Colombina 10-1-6, 10-1-7)—which again constituted an advance on the original *Abecedarium*, including an alphabetic list not only of authors and titles but also of the first line of each work—*incipits*—in a move, Juan Pérez confirms, designed to engineer out the duplication caused by unscrupulous printers simply issuing the same work under variant titles:

> And this was an excellent design for this purpose and also for the acquisition of books, to avoid the deception of booksellers, who frequently and maliciously, in order to sell a book as a new work, remove the name of the author and sell it without it, or under the name of another; but if they look up the *incipit* in these indexes, they will not be deceived; and thus it happened to my lord don Hernando Colón who, when in search of these books, some booksellers tried to sell him a book of law by Juan Andrés as if it was by someone else, and he looked at the *incipit* and saw that it was by Juan Andrés, and told this to the bookseller who acknowledged it was true and even begged him not to tell anybody else because he would never sell it if this were known; so this was a great design.[35]

This charming anecdote, in which we glimpse Hernando holding a sheepish bookseller to account, suggests the contribution of bibliographers such as Hernando to the creation of a stable "author function" in the face of an opposing pull by publishers to muddy the waters of authority and authorship by recycling the same material under different guises. The prolific library lived under constant threat of being flooded with duplicate materials which would undermine the usefulness of its collections, making bibliographers a powerful force for the construction of stable textual and authorial identities.[36]

Hernando's next project seems also to have been prompted, at least in part, by the shortcomings of book titles as descriptive labels: it was all very well to come up with an alphabetic list of titles, and yet "there are many books with grandiose and swollen titles which do not treat of what they promise" (*hay muchos libros de grandes y hinchados títulos y después no tractan lo que prometen*), another ruse of untrustworthy publishers and booksellers. Hernando's response to this was to begin the *Libro de los Epítomes,* comprised of "sumas de lo que cada libro contiene difusamente." This project seems to have gotten underway shortly after Hernando's return from his first continental tour in 1522; writing to Charles V around 1536/7 Hernando suggests the project has been going for fifteen years, and a note made on 25 March 1524 suggests that somewhat over 1,000 entries had been completed by that date.[37] Juan Pérez describes three volumes of *Epítomes*—two rough quarto manuscripts and a folio into which the first quarto had been copied in a neat hand—the quartos surviving in partial form until this day in the Biblioteca Colombina in Seville (fig. 20), while the scribal folio volume appears to have left the collection by the early seventeenth century, eventually coming to form part of the Arnamagnæan Collection in Copenhagen (as AM 377 fol.), where it was finally identified in 2019 (figs. 21, 22). The two quarto volumes contain 558 densely written leaves of epitomes (many of them loose and sporadically covering epitome numbers between 509 and 3130), bound with twelve pages that actually belong with the *Libro de las Materias.*[38] The gatherings are worn on the first and last folios, suggesting these rough notes were bound together after composition. The Copenhagen folio manuscript, on the other hand, has over 2,000 pages of clear, neatly spaced entries, beginning part way through the epitome numbered 140 and ending part way through number 2330. The fact that the first part of the manuscript is missing explains why it went unidentified for so long, as there is no obvious link to Hernando's collections without knowledge of his catalogues and the epitome numbers contained in them, which match the Copenhagen manuscript precisely. The last few pages of the folio are badly damaged, making reading difficult in the last few entries, but otherwise the manuscript is well preserved and easy to read, being the product of several hands and containing occasional marginal notes by Hernando himself, mostly making corrections to the scribal text and noting that they have been checked against the original, rough entry in the quartos.[39] The nearly 2,200 entries that survive between the quarto and folio manuscripts—a little under two-thirds of the 3,500 mentioned as having been completed by Hernando's death—are mostly of about a half page in the folio but range from a few lines to thirty pages (for the complete works of Plato), headed with details of the author, title, and (usually) year of printing or composition, followed by a summary of the doctrinal content, though with occasional comments on the author's style.[40] Entries in the Copenhagen manuscript also often contain, especially in its later stretches, short biographical sketches of the author when his or her identity is known. Each epitome is given a number (according to the order in which it was created), allowing for the epitomes to be cross-referenced using this number in the other catalogues; the epitome numbers are distinguished in the *Abecedarium* by being written inside a box. It is clear from the surviving records that the project intended to distill not only the learned works but everything, including the prognostications Hernando held so dear; even titles such as *La Bella mal mariada* were summarized.[41] Most of the entries in the quarto are written by a single, unidentified hand, with only a single one (fol. 252) in Hernando's own hand; this may mean that these epitomes are the work of one of the *sumistas* whose recruitment and employment is laid out in detail in Hernando's testament or simply that Hernando passed on his own rough notes to a scribe to be copied into the quarto gatherings for the *Libro de los Epítomes*. The latter possibility seems likely given the survival, in a Colombina volume, later given the title *Compendia Diversorum Librorum*, of rough epitomes in Hernando's own hand.[42] It seems likely that the most intensive activity on the *Epítomes* took place during the first years, given that the 1,000 entries had been completed by 1524, and the total number estimated by Hernando in his *Memorial al Emperador* in the mid-1530s is only 3,500.[43]

While Juan Pérez observes that the usefulness of this undertaking is obvious (*está muy notorio*), we are fortunate that he goes on to spell out exactly what Hernando had in mind in creating it: "The great benefit of this book of epitomes is very obvious because it allows you to know briefly

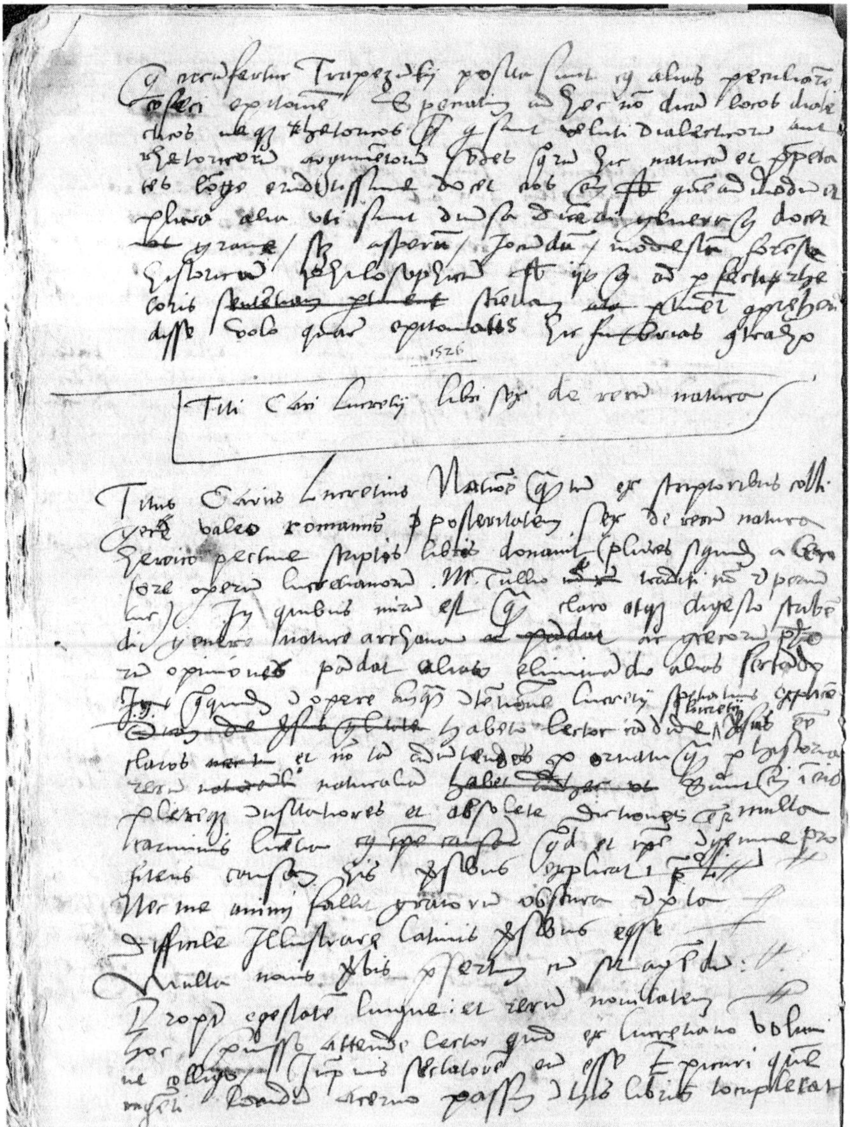

FIG. 20. Lucretius's *De rerum natura,* epitome 1526 in the Sevillian draft copy of the *Libro de los Epítomes* (© Cabildo Catedral de Sevilla)

Ennius et [illegible] nonnulli Empedocles qui dixerunt ab
Epicuro [illegible] rerum principio. Nam Empedocles quatuor ele-
menta rerum primordia esse [illegible] sed [illegible] hoc [illegible]
[illegible] Themistius [illegible] habes [illegible] odium et amo-
rem [illegible] reddidit [illegible] capitulo [illegible]
[illegible] originalibus [illegible] Themistius Epicurus [illegible]
duo [illegible] rerum posuit principia corpus sc. atque inane [illegible]
[illegible] spiritu quod est aut coniungit aut coniungitur. Corpus autem
atomis Epicuri et Lucretius [illegible] [illegible] minutissimas
[illegible] vocant [illegible] hoc [illegible] in principium
[illegible] et atomi dicte sunt. [illegible] Lucretius investigans
[illegible] et minutiores [illegible] corpusculis [illegible] per
fenestras solis radiis videmus. Inane [illegible]
[illegible] Epicuro [illegible] atomi [illegible]
Epicurorum fantasmata [illegible] ex istis duobus
[illegible] velle [illegible] aerem aquam et terram et
ex his aliquam [illegible] corpus et inane duo elemen-
ta [illegible] composita [illegible] et aliis duobus
[illegible] aliis [illegible] Hinc constat Epicu-
[illegible] opinari [illegible] posse [illegible] non est
[illegible] et Lucretius [illegible] rerum [illegible] natura [illegible]
[illegible] post [illegible] et [illegible] proponit [illegible]
[illegible] diminutas [illegible] atomis
[illegible] nullam [illegible] in spiritu aut [illegible]
[illegible] nullam [illegible]
[illegible] figuram et magnitudinem ac gravitatem quod [illegible]
[illegible] atomorum [illegible]
[illegible] atomi [illegible] aliud [illegible] ex corpo-
[illegible] atomus [illegible]
biles [illegible] atomos [illegible] opinari [illegible] aut [illegible]
[illegible] valent [illegible] atomorum [illegible]
[illegible] Epicurus [illegible] Epicuro
[illegible] Lucretius animam [illegible] atomis [illegible]
[illegible] corporeas [illegible]
[illegible] calor [illegible] vapor ac
quartum [illegible] quoddam [illegible]
[illegible] tenuissimum [illegible]
[illegible] atque [illegible] mortales [illegible]
[illegible] esse mortales videntur [illegible]

468

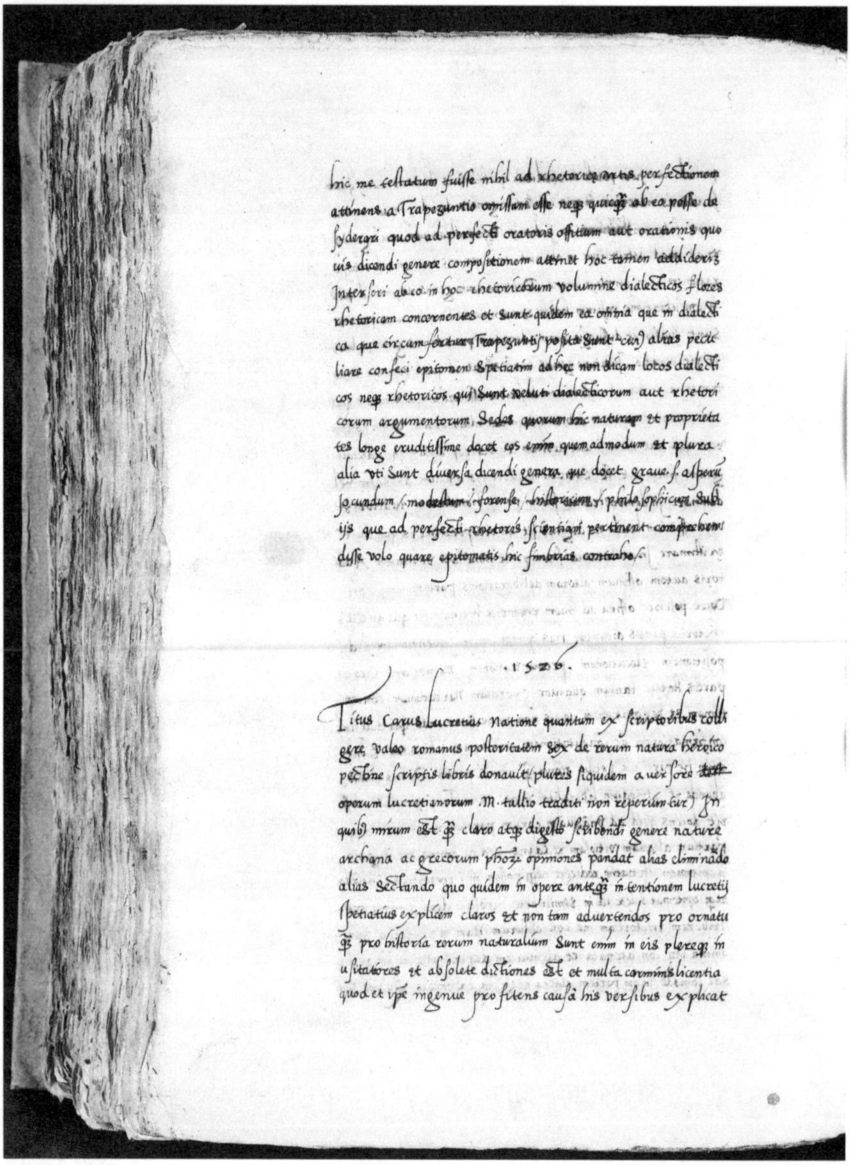

FIG. 21. *De rerum natura*, epitome 1526 in the Copenhagen fair copy of the *Libro de los Epítomes* (Copenhagen, Arnamagnæan Collection, AM 377 fol., fols. 532v–533r. Photo: Suzanne Reitz. Used with permission.)

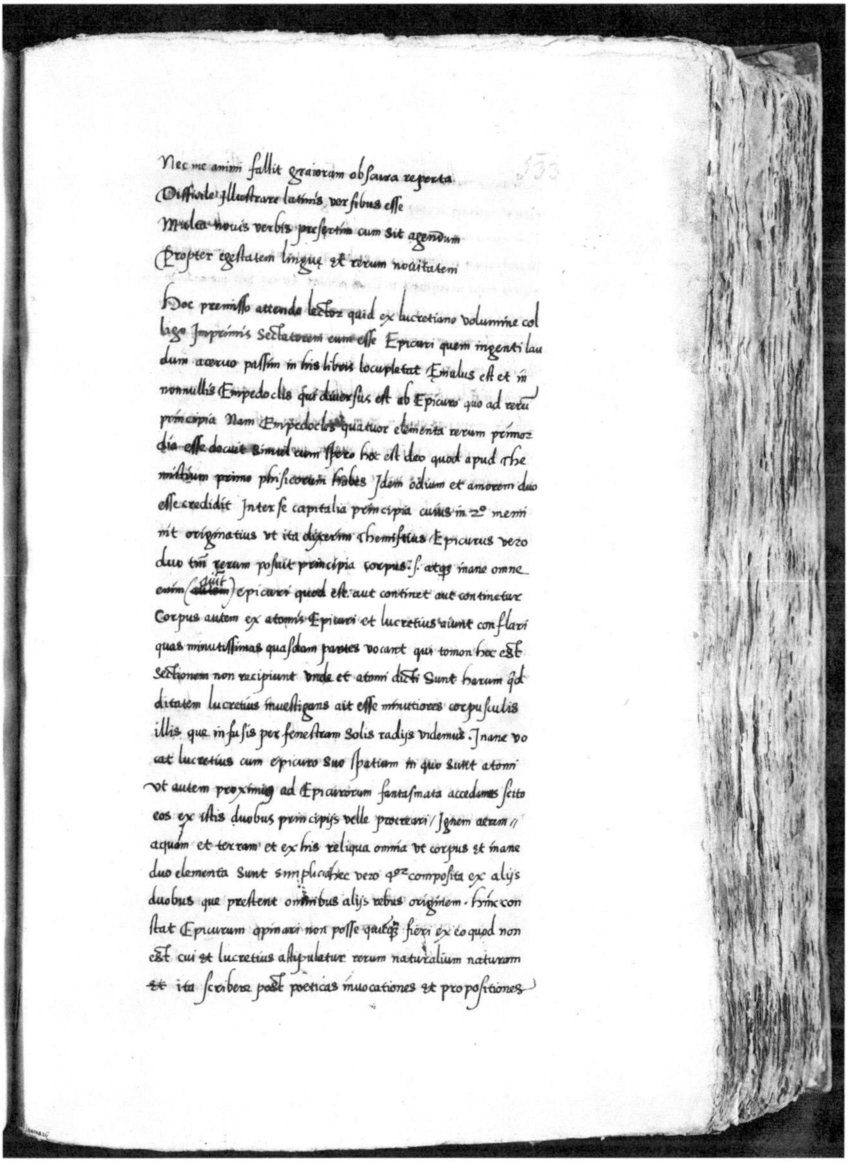

533

Nec me animi fallit graiorum obscura reperta
Difficile illustrare latinis versibus esse
Multa novis verbis presertim cum sit agendum
Propter egestatem linguę et rerum novitatem

Hoc premisso attende lector quid ex lucretiano volumine col
ligo Imprimis sectatorem eum esse Epicuri quem ingenti lau
dum acervo passim in his libris locupletat Emulus est et in
nonnullis Empedoclis qui diversus est ab Epicuro quo ad reru
principia Nam Empedocles quattuor elementa rerum primor
dia esse docuit simul cum sfero hoc est deo quod apud the
mistium primo phisicorum habes Idem odium et amorem duo
esse credidit Inter se capitalia principia cuius in 2° memi
nit originatius ut ita dixerim themistius Epicurus vero
duo tm rerum posuit principia corpus . s . atque inane omne
enim (sunt ~~autem~~) epicurei quod est aut continet aut continetur
Corpus autem ex atomis Epicuri et lucretius aiunt conflari
quas minutissimas quasdam partes vocant qui tomon hoc est
sectionem non recipiunt unde et atomi dicti sunt harum qd
ditatem lucretius investigans ait esse minutiores corpusculis
illis que in fusis per fenestram solis radijs videmus . Inane vo
cat lucretius cum epicuro suo spatium in quo sunt atomi
Ut autem proximius ad Epicureorum fantasmata accedamus scito
eos ex illis duobus principijs velle procreari / Ignem aerem //
aquam et terram et ex his reliqua omnia ut corpus et inane
duo elementa sunt simplicia hec vero 4or composita ex alijs
duobus que prestent omnibus alijs rebus originem . hinc con
stat Epicurum opinari non posse quicque fieri ex eo quod non
est cui et lucretius astipulatur rerum naturalium naturam
et ita scribere post poeticas invocationes et propositiones

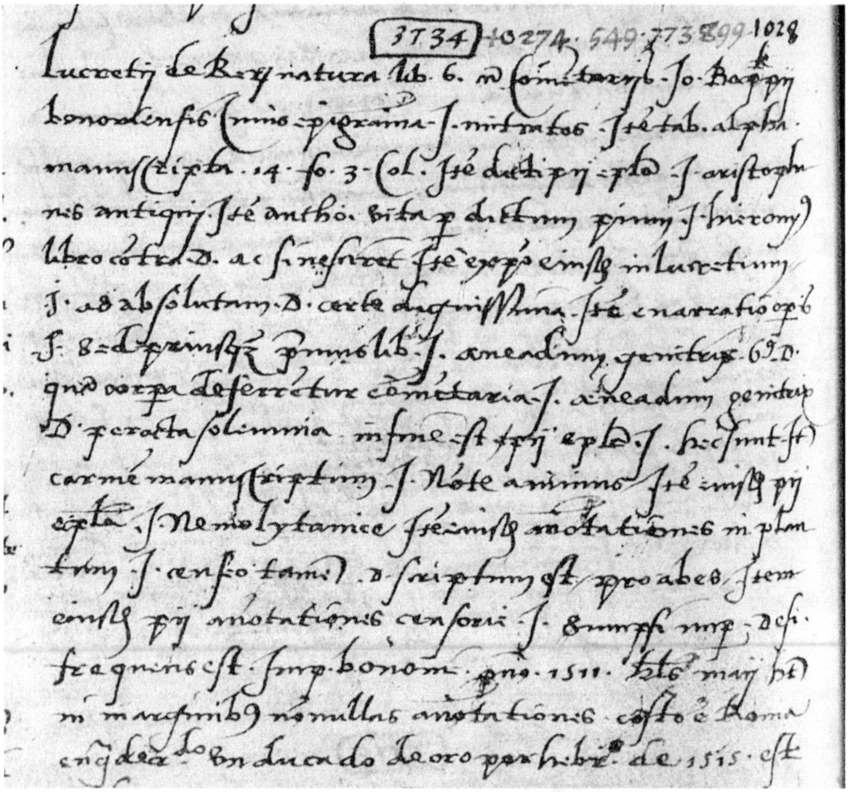

FIG. 22. Entry for Lucretius in the *Registrum B* (© Cabildo Catedral de Sevilla)

that which the book treats more diffusely, and if a person cannot afford to have many books to read, at least he will have one that will give him a sense of the contents of many books, and this allows him, if he finds the book and the subject it treats fitting, to buy it, and if he does not, then he will leave it, and will not be cheated in buying it, since there are many books of grand and swollen titles which then do not deal with what [the title] promises, and printers do this to swindle [*por engañar*]."[44] The *Libro de los Epítomes,* then, offered a way not only to avoid being tricked by book titles when navigating the library, but also to distribute the benefits of the library more widely: the volume is envisaged here not only in the hands of the library's representatives, providing them with a distillation of its knowledge when they are absent from it, but also in the hands of a reader compiling his own library, who has yet to decide whether or not to buy the volumes contained in Hernando's collection. It was, like the *Libro de las Profecías*, which he worked on with his father, a portable distillation of a cultural reservoir, allowing the works in the library to be used at a distance. Hernando intended his project not merely to improve the functioning of his own library but to provide a corrective to the cancerous growth of information in the marketplace, steering book buyers away from works with deceptive titles and unoriginal contents. Beyond providing a fascinating insight into Hernando's intentions, the *Libro de los Epítomes* offers a potential treasure trove for understanding the early modern book world, not only for the summaries it provides of books otherwise lost but also for reading and summarizing practices; for all that Juan Pérez suggests that the books for summarizing were selected "at random" (*ellos se iban sacando a reo*), there is a clear preference for philosophical and theological works (though slighter works are also treated) and clear potential for the discernment of a more purposive mode of proceeding. Tantalizingly, the surviving sections of the *Epítomes* contain extensive epitomes of (among other things) Strabo and Lucretius, with the latter being summarized in sections on each of the six books over as many pages, offering unusual insight into how these works were being read at the center of Hernando's knowledge-mapping operation.[45] The discovery of the beautifully preserved folio manuscript in Copenhagen more than triples the number of epitomes previously available to scholars and greatly expands the range of genres and topics treated. Work on the *Libro de los Epítomes* is only just beginning, with both Seville and Copenhagen manuscripts undergoing digitization (the Colombina volume after much-needed restoration work) and an international project underway to study the contents and procedural logics of these treasure troves.

Like the alphabetical lists of titles and authors, the *Epítomes* had the significant shortcoming of requiring the user to know which book they were looking for before proceeding—so while it would be immensely useful to the book buyer in the scenario envisioned by Juan Pérez, allowing them a preview of the book they were considering, it would not (for instance) be of much use to someone inquiring about a topic but without a particular author or title in mind. Hernando's response to this was the *Libro de las Materias*, a concordance or subject index to the library as a whole, which seems to have been started at the same time as the *Epítomes* and to have progressed alongside it, often being mentioned by Hernando and Juan

Pérez together. The *Materias* was, in a sense, the amalgamation of two existing practices, both of which Hernando had absorbed during his education at the court and in Rome: the compilation of book indices—which were increasingly appearing in printed books, and which Hernando went to great efforts to supply for many of his volumes lacking them—and the gathering of commonplaces. As with many humanists, Hernando kept a commonplace book recording authoritative pronouncements on particular subjects—*sententiae*—and his commonplace book survives today as Colombina 7-2-60. Though the date of this volume is unclear, it is likely from his early life (not least because its usefulness would be superseded, after the early 1520s, by the *Materias*). As with so many of Hernando's projects, his commonplace book is interesting not only as a witness to his use of the reading technologies of the day but also for how it mingles commonplacing with other practices, practices which similarly mingled in his design for the library: the commonplace book contains not only *sententiae* under headings listed at the beginning (often in pairs of opposites—*Bellum-pax, cura-negligentia, caro-spiritus,* and so on) but also lists of astrological symbols, a table of world climate types, and a series of diagrammatic knowledge trees showing the divisions of knowledge within astronomy and medicine, among several others (of which more below).[46]

In Hernando's characteristic fashion, however, the *Materias* differed from traditional commonplacing and indexing practices both in scale and in the structure it imagined for knowledge. Whereas the commonplace book provided humanist readers with the best that was thought and said on a particular topic, giving them the essence of authoritative thought with which to populate their own orations and writings, the *Libro de las Materias* made no particular qualitative judgment on the materials being gathered, creating instead (in the manner of a book index) a web of connections between similar materials in the library. In fact, the analogy that occurred to Hernando when describing this project to Charles V was neither the book index nor the commonplace book but instead the compendium of legal maxims by Giovanni Bertachino: the *Materias* was not an engine for reproducing *auctoritas* but rather a guide to precedents. In the words of Juan Pérez, it seemed reasonable to suppose that every author has a particular topic in mind (*siempre tomo un intento*), even if he also treats a variety of other topics; the compilers of the *Materias,* then, were to note for each book the main subjects treated, marking whether the subject was treated briefly or at length (*b—brebiter; d—difuse; pt—per totum*), and to register these subjects in a rough alphabetical volume which would be successively refined into neater and more accurate alphabetical registers. As an example, Juan Pérez notes that Erasmus's *Lengua* would be logged as treating *lingue prabe incomoda* and *lingue bone comoda* at great length, as well as dealing briefly with the natural history of the asp, "que es çierto género de bívora ponzoñosa" (which is a particular kind of poisonous viper).[47]

Beginning roughly at the same time as the *Epítomes*—indeed Hernando's description suggests that books may have been entered into the two registers at the same time, as seems logical—the number of volumes registered in the *Materias* had reached 3,824 by the time he departed for his second tour of the continent in 1529.[48] While Juan Pérez describes four rough volumes of *Materias* and four neat volumes into which they were being copied, what survives today consists of two rough quarto volumes (of 218 and 625 folios), 1,000 loose quarto pages, and two neat folio volumes (of 636 and 531 folios).[49] As with the *Epítomes,* the entries in the rough quarto volumes are each given a number (in the order of creation, with these numbers cross-referenced elsewhere and distinguished by being written inside in an open-topped box), followed by a few words or short phrases indicating the main doctrinal content of the work; the first 1,725 of these are missing, suggesting that perhaps around half of the original material survives. The entries in the *Materias*—which seem, according to marginal entries, to have been largely the work of an otherwise-unknown "Maestro Ortega"—were then transferred into the neat, folio volumes, which consist of alphabetical lists of keywords followed by the author's name, the name of the work, and the number of the entry in the rough volumes.[50] The first folio volume matches Juan Pérez's description, for the most part leaving one side of each page blank to allow the entries to be cut out into strips and pasted into a more accurately alphabetized register, but the second volume has writing on both sides, perhaps suggesting that this intention had been abandoned.[51]

While these projects of the early 1520s pushed toward the dematerialization of the library—breaking down the divisions into books by creating links between similar subject matters, and indeed using the epitomes to weed out unnecessary books or even make books superfluous altogether—

from the late 1520s on there is a marked turn of Hernando's attention toward the physical form of the library, perhaps understandably coinciding with the construction of a library building at the Puerta de Goles from 1526. Among these initiatives were the development of a series of book symbols for use in the catalogues, symbols that arrestingly focus (like symbols on a map) not on the textual contents of the book but on its physical characteristics (format, layout, typography), a design for the physical space of the library, and the beginnings of a final, subject-oriented cataloguing system (the *Tabla de Autores y Ciencias* or *Annotaciones*) that was also a shelving order for the books, whose storage until then had not been strictly governed by content. These three elements seem to have been developed alongside each other, with the biblioglyphs being developed for the *Tabla de Ciencias* and that table in turn dictating the layout of the library. This final phase in Hernando's creation witnesses an escalation of the previous tendency to abstract and tabulate the contents of the library and at the same time was a move to reinstate physical and intuitive experience as a key component in the acquisition of knowledge, to turn the basic act of wandering (moving, looking, comparing) into a way of exploring the thought of the world. The final form of the library would create a coupling between man's instincts and the abstract, symbolic, exponentially expanding realm of data to which he now had access.

The most distinctive innovation of the *Tabla de Ciencias* was that it would no longer be tied to the physical form of the codex: rather, as Juan Pérez notes, it was composed of about ten thousand "manojos de papeles cortados y ensartados" (bundles of cut paper strung together), each of which contained up to thirty pieces of bibliographic information on the title in question and was headed by the *ciencia* to which the book was felt primarily to belong.[52] While the idea of cutting data into strips had been employed in previous projects—notably the cosmographic *vocabulario* and the *Libro de las Materias*—the idea had previously been to paste these slips back into a volume in a particular order. The *Tabla,* as suggested by the name used by Juan Pérez, holds back from fixing the order of the books: a working organization of "sciences" does seem to have been arrived at, in order to guide the storage of books in the library, but the unbound nature of the slips allowed for the possibility of perpetual rearrangement. While in part this must have been a reaction to the frustrating way in which any fixed catalogue becomes obsolete with the introduction of new books—just as a finished map could not absorb new information—it also made it possible to rearrange the way knowledge was structured in the library. The fact that these slips were unbound, however, likely contributed to the disappearance of the entire *Tabla:* it seems not a single one of the ten thousand slips survives today.

The bibliographic symbols written on the *Annotaciones* used a combination of basic geometric shapes (lines, circles, squares, triangles) to convey a vast amount of bibliographic information, starting with format (*marca real*, folio, quarto, octavo, sexidecimo) and length:

broadsheet
ultrapica (<5 pages)
tractatus (5–10 pages)
tractatulos (10–20 pages)
liber parvus (20–40 pages)
liber mediocris (40–80 pages)
liber magnus (>80 pages)[53]

The symbols further provide information on the volume's use (or not) of columns, arguments, an index; whether it is written in verse; whether manuscripts are rough or neat copies; whether the book is complete, damaged, translated, a response to another work, or pseudonymous. There were also numbers and abbreviations that indicated where the text was printed, in which year and in which language, and whether it had prologues or epistles. Intriguingly, the symbols also tell the reader the length of other texts that are bound with the volume. As has already been suggested, these symbols are a striking confirmation of how "editorial genres" worked in the world of early print. In creating them Hernando was attempting to reinstate, in the abstract environment of the *Tabla*, a replacement for the unconscious awareness that comes from being in the presence of a book. The development of the biblioglyphs makes clear that these physical characteristics—format, length, layout—were components of a language through which the print trade had already created a de facto classification system for the texts with which they worked, creating visually distinct objects that were also understood to play different roles in the world. From the *obrezilla* in verse to the *liber magnus* with its infrastructure of paratexts, these print products transformed the way in which the world was treated by the text into a way of handling the text itself.

It is clear from Juan Pérez's description that the *Tabla de Ciencias* was also intended to facilitate a rearrangement of the library into subject order: "It is important to be aware that up until now the books were all kept together and the sciences mixed up and confused among them, and at that time they had this number which we refer to as the old one; now they have been arranged according to sciences so that all the books that correspond to a science are together."[54] What is not clear, however, is how far this project had progressed during Hernando's lifetime: Juan Pérez, writing after Hernando's death, seems to suggest that the haphazard arrangement of books had continued "until now," and this accords with Hernando's own description of the arrangement as something yet to be completed. He wrote in his *testamento,* on which he was working in the final months of his life, that "as regards the arrangement of the books, I hope that our Lord will grant me life and means to build a large room and place in it, starting at the bottom of the walls, cases [*caxones*] just as the books are now arranged in them, on end [*de canto*] each of them with their title, name, and number [showing outward]. The subjects must be separated according to the table of sciences."[55] While the rearrangements of the books had perhaps not commenced during Hernando's life, awaiting the transformation of the original series of library rooms into a single large room with a continuous sequence of shelves, it seems that the division of books into *ciencias* was already well underway, as confirmed by the conversion tables that occupy fols. 195r–243v of the *Registrum B,* and which gives for each *Registrum B* number up to 15344 (with very few gaps) an equivalent number in the *Tabla de Ciencias* and hence the intended order of the books on the library shelves. These tables allow us to reverse, in some sense, the tragic loss of the *Tabla de Ciencias* and to reconstruct for the first time the order of knowledge as Hernando envisioned it working in his library.

Hernando had been thinking about subject classification of his library for quite some time, with sketches of early subject headings appearing in the *Registrum A/Memorial de los Libros Naufragados* as well as in the margins of the *Itinerario* or *Descripción.* In addition, his commonplace book contains a series of diagrammatic divisions of knowledge in the fields of astronomy and medicine. While it is not clear what relationship there was between these early sketches of knowledge organization and the final scheme, it does indicate that from an early stage Hernando was building on the traditional ways of organizing knowledge, combining the parts of the *trivium* and *quadrivium* with the schools of the university and also employing Aristotelian methods for the sequential division of topics. So while Hernando's jottings in the *Itinerario* and his subject descriptors in the *Registrum A* contain many of the same fundamental divisions that were to be seen in (for instance) the schemes for the Vatican library—*poesía, gramática, lógica, geometría, aritmética, retórica, filosofía, astrología, teología*—his labels in the *Registrum A* also contain subdivisions of these (*theologia biblica, theologia moralis,* and so on), just as the divisions of astronomy and medicine in the *Loci Communes* proceed through the traditional mode of divisions (*Medicina>theorice/practice,* and so on). The reconstructed numerical order of the *Tabla* does not, of course, tell us what the formal categories or subdivisions were, but most of the rough overall structure is fairly easily discerned (table 2).[56]

While the general subject areas can be discerned from the preponderance of books falling within each sequence, there are many titles in any given group whose placement there is somewhat surprising. Although a fragment on which Hernando was working out subject orders (10-1-3) suggests that numbers 3600–4100 were given over to natural philosophy, the sequence contains a variety of material that does not seem to belong. On the other hand, none of the volumes that survive in the Colombina today fall in the range between 8948 and 9507, though sampling and the fragmentary draft order indicates that this group may have been made up of Hebrew and Arabic texts, suggesting that Hernando may have had a substantial collection of Hebraica and Arabic works which was removed or destroyed en masse after his death.[57]

The number sequence provided for the *Tabla* in the *Registrum B,* and tabulated for the first time in a database generated for this project and which will eventually form the basis for a digital resource, allows us to reconstruct a number of features of the library during Hernando's lifetime, including (for instance) establishing which of the *obrezillas* were bound together (and hence given the same shelf number) and studying the organization of volumes within these broad divisions in order to discern more specific subdivisions of knowledge in Hernando's scheme. They also allow us to reconstruct the physical space of Hernando's library, in combination

TABLE 2
Tabla Restructured Numerical Order

Numbers	Subject
1–400	Grammar
400–1000	Oratory/Rhetoric
1000–1400	History
1400–2000	Poetry
2000–2600	Philosophy
2600–3000	Mathematics
3000–3200	Music
3200–3500	Astronomy
4100–4600	Medicine
4600–5000	Moral Philosophy
5000–5900	Law
5900–6500	Sermons
6500–6800	Liturgy and Dogma
6800–8500	The Bible (with commentaries, lectures, etc.)
8500–8900	Greek
9500–10000	Catalan
10500–11300	Italian
11300–11900	French

with Juan Pérez's description of the furniture of the library, which was orchestrated to further translate the project of knowledge classification into a haptic experience. As Juan Pérez makes clear, though, this first-hand, immanent experience of the structure of knowledge was something reserved to the librarians themselves, kept from the common reader by a metal grille standing six feet from the bookshelves. Hernando specified that the grille should be mesh, rather than simply vertical bars, to allow readers to reach from their allotted benches through the iron cage to the lectern where their chosen book would be placed. Yet with six feet between them and the shelves of books, readers would be forever kept from the mysteries of browsing, reliant on the transitional medium of the catalogues to navigate the realm of knowledge. Hernando anticipated the objections that this would raise from frustrated readers: "And if they say that they cannot study the book with ease in this way, I say that this library is not designed as much for common study as for the safeguarding of all books and for the elaboration of the tables of authors, and sciences, and epitomes and subject matters. And for common readers who want to resolve doubts, or find something remarkable, or study something in depth, there are no lack of institutions and books for them to turn to. For otherwise it will be impossible to keep the books safe although they are held with a hundred chains."[58]

Much as Hernando recognizes the desirability of studying a matter *at length*—following it to its logical conclusions, surveying its neighboring areas—this privilege was reserved to the inducted few, so as to preserve that delicate suspension in which the raw materials of the library remain forever secure and yet moveable to meet the requirements of new materials and new organizational schemes. The grille serves, rather like the grid of longitudinal and latitudinal lines on a map, to keep a solid structure for the whole while allowing the parts to drift around within it, moving ever closer to a final order that is "más cierto" and "más verdadero" than the ones that came before.

This impression, of the librarians as initiates to a mystery, at whose heart is the preservation of an intricate and developing picture of the world, is reinforced by many of the remaining rules provided for the library. The *sumistas,* recruited from Salamanca by advertisements placed during the examinations, would be required to commit to a minimum of three years in the library, the first of which would take the form of an apprenticeship; during the following two they would be let loose to follow their own paths through the library, restricted only to the rules laid down for populating the catalogues as they went about their reading. For this they would receive a base salary of ten thousand *maravedís* a year for a minimum of two hours of reading a day, with a further twenty *ducados* for each additional hour—up to a maximum of six hours, as they will not (Hernando surmises) work at the required level of precision for any longer than that. The *sumista* would also be provided with a cell adjacent to the library, with a desk, a cot bed, linen, mattresses, sheets, pillows, covers, blankets, a chest, a chair, a bench, and a cupboard for his books and writings. The arrangements were designed to reduce the inconveniences arising from human weaknesses (the tendency to fatigue, coupled with the need for money, leading to sloppy work), to extract from the *sumistas* the optimal amount of concentrated effort of which a person is likely to be capable, using regimes inherited from the monastic foundations of the Middle Ages which worked to clear away the distractions of the flesh impeding the life of the spirit. This environment was designed to reduce human error, but Hernando did not trust that it would in itself be enough, and he instituted a system of fines for delinquency and the disappearance of library materials, to be overseen by a legally qualified *depositario* (along the lines of an institutional visitor), and (more than this) to be further guaranteed by a failsafe store in a separate location of duplicate copies as backup should the copies in the library go missing. Once again, this unique arrangement for guaranteeing the library holdings gestures toward the crucial and complex task of ensuring that the library remained *complete* without allowing for any *duplication* which could open a disastrous road to cancerous distortions in the library's image of the world. The processes for comparing editions and retaining the most up-to-date one (while holding others in reserve) is very much the bibliographical equivalent of collating cartographic and lexicographical data which Hernando had designed in his previous projects.

It is clear as one follows Hernando's projects from beginning to end that they are all, in their own ways, attempts to solve the problem posed by man's inability to keep more than a certain portion of the world in mind at any one time. In the stead of an almost infinite number of places, transactions, ideas, and writings, these projects develop systems of assigning each discrete entity with a unique identifier—a coordinate, a registry number, a spelling—which prevents them from being confused with other, similar entities and allows the human to substitute for a knowledge of each individual thing a knowledge of the methods of retrieval. The more dimensions one allows, the more entities can be similar in one way while differing in another—just as latitude and longitude are required to fix a place on the exterior of a sphere, and altitude would also be needed for subterranean or submarine locations. Similarly, the combination of Hernando's catalogues allows for works to be grouped by subject matter and author, and it even (using the *materias*) allows the subjects treated within works to be grouped regardless of subject matter and author (as one might study similar altitudes or depths together, regardless of latitude or longitude). The combination of these categories transforms the near-infinite space of the library from an abstract and inhibiting concept into a usable expanse, and the "world" from a conceptual thing into something that can be documented and charted—through acts of measuring which are themselves reliant on the material forms of documents and charts. This coordination, then, allows the library to become a picture of knowledge in many dimensions, a sculpture of the knowable.

Hernando borrowed from the merchants of early modern Europe not only many of the ideas of fluctuating values and actuarial tabulation but also the networks by which the individual could be connected to the wider world. Hernando's instructions on how to acquire books for his library assume that the general trade infrastructure of Europe would remain relatively stable—as it had since the time of the Middle Kingdom in the eighth century—while allowing for radical transitions in the nature of the *print* trade. By not fixing particular publishers or booksellers as his suppliers but rather leaving the decisions on *what* to acquire to local agents, Hernando reveals his belief in the far greater relative stability of channels of communication to the content of what was communicated through them. Financial instruments, cosmographic observations, and textual products would all change, but they would all (until the invention of technologies to overcome the geographic obstacles of earth and water) rely on the same channels of communication. His library reached out into the world with well-fashioned limbs, even as it prepared for them to touch the unknown.

Needless to say, the constructions of these counterintuitive frameworks—in which value, meaning, location, and significance are understood to be radically in flux—required an environment which translated these things back into intuitive, immanent experiences of stable, fixed things. Just as the graticule of the Ptolemaic map provides a fixed and universal sphere while allowing for inevitable fluctuations arising from fallible human reports and observations, so the construction of shelves in subject order allowed for the human wanderer in the library to experience knowledge at first hand—as a matter of location and relations of distance/proximity, laying the groundwork for that apparent serendipity characteristic of the library experience—while also cutting the *essence* of what was being navigated free from any fixed moorings. The rules for the conduct of *sumistas* complete the *form of life* of this little world, providing certain axiomatic regulations which would combine with the form of the library to produce an understanding of the world that was at once to hand—immediate, intuitive—and connected to the entire globe through its representation in the library, like the monk who travels the globe through a map.

CHAPTER FIVE

AFTER HERNANDO

Hernando's vision came to fruition in a house and a garden by the Guadalquivir, the waterway that carried ships and their goods, precious metals and information from the other side of the Ocean Sea, right into the heart of the Spanish Empire. The Sevillian historian Juan de Mal Lara described it this way: "This gate (which used to be called of *Hercules,* and now of *Goles*) was neglected and low, covered with earth halfway up, and in front of it there was a large mound of dirt, where don Fernando Colón, the son of don Cristóbal Colón, who discovered the West Indies, started to build a house and plant a garden of more than five thousand trees along the river, beautifying the city on those parts, and refreshing the riverbanks. He put together in this house almost 20,000 books, and he planned to turn it into a veritable Mount Parnassus, both on account of the fresh and lush gardens, and also the buildings and the multitude of books. Which books are now in the Cathedral, in a room that runs from the tower to the sanctuary."[1]

This description confirms Hernando's scheme to create a typically humanist villa—a model he had found in works like Erasmus's *Antibarbari*—with a garden full of exotic new plants brought from all over the globe, an oasis for the pursuit of knowledge in a large tract of land which had, alongside the main villa, smaller buildings for the use of staff. However ambitious and grand Hernando's house and gardens were, at the time of his death they were mortgaged for 450,000 *maravedís,* an amount his heir and nephew Don Luis refused to pay. Hernando's creditor transferred the debt to two Genoese merchants, Franco Leardo and Pero Benito de Basiniana, and they in turn passed it over to the banker Pedro Juan Leardo. The house and gardens soon changed hands, and they were eventually demolished, being absorbed back into the same channels of finance from which they had first grown.[2]

Although his executor declared that Don Hernando had provided money for the maintenance and expansion of the library, in truth the financial situation he left behind was far from buoyant, and the instructions he carefully recorded in his will for the future of the collection could never be implemented.[3] All the evidence seems to indicate that Hernando had exhausted his fortune and energies not just in putting together his fabulous library but in defending the interests of a family from whose wealth he never received a fair share. Years earlier Hernando had willingly renounced to his brother his rightful part of his father's legacy in exchange for the promise of an annuity of 200,000 *maravedís*. The document was signed on 12 June 1520, when Hernando was about to embark with Charles V on his voyage to Aachen—a trip that would become his most fabulous shopping spree, likely spurred on by the financial agreement with his brother and also the knowledge that he would soon receive money from the future emperor. But the money from his brother never materialized, and a few years later Diego moved to annul the agreement. Although in all the public documents he signed, Don Diego, the second admiral, paid lip service to the great and useful services his brother had provided for his family, he always failed to put his money where his notarial documents were.[4]

Soon after Hernando's death, the Cathedral Chapter, knowing it was listed as residuary heir after Don Luis Colón, son of Diego and third Admiral of the Ocean Sea, took an interest in the library. Don Luis, seventeen at the time, was away in Hispaniola, and the Cathedral Chapter sent him several official requests, politely inquiring whether he intended to take charge of his uncle's books, which still lay at the Casa de Goles.[5] For five years Don Luis failed to answer these requests. The bureaucratic dispute between the family heir and the cathedral thus remained at a stalemate until Don Luis's mother and legal representative, Doña María Álvarez de Toledo, decided to move the books out of the Casa de Goles and deposit them in the Dominican convent of San Pablo. Doña María, the granddaughter of the first Duke of Alba, had powerful family networks that extended to the convent through the presence of her brother, Antonio de Toledo, as one of the Dominican friars. The legal document that recorded the deposit of the books in the convent was signed before the notary public Pedro de Castellanos on 7 April 1544.[6] The books were received by friar Vicente Calvo and Father Jerónimo Garrido, who (in the words of the contract) were to "commit to receive the books into their custody, as well as all other things related to them, which at this moment were all in his houses at the Puerta de Goles, and to *position and preserve them in the same order.*"[7]

Since the inventory made when the books were deposited in San Pablo has not survived, it is impossible to confirm whether the erosion of the collection began over the course of the eight years the collection was stored there. The French-American scholar Henry Harrisse (1829–1910) speculates that many important documents went missing during this period—including the map that accompanied Toscanelli's letter in the copy of Piccolomini's *Historia.* We do know that the Dominican Bartolomé de las Casas, who had been consecrated as bishop of Chiapas in Seville on 26 March 1544, had full access to all the books and documents and used them as the basis of his writings, in particular for the chapters in his *Historia de las Indias* that dealt with the first voyages of Columbus. As only the Dominican friars, the Columbus family, and their agent Marcos Felipe enjoyed full access to the books while they were at San Pablo, the coincidence that gave las Casas access to Hernando's extraordinary Columbian collection must be considered a great moment of historical serendipity.[8] No better fate, at this point, could have been devised for Hernando's documents, than falling into the hands of one of the most illustrious, humane, and prolific early historians of the Americas.

The Cathedral Chapter and the Dominicans of San Pablo subsequently became embroiled in a legal dispute, which was finally resolved by the Royal Chancery in Granada in March 1552 in favor of the former. As a result the books were carefully moved to the cathedral under the strict watch of several witnesses, though only after the Chapter paid a hefty deposit of ten thousand ducats. So thorough was the process—with the creation of two inventories that recorded the books first on their way out of San Pablo, and then again when they were deposited at their final destination—that it took several weeks to move the collections from the convent to the cathedral, where they became integrated with the preexisting Biblioteca Capitular in 1557. They have shared the same space since then. Once again, these two inventories have not survived. The disappearance of books, the beginning of which Harrisse dated to the period at the convent of San Pablo, demonstrably continued after their removal to the cathedral. The situation became so serious that it led to the suppression of the office of librarian by the Cathedral Chapter—the two librarians who had been appointed to take care of the collections in 1557 were held responsible for the thefts and fired in 1567.[9] We can assume from this that the losses were substantial enough by this stage to have been hard to disguise. The Chapter failed to appoint a new librarian, and although the Inquisition appears to have prompted the creation of some ad hoc inventories during the rest of the sixteenth century and the early years of the seventeenth century, the books were left without any competent, official administrators until well into the seventeenth century.

Juan Guillén, the most recent historian of the Capitular and Colombina libraries, makes a valiant effort to exonerate the administrators in the Cathedral Chapter for neglecting their duty as custodians of the books. His volume, however, relies on a useful profusion of primary documents from the cathedral archives and other related records, which he knew very well, and the rigorous evidence that he himself provides acts as witness against him.[10] Guillén identifies two fatal flaws that arose from the moment Hernando's books came to the cathedral. The first was their incorporation within the preexisting collection, the Biblioteca Capitular, which, by combining two rather large collections with no clear criteria for their proper arrangements, destroyed the character of both collections as well as key evidence regarding their histories. This led to a second problem—the obsolescence of Hernando's classification systems, which fell out of use, meaning that the collection swiftly departed from its initial organization and thus there was little sense of how much of the original collection had disappeared.[11]

The earliest direct testimony about the collection in the cathedral comes from another Sevillian historian, Argote de Molina, who described the situation of the library at the end of the sixteenth century in rather unflattering terms: "[Don Hernando] donated his library to the Cathedral Church of Seville, where the books are now locked in a room atop the Nave of the Lizard, and what was left for the profit and study of learned scholars is now [of] no use or profit for anybody."[12] This assertion by Argote de Molina has been disputed by Guillén and by Gil, who argue that whereas it is true that the administration of the collection was deficient, it is far from accurate to say that the books were not at the disposal of a learned readership. It might not have been a public collection, but there were members of the Cathedral Chapter during these decades whose intellectual prestige, they argue, is beyond dispute (though they provide no concrete evidence that the books were in use by these figures). The books, they add, must have been available for the religious communities attached to the cathedral—the so-called *prebendados,* a category which included, among others, administrative staff, preachers, priests, and also members of several religious orders. To these we should add the students of the religious schools of San Miguel, Santa María de Jesús, Santo Tomás, and San Hermenegildo.[13] Actually, Wagner suggested that the use of the books by members of these communities may account in part for the disappearance of a number of volumes: since the members of the Cathedral Chapter, and other members of the church associated with it (about three hundred of them in the sixteenth century), enjoyed the privilege of borrowing the books and taking them to their respective monasteries and convents, many of the volumes were removed from the library. Without a proper borrowing policy or record, their return was never enforced, and after the death of the readers, the books found in their cells were often simply incorporated into the libraries of their respective orders.[14] Finally, and as a result of the *amortizaciones* of the nineteenth century, many of these libraries were seized by the state and incorporated as part of public Sevillian libraries, such as the municipal library and the university library—where some of Hernando's books are still preserved to this day.[15]

A hundred years later the description of Argote de Molina was repeated by another Sevillian historian, Diego Ortiz de Zúñiga (1636–80), who praised the ebony shelves and the frescoes that decorated the library's ceiling but hastened to add that the library had fallen prey to "the ravages of time, [and was] more forgotten, less frequented than its original owner would have wished, difficult to visit, and susceptible to decay."[16] During the sixteenth and seventeenth centuries there were important projects devoted to the embellishment and expansion of the cathedral and its annexes—which included the belfry that was added on top of the original minaret with the new and spectacular bronze statute popularly known as the Giraldillo, as well as the remarkable neoclassical chapels.

In April 1569 King Philip II urged the dean of the cathedral to send him all the papers that Hernando had put together for the elaboration of the universal navigation chart in 1526. There is some indirect evidence that these documents may have been taken to El Escorial.[17] Philip II also requested some important medieval manuscripts from the Capitular to serve as the foundation of a new edition of the works of Saint Isidore, the jewels in the crown of the Capitular collection before the arrival of Hernando's books. To judge by the titles that the king requested, this new edition was part of a doctrinal counterattack to the Reformation, to reassert the primacy of Catholicism, and within it the central and foundational role of the Hispanic church, represented by the work of one of its earliest authorities, the Sevillian encyclopedist Saint Isidore. There are also hints that some books may have been taken from the collection by order of Philip II when he was putting together his own royal library in El Escorial.[18] These requests were the local beginnings of an exodus of the books from Hernando's collection, many of which were eventually scattered across the world, parallel to the growing importance of Renaissance culture as a totem of European identity and central to European imperialist claims of exceptionalism. Henry Harrisse in his denunciation of the theft and illegal sale of printed books and manuscripts from Hernando's collection (1885) included a detailed list of some Hernandine items that showed up in Paris ca. 1884–85, including a few which were acquired by the National Library of France and are still there. The collection at the Giorgio Cini Foundation in Venice also has several of Hernando's *obrezillas* that found their way back to Italy—more than three hundred years after their purchase—from Hernando's Sevillian collection via France and their sale in Paris.[19] One title at least has been identified at the John Carter Brown Library in Rhode Island, and there are two books at the Pierpont Morgan Library in

New York that might have belonged to Hernando.[20] There are also books from Hernando's original collection at the Biblioteca Nacional in Madrid, the University Library in Seville, and the library at the Complutense University of Madrid (from the old university of Alcalá and its colleges).[21]

The Inquisition

Historical forces also had an impact on the collection. The treatment of Hernando's copy of Erasmus's *Antibarbari* by the Inquisition is an excellent example. The *Antibarbarorum libri duo* deals, inter alia, with the reform of the disciplines and the redesign of the curriculum, and Hernando's prized copy was a gift to him directly from the hands of its author. Hernando brought it from the Netherlands to Seville, where years later it was expurgated by the censors, thus becoming a textual battleground between the new ideas regarding learning and knowledge, and those who wished to oppose or modify them. Hernando's 1518 edition of Pomponius Mela's *De situ orbis* was a replacement for the copy he had lost in the shipwreck, but it too could not be saved from the hands of censorship (figs. 23 and 24).[22] The manuscript notes suggest that it was expurgated in 1662, following its inclusion in the index of 1640: the objections of the Inquisition regard the commentator, Joachim Vadian, a Swiss reformer and fellow bibliophile who bequeathed his library to his hometown, St. Gallen.[23] Frobenius's 1521 Basel edition of Lucian, translated into Latin by (among others) Erasmus and Thomas More, is another significant title that was submitted to a vigorous process of expurgation (figs. 25 and 26).[24] Other Erasmian volumes that show some traces of censorship include an edition of his *Adagia* (Sélestat, 1521, Colombina 12-2-40) and his edition of Suetonius's *Vita duodecim caesarum* (Basel: Frobenius, 1518, Colombina 13-5-9). The Suetonius in particular has manuscript notes that trace its expurgation at the hands of one of the canons in the cathedral, Andrés de León, appointed librarian in 1661. His combined duties should not come as a surprise, since virtually all the Sevillian archbishops of this age were also General Inquisitors—including the notoriously zealous Fernando de Valdés (1546–68). Andrés de León's predecessor, Antonio del Corro (d. 1556), was also both an Inquisitor and a librarian in the cathedral. The anxious desire of del Corro to seem beyond reproach makes sense in light of the activities of his even

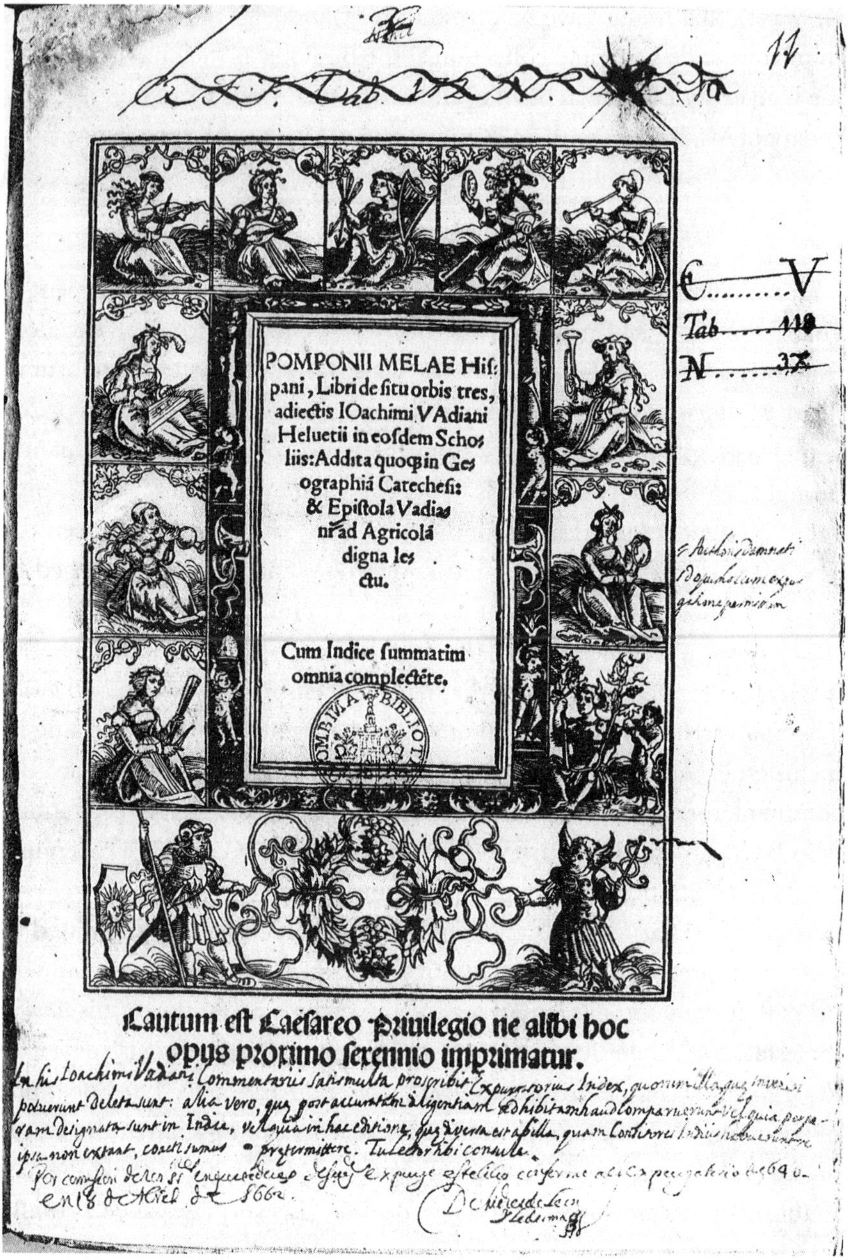

POMPONII MELAE His-
pani, Libri de situ orbis tres,
adiectis IOachimi VAdiani
Heluetii in eosdem Scho-
liis: Addita quoq; in Ge-
ographiá Catechesi:
& Epistola Vadia-
ni ad Agricolá
digna le-
ctu.

Cum Indice summatim
omnia complectête.

Cautum est Caesareo privilegio ne alibi hoc
opus proximo serennio imprimatur.

FIG. 23. Title page of the expurgated copy of Mela's *De situ orbis*, Hernando's replacement of the copy he had lost in the shipwreck (© Cabildo Catedral de Sevilla)

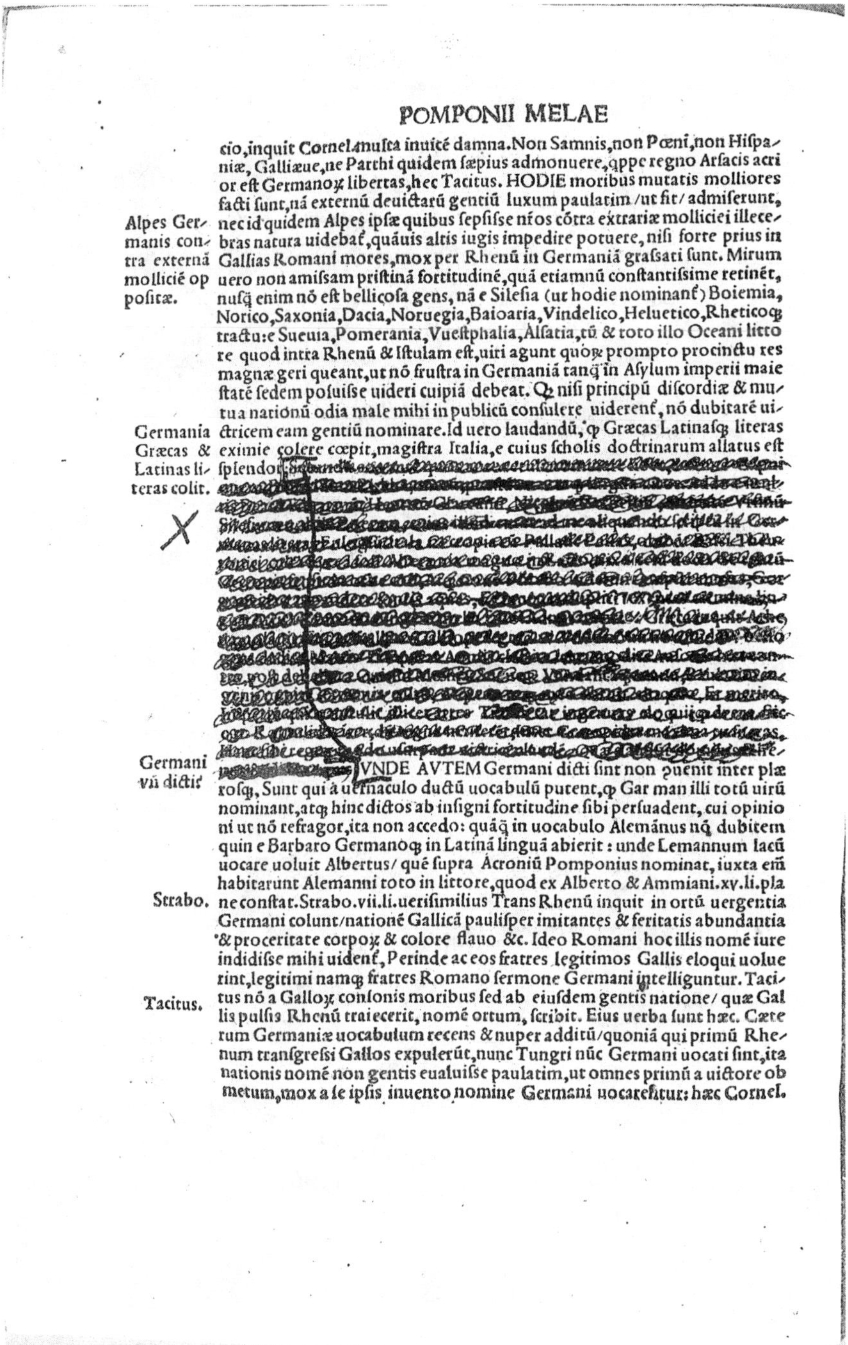
POMPONII MELAE

cio,inquit Cornel.inulta inuicé damna.Non Samnis,non Pœni,non Hispaniæ, Galliæue,ne Parthi quidem sæpius admonuere,qppe regno Arsacis acrior est Germanoꝝ libertas,hec Tacitus. HODIE moribus mutatis molliores facti sunt,ná externũ deuictarũ gentiũ luxum paulatim /ut fit/ admiserunt, nec id quidem Alpes ipsæ quibus sepsisse nr̃os cõtra extrariæ molliciei illecebras natura uidebat,quãuis altis iugis impedire potuere, nisi forte prius in Gallias Romani mores,mox per Rhenũ in Germaniá grassati sunt. Mirum uero non amissam pristiná fortitudiné,quá etiamnũ constantissime retinét, nusq̃ enim nõ est bellicosa gens, ná e Silesia (ut hodie nominant) Boiemia, Norico,Saxonia,Dacia,Noruegia,Baioaria,Vindelico,Heluetico,Rheticoq; tractu:e Sueuia,Pomerania,Vuestphalia,Alsatia,tũ & toto illo Oceani littore quod intra Rhenũ & Istulam est,uiri agunt quoꝝ prompto procinctu res magnæ geri queant,ut nõ frustra in Germaniá tanq̃ in Asylum imperii maiestaté sedem posuisse uideri cuipiá debeat. Q nisi principũ discordiæ & mutua nationũ odia male mihi in publicũ consulere uiderent, nõ dubitaré uictricem eam gentiũ nominare.Id uero laudandũ, q Græcas Latinasq; literas eximie colere cœpit,magistra Italia,e cuius scholis doctrinarum allatus est splendor [illegible]

Alpes Germanis contra externá mollicié opositæ.

Germania Græcas & Latinas literas colit.

Germani vñ dicti.

UNDE AUTEM Germani dicti sint non ꝯuenit inter plærosq;, Sunt qui á uernaculo ductũ uocabulũ putent,q Gar man illi totũ uirũ nominant,atq; hinc dictos ab insigni fortitudine sibi persuadent, cui opinioni ut nõ refragor,ita non accedo: quáq̃ in uocabulo Alemánus nõ dubitem quin e Barbaro Germanoq; in Latiná linguá abierit: unde Lemannum lacũ uocare uoluit Albertus/ qué supra Acroniũ Pomponius nominat, iuxta eũ habitarunt Alemanni toto in littore,quod ex Alberto & Ammiani.xv.li.plane constat.Strabo.vii.li.uerisimilius Trans Rhenũ inquit in ortũ uergentia Germani colunt/nationé Gallicá paulisper imitantes & feritatis abundantia & proceritate corpoꝝ & colore flauo &c. Ideo Romani hoc illis nomé iure indidisse mihi uident, Perinde ac eos fratres legitimos Gallis eloqui uoluerint,legitimi namq; fratres Romano sermone Germani intelliguntur. Tacitus nõ a Galloꝝ consonis moribus sed ab eiusdem gentis natione/ quæ Gallis pulsis Rhenũ traiecerit, nomé ortum, scribit. Eius uerba sunt hæc. Cæterum Germaniæ uocabulum recens & nuper additũ/quoniá qui primũ Rhenum transgressi Gallos expulerũt,nunc Tungri nũc Germani uocati sint,ita nationis nomé non gentis eualuisse paulatim,ut omnes primũ a uictore ob metum,mox a se ipsis inuento nomine Germani uocarentur: hæc Cornel.

Strabo.

Tacitus.

FIG. 24. An expurgated passage in Hernando's 1518 edition of Pomponius Mela's *De situ orbis* (© Cabildo Catedral de Sevilla)

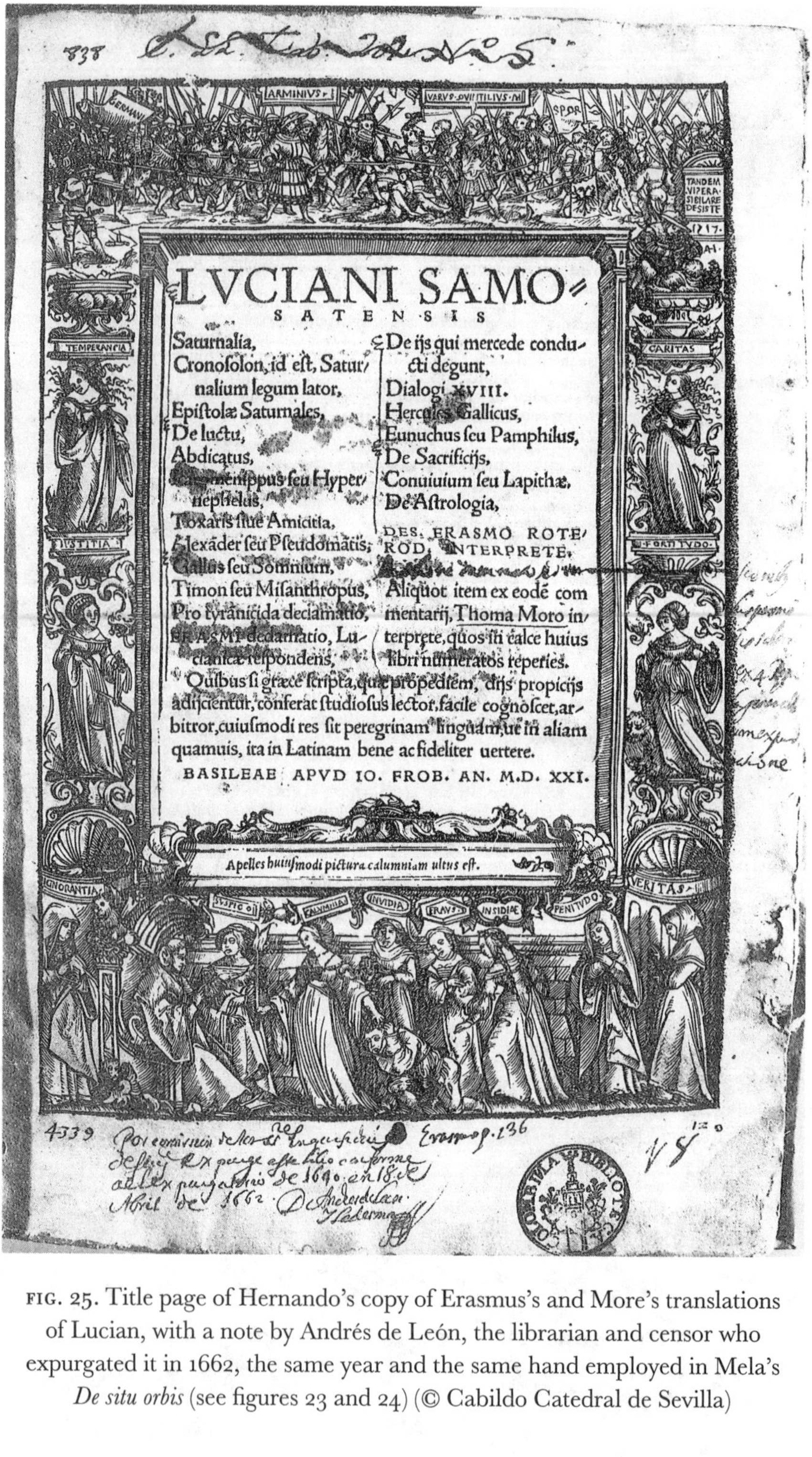

LVCIANI SAMO=
SATENSIS

Saturnalia,
Cronosolon, id est, Saturnalium legum lator,
Epistolæ Saturnales,
De luctu,
Abdicatus,
Icaromenippus seu Hypernephelus,
Toxaris siue Amicitia,
Alexader seu Pseudomatis,
Gallus seu Somnium,
Timon seu Misanthropus,
Pro tyrannicida declamatio,
ERASMI declamatio, Lucianicæ respondens,
De ijs qui mercede conducti degunt,
Dialogi XVIII.
Hercules Gallicus,
Eunuchus seu Pamphilus,
De Sacrificijs,
Conuiuium seu Lapithæ,
De Astrologia,

DES. ERASMO ROTEROD. INTERPRETE.

Aliquot item ex eodē commentarij, Thoma Moro interprete, quos in calce huius libri numeratos reperies.

Quibus si græce scripta, quæ propediem, dijs propicijs adijcientur, conferat studiosus lector, facile cognoscet, arbitror, cuiusmodi res sit peregrinam linguam, ut in aliam quamuis, ita in Latinam bene ac fideliter uertere.

BASILEAE APVD IO. FROB. AN. M.D. XXI.

Apelles huiusmodi pictura calumniam ultus est.

FIG. 25. Title page of Hernando's copy of Erasmus's and More's translations of Lucian, with a note by Andrés de León, the librarian and censor who expurgated it in 1662, the same year and the same hand employed in Mela's *De situ orbis* (see figures 23 and 24) (© Cabildo Catedral de Sevilla)

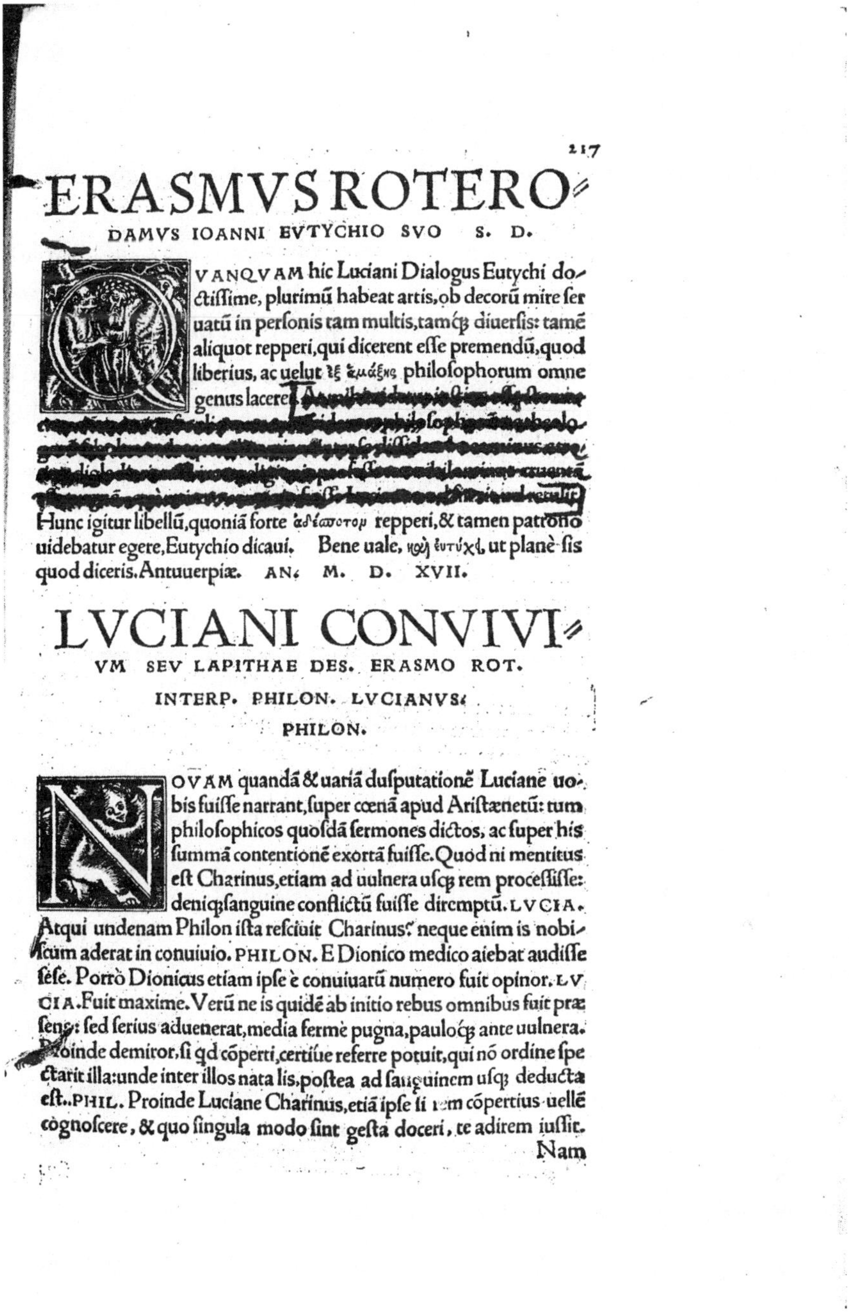
217

ERASMVS ROTERODAMVS IOANNI EVTYCHIO SVO S. D.

QVANQVAM hic Luciani Dialogus Eutychi doctissime, plurimũ habeat artis, ob decorũ mire seruatũ in personis tam multis, tamq̃ diuersis: tamẽ aliquot repperi, qui dicerent esse premendũ, quod liberius, ac uelut ἐξ ἁμάξης philosophorum omne genus lacere[illegible]

Hunc igitur libellũ, quoniã forte ἀδέσποτον repperi, & tamen patrono uidebatur egere, Eutychio dicaui. Bene uale, καὶ εὐτύχει, ut planè sis quod diceris. Antuuerpiæ. AN. M. D. XVII.

LVCIANI CONVIVIVM SEV LAPITHAE DES. ERASMO ROT. INTERP. PHILON. LVCIANVS. PHILON.

NOVAM quandã & uariã disputationẽ Luciane uobis fuisse narrant, super cœnã apud Aristænetũ: tum philosophicos quosdã sermones dictos, ac super his summã contentionẽ exortã fuisse. Quod ni mentitus est Charinus, etiam ad uulnera usq̃ rem processisse: deniq̃ sanguine conflictũ fuisse diremptũ. LVCIA. Atqui undenam Philon ista resciuit Charinus? neque enim is nobiscum aderat in conuiuio. PHILON. E Dionico medico aiebat audisse sese. Porrò Dionicus etiam ipse è conuiuarũ numero fuit opinor. LVCIA. Fuit maxime. Verũ ne is quidẽ ab initio rebus omnibus fuit præsens: sed serius aduenerat, media fermè pugna, pauloq̃ ante uulnera. Proinde demiror, si qd cõperti, certiúe referre potuit, qui nõ ordine spectarit illa: unde inter illos nata lis, postea ad sanguinem usq̃ deducta est. PHIL. Proinde Luciane Charinus, etiã ipse si [illegible] cõpertius uellẽ cognoscere, & quo singula modo sint gesta doceri, te adirem iussit. Nam

FIG. 26. An expurgated passage in a text by Erasmus in Hernando's copy of Lucian (© Cabildo Catedral de Sevilla)

more notorious illegitimate son, Antonio del Corro (1527–91), a Sevillian Lutheran who was forced into exile in a succession of European countries and ended up a don at Oxford.[25]

Seville, along with Valladolid, had by this time become an active center of Spanish Lutheranism, to the great alarm of the retired king Charles V and his son King Philip II, who now saw the arch-enemy they had been fighting for years in northern Europe making important doctrinal inroads at home. These Lutheran groups in Seville and Valladolid were detected by the authorities in 1557, and, significantly, the first document that records an inquiry into the collections housed at the cathedral dates from March of 1558. Although no proper new catalogue had been made of the books since they had been moved to the cathedral, there are documents that indicate that inventories were made over the course of the second half of the sixteenth century (in 1558, 1563, 1584, and 1591) with the exclusive purpose of expurgating the collections.[26] Guillén assigns to this period the expurgation of Erasmus's *Antibarbari* and the very likely (although undocumented) destruction of other potentially suspicious volumes; to this period perhaps also belongs the wholesale disappearance of Hernando's Hebrew collections, detected in our reconstruction of his final shelf order. The Inquisitorial process continued well into the seventeenth century: after the publication in 1612 of a new edition of the *Índice de libros prohibidos,* the Inquisition sent a renewed request to the Chapter for the expurgation of the books in its collections. Another new *Índice* set in motion yet another expurgation in 1640, a process that dragged on for several years, until 1662. Klaus Wagner has traced some of the books eliminated from Hernando's collection by the Inquisition while documenting the expurgations that took place in the mid-seventeenth century.[27] Whatever had survived of the considerable collection of titles related to the Reformation controversy, a number of which were lost at sea in 1522, had already been eliminated by the time Juan de Loaysa created his new catalogue in 1684.

Another volume that left the library during this period was the neat, scribal copy of the *Libro de los Epítomes,* recently rediscovered among the holdings of the Arnamagnæan Collection in Copenhagen, where it bears the shelf mark AM 377 fol.[28] The manuscript, which has been in the collection at least since the death of its founder Árni Magnússon in 1730 and was unidentified owing to its missing initial pages, may have been previously owned by Cornelius Lerche, Danish ambassador to Spain 1650–53 and 1658–62, the auction catalogue of whose collection contains a description that matches the *Libro de los Epítomes* (if only in general terms)—though there are also other established routes through which Magnusson acquired Spanish manuscripts, including from the Danish nobleman Jens Rosenkrantz. Whatever the route through which the manuscript reached Copenhagen, it appears likely that it resided for a period in the library of Gaspar de Guzmán, Count-Duke of Olivares; a shelf mark (E.5) appearing on the first folio of the present manuscript matches an entry in the 1627 inventory of Olivares's library. Olivares's extraordinary power during his ascendancy under Philip IV would have provided ample opportunity for him to remove anything that interested him from Hernando's collections, and it is possible that a further study of the 1627 inventory will reveal a wider pattern of depredations.

Loaysa

For more than a century the books had languished in the rooms atop the so-called Nave of the Lizard in the cathedral, but in 1678 the space where they were kept underwent a series of reforms. It was the first serious intervention in the library's infrastructure since its installation in the cathedral in 1557, and it included the first inventory to survive since Hernando's original catalogues, one undertaken by the librarian Loaysa.[29] By the time Loaysa made his list, only around five thousand titles remained from the original number in excess of fifteen thousand. In 1993 Marín Martínez confirmed that around five thousand titles remained of the original collection—around the same number found in the most recent catalogues of manuscripts and printed books that once belonged to Hernando.[30]

Loaysa found the books in a considerable state of disarray—a result of the refurbishment of the space where they had been deposited, compounded by years of use by the *prebendados* without the supervision and care of a diligent librarian, who could have regulated the organization, storage, and circulation of the books.[31] The new librarian helped to preserve many books that otherwise would have been lost or irreparably damaged—he claimed, for instance, to have rebound more than two thousand of them, though his work sadly meant that almost all of the original bindings were lost.[32] His zeal for the regularization of the collection also led to the cutting down of many volumes as they were rebound, damaging or removing entirely many of the manuscript notes made in the original volumes. He also rearranged the shelf order of the books. According to his inventory, to the left of the entrance ("desde la mano izquierda como se entra en la librería") were the shelves with the following subjects: grammar, rhetoric, history, philosophy, astrology, music, medicine, civil and canon law; on the right were "teología moral, escolástica, Sagrada Escritura, doctrina piadosa, oficio divino" and a section which he called "tratados varios *diversorum*" and finally "tratados y libros sueltos o fragmentos." This order preserves some of the original sections of Hernando's final arrangements, though others are missing, making the logic of the divisions unclear. Loaysa describes how the room was rebuilt and redecorated, to the tune of seven thousand *ducados,* including a portrait of King Ferdinand, patron saint of Seville, by Bartolomé Estaban Murillo, in memory of the other illustrious Ferdinand who bequeathed his library to the city.[33]

We are indebted to Loaysa, then, for a salvage operation that ensured the survival of most of the books and materials we can still consult today, though further depredations were to come. After Loaysa's death in 1709, the books were again abandoned. The indicting evidence provided by Guillén in his history of the Colombina and Capitular libraries piles up, alongside his timid but constant attempts to attenuate the guilt of those ultimately responsible for the care of the books. For decades after Loaysa's death there was a constant flow of documents and reports sent to the Chapter, requesting the appointment of a librarian and proposing not only the proper care of the books but also measures to secure them against the losses and thefts that continued to take place. The situation deteriorated to a point where the keys to the library were handed over to the cleaners of the cathedral, and the books ended up sharing space with brooms, cleaning supplies, and other implements for the daily upkeep of the cathedral. This returned the books once more to the undistinguished state in which they existed when Hernando first took the core of the collections to Santo Domingo in 1509.[34]

The Eighteenth and Nineteenth Centuries

The next testimony to the neglect that the books were suffering can be found in a report the Chapter requested from its archivist, Ignacio de Valencia. Dated 25 August 1788, it also includes a brief history of the library. De Valencia points out that during the sixteenth century the Chapter spent considerable funds on beautiful new shelves (*estantes primorosos*) and the decoration of the room (*mandó adornar la pieza en que estaban con varias pinturas del insigne sevillano Luis de Vargas*). But his report also laments that many volumes, owing to the negligence of the custodians, were left in inexperienced and unqualified hands and vanished either by theft or by loans that were never recorded, and that the remaining books had been damaged by moths and humidity.[35] The bibliographer and scholar Bartolomé José Gallardo (1776–1852) recorded the testimony of Rafael Tabares, one of the librarians in the early eighteenth century, to the effect that "as a boy he went there with others to play, and they amused themselves leafing through the illuminated books and prints, in particular the ancient liturgical manuscripts, some of which had lovely illustrations in beautiful colors."[36]

A new librarian, Diego Alejandro Gálvez, was finally appointed on 3 September 1759. With Gálvez also came some funds to move the collection to the Patio de los Naranjos in the opposite wing of the cathedral complex. De Valencia reports that the shelves were renovated and wire mesh was installed as well as locks, in an attempt to protect the books. Moths and humidity, however, continued to wreak havoc: de Valencia reckoned that during this period around three hundred volumes perished on account of the lack of proper care, airing, and cleaning. Rafael Tabares, who was appointed by Gálvez as his assistant in 1777, further reported that many of the books were taken as the library was decanted from one space to another. The bleeding and destruction continued slowly but unabatedly.[37] In an episode with decidedly Sisyphean overtones, Gálvez took up the task of reordering the books after they had been moved to the new space. For this task he had a paucity of funds and the help of just two assistants—the aforementioned Rafael Tabares and Juan Nemopuceno González de León, who soon fell ill and quit, leaving Tabares and Gálvez to face this labor alone. As Loaysa had done before them, they restored some damaged books, and they created a new catalogue, a remarkable *Índice de impresos y manuscritos* (figs. 27 and 28). Their work represented a much-needed advance on the labors of Loaysa a century before. The rearrangement of the books and the work on the catalogue dragged on from 1777 to 1790. Finally, on 28 April 1790, Gálvez and Tabares completed their three-volume manuscript catalogue. The documentation strongly suggests that Rafael Tabares is the unsung hero of these years, during which he was very much on the front line, as it were, in the diligent reorganization of the books and the elaboration of the new catalogues—when he could find time between the time-consuming task of copying manuscripts at the request of prominent scholars and administrators.

After the death of Gálvez and Tabares, Nicolas Maestre Tous de Monsalve ran the library between 1803 and 1841, followed by Antonio María Araoz, who was in charge between 1841 and 1859. These were tumultuous years in Spain, with first the Napoleonic invasion, then the War of Independence and decades of political instability—including the *desamortizaciones* (the first of them in 1836, the second in 1855), a series of expropriations which affected the property of the church and its economic resources, including its art collections and libraries. The *desamortizaciones* responded not just to the general secularizing policies of nineteenth-century liberal revolutions, but also to an urgent need of funds to assuage the national debt; the result was that the economic situation of the Cathedral Chapter (and the country more generally) became even more dire. The Colombina was no exception to this. External agents, in concert with the state, began to intervene in response to this desperate situation: one of the administrators of the library, José María Fernández y Velasco (1808–79), managed to obtain some exceptional subsidies from Queen Isabel II and the Duke of Veragua around 1871–72—the shelves where the books are stored today date from these years.[38] The Duke of Veragua, a direct descendant of the Columbus family, appears in connection with the library in 1856, the first time since Hernando's death that a member of the family manifested any interest in the collection. In a letter sent to the Chapter on 13 October of that year, he offered to help with the management, while also requesting permission to "visit and inspect the Colombina Library, in accordance with my right, as successor and representative of its founder, and that, to this end, I shall have access to as many books, papers, and documents, as

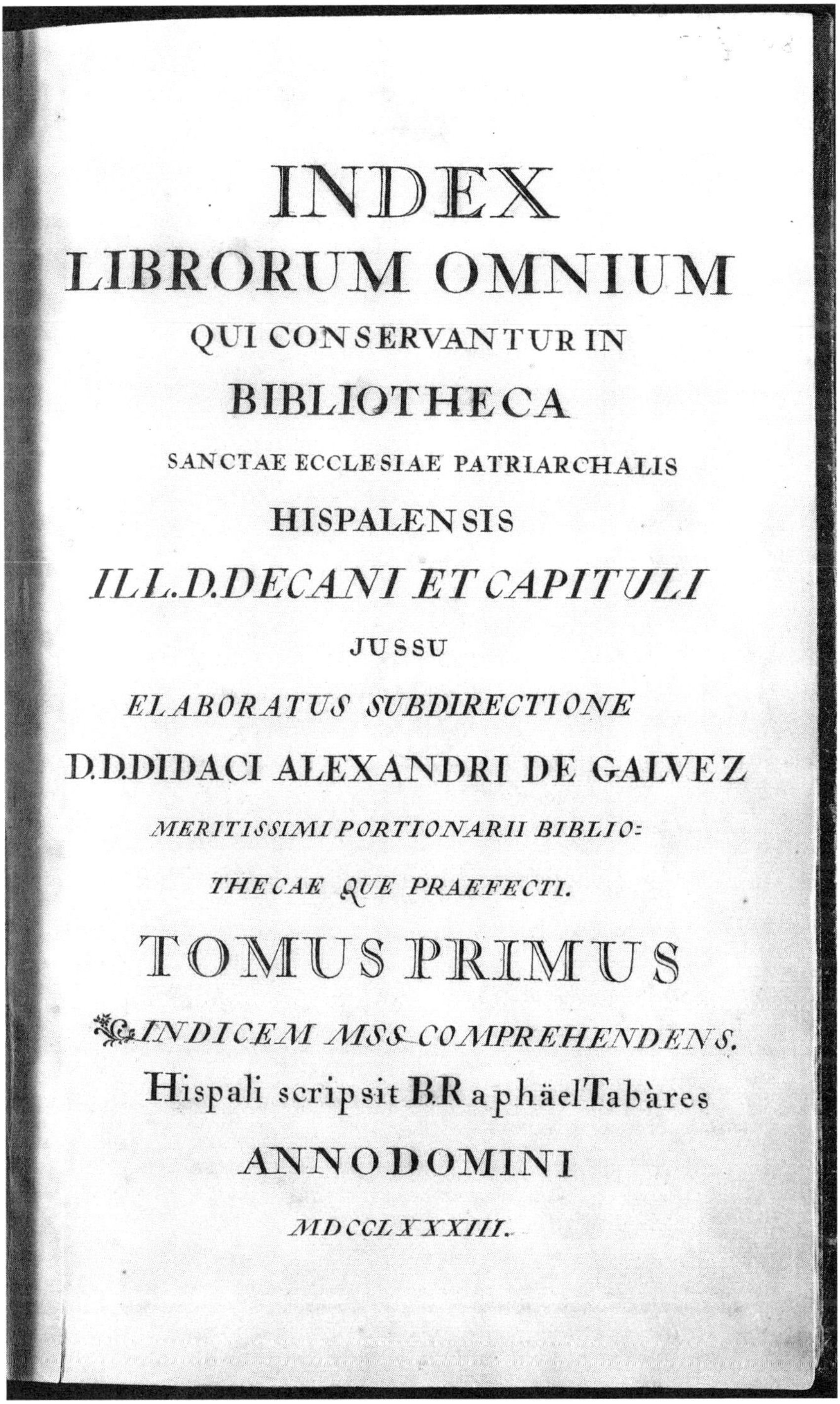

INDEX
LIBRORUM OMNIUM
QUI CONSERVANTUR IN
BIBLIOTHECA
SANCTAE ECCLESIAE PATRIARCHALIS
HISPALENSIS
ILL.D.DECANI ET CAPITULI
JUSSU
ELABORATUS SUBDIRECTIONE
D.D.DIDACI ALEXANDRI DE GALVEZ
MERITISSIMI PORTIONARII BIBLIO:
THECAE QUE PRAEFECTI.
TOMUS PRIMUS
INDICEM MSS COMPREHENDENS.
Hispali scripsit B.Raphäel Tabàres
ANNO DOMINI
MDCCLXXXIII.

FIG. 27. Title page of Gálvez and Tabares's 1783 catalogue (© Cabildo Catedral de Sevilla)

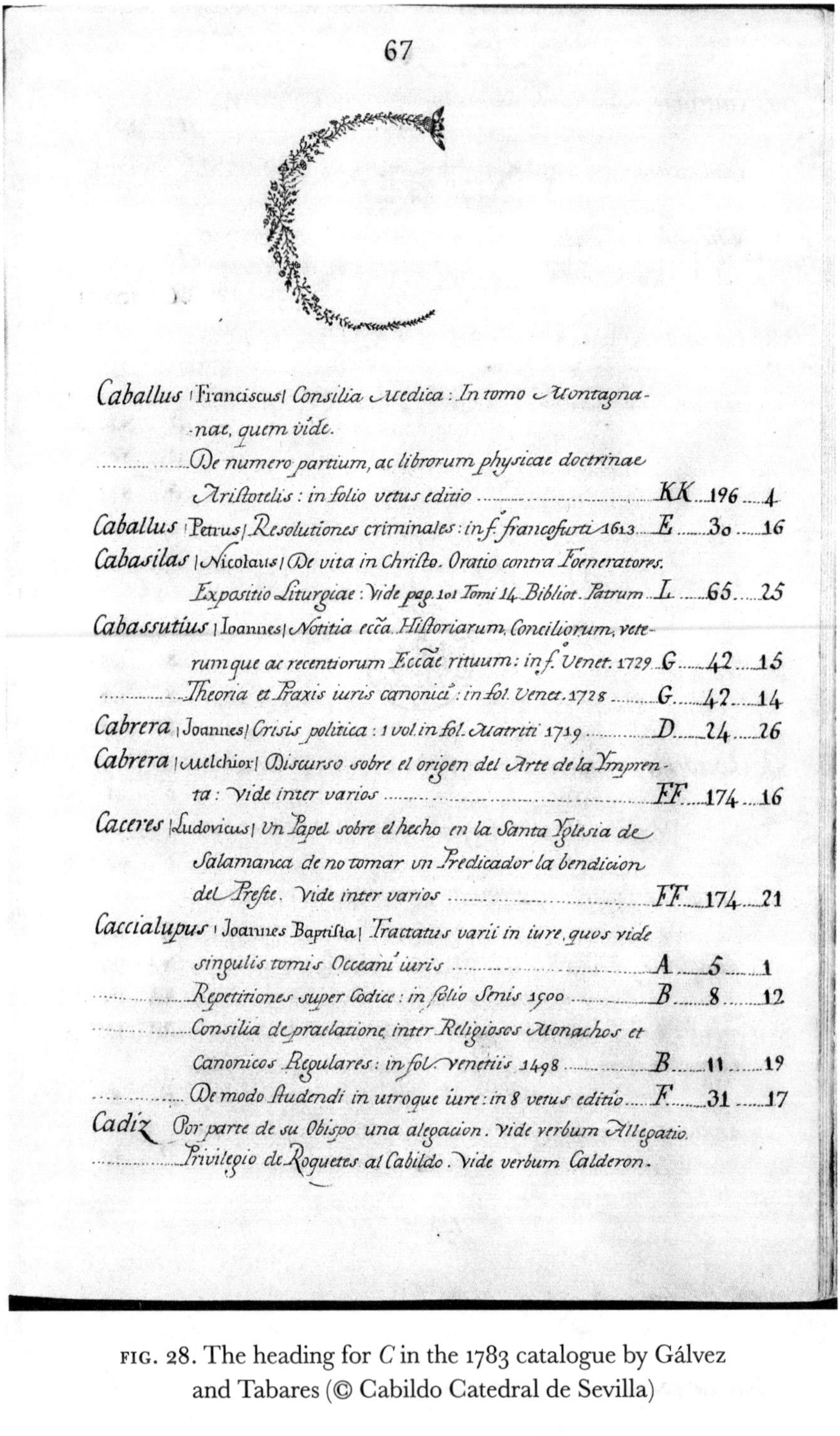

67

C

Caballus | Franciscus | Consilia Medica: In tomo Montagna-
-nae, quem vide.
.... De numero partium, ac librorum physicae doctrinae
Aristotelis: in folio vetus editio .... KK ... 196 ... 4
Caballus | Petrus | Resolutiones criminales: in f. francofurti 1613 ... E ... 30 ... 16
Cabasilas | Nicolaus | De vita in Christo. Oratio contra Foeneratores.
Expositio Liturgiae: Vide pag. 101 Tomi 14 Bibliot. Patrum ... L ... 65 ... 25
Cabassutius | Ioannes | Notitia ecca. Historiarum, Conciliorum, vete-
rumque ac recentiorum Eccae rituum: in f. Venet. 1729 ... G ... 42 ... 15
.... Theoria et Praxis iuris canonici: in fol. Venet. 1728 .... G ... 42 ... 14
Cabrera | Joannes | Crisis politica: 1 vol. in fol. Matriti 1719 .... D ... 24 ... 26
Cabrera | Melchior | Discurso sobre el origen del Arte de la Ympren-
ta: Vide inter varios .... FF ... 174 ... 16
Caceres | Ludovicus | Un Papel sobre el hecho en la Santa Yglesia de
Salamanca de no tomar un Predicador la bendicion
del Preste. Vide inter varios .... FF ... 174 ... 21
Caccialupus | Joannes Baptista | Tractatus varii in iure, quos vide
singulis tomis Occeani iuris .... A ... 5 ... 1
.... Repetitiones super Codice: in folio Senis 1500 .... B ... 8 ... 12
.... Consilia de pralatione inter Religiosos Monachos et
Canonicos Regulares: in fol. venetiis 1498 .... B ... 11 ... 19
.... De modo studendi in utroque iure: in 8 vetus editio ...... F ... 31 ... 17
Cadiz Por parte de su Obispo una alegacion. Vide verbum Allegatio.
.... Privilegio de Roquetes al Cabildo. Vide verbum Calderon.

FIG. 28. The heading for *C* in the 1783 catalogue by Gálvez and Tabares (© Cabildo Catedral de Sevilla)

are necessary to be informed about its current condition."[39] This reference to the duke's rights as a member of the Columbus family and his declared intention to conduct an inspection of the state of the collection alarmed the Chapter, which immediately commissioned a working group to draw up a preemptive legal report in support of the legitimacy of its ownership and custody of the collection. Things did not progress beyond this exchange, and the duke did not push his claims any further, though he eventually intervened with the government to obtain further funds for the maintenance of the library in its existing location.

These subsidies from the crown and the government are indicative of the ambiguous administrative situation the library found itself in after the French invasion, the political turmoil that followed, and the series of liberal governments, some of which made efforts to take control of church property. As part of this general trend, there was a struggle between civic authorities and the church over who should own and manage the library. After a royal decree issued in 1850, the administration and upkeep of the library relied more than ever on the funds that came from the government, which thus exerted increasing pressure to nationalize the collection. This threat finally encouraged the diocese to include the library in its budget for 1859, although the portion of the episcopal budget that it received was somewhat meager.[40]

This situation reached a climax in January 1869. Queen Isabel II was deposed by the liberal revolution of 1868, and the new government issued a decree seizing all the libraries, archives, and art collections that belonged to the church. For the first time, the Chapter library and Hernando's collection came under the direct jurisdiction and control of the state. The deposition of Queen Isabel II and then of her successor King Amadeo de Saboya led to the proclamation of the short-lived republic of 1873–74. The swift restoration of the monarchy, however, returned ownership of the collections to the Chapter. Yet the government proposed a sort of mixed administration rather than full restitution: the state would fund and run the collection in the same way it did for all the other libraries that belonged to the nation, while preserving ultimate ownership by the church. The Chapter, however, wary as ever of any creeping process of appropriation, rejected the offer.

Toward the end of the nineteenth century, thefts started again, but this time the scandal became public.[41] Henry Harrisse denounced the appearance in Paris of a series of books and manuscripts, apparently from the Colombina, first in an article in the *Revue Critique d'Histoire et de Litterature* (18 May 1885) and afterward in his *Grandeur et Decadence de la Colombine* (Paris, 1885). To judge by the figures suggested by Harrisse, the number of books up for sale in Paris was higher than four hundred, including not a few of the rare and precious *obrezillas*.[42] At least five of them had been offered to the National Library in Paris for one thousand francs: the director of the Parisian library sent a letter to the dean of Seville Cathedral on 18 May 1885 (the same date as Harrisse's article), declaring that he had been offered these five works, which appeared to belong to the Colombina. The director offered to return them to Seville if he could get the one thousand francs he had paid for them. The dean answered back, requesting further details before he could make a decision on the payment—details which were never sent, leaving the books in the National Library in Paris to this day.

News of the book sales soon spread from Harrisse and the French press, to the press in Madrid, then parliament, and finally the local Sevillian press. It raised again the question of the ownership of the collection, or at least the need for the state to supervise its administration, in line with the proposal made soon after the Restoration—that is, the ownership would remain with the Chapter and the church, but supervision and administration of the collection would pass to the state. In late 1885 and early 1886, in the middle of this controversy, more evidence of thefts came to light, which intensified the scandal. It was compounded by a medieval missal from the Chapter library showing up for sale in London in 1886. The manuscript had been offered to the British Museum by one Mr. Allfeld, who claimed he had bought it in Paris. The same year other items from the collection surfaced in Rome.[43] These developments took place under the watch of a new librarian, Servando Arbolí, who had been appointed in 1884. In 1888, once the dust had begun to settle, Arbolí set about the elaboration of a new catalogue, which was completed by his successors and finally published in 1948.

Hernandine Studies

In the nineteenth century Romantic travelers discovered Spain, seeing it as an exotic destination, a misplaced oriental jewel in southern Europe, and therefore a fitting subject for fiction, travelogues, and historical research. Washington Irving was among the most prominent and prolific of these authors: he was probably the first non-Spanish scholar to examine Spanish archives systematically in search of information about Columbus. His sensationally successful *A History of the Life and Voyages of Christopher Columbus,* first published in 1828, was the prelude to a renewed interest in the famous explorer and his voyages, an interest that eventually extended to his son. On its title page Irving's biography features the verses from Seneca's *Medea,* which Hernando also interpreted as a pagan prophecy of his father's discoveries. In his introduction Irving acknowledges that he was spurred into taking up this project by the impending publication of a collection of documents compiled by Martín Fernández de Navarrete (1765–1844). The five-volume *Colección de los viages y descubrimientos que hicieron por mar los españoles desde fines del siglo XV* gathered a vast number of primary sources concerning the age of discovery, with a special emphasis on Columbus, and became a fundamental resource for further historical research. In 1850 his grandson, Eustaquio Fernández de Navarrete (1820–66), published a similar compilation of archival documents about Hernando's life, which was to Harrisse what the grandfather's publication had been to Irving. If Harrisse, and the scandal of the missing volumes, gave Hernando a national and international reputation, whatever Harrisse and those who followed in his wake achieved relied heavily on the work of Eustaquio Fernández de Navarrete. His collection of primary sources, together with the 1941 publication by Hernández Díaz and Muro Orejón, constituted the starting point for much subsequent research.

Henry Harrisse's approach to the Colombina was part of his general interest in American studies, early modern exploration, and Hernando's father—including an early interest in the relations between Columbus and the Casa di San Giorgio. In addition to his work on Columbus and early printed reports of exploration in America, Harrisse published books on the Cabots (father and son), Vespucci, and Verrazano. His account of Hernando's life and work is therefore rooted in a thorough knowledge of the historical context and a close familiarity with all the primary sources. After an early start as a not very successful lawyer in Chicago and New York, Harrisse encountered another collector, the American bibliophile Samuel L. Barlowe, who determined the course of his future career. At Barlowe's behest Harrisse put together his first major work in the field of American bibliographical studies, the *Bibliotheca Americana Vetustissima* (1866), a collection of sources containing news on the discovery of the new continent printed between 1492 and 1551. The bibliographical nature of this early accomplishment could not but incline Harrisse to the work of another obsessive bibliographer, Hernando. This took him to Seville in 1870, where his research first bore fruit in his *Don Fernando Colón, historiador de su padre*. After Seville he moved to Paris, where he was associated with Ernest Renan (whose work he had also studied), George Sand (with whom he corresponded), and Gustave Flaubert. In 1872 he published a French version of his monograph on Hernando Colón (*Fernand Colomb, sa vie, ses oeuvres*), with a dedication to his "ami Ernest Renan." Although its title is somewhat misleading—most of the book is dedicated to the question of the authorship of *Historia del Almirante*—it was the first major work dedicated to Hernando by an international scholar for a non-Spanish readership. With access to the primary sources available at the Colombina—the catalogues as well as Hernando's books—Harrisse was the first to use Hernando's manuscript notes in his books to trace the itineraries he followed in his travels around Europe.[44] With all its shortcomings, the main body of Harrisse's 1871 monograph and its appendixes—which include the *Memorial al Emperador*, a new transcription of Hernando's testament (which had already been published by Fernández de Navarrete), and the *Declaraciones de Marcos Felipe*—provided extremely useful starting points for those interested in Hernando and his collection, though it did not prompt the widespread international recognition of the collection that Harrisse might have hoped.

After Harrisse's publications, no major work was dedicated to Hernando and his books until 1913, when Jean Babelon published a catalogue of Hernando's French books. The decades that followed saw the publication of research that almost universally saw Hernando in the shadow of his father, first, and then of his brother Diego—above all with respect to the controversy over the authorship of the *Historie della vita e dei fatti di Cristoforo*

Colombo. Rumeu de Armas's *Hernando Colón, historiador del descubrimiento de América* is probably the most comprehensive account of this controversy, and it includes also important information about Hernando's life.[45] Interest in Hernando as a historian coexisted with publications about partial aspects of his library—such as surveys of specific subcollections within it, which had started in 1913 with Jean Babelon, who included some publications on his musical collection.[46] There are two exceptions to this approach. One is a collection of primary sources compiled by José Hernández Díaz and Antonio Muro Orejón and published in 1941, which brings together notarial documents illustrating Hernando's life and legacy. A fundamental resource for any Hernandista, it records important documents, many of which had not been taken into consideration before—for instance, those which provide information about the financial situation of Hernando at the time of his death, which determined to a great degree the eventual fate of his books. The other is the massive tome, also with a wealth of primary sources, by Tomás Marín Martínez, published in 1970. The first major critical monograph devoted to Hernando's books and catalogues, it surveys in great detail earlier scholarship and focuses, above all, on his collection and, for the first time, the methods he employed in its classification.[47]

Another foreign scholar who settled in Seville during the second half of the twentieth century, the German-born Klaus Wagner, became a prolific scholar of Hernando's collection. Although Wagner never produced the monograph that his familiarity with the collection and other related primary sources might have facilitated, he published a series of important and useful articles and, above all, repertories of partial aspects of Hernando's library, such as his Italian books (including those that Hernando purchased from Marin Sanudo), astrological prognostications, and publications showing the presence of the Lutheran controversy in the collection.[48]

1986

Interest in the collection had been slowly gaining momentum among specialists ever since Harrisse drew attention to the thefts in 1885 when, one hundred years later, another traumatic event occurred. On the night of

8 January 1986, a storm caused the library ceiling to collapse. The broken beams and the rubble fell from the roof, hitting a number of the shelves and also damaging illuminated manuscripts on display in the middle of the room. It was a severe shock to Seville, which was in the middle of preparations for the 1992 commemoration of the five hundredth anniversary of Columbus's First Voyage. Significant amounts of public and private funds, and institutional and political capital, were being invested in an international fair (the EXPO 92) which involved the restoration of local monuments, including the cathedral, and the creation of new infrastructure to house the different national pavilions on the grounds of the nearby monastery of the Cartuja de las Cuevas, the so-called Island of La Cartuja—across the river from the original location of Hernando's Casa de Goles—where his father had kept some of his personal archive during his life and where he had first been buried.

The regional government immediately intervened to support repair of the facilities and the recovery and restoration of as many books as possible. Urgent plans were made to redefine the administrative structure of the collections: the archdiocese of Seville and the Cathedral Chapter created the Fundación Capitular Colombina in 1991, a single administrative unit that oversees the Biblioteca Capitular and the Biblioteca Colombina, and in 1992 the Institución Colombina, which still runs the library. In an echo of the public reaction to the books stolen in the nineteenth century, the local and the national press denounced the precarious situation of the collections. It came to the attention of the public that, even before the collapse of the roof, the facilities that housed the library, including the reading room used by researchers, had no electricity. The roof, which had been restored several decades before (around 1948), had collapsed previously, in 1956, although with apparently no damage to the books. According to local press reports, the roof had for some time shown alarming signs of water damage that went unheeded. This is all the more striking since many other parts of the cathedral complex were at the time undergoing restoration, with a view to the visitors who would flock to Seville for the commemorations of 1992.[49]

In an article published in 1990 Klaus Wagner and Juan Guillén reckoned that the number of books affected, most of them from the Chapter library, amounted to around one thousand—although they claimed the extent of the damage was not as serious as originally thought. Technical support from experts at the National Library in Madrid was instrumental in acting quickly to repair the books that had suffered the most damage. The disaster also prompted a close examination of the rest of the books and the conditions in which they had been stored, showing that they had been exposed for decades to humidity and the depredations of moths and microorganisms.[50]

The combined effect of the collapse of the roof and the preparations for the commemoration of 1992, alongside the decisive action taken by Juan Guillén—who had been appointed as director of the library only a month before the accident—led to a series of important publications about the collection which have facilitated the work of researchers: new updated catalogues, first in print and now available online, were put together by a team of librarians who helped to salvage the books after the ceiling collapse.[51] Partial accounts and commemorative publications to familiarize the reading public with the collection started to appear, alongside specialized essays. One of the most valuable was Juan Gil's edition of Hernando's copy of *Marco Polo,* a book that had belonged to his father and which features manuscript notes by several hands, contributing to a proper understanding of Hernando's outlook and that of his family in terms of their reading strategies.[52] One of the most interesting recent publications is Juan Guillén's *Historia de las Bibliotecas Capitular y Colombina* (2006), the result of an exhaustive process of research in the archives of the cathedral and in the library itself, and a volume that provides a guide to researchers with easy access to some of the most relevant primary sources that document the history of the two collections. Finally, the *Catálogo concordado,* an ambitious project for a comprehensive collation of Hernando's own catalogues by a team of librarians and paleographers coordinated by Marín Martínez, Klaus Wagner, and José Manuel Ruiz Asencio, bore its first fruits in 1993 with the publication of two of a proposed total of seven volumes. Regrettably, the publication of this *Catálogo concordado* has been halted for twenty-five years now, a time during which none of the promised new volumes have been published.

Beyond Spain, an important aspect of Hernando's collections was brought to the attention of Anglo-American academia, and of visitors to the British Museum, with the 2004 exhibition on Hernando's prints curated by Mark P. McDonald. Other than McDonald, the Anglo-American world has virtually ignored Hernando's collection, including, of course, his emphasis on *obrezillas* and the insights these provide to the early modern world of print and of knowledge. By comparison with other libraries and catalogues, Hernando's collection was far more comprehensive and more ambitious. Yet recent accounts of the most prominent bibliographies of the sixteenth century fail to mention Hernando's library and catalogues, with some even singling out ephemera as one of the most relevant absences in early modern catalogues, given their lack of intellectual prestige and the fact that they tended to be associated with polemics and scurrility. That Hernando chose to collect them and valued them particularly in his will underlines the exceptionality of his vision, a vision whose invisibility outside of the world of Spanish bibliographers this book and the biography by Edward Wilson-Lee have sought to remedy.[53] The recent discovery of the *Libro de los Epítomes* and its forthcoming critical edition demonstrates that Hernando's books and catalogues remain a fabulous source of unexplored material that will yield new insights for decades to come.

Hernando's collection reached its crescendo at a watershed moment, on the threshold of a new world in science and communication. His library was an ambitious and innovative project that sought to hoard and classify information in an unprecedentedly comprehensive way. But it also had very deep roots in well-established millenarian and universalist dreams founded, inter alia, on the prophecy of the book of Daniel: the four empires whose chronographic path prove that imperium wends its way westward—Assyrian, Persian, Greek, and Roman, mirrored (for instance) in Pedro Mexía's genealogy of Roman emperors down to Charles V in his *Historia imperial y cesárea* (Seville, 1545). In spite of its originality and ambition, and in spite of the cultural and political capital it would have brought to the institution that housed it—the Sevillian cathedral—and to the monarchy it sought to serve since its very inception, the Biblioteca Hernandina never had a chance to survive, grow, and flourish. It was deprived of the chance to act as a repository and a witness to the forthcoming host of books and theories that struggled to make sense of the New World and the new science—much of which was founded on the knowledge Hernando had accumulated in his collection. It is true that Hernando did not live to see the impending scientific revolutions, but it is also true that much of the traditional worldview curated in his Casa de Goles and recorded in his catalogues long survived and coexisted with the theories proposed by the new science of Galileo and Newton. The early age of print carried over traditions that had circulated profusely in manuscript and now coexisted with novel ideas formulated for the first time in print. This hybrid furnished Hernando's library, but it also outlasted him.

This intersection of cartography with history, science, and myth, of the disciplines of space and time within a millenarian outlook, would find continuity in the work of one of the cosmographers employed at the Casa de Contratación after Hernando's death. Jerónimo de Chaves, the son of Alonso de Chaves, one of Hernando's most important collaborators in the Sevillian mapmaking factory, later became the first professor of cosmography at the Casa de Contratación, and during his tenure there he published *Chronographia o reportorio de los tiempos* (1548), a combination of methods for the measurement and partition of time with a physical description and a history of the world and its ages, heavy with millenarian connotations—a worthy heir to d'Ailly's and Piccolomini's legacy, those founding volumes in Hernando's collection, which Jerónimo de Chaves updated with the knowledge he acquired from his own father's *Espejo de navegantes*.

Jerónimo de Chaves's work is thus the axis that connects the Casa de Contratación to the milieu Hernando helped establish with the emerging chronographic and scientific tradition, seeking to make sense of the new global world that had gradually emerged during the age of exploration, as well as the history that was believed to precede this event horizon. Scaliger's *De emendatione temporum* (1583) combines a series of disciplines—philology, astronomy, chronography and is the result of information culled from a close reading of manuscript and printed sources and also from a vast network of global correspondents, most of them Dutch merchants—the same works and networks that Hernando used as he painstakingly gathered information for his own project. A few years after Scaliger's work, Benito Arias Montano (1527–98) was still using biblical teleological patterns to make sense of the world: in the *mappamundi* that he included in his *Antiquitatum iudaicarum libri ix* (Leiden, 1593) he traced the migration of Noah's sons to North and South America and identified Peru as the site of the biblical Ophir. A scholar and an encyclopedist, Montano also suggested the design of the frescoes in the library of El Escorial, where some of Hernando's books may have been taken. This series of concerns became widespread: a few decades later Sir Walter Raleigh's *History of the World* (1614) combined exploration, universalism, cartography, and chronography, and in his plans for American colonization, Raleigh sought the advice of the astronomer and mathematician Thomas Harriot, who in turn worked on a dictionary of Algonquin, using the information that the natives brought back to England from Arthur Barlowe's American expedition of 1584. After his release from his imprisonment at the Tower of London in 1616 Raleigh still had time and energy to organize an expedition in search of El Dorado to the Orinoco, the same place where about a century before Hernando's father claimed he had found Eden. In 1643, Hugo Grotius's *De origine gentium Americanum* also engaged in biblical ethnography and chronography, tracing the origin of the peoples of the world back to Noah and the Tower of Babel, synthesizing the vast new cartographies with the traditional T-O maps of the world that are found in the *Etymologiae* of Saint Isidore and the universal demography (descended from Japheth, Shem, and Ham) adumbrated in them. For many decades after Hernando's death, then, and even as they laid the foundations for Europe's proclaimed modernity, European scholars remained engaged in the sort of chronographic, cosmographic, and bibliographic interpretation of America and the new global worlds which Hernando had taken up with his comprehensive canon of books and the universal scope of his cartographic, lexicographic, and catalogic projects.

When it comes to assessing the place of the Biblioteca Hernandina in the redesign of knowledge between the end of the fifteenth century and the early years of the sixteenth century, in the revolution of communication and technology the invention of print brought about, and in the changes in the relations between Europe and the rest of the globe in the early age of exploration, it is indisputable that Hernando's collection predates most of the works that are usually acknowledged as agents of these changes. For instance, Hernando died four years before the issue of Copernicus's *De revolutionibus orbium coelestium* (Nuremberg, 1543), he did not live to see the publication of Vesalius's *De humani corporis fabrica* (Basel, 1555), nor did he witness the revolution in cosmology brought about by Galileo, even though his collection was primed to absorb these new ideas and integrate them into existing thinking. The twenty-first-century historian who contemplates with some melancholy the almost tragic fate of his universal library cannot but imagine what a great collection it could have become if Hernando's financial situation should have been more buoyant, if the Spanish situation had been more favorable, and if his heirs had followed his instructions, stocking his shelves with these new iconic volumes in the history of science and knowledge alongside the myriad of pamphlets which reshaped the politics and culture—high, middle, and low—of early modern Europe.

For Hernando was, in many respects, decidedly ahead of his own times. Between 1545 and 1549, Conrad Gessner published his *Bibliotheca universalis, sive, Catalogus omnium scriptorium locupletissimus in tribus linguis Latina, Graeca et Hebraica.* Unlike Hernando's collection, this bibliographic blueprint was limited to the three great languages of learning—Latin, Greek, and Hebrew—and did not heed the increasing mass of printed matter that was being produced in the vernacular, let alone Hernando's treasured *obrezillas.*[54] It would be even longer before the Florentine Francesco Marucelli (1625–1705), in the middle of the seventeenth century, started to compile a bibliographical catalogue with summaries of all the disciplines of his age—his *Mare Magnum Omnium Materiarum,* which his nephew and librarian enlarged after his death until it reached 111 manuscript volumes in its final version, already well into the eighteenth century. Marucelli, who insisted on buying inexpensive but useful editions, was more interested in content than in luxury or collector's items. Yet his library amounted in the end to only six thousand titles—less than half of what Hernando gathered.

Hernando's testament and Juan Pérez's *Memoria* are two unparalleled texts in the history of libraries; they do not simply predate subsequent projects but stand out among them for being extremely practical, material maps that couple an ambitious plan for an omnicomprehensive collection—not just a bibliography or an academic library—with a precise description of its different catalogues, a financial scheme, and instructions for its future administration, from the international routes the factors should employ in the enlargement of the collection down to the number of pillows the librarian should have in his bedroom. Although it would take almost a hundred years for Justus Lipsius to publish a brief treatise, *De bibliothecis syntagma* of 1602, which is considered a landmark in the history of libraries and inspired Federico Borromeo to found the Biblioteca

Ambrosiana in 1609, as well as Gabriel Naude's 1627 *Advis pour dresser une bibliotheque,* Lipsius's booklet in the end is an academically compendious history of classical libraries put forth as examples for emulation by European patrons and takes no account of the revolutionary innovations suggested by Hernando.[55]

Hernando's universal library, and his catalogues, also predate the equally ambitious plan of publications and editions of the Venetian Academy, which in 1558 published a *Somma delle Opere che in tutte le scienze et arti piu nobili, et in varie lingue ha da mandare in luce l'Academia Venetiana,* a project of publications that would reduce to a condensed summary the most important works in all disciplines, to facilitate communication and learning. This summary and reduction to the basics was to be carried out by the anatomization of disciplines and their display in branching diagrams—of the sort employed by Hernando in his *Loci Communes* and also similar to the methods proposed by Poliziano in his *Panemistemon.*[56] His catalogues prefigure instruments like Giulio Camillo's *Trattato delle materie* (1579) and other similar "rhetorical machines," which seek to classify subject matters, disciplines, and topics in tabular or diagrammatic format—visual, geometrical, or reticular displays that combined different modular elements of the previously anatomized disciplines into rational and ordered cartographies of knowledge.[57]

Hernando's obsession with storing, sorting, selecting, and summarizing involved not just alphabetical and numerical indexes, or information about the place of publication, the publisher, price, and exchange rates. As we have seen, his catalogues also included very detailed descriptions of the physical format of the printed product in question—such as its size and the number of quires. He was also a pioneer in recording the paratexts in his catalogues, devising an abundant and very detailed list of symbols to classify books according to these elements, such as prologues in prose, paratexts in verse, incipits, explicits, whether the book in question had an argument for each of its chapters (*capítulos epitomáticos*), whether the book had been translated or was an original version.[58]

But Hernando was far more than an obsessive, bookish collector: his habits evince the mentality of a merchant or an entrepreneur with a long-term plan in mind, proven by his suggestion that with the extra copies, and after duplicates have turned into a backup copy for the library—not just one, but *two* universal repositories of knowledge—the triplicates should be put up for sale through a bookseller who would make a profit for himself and eventually for the library too. With this profit, the library could then afford to pay for its own employees and gain an independent source of income to keep buying books. With this long-term business plan the library had the potential to become self-sufficient: a self-perpetuating repository of knowledge and an ongoing rhetorical machine.[59] This entrepreneurial outlook is further emphasized by Hernando's avowed reasons for resorting to Genoese merchants and bankers, or to merchants of any nationality whatsoever if the former were not available—for, he says, they all have the right disposition and know-how (*ynteligencia*) to communicate with others and to make deals with strangers.[60] In short, Hernando emerges not as a scholar or collector divorced from the processes of the age, but as a master planner whose only impediment was that his vision was only compatible with the universal, a vision the scale of which guaranteed its eventual collapse.

Hernando lived through a period during which this fixation of the universal in a single spot was constantly elusive—even more than it already is by nature. In the same way in which Peter Martyr and his readers could hardly keep up with the news that came from the New World and made his *Decades* into a work in progress requiring constant new editions, cartographers in these same years also struggled to fix into reliable maps the incoming flow of data about physical spaces that were in a ceaseless process of expansion. This overwhelming flow of new information included anthropological Others and alien cultural phenomena that defied the existing stock of Western categories not just for their interpretation but even for their representation. As discursive knowledge moved in the shifting and restless space of the library, so the visual languages of the map contended in cartographic spaces. Christian Jacob describes maps as dynamic processes, and there are few maps more dynamic and fluid than those being produced in the early sixteenth century. Perhaps foremost among these was the *Padrón Real,* which was under permanent revision and redesign as a result of the constant flow of new information conveyed by the pilots. As a map of knowledge, Hernando's collection was similarly conceived to be under constant revision and expansion—as the provisions in his testament demonstrate—and his catalogues are also the result of the dynamic processes emerging from the purchase, transport, and classification of the materials he acquired for his library.

The ambition to map time, the cosmos, knowledge, and even human societies—and to hold them in clocks, charts, dictionaries, encyclopedias, libraries, catalogues, and representative political institutions, all of them conceived under the species of mirrors where they could be apprehended and somehow kept under a semblance of control—evokes Jorge Luis Borges's paradoxical tropes of impossibly faithful and transparent representational techniques, artifacts, and institutions in short stories like "The Library of Babel," "The Congress," or "On Exactitude in Science." The utopian universalism of Hernando's library survives only as a trace of something glimpsed but not achieved, yet it is eloquently witnessed in his final documents: his letter to the emperor, his will, and the *Memoria* by Juan Pérez. If Borges's map in his "On Exactitude in Science," like the empire that produced it, survives only in scattered remains, then the remnants of Hernando's library and the universal cosmographies that ran alongside them are similar fragments, attesting to a vision of the world that has disappeared yet continues forcefully to underpin many assumptions today.

APPENDIXES

PRIMARY TEXTS

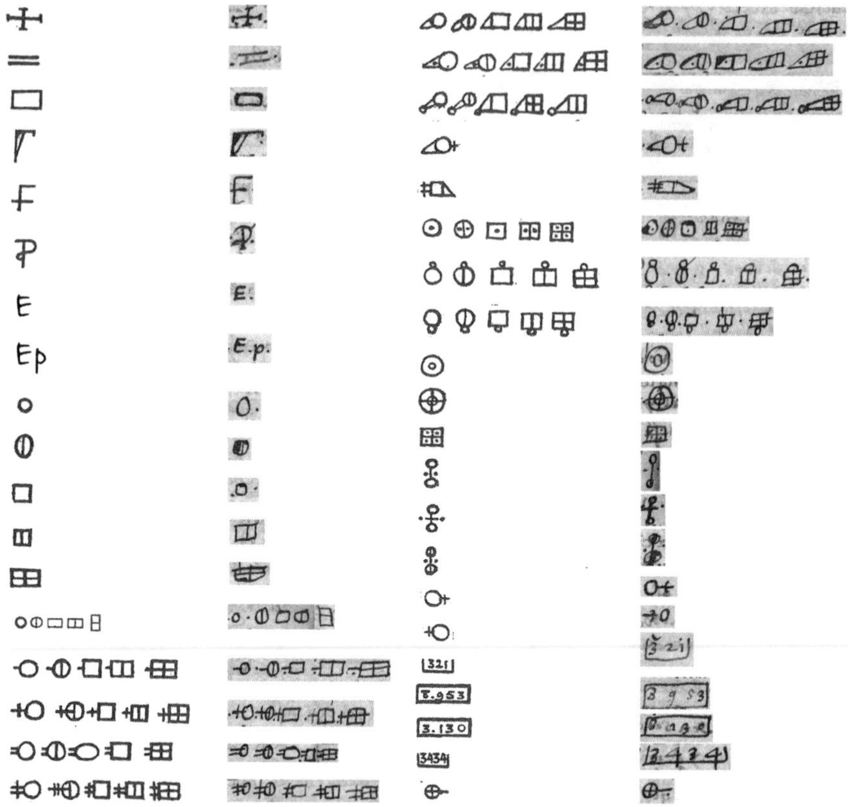

FIG. 29. A table of symbols in the manuscript of the *Memoria* in the Biblioteca del Palacio Real, Madrid, alongside the symbols as redrawn by Guy Beaujouan (Guy Beaujouan, "Fernand Colomb et le marché du livre scientifique à Lyon en 1535–1536," in *Lyon: cite de savants,* Actes du 112e Congrès national des sociétés savantes [Lyon, 1987], section d'Histoire des sciences et des techniques, tome 1 [Paris: Éditions du CTHS, 1988], pp. 55–63.)

ONE

Juan Pérez's Memoria

This lengthy description of Hernando's registers—both those that recorded and arranged the contents of the library and those that pertained to lexicography and cosmography—is preserved in a contemporary (but not autograph) manuscript miscellany in the Real Biblioteca de España (MS 652), a volume that contains a number of other works either by Hernando or from his milieu (see chapter 4). Though it is unclear when the bachiller *Juan Pérez entered Hernando's employment—and little more is known of him than what can be gleaned from the documents in this appendix—it is clear that by the time of Hernando's death he was the most trusted assistant in the library, and Hernando's will makes specific provision for Juan Pérez to continue his tasks in the library after the death of the founder. It is clear from internal evidence that the* Memoria de las Obras y Libros de don Hernando Colón *was written between Hernando's death in July 1539 and the removal of the books from the Casa de Colón in 1544, though no more specific date has yet been fixed.*

Although the document is perhaps the most fascinating and detailed description of a sixteenth-century library—and one of the greatest libraries of the age, at that—Juan Pérez's style is rather rambling and repetitive, and it is almost entirely lacking in punctuation. He is also rather vague in his use of terminology, at times falling back on circumlocutions to describe elements of the library, and at others using the same term to describe a number of distinct things. In attempting to provide a readable version of the document, we have silently added punctuation and lightly disentangled the syntax or adapted the phrasing while departing as little as possible from the original sense. We occasionally add a word, enclosed in square brackets, to make the meaning clear, and when the import of a word or phrase is ambiguous we provide the original Spanish (in italics, between square brackets) after a translation of the most likely meaning. Some particularly problematic words are discussed in notes.[1]

Memorandum of the works and books that don Hernando Colón my lord, who is in Heaven, started by his own hand and labor (and not including others that are already complete), and they are kept in the library within the theology room; above each of them there is written what they are and their purpose, and they are as follows:

(1)

In the first place, because it was my lord don Hernando Colón's purpose to make a cosmography of Spain, and in it to describe all the particulars and the memorable things that are there, and for this purpose it was necessary to send around all the towns of Spain certain people to gather information from the residents in each town about the size of the population and about all the rest there was in each of them which deserved to be remembered, and once this information had been gathered, they should have it validated by a notary public and by reliable witnesses. There is in the library a manuscript, in quarto, bound in black leather and tied up, which is the record of all these memorable things I have just mentioned and of the notarial documents attached to them as their certification, which is a sort of prototype or original from which seven other books were compiled, which we shall now mention.

(2)

There are besides seven other additional volumes, as I have just mentioned, in quarto, written by hand and bound in wooden boards and embossed leather, bound with leather straps, which proceed alphabetically from *a* to *c;* and in them is contained the cosmography of Spain which had already been started, and in them are all the remarkable things that exist in each of the towns which are recorded there, and I say this because not all of them are here, because this [project] was never completed. It would have been of great benefit to know about the excellencies of Spain, since there is no Christian generation that has not made such description and figure [*discriçión y figura*] even of its smallest town, so that those who have never been in Rome, Jerusalem, Babylon, Paris, or Antwerp, and all the rest of them, can know about the shape of its location, and how big it is, and can recount it as if they had been in there, and even better than that, because particularities are better perceived in a drawing; so that only our Spain, or better said Castile, has lacked this, or at least has come very short [of this sort of record]. Seeing this my lord Don Hernando would take up this immense task and great expense, but envy kept him from bringing it to an end.

The manner of proceeding to find whatever is being looked for in the completed part is by looking up the first letter of the name of the city they want to search, and in its proper place they will find it, because as I have said it proceeds alphabetically, so that if someone wants to know about Seville, what it is like, or its population, its location and its estates [*heredades*] or, in sum, what memorable things there are in it, must proceed to the letter *s* and there he will find in its right order all he would like to know about it, about the local parishes, how many leagues it is from each of them, and which roads lead from one to the other, and everything else he would like to know. And these seven books have many blank spaces because as I have said they had not been finished.

(3)

My lord don Hernando also planned to collect there all the drawings, paintings, or images[2] he could find, as he did with a large number of them; and it was necessary to order them to keep a record of those that had been bought so that the same painting was not bought twice. And to this effect he made three manuscript books in quarto, bound in white parchment,[3] all of which are tied together in the library in the place I mentioned above, and they are records of all the drawings or paintings that there are in the library and in the chests, classified according to the following order: if the painting is small, being of an entire sheet divided in sixteen parts, it is called sexto-decimo;[4] and if it is mid-sized, a whole sheet divided in eight parts, it is called octavo; and if larger, a whole sheet [*pliego*] divided in four, it is called a picture [*figura*] in quarto; and if it is as big as a single sheet [*pliego*], it is called a folio picture [*figura de un pliego*]; and if it is very big, an uncut sheet [*marca real*], it is called a broadside picture [*figura en marca*]; and in these names we find all the different pictures [*figuras*] there are.

I already said that the purpose of these books is to know which [pictures] there are [in the collection] so that the same painting is not purchased twice. The way in which it was described was to take the picture that would be recorded and if it was a sheet [*pliego*] divided in four parts, it [i.e., the catalogue section] said "quarto," and if there was in it one, or two, or more figures, it said "quarto with two figures," and if they were dressed, it said "dressed," and if they were naked, then this was used in the title, and then [starting] on another line it recorded all the features of the painting in question and of its figures; so that if the painting is in quarto and with four naked males, its title records: "quarto, with four naked men," and then below it includes all the rest of the most important features of the picture [*figura*] in question, saying thus: "a man and a woman, naked, sitting, and he has his right hand on his thigh and her thumb is not visible and the left arm is leaning on the elbow with the hand holding the left cheek, the feet are crossed, and next to the left knee he is touching the handle of an axe; she holds two children with her right hand, and she has a spindle"; and so with all the rest of its main features. The purpose of this was that, were they to bring a painting to be sold and we wanted to purchase it, since there are many of them, we would not know whether this particular one was in the library, and so seeing the figures or objects it [i.e., the painting or engraving] has, and its features, they would see whether it was there by consulting with these books and checking the size, and if it was not, it should be bought immediately, and if it was, then it would not be bought twice.

(4)

My lord don Hernando, who is in Heaven, also had a great desire to collect many books, indeed all those he could find (as he in fact did) [*lo puso por la obra*], and he gathered and stored in his library most of those which had been printed until his own days and left rent so that any others that emerged could be purchased. This keen desire that he had was and still is worthy of admiration, and from it comes and always will come incomparable profit, although many thoughtlessly have cheated it of its fame or ignored it, since they thought that the money and the time spent in this truly holy work would have been better employed in falconry or in other more knightly endeavors, and although they do not say so in plain terms, this is what they actually mean, because they do not approve of what he did. But setting them aside, I say this work is, as I have said, worthy of great admiration and so that I can express my feelings, I wish the Holy Ghost would illuminate my understanding and enliven my tongue to be able to tell it as I feel it, because trying to magnify or laud it is madness, since the task speaks for itself; for the work and effort employed in collecting these books, and the expense was so much, and so big, that it could not be either expressed nor even felt unless one were involved in it.

But leaving all of this aside for some other time and place, and getting down to what is more to our purpose, namely the benefit that results from these books, I say that beyond my lord don Hernando's proposal to employ time and energy in such a virtuous work as it was to study and apply himself in things of knowledge and make good use of his talents [*dar cuenta de su talento*], and besides wishing that knowledge would be preserved here [*aquí se conservasen las ciencias*] so that it would not perish in our Spain and so that those who are learned and inclined to virtue could here find remedy for their doubts, and books that perhaps even with a lot of effort could not be found, and besides many other sorts of benefits that he intended, as appears in his testament, the main wish he had was the promotion of knowledge [*sçiençias*] so that one could become very and truly knowledgeable [*sabio*] in as short time as possible and with the least possible effort, for it weighed upon him, as truly it should weigh upon us all, that there were so many books about law, when in truth to say, with just one, or at least with four at most, if they were properly conceived, one could rule/order [*regir*] the world; and so in medicine too one [book] would suffice to cure all natural diseases, and the same in grammar: a well-thought-out art [of grammar] would suffice to teach it, and so in the rest of disciplines [*sçiençias*]; and so he proposed, and many times did he tell me, that he planned, if only God would grant him life and means, to leave in this house a dozen scholars, whom he called *sumistas,* with very good salaries, so that there would be excellent men who would summarize or facilitate the understanding of disciplines [*sçiençias*] by reducing them to greater brevity and ease of understanding. For were this to be done, anyone can imagine the huge profit that would accrue to us from it [*juzgue cada uno el demasiado provecho de que aquí nos veniera*].

And so to put into effect what he so desired it was necessary to establish some foretastes or foundations and open some new path upon which those tasks that lay ahead could be framed, and so he took up and began four most marvelous works, the first of epitomes, the second of subject matters [*materias*], the third one authors, the fourth topics [*sçiençias*], which were begun, and to a great extent completed, and they are in the library in the aforementioned place, as follows:

There are two old books in quarto, manuscripts, in a very bad hand,[5] bound in parchment and tied together, which are the epitomes of the books in the library, which is to say summaries of what each book contains at greater length. And one of them is transcribed into another large book that there is, which I shall mention later; although those of which fair copies[6] were made are not all corrected; they should be corrected as I shall say below.

Of the other one, which is the smaller, there is no fair copy. So one of them needs to be corrected and compared with the other big one to see if it is properly transcribed, and this will be easily done on account of the numeric order they have, as the numeration of these epitomes in the small book correspond to the same numbers of the epitomes in the large book, which numbers are at the top of the epitome by way of a title; and the other book of epitomes of which there is no fair copy will have to be made into a fair copy, for it is in a very bad hand and corrected in the same order I said the other one should be corrected.

(5)

There is besides a large book with folio pages[7] bound in white parchment, manuscript, in a good hand, which was mentioned above, which contains the clean copies of the epitomes transcribed from the old one we mentioned, the one in quarto and in a very bad hand; this [folio], as has been mentioned, needs to be corrected. But be aware that at the beginning there are some epitomes with two numbers, one within a box and the other not, in this manner

153 [25]

The first number, which is not in the box, is the number that corresponds to the order in which the epitome had been produced and does not correspond to its order in the library, because they were taken out at random, and so sometimes a book with number 5632 in the library was taken out, but in the epitomes that was not its number; rather if before this one thirty epitomes of other books had been produced, this one was numbered thirty-one because there were no other epitomes but these, and so on with the rest. The other number I mentioned, in the box, is of no use any more because it was to show in the book of subject matters [*libro de las materias*], which I shall describe later on, under which number that book's matters had been entered; and [the numbers] are not of any use for this any more because you can find this out in the index [*Índice Numeral* or *Registrum B*]. Be aware that toward the end of this book of epitomes, in some new quires, in many epitomes you will find two numbers, one at the very top; only this one corresponds to the original epitome from which it was transcribed, which will serve to correct it with that corresponding number; the other number (which goes after the name of the author who composed that book from which the epitome was produced) is the number that this book had in the library according to the old numeration, which can be used to find that book in question in the library according to the instructions that I will provide shortly. And it is true that, although I have said that the epitomes that have been transcribed into a clean copy must be corrected, not all of them [require this] since some of them have already been revised: they are those who have the note *vidi* next to them in the margin, which means that the epitome has been revised and corrected, and there are others corrected by myself and the Master [*el maestro*]:[8] they have no marker, but it is easy to see that there are in them some parts which are erased and amended on the margin.

The great benefit of this book of epitomes is very obvious because it allows you to know in brief that which the book treats more diffusely, and if a person cannot afford to have many books to read, at least he will have one that will give him a sense of the contents of many books, and this allows him, if he finds the book and the subject it treats fitting, to buy it, and if he does not, then he will leave it, and will not be cheated in buying it, since there are many books of grand and swollen titles which then do not deal with what [the title] promises, and printers do this to swindle [*por engañar*]. So if you have this book of epitomes they will not deceive you because if you want to know, say, what Erasmus's *Silenus* is all about, you can go to this book's epitome and there you will briefly find all the substance of its contents. The way in which they have to be searched and found will be recounted when we deal with the indexes [*Índice Numeral*] that are there to search for books in the library.

So everybody can now judge whether this was a great foundation for what I mentioned above, which was the facilitation of knowledge [*sçiençias*], and consider what great effort and cost he employed in this, and you will see whether he spent his time properly, he who devoted so much industry to such great good, and invested his life and property in it.

(6)

The second book, which we said my lord Don Hernando, who is in Heaven, had meant to make in order to fulfill his desire, was of subject matters [*materias*], and accordingly he left four old books in quarto, manuscript, in a bad hand, bound in old parchment, which deal with subject matters and are now all tied together, from which another four books have been transcribed, which we shall mention later, which are in alphabetical order and whose purpose will be described below. These four books I just mentioned are not completely transcribed in the other four large books, and whatever is transcribed has a long stroke like this one

in the margin; the lines that lack this mark need to be transcribed taking the first letter and searching for it in the other large books and there record them in their proper place in alphabetical order, so that if a certain subject matter begins *Cristi* [*sic*] *passio*, they must go under the letter *c* in the large books and they will check whether it is transcribed, and if it is not, they will have to put it in its proper place, considering all the letters—by which I mean that they must keep an alphabetical order in all its letters, syllables, and dictions;[9] the numbers that are in these four books correspond to the order in which they were recorded [*que se sacaban*]—not that of the library, but rather according to the time at which it was done; their purpose is to facilitate a search of their subject matters, since in the index we can find those same numbers with a certain marking, as we shall explain when we deal with that.

(7)

There are besides four other large books that have been taken from these four small ones we mentioned above, which are gatherings of manuscript folios, in a reasonably good hand, bound in white parchment and with bands in black leather where the stitches [*puntadas*] are, which are in the library in the aforementioned place, and each of them is bound by itself, and they go in alphabetic order from *a* till the end; their name is, as I have said, books of subject matters, although they would be best referred to as *annotations;* their advantage is considerable as their contents demonstrate. The way in which they are produced is as follows:

Any author who composes a work always has a particular intention, although under this he always deals with other matters that aid and serve his ultimate purpose. So on those things which are his main subject and on its most notable related topics three or four annotations are elaborated, according to the most remarkable matters within the book and what they concern, in the following way: if Erasmus in his *Lengua* deals with the harm that comes from the improper use of language and the benefits from good use, then two annotations must be made, which will read thus: "lingue prabe [*sic*] incomoda [*sic*] difuse docet Erasmus in sua lingua 4329; and the other one: lingue bone comoda [*sic*] difuse çentur (= docentur), in lingua Erasmi 4329"; and this number is that which this book (where these things are dealt with) has in the library; and be aware that such annotations always begin with the most common term for the subjects dealt with in it, so that whoever wishes to find it can do so more easily; because although I might wish to use something similar to lingua, I will not use [a difficult phrase such as] *oris incommoda* for the entry, just as in many other examples we could bring forth. It is true that many other annotations could be made about a book such as Erasmus's *Lengua,* since it deals with many other remarkable things which are good to know, such as the nature of the asp, which is a certain kind of poisonous snake, and we would say: *aspidis naturam breviter doçet Erasmus in sira (= sua) lingua.* It should also be considered that the same annotation could begin with two very common terms, and such annotation can be recorded twice so that whoever wants to can find it in this way: there being a book that deals with the *Encarnaçione* [*sic*], some will think of it being under *Jesuchristi,* others rather that it is under *Cristi* [*sic*]; so that no one is misled, and so it can be more easily found, it will be recorded in two different places in the following manner: one will say *Cristi, etc.,* the other one will say *Jesuchristi;* the first one will be recorded under *c,* and the second one under *i* so that they will more easily find it either in one place or the other and cannot miss it, because if it were to be placed only in one of them perhaps they would search it in the other one, and not finding it, they would think that there was no such subject matter and they would be left without the benefit that might come from it.

These aforesaid books have their numbers after the subject matter, which are those that identify the books in the library according to an old numbering so that if, once the subject matter has been located, someone would consult the book itself, he can find it easily, because although now they may not have the same numbers they used to have, they serve as guides and aids to find it in the supplement that shall be mentioned later on. Also be aware that in these books there are some abbreviations, and so wherever you come across a *b,* it means *brebter* [*sic*], and a *d* means *difuse,* and where there is a *p t* this means *per totun* [*sic*], because it was necessary and very helpful to record whether such an author or book that deals with such a matter does so briefly or diffusely or throughout, so that anyone searching in it, can know in what manner it is dealt with. They will also find in these subject matters boxes like this

which were intended to include other numbers, which are not yet entered, to cross-reference other books that dealt with the same subject matter; it remains to decide what is best, since they were left imperfect and unpolished because the plan was to make them briefer and in a different way, if death had not precluded it, but even in their current state they are very useful and very beneficial. You will also find now that they were returning to transcribe these subject matters, leaving one side of the leaf blank, as can be seen in the first volume, and this was because, since they should go in alphabetical order and they could not the first time be arranged with much accuracy, they were to be cut again as slips of paper and arranged in their alphabetical order, and that is the reason why one side of the leaf is left blank, because [otherwise], if they were to be cut as required, they would cut the letters on one of the sides; this is the reason why it was necessary to do this.

The great benefit of these [annotations on] subject matters was very obvious and so it was praised by all the scholars who have seen them, because thanks to them many admirable things may come to be known, and who treats of them in the best way, and where, so if one, for example, would like to compose a sermon or write on the passion, he can go to *Cristi posione* [*sic*], etc., and there he would see in great abundance who and how many have dealt with this subject, and who does so copiously and who does so briefly; and if someone were to compose an oration in praise of Spain, by going to *Hispanie laudes,* etc., there he will find what he desires. See, then, whether this is of little profit: to provide everything which is searched for, all of it properly cooked and even (as the saying goes) chewed up [*darle guisado todo lo que busca y aun como suelen dezir dárselo mascado*]; see, therefore, whether much is owed to one who procured so much good, since in what has already been done not a little effort and money was employed, and all directed toward the common good.

(8)

Table of sciences and authors.[10] There are besides in the library some slips of paper strung together [*manojos de papeles cortados y ensartados*], which go almost from the first book in the library to a little over ten thousand, although in between some are missing and there are some others beyond ten thousand; we call these annotations [*anotaçiones*] and they were to be used to compose the table of the sciences and authors, to know how many authors have written about which sciences; and these constitute the two last books I mentioned above (calling them authors and sciences), but bringing the authors together and the disciplines aside, as we will see in the instruction there is for it [*o poner los auctores solos y las sçiençias aparte commo se verá por la instrucción que hay para ello*].[11]

These slips or annotations as I have said before are arranged according to the library number, in the following manner: taking the book, the science with which it deals is looked into, and then this and the subdiscipline to which it corresponds are recorded, so that, if a book consists in an exposition of the Psalms, then we must give [the annotation] *theologia psalmorum* as a title, and then the annotation would begin with the name of the author of the book, if there is one, and if there is no author, the title of the work, and after this the substance of what it is about in two words, or in the shortest way possible, and then the incipit of the book, with its corresponding symbol,[12] and then the ending of the book with its corresponding symbol too, and then what prologues, and epistles, and epigrams it has, and after this the name of the place where it was printed, abbreviated according to the conventions for the towns where there are printers, and then the year of printing in figures, and then the number in the library underlined in the following manner 5342 (= 5342), and then its dimensions using the appropriate symbols, as explained in great detail in two sets of instructions that there are, both of them treating the same thing, in the hand of my lord don Hernando: one of which I have in the library, and the other one is kept by the *licenciado* Marcos Felipe.

But since these annotations include many symbols, used within them and also elsewhere, it is fitting to say something about them so that the memory of them is not lost, and what I shall say about them here applies wherever they are found.

Anywhere in these annotations where this symbol is found

means that what is written afterward is the opening of the author or work in question, until we reach another one like this

which means that what is after this sign is the end, and thus ends the author or work in question. And if there is a prologue in the work, we use this sign

and then the first word of the prologue in question; and this sign

means that it has an epistle, and then follows the first word of the epistle in question; and this sign

means that the work in question has an epigram, and then follows the first word of the epigram in question; but be advised that if there are two or more prologues, they are recorded by means of a number, in the following manner

quoniam, 2 antiqui

which means that the work in question has two prologues, and the first one begins *quoniam* and the second one *antiqui,* and the same applies to the epistles and the epigrams, but with this difference, that if the epistles in question are either one, or both of them, at the end, we underline the ones at the end in the following manner

vehementer, 2 (= 2) cum sepe

which means that the book in question has two epistles, one at the beginning that commences *vehementer,* and the other one, because it is at the end, its number is underlined, and it begins *cum sepe;* and if both were at the end, both symbols [i.e., numbers] would be underlined; and this applies as much to epigrams as to prologues, although no prologue is ever placed at the end. And be aware that we label any text in prose an epistle, even one which is not a prologue as such, indeed it might be the prayer of a saint; and we label anything written in verse an epigram, even if it is a distich or any other kind of verse. And then after these symbols comes the name of the place where the book was printed, abbreviated according to the abbreviations that are listed on a sheet posted in the library [*un papel que está enclavado en la librería*], and after the name the year when it was printed, in this way: P1532 it means that it was printed in Paris in the year of one thousand and five hundred and thirty and two years; and so *L.* means Lyon in France, *AL.* Alcalá, and so on with the rest. Then after this comes the size of the books with their respective symbols, as follows:

means that the book in question is a royal folio [*marca real*],[13] which is the large size, and the following

means folio, of the standard size, and this one

means that it is the quarto, from a sheet divided in four parts, and this one

means octavo, which is a sheet divided into eight different parts, and this one

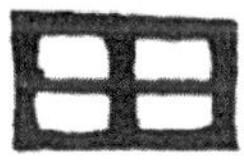

means sexto-decimo, which is a sheet divided into sixteen parts, because in these different sizes are all books made. There are other signs for the volume [of the books] which are used alongside these of size, in the following manner

meaning that the book in question uses half a sheet, because the first one is the sign of half a sheet, and the second one a folio using half a sheet, the third one a quarto using half a sheet, the fourth one an octavo using half a sheet, the fifth is sexto-decimo using half a sheet, according to what has been said.[14] There are other ones, which are the following

which mean that the book in question is a single page, and its size according to its respective sign; these

mean that the work in question is *ultrapica* [a pamphlet] which is more than one page [*pliego*] and less than five; these

mean that the work in question has five pages or more and less than ten, which we call *tractatus;* these

mean that the work in question has ten pages or more, but less than twenty, which we call *tractatulos;* these

mean that such books have twenty pages [*pliegos*] or more, but less than forty, which we call *liber paruus;* these

with a point in the middle of the triangle mean that the book in question has forty pages or more, but less than eighty, which we call *liber mediocris;* these

mean that the book has more than eighty pages, which we call *liber magnus*. These same symbols can also be placed on the other side [*se postponen*], in the following way

which means that the book in question is in royal folio [*marca real*] and it is between twenty and forty pages and that another one which is next to it is of two pages or three, up to five; and this one

means a book in quarto of more than ten pages, but less than twenty, which is next to another small book of twenty pages or more but less than forty; and so on with the other signs whether they are on the other side or not. There are also sometimes in these symbols a dot or two inside, in the following manner

which means that the books in question are in two columns, and if they did not have it the line runs to the end of the page; there are some others in the following manner

which means that the books in question have arguments [*capitulos epitomáticos*], chapters into which they are divided, and I mean "arguments" when they provide a brief summary of the contents of each chapter; and although it may say "Chapter Twelve" in large print, if it does not say what it is about, it is not considered as composed with arguments [*capítulos epitomáticos*] and thus this sign will not be used for those books that do not have such chapters; there are also these ones

which mean such books have indexes or alphabetic tables of the most relevant matters or vocabulary, and be aware that although there may be indexes, if they are not in alphabetic order, these symbols should not be used. Then, toward the end, after these said symbols, comes the number which the book in question has in the library, underlined in the following way 5342, whose purpose is to locate the book for whoever is searching for it in the *Fernandina Library*—because that is, and should be, the name of our library.

In the margins of these annotations there are also certain symbols to identify the language in which the book in question is written, as books in all languages are included in the library, in the following manner: *Ita.* means Italian, *espa.* Spanish, *grec.* Greek, *heb.* Hebrew, *cat.* Catalan, *ax.* Arabic, *gall.* French, *bar.* Barbaric, and we call Barbaric all the other languages, such as German, Flemish, Hungarian, etc., and they are underlined with two lines [*virgulitas*] to differentiate them, lest someone think it has to be amended.[15] There are other symbols, for instance a poetry book will have this sign:

in the margin, and one which is half poetry and half prose will have this symbol:

A manuscript will have this symbol

in the margin if the writing is good, because if it is in a [bad] hand, it will feature these little points in the following manner

which means it is written in a bad hand. Incomplete books [*libros faltos*] will also bear this symbol

in the margin, which means that such book lacks some pages, or quires [*cuaderno*], at the beginning or the end; but if the book is also damaged, the symbol will be like this

and crossed; and if it is stained, the symbol will be like this

with points. In the margins they will also find this symbol

which are two long lines and this is to distinguish authors from translators, because the symbol of two lines means that it is a translator who rendered the text from Greek to Latin, or from Latin into Romance, or into any other tongue. They may also find a cross in the following manner

in the margins, which we call *pro vel contra,* and it marks a book where some author defends another, or rebuts [*impugna*] him, so one can identify who wrote against Erasmus and who defended him, and who against Luther, and so on with the rest; therefore, whoever has this symbol is opposing or defending another. There is also this symbol

which is to supplement the names, because many are better known for their sobriquets than by their own names, and so Calepinus is better known by this name rather than Ambrosius, which is his actual name, and because in the index and in these annotations he is under his own name which is Ambrosius Calepinus, it was necessary to create a supplement in the following manner

Calepinus Ambrosius (= Ambrosius)

underlining the name that must be used for the search, which means that if you are looking for Calepinus, you will find him under this his name which is Ambrosius Calepinus, and so with the rest; and also for the works which are better known for their names, and so for *Cornucopia* we shall say

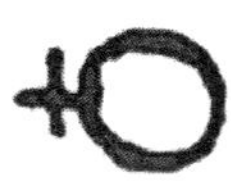

Cornucopia: Nicolhai Peroti Cornucopia

which means that you can find it under the name of its author, and the same with the others.

The benefit of these annotations is incomparable, both for the organization of the library and otherwise, because, since the intent of its founder was to collect all the books that have been written and always buy the best latest editions, it is useful to have a record to know how the book begins, and how it ends, and which epistles, prologues, and epigrams it has, and information about the edition [*y qué impresión*] and dimensions [*grandor*], because although there may be a copy of the same book in the library, if by chance there is another one which is more complete, it was his [i.e., Hernando's] will, that it should be bought. So, let the learned consider whether it is good or not to have a book with all the authors that exist and with information about the disciplines they wrote on, and if they approve of this, let them be grateful and hold in great esteem the thought and the effort that has been invested, and which will be invested until the entire task is completed, and let them also pray to God for the soul of him who devoted himself to this task and who left funds to complete it, and also for the souls of those who did so much good in giving us a gentleman like him in today's world.

(9)

Since in all things my lord don Hernando Colón, who is in Heaven, was so provident, he did not wish his library to be a dead library, as the rest are, where, before finding a book, the user must look up and down all the shelves and books, and read all the titles. In order to deal with this, he arranged it so that once a book had been requested, it could be handed over, and so he left two books in manuscript pages [*pliego*], bound in wooden boards [*tablas de madera*] and black leather, which are the general indexes of authors and books and *incipits* of the books in the library, and they are arranged in alphabetical order. The first and largest goes from *a* to *j*, the second, and smaller, goes from *l* to *z*. In these, as I have said, there are names of authors, names of works with no author, and all the *incipits* of these authors and the works, and all of it in proper alphabetical order, so that if one were to search for a book which is in the library, knowing that the name will show up if it is there, then he will obtain it very easily by looking it up by its number that is in the same book, and if the user does not know how it begins they will give it to him using the same method; and this was an excellent design for this purpose and also for the acquisition of books, to avoid the deception of booksellers, who frequently and maliciously, in order to sell a book as a new work, remove the name of the author and sell it without it, or under the name of another; but if they look up the *incipit* in these indexes, they will not be deceived; and thus happened to my lord don Hernando Colón who, when in search of these books, some booksellers tried to sell him a book of law by Juan Andrés as if it was by someone else, and he looked at the *incipit* and saw that it was by Juan Andrés, and told this to the bookseller who acknowledged it was true and even begged him not to tell anybody else because he would never sell it if this were known; so this was a great design.

It is important to be aware that many authors in this index have two, three, or even four different numbers, each of them identified with symbols in the following manner

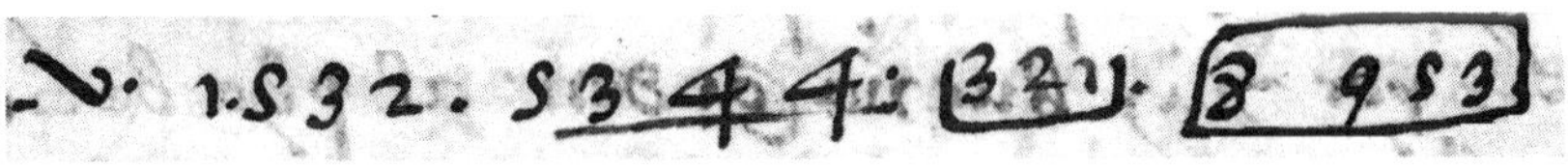

Note that the number which is not underlined and has a single letter before it, indicates the edition, conforming to what I said about the annotations; it says it was printed in Venice and that is why it has a *v* and the year of a thousand and five hundred and thirty-two; the second number which is underlined in the following manner 5344 is the number that the book has in the library, so that it can be found when it is requested, and this according to the old numbers; the third one, between three lines in this manner

and it is the number that the subject matter of the book in question has in the Book of Subject Matters [*Libro de las Materias*], which we mentioned above, and it means that in this number you must go and search its matters; the fourth number which is in the box, in this manner

is the number that it has in the epitome of the author in question in the book of epitomes which I mentioned above, and it indicates that at the epitome that has that number they will find the epitome of this author; so that according to these cross-references [*esta remision*] they can search and find all they may want to know about that book in question, because if the index says

Erasmus adagia seu prouerbia

it means that under number 2466 and under number 12910 they will find this book in the library, and that it was printed in Basel, which is what *b* means, and in the year 1533, and that its subject matter will be found in the Book of Subject Matters [*Libro de las Materias*] under number

and that the epitome of the book in question they will find in the book of epitomes under number

3130

And since there are books in the library which are duplicated, and whose subject matters and epitomes, for lack of attention, were recorded twice, so these numbers will appear twice, which means that they will find it in the library or in the subject matters or in the epitomes as shown by the sign that the number was duplicated, and so they will see that the book we demarcate with two underlined numbers, which means that it appears twice in the library under those names; and also, because there are many books which lack information about the place of publication, or about which there is no record of subject matters, nor an epitome, they will simply be identified by one number and this will be the library number, by which I mean the old number, because it is important to be aware that up until now the books were all kept together and the sciences mixed up and confused among them, and at that time they had this number which we refer to as the old one; now they have been arranged according to sciences so that all the books that correspond to a science are together, and those old numbers we had are of no use now, because the one that was 771 is the first one now; but eliminating these numbers now would be a great problem, since the epitomes and subject matters and the tables of disciplines and authors all of them cross-reference each other using those old numbers, so it would confound everything. In order to solve this there is now a supplement in such an order that the old numbers can be used to find the new ones, in the following way: the first book which is now in the library was before 771 according to the old order, and now, according to the new one it comes first, and therefore we make a numbered list [*numeral*] that includes all the numbers from the books between 1 and 15332, and it says:

771.1̄

which means that the former number 771 now is the first one, so that once the old number it used to have has been located in the index, I can go to the supplement and look it up, and this number takes me to the new current number, saying: 771, 1̄, and there will also be another record in inverse order, with the new number first, before the old one, in the following manner

1̄.771

so that by the new number we can identify the old one, and with the old one, we can identify the new, and the way we recorded this was by adding a line on top of the new one, and underlining the old one, so we know which is the old and which is the new. Note also that the incipit [entries] of books do not have this distinction in numbers we spoke of above because it is enough that the author [entry] bears it, because the incipit is only used to search for books, and this incipit can also be found in the supplement according to the method we mentioned above. It is also important to know that because in many places these indexes were very cramped and the writing was so compressed that new works could not be written in, it was necessary to create a supplement (for the works which did not fit in their proper alphabetical place) which is in the main body of the indexes, toward the end of it, in the same alphabetical order, and whenever you find something recorded with the following symbol on the margin

understand that in this place there should be other works, but because there was not enough space for them, they went in the supplement, and they will find it under the first letter of the author or the work, as they will see with the works of Saint Jerome or Erasmus, or in many others that have the said symbol. Consider thus the great advantage of these indexes and judge for yourself the effort that was invested thus in collecting so many books from foreign lands in times of so many wars and so much dissension, and in recording them and providing them with the marvelous order I have mentioned, so that any book can be found easily and with no effort, and you will see that it is a project never seen before our times, of great marvelous artifice and immense benefit, and therefore worthy of immortal fame and eternal praise, and its author deserving of sempiternal glory.

(10)

Besides these two aforementioned indexes there is in the library a large book bound in wooden boards and red leather, which has a manuscript part, in a small and very good hand, which is also an index of books but not in alphabetical but in numerical order, by which I mean the number that the books have in the library in the following manner which starts with the numbers and says

1

is such a book and its author was such and such, and it has such an incipit and such ending, it has such epistles and such epigrams and it was published in such place, and it has such format, its price was such in such place, so that all the information about the book is recorded there, and all things which are relevant about it and which must be recorded, and this was done from the first book up to 4231, and because afterward the number of books grew to a great quantity, it could not be continued and its composition was abandoned, except for the numbers which were continued, until the last one which is in the library, and so most of its numbers are on blank pages. This was used for the purchase of the books, to know what any new book brings, whether more or less material, and also in case a book was lost or stolen, we could identify it to buy again, and this could be very easily known in the following manner: knowing that a book was missing whose number was 3215, they went to the book with this number and the record gave all the particulars of such a book, as I have explained, and from this record it was known what should be purchased; this information could not be known from the other indexes, because they are arranged in alphabetical order by author, and this one is the numeral order of the books; and although [the books] were not recorded [in detail] there, as I have just said, above 4231, and the rest are only numbers, a measure was taken such that by the number alone the book could be identified, with certain numbers in small writing which referred to the column [numbers] in the other indexes in the following manner: if there is 4232 and then 175, this means that you should go to the [alphabetical] index and in column 175 you will find that number 4232 and by that number you will find out which book it is. But since this was never completed, and there are already other new numbers and new measures are required to gather this information, because it is very necessary for the library, nothing else will be specified here, although whoever wants to know something or make inquiries can do so using this method.

There is besides in this book [*Registrum B*] the new supplement that is being made for the books, in numeral order, in the arrangement I described above, in the [section on the] indexes of the library. Therefore this book was a marvelous instrument for the use of the library.

(11)

There are besides five other books in quarto pages [*cuarto de pliego*], bound in parchment, manuscript in a reasonable hand, in which are all the names of the authors and works, or books whose author is unknown, and they have their own names all in alphabetical order, with the numbers they have in the library according to the old number (which now must be converted to the new one), and also the number of the epitome and the number of the subject matter and the name of the place where it was printed and the size of the book, with all the symbols and abbreviations for these things, as I mentioned [in the section] about the indexes of the library. Whoever wants to know must go back to what I said or to the first or second page of one of these five books, and there he will find all that can be known about was has been written.[16]

There is besides another small sixth book in the same manner as these ones, which is a supplement for these five, I mean that the authors that could not be found in their proper place will be found in this supplement under their respective letters because it is also in alphabetic order, and the reason was the one I mentioned in the [section on the] indexes: since in many parts within the indexes there was not enough space for the new authors and works, it was necessary to create a supplement within them, and a symbol that referred to them in the place where they should be found, and thus it was done as I have said. But since these five books were transcribed from the indexes, those who transcribed them did not know about the sign [*aviso,* i.e., the sign that referred them to the proper place in the new numeration], or did not become aware of it, when they found the sign, they did not search for it to put it in its proper place, and so it was necessary to transcribe also the supplement to the indexes, and so this sixth volume I mentioned was transcribed, in the same alphabetical order, where you will find all the authors and the works that are missing in the other five, and so they will find that in them that the works of Saint Jerome are missing, but they can find them in the supplement under the letter *h.* Note that in the supplement of the indexes there are some authors that are not arranged alphabetically, but that they are in the end, each of them on their own, such as Erasmus, Lucian, Saint Thomas, Symphorien, the works of Our Lady, musical works, and some others, that are also in this supplement in the same manner, and so the works by Galen will not be found in their proper place, nor in the supplement, but set apart, toward the end of the supplement, and so with all the others. And not even this supplement is yet complete, and part of it is even faulty because many works which are in the other supplement are not in this one, since it was a very arduous task, don Hernando my lord left it to a young man, who did it and mangled it, and he transcribed some titles as though they were incipits of the books and left them thus, and other incipits of the books he thought were titles and recorded them accordingly; all of it must be revised and corrected.

These five works with the sixth (which is the supplement to them) were meant to furnish the table of authors that was being made, and for this purpose a blank was left between one author and the next so that new ones could be put there; and this is the reason why they are not written on more than one side, because they would have to be cut out and put in numeric order or by sciences as I said of the others above; but now this will only serve as an index of the authors alone, and not of *incipits* like the general indexes, which have everything in them; and if the indexes are taken off for use when buying books these ones will stay in the library to find authors that are being looked for.

(12)

There is besides a book in quarto of a sheet, manuscript, bound in white parchment, in horizontal format, in the manner of music books, which was meant for the index of authors and sciences [*sçiençias*] and had certain numbers that referred to the subject matters, but since this is being now done in a different way, it seems that this one is not and will not be of use, as the manuscript note by lord don Hernando (who is in Heaven), says, that it will be of no use.

(13)

As I said above, all the intent of don Hernando my lord was to facilitate knowledge [*sçiençias*] and thus he wanted to make a vocabulary, taking from all the others the pith and the best of them, and so he began it, and left in the library a big book in paper folios [*pliego de papel*], in manuscript of his own hand, bound in white parchment, and with very large margins, which is the dictionary or vocabulary in alphabetical order and it does not have anything other than *a* and a little of *b*, and in it are specified all the meanings that a word [*dicción*] has, and which authors use it, and in which parts [of their works], importing into all the authorities; which would be of great profit if it could be finished, as would all the rest, but death, envious of our fortune [*provecho*], would not let him reach beyond *b*. The blank margins were left thus on purpose so that if any authority was found for the definition of a word, it could be written there. It has at the beginning an alphabetical table of some words [*dicciones*] that are in it, with their number, which refers to the pages [*planas*] where such a phrase [*dicción*] or word is treated, and each leaf has two numbers, with each page [*plana*] its own. This is a work of great benefit and proves the great knowledge and experience of its author.

(14)

There is besides another large book of manuscript pages, bound in white parchment, which is the memorandum of books from numbers 825 to 2562, which lord don Hernando, who is in Heaven, bought in Venice, and sent here to his library; and, fearing that which did eventually happen, he kept custody of this memorandum of them, in which is the name of the author who wrote the book, or the work if there was no author, and the *incipit* and the *explicit,* and the prologues, and epistles and epigrams and the place of publication and the size and where it had been bought and how much it had cost; but these books, alongside many drawings and most excellent pictures, were lost in a carrack that sank, and only this memorandum remained of them, which will be used to know whether these books have been repurchased or not, because to say the truth many of these, it is believed, have been repurchased. The way in which this can be done is by looking up the name of the author or the work that you wish to find, and then they will see whether it is in the index, and if they find it there, it means that it has been repurchased; then they will take the number that the book in question has in the library and must annotate it on the margin of this book (near the author in question) within a box, which signals that that book with the number in the box has already been repurchased, and that the number above it is of no use because [that copy] was lost and another one obtained in its place; and in this manner, after revising everything, those which do not have the said symbol have not been repurchased; it will then be necessary to repurchase them and give them an appropriate number because, as I have said, the number that they have in this volume is useless because others have already been assigned these numbers.

(15)

There are besides two very large books, in giant folio (*marca real*), bound in wooden boards and red leather, and one of them has no writing but only lines and numbers, the other one has some writing, with the same numbers, lines, and symbols. These were meant to be very general indexes of brief [entries on] everything that has been written until now, with their letters and symbols so they could be found according to the instructions which are now in the hands of the *licenciado* Marcos Felipe. But they will be of no use any more unless another don Hernando comes back to life [*sic*], because it is a work that requires great learning, I mean great knowledge, and great experience, and great memory and wit, and extended and great effort and expense, and death took away the one who had all of this, and thus deprived us of such great benefit as would emanate from this, and for our sins he was taken from us.

(16)

There are besides three small paper books [*de pliego*] which are all tied together, manuscript, bound in old parchment, which are of no use because what they contain dates back to when the books started to be purchased, and is already transcribed elsewhere, particularly in the index I mentioned which is ordered by numbers.

These are the works that don Hernando Colón my lord left unfinished which are now in the library, without considering many others he left, some of them unfinished, some of them completed but not yet registered. May Our Lord grant him Glory for the effort that in the advancement of letters he took up for the common good, and may He also grant us grace to serve him and embrace virtue, and praying God for the soul of him who left so much good, and of his ancestors, and may he grant us glory too afterward, amen.

TWO
Hernando's Will

These extensive sections of Hernando's will deal with his plans for the library after his death and provide us with important details on the running of the library during his lifetime and the stage reached in various projects pertaining to it.[1]

I leave all my books in custody of the admiral don Luis Colón, my nephew, and to his heirs and successors in his admiralship, as long as the conditions and instructions that I shall describe below are respected; if they are not kept the custody will go to the church and monasteries that I shall list in the proper order. . . . I attach [*anexo*] my property to the library.

[After several paragraphs listing numerous outstanding debts which must be paid before the estate is disposed of, Hernando outlines his central legacy to his library.]

I leave whatever remains of my property and wealth for the maintenance and augmentation of the library. And a month after my death those responsible for the expenses and administration of my household should reckon and establish its value, alongside my executor and three suitable persons under oath, including the house, gardens, and all the items within them, and then calculate how much can be bought in public annuities. And if the lord admiral aforesaid wishes to take charge of the goods, house, and orchard, the equivalent amount must be dedicated to the upkeep of the said library, or he must commit [an amount from] his own income, so that the said amount is secured and available to the satisfaction of my executors. . . .

The income to be spent in the library . . .

The first expense each year will be employed in the purchase of printed books here in Seville or in Salamanca which are not in the collection, or if they are, only those cases in which the new ones are more complete editions; and manuscripts must be bought at moderate prices. And no more than half of the yearly income will be spent in the purchase of books, for the other half will be employed in bindings, and stalls [*bancos*][2] and chains and other implements for the library. And when the yearly income reaches thirty thousand *maravedís,* ten thousand will be spent on books, another ten thousand on bindings, and the other ten thousand will be paid to the best Latin scholar who applies for the post, whose task will be to continue with the tables of authors and sciences and epitomes and subject matters according to the instructions that I have left for this purpose. And in this task he must employ two hours each day.

What to do with the extra income

In case the rent exceeds these thirty thousand *maravedís,* the equivalent percentage must be increased and employed in each of the three areas described above, but if there is no reason to overspend, then the remaining funds must be invested until the benefits afford the purchase of an annuity of ten thousand *maravedís* or more.

Hiring new *sumistas* if there is a surplus

If the income exceeds thirty thousand, the third to be spent on a scholar or scholars will be increased to twenty ducats per [daily] hour whenever there is enough for it, so that if the scholar who was paid ten thousand for two hours [of work a day] would be capable and willing to work an extra hour, he will be paid twenty ducats more, and another twenty if he works for four hours [in total], and so on, but never beyond six hours—even if he is willing to do so, and there is enough income, since it is certain that he will not work as he should for such a long time.

Fines and rewards for the *sumista*[3]

If the *sumista* works fewer hours than initially agreed, this must be docked from his wages, and increased if he happens to work overtime.

Room and bed for the *sumista*

The *sumista* will have a room near the library with a table and a cot bed [*cama de campo*] of mine with bed linen and a pallet and two mattresses, four white sheets and pillows, a bed cover, a blanket, a chest, a chair and a wooden bench to sit, and a big cupboard for books and documents. The door must be repaired and all this furniture must be in proper condition for ready use, and whatever must be renewed or replaced, it must be bought with the third that was allotted for bindings and other implements for the library.

How the *sumista* is to be appointed

This master or scholar must pass an exam in Salamanca, after the post is advertised a month earlier in Alcalá. And he will be under obligation to hold tenure for three years, of which one will be employed in training in the necessary skills, and the other two he will do whatever he pleases as long as he follows the procedures established in the library, a copy of which will be made available in Salamanca at the time of the exam.

Monthly Visitation

The person holding custody next in succession must send for a day or so at the end of each month a learned person [the Visitor] who can oversee how these tasks are performed, and upon his conscience [the custodian] must send the fittest person he can find and for those twelve visits [the Visitor] will be paid a salary of twelve ducats, and each time he must employ an entire day in the task.

Corrections of the custodian and the *sumista*

Whatever faults are found attributable to the custodian and the *sumista* in the library (for that is how the scholar or scholars in charge of this will be called) will be recorded in a white bound volume, so they know what needs to be fixed, and at the end of the year the book will provide an account to the next Visitor so that he can know whether he who preceded him made impositions during his commission or whether there is anything he must require them to do or to mend.

How the books are to be arranged

As regards the arrangement of the books, I hope that our Lord will grant me life and means to build a large room and place in it, starting at the bottom of the walls, cases [*caxones*] just as the books are now arranged in them, on end [*de canto*] each of them with their title, name, and number [showing outward]. The subjects must be separated according to the table of sciences. Six feet away from the wall, which is two *varas* [thirty-three inches], the whole way around, there will be an iron grille so that whoever enters the room cannot reach the books, and within this grille toward where the books are there will be attached to the grille a high lectern like those which are used in libraries, and here as many books as can fit within it will be put, of the relevant subject. And on the other side of the grille, in the middle of the room, there will be a bench at a distance of a foot from the grille for visitors to the library, so that those sitting on it can read the books on the other side of the grille and put their hands between the bars to turn the pages. But note that the grille must not have vertical bars, but a mesh with space only to put your hand through.

Keeping the books for those in the library

Since some will want to see or read some of the books on the shelves and will not be able to reach them, I say that the librarian will put the requested book on the lectern, and after they have read it, he will return it to its proper place. And if they say that they cannot study the book with ease in this way, I say that this library is not designed as much for common study as for the safeguarding of all books and for the elaboration of the tables of authors, and sciences, and epitomes, and subject matters. And for common readers who want to resolve doubts, or find something remarkable, or study something in depth, there are no lack of institutions and books for them to turn to. For otherwise it will be impossible to keep the books safe although they are held with a hundred chains.

The librarian must have a catalogue of all the books

This librarian will have a record of all the books, each with its own number, in a book in numeral order, saying number 1 is such book, and 2 such another, and so one after another until the last one. And another book will also record the names of the authors, arranged in the same order they have in that book [i.e., in alphabetical order], with information about the edition and the *incipit* in the same order as in the index which is now made, so that by the numeric register an account can easily be kept, and by the number of the author we can know which one is missing, if indeed something is missing.

A record of duplicates

Besides this book there must be another one that records all the new books which are bought, and those which are discarded from the library because there are new, better [editions]. And the Visitor will use this record to take a count of the books, and he will be able to check whether they have been recorded in the numeric register, which must be kept by the librarian, and whether they were put in their right place.

Book of expenses

The custodian will have another book that will record all the expenses incurred in the library, so that at the end of the month the Visitor can verify it. And at the end of the year he will make a final account of the twelve months, to see if the income and the expenses are balanced, or whether there has been a deposit that will need to be balanced at the end of the second year.

The custodian must be an attorney

The custodian will have power of attorney to represent the interests of the library at court and out of it too. He will not have power, however, to donate or exchange nor alienate anything from the library, unless it is something superfluous and he has the approval of the Visitor, so that a proper estimate can be made of the value or price of the items sold or exchanged.

He must not lend nor lose books

Neither the said custodian, nor anybody else, can give nor lend any book, nor allow any of them out of the library, under the following penalty: that for each book that he gives away, or which goes missing through his fault or with his agreement, he must pay ten gold ducats, half of them for the next custodian, the other half for the library itself. And if he is responsible for the alienation or loss of ten books, besides the ten ducats for each of the books, if he does not seek out and restore the books to the library within two years, he will consequently lose the administration and custody of the library as a whole and the rents and everything else annexed to them. And the office will be bestowed on the next custodian who will accept it with the same conditions and penalties and commitment to abide by them.

The labeling of the books

In the first opening [*tabla*] of each book it will say: "Don Fernando Colón, son of don Cristobal Colón, the First Admiral, who discovered the Indies, left this book for the use and profit of all who come after, pray for him." And if this book is to be replaced by a better edition, it should say: "This book was exchanged, and it replaced another left here by don Fernando Colón, son of don Cristobal Colón, the First Admiral, who discovered the Indies, because he ordered it be done thus whenever another version of the same thing with some improvement was found."

Memorial of the founder

In the most commodious and visible part of the library there will be a tablet, similar to the design for my tombstone, except for the first two words that say "here lies," and in their place it will say "in memory of don Hernando," and so on. This stone will not be as big as my tombstone, but half the size. And it would appear that the most suitable place will be above the main entrance, or right opposite it, within the library, on the wall, and with its crest above it, also in stone or in marble.

Order to acquire books from different places

If the custodian planned always to acquire books here in Seville or in Salamanca, there would be an infinite number of books that would not come to his notice nor be included in the library, because they won't make it to these places; so I say that there should be a procedure which I have myself begun to shape, which will be as follows: that whereas for all sorts of books printed in Christendom booksellers always go to one of these six cities—which are Rome, Venice, Nuremberg, Antwerp, Paris, and Lyon—I say that by mediation of merchants who live here in Seville we must establish relations with some bank or important merchant in Lyon, and give him a hundred ducats in deposit, so that he may contact his agents in each of the other five cities, and send them the identical order, that they must enjoin a bookseller they trust to sell them every April books to the value of twelve ducats, at the trade price. These must be the most newly published and those never printed before. But because these books may cost more or less than the said twelve ducats, they must instruct the bookseller not to buy during that year more with the fifteen [*sic,* i.e., twelve] ducats than small books, and as far as large new books that exceed that price, they must be recorded in a document, each of them with their title and author, the price and the size—saying whether it is quarto or folio, and that it has been published in such a location—so that alongside those small books that make up the twelve ducats this record can be sent so they can respond from here in Seville whether they are to be sent or not.

In this manner every year in April in these said five cities—Rome, Venice, Nuremberg, Antwerp, and Paris—a bookseller will give to his partner the merchant books to the value of the said twelve ducats. And as regards the price, they cannot but do what wholesalers do with others whom they send books to other cities, to wit, they send them the record of all the books they are sending with the price attached to each of them, upon their conscience and good credit, the merchant in each of these said cities needs do no more than receive the books in their package or bundle and send them to Lyon to their contact alongside their record and that of those which have not been sent.

Then the said merchant in Lyon will receive all the books and pay his agents the principal and the costs of transport, and he will also take from a bookseller-partner in Lyon as many books as corresponds to the rest of the money, once he has paid his five correspondents. So that if the five correspondents sent him sixty ducats in books, and the transportation costs were ten ducats, and the remainder is thirty, then out of those thirty he will pay the transportation costs of the mule driver who will bring them to the trade fair in Medina del Campo. And the rest he will spend in books, which will normally be about seventeen or eighteen ducats, as the usual cost of transportation for a load of books carried by mule is around twelve or thirteen ducats. And once the load arrives at the fair in Medina, the agent in that city will receive them, send back the said one hundred ducats [to Lyon], and send the books on to Seville.

And I say that he must be paid the said one hundred ducats because the first one hundred were paid as a deposit and as a guarantee that each year this one hundred ducats will be received and paid in books, and having it always paid in advance is a sort of gratuity for the work he does in receiving them and then sending them on.

The booksellers responsible for the provision of the books in these six cities should be directed to be sure to buy all the little works [*obrezillas*] of any quality whatsoever, and that only once they have acquired these first, will they then buy larger ones up to the said amount [i.e., twelve ducats]. And since, as we mentioned above, it could be the case that there are not enough new publications in a given year to spend twelve ducats on them, in those cases they should spend until this limit on all the manuscripts which are not available in print, as long as they do not cost more than they would if they had gone into print. And I say this because it could happen that, for not knowing the book, they could end up sending a manuscript not worth ten *reales* having paid ten ducats, and they could also buy books that are reprinted with some additional glosses or alphabetic indexes or epitomes. Each of them must also be warned against sending books printed in or close to a city other than theirs: for instance, the agent in Rome must not send books printed in Venice or Milan, because this must be done by the agent in Venice, and the agent in Nuremberg should not send books printed in Paris or Lyon.

The merchants who act as agents in these six cities should be directed not to select or choose a bookseller of large and expensive books, in the first place because they do not deal with, nor care about, works in small format [*obrezillas*], with ballads or proverbs and other similar things, which must also find their place in the library. Since these are wealthy booksellers, they deal with what they have in their shops, and they have no interest in finding or searching out what is available elsewhere. In the second place because if they have some works in large, expensive format, they are easy to find, whereas the small ones are more difficult to search for, and also because a large bookseller will not care as much for this small commission as it is a small one, and he will refuse to keep a record of the books he has sent to avoid sending the same again; for each of these booksellers should record in their registers the reports or details of the books he sends, to keep a permanent account of them, and thus avoiding sending duplicates in the future.

In spite of these and other procedures, it will be impossible to avoid many duplicates in the library. I say that these duplicates should be stored in their chests, and the alphabetic table of the authors must record, next to the name of the author in question, the number of the chest where it is, in a square, and to differentiate it from the rest, this square will have two little circles in the corners, so as not to confuse it with the number of epitomes. And these chests will be stored in some monastery in an elevated place, on wooden legs to avoid any sort of damage, and two or three times a year each chest will be opened and the books will be taken out and then back again, to air them. And they will be left thus in deposit so that, in case one of the copies is stolen, the duplicate can be put in its place. And also so that in time, the library itself can be duplicated, so that—may God avoid this—in case the collection is destroyed by fire or in some other way, its double can replace it.

And since, in due time, it could be that many books will not just have duplicates, but triplicates, in these cases there should be a bookseller or a bookbinder who takes an inventory of these books and puts them up for sale, for a price that leaves some profit for him. In this way the triplicates, far from being a problem, in time will become quite useful, since this bookstore will have a large and varied supply of books from many different parts of the world, so that with the growth of business he may end up in a position to import more books. So that, if right now books for a value of twelve ducats are sent from each city, then it could become a hundred, the profit would grow, and the store could hire its own factor to travel around the said cities, and also some others (as I did myself) and so these occasional trips would be more worthwhile than always relying on what the booksellers decide to send.

And even without this store, every six years or so, the custodian should send one of the *sumistas* to Naples by sea so that there, bookstore by bookstore, and book by book, he could look if there is something that is not in the library and so buy it, in order to buy small works of a value of one *real* or below it, even if they were printed in France or in Germany, or anywhere else, because there are always a thousand obstacles to finding them, even if you return to the same workshop where they were printed. But if they are books of one *real* or more printed in Rome, or Lombardy, or France, or Germany, he should not buy them in Naples. Instead he should record them, their size and their publication details, in order to buy them afterward, closer to the places where they had been originally printed. And the *sumista* who does this must take with him the index or table of all the books that there is in the library, I mean the records of authors and incipits [*Abecedarium B*], so that he can compare each book he buys with these tables to see if there is a copy already. And he must also check whether the book offered him is a better edition, or of a better quality than the copy in the library—for the collection should always be improving. And he must also record the name of the booksellers whose bookshops he has searched, and what each book cost him, and on which day, and in which place, as I used to, recording all of this at the back of every book. And he will tell each of these booksellers that he is the *sumista* of the Fernandina Library, and that he beseeches them that if there is some new manuscript or printed book or work that comes to hand, they send it to such a bookseller, who is responsible for purchasing books for this library, and he will get paid a fair price whatever it is, and the appointed bookseller must be the one in the closest of the said six cities where the agents are based.

And once the *sumista* has done this job in Naples, without leaving one single store unsearched, book by book, he shall go on his own horse with the post that leaves every Sunday for Rome, and once in Rome he will do the same, and from Rome, with another post, he will go to Siena, and from Siena to Pisa, and from Pisa to Luca, and from Luca to Florence, and in each town he will perform the same tasks I have just described above.

And since he will have to buy books in each of these places, and to transport them from one to another would be very difficult, he should seek assistance from the Genoese. I mean that he must inquire in these places whether there are Genoese merchants, and if there is one, he must tell him "that he is a *sumista* of the Fernandina Library, founded by don Fernando Colón, son of don Christobal Colón, native of Genoa and First Admiral, who discovered the Indies, and since they are the founder's countrymen, he asks them to favor his requests (as [the founder] directed and ordered his *sumistas* to do), that he makes in [Hernando's] name, for [Hernando] knew he would always find help among his compatriots." And I can say for certain that there will not be a major city where you will not find Genoese merchants, to whom he can address himself and leave the books he has bought under their care, either bundled together or in a chest, to send them anywhere he wishes to, and to aid him in any other matter he requires. And in this he will also have as an aid letters of introduction from among them [i.e., the networks of Genoese merchants].

And as regards the convenience of gathering all the books that are purchased in different places in order for them to be sent to Seville—since they cannot be sent from each individual place where they are purchased—I say that all of those bought in Naples, and Rome, and Siena, and Pisa, and Luca, and Florence can be sent to Rome in their packets by the Genoese merchants in each of these cities. In the event that there is no Genoese merchant in one of these cities, the Genoese in the previous city should contact his local agent and partner, recommending the *sumista*. For instance, if there is no Genoese in Siena that can be contacted by the

Genoese in Rome, the latter will undoubtedly have some factor or correspondent of whatever origin, who, out of respect for the correspondent from Rome will aid him [i.e., the *sumista*]. And in case there is none of these, there is no doubt that there is no town where some honest merchant will not be pleased to aid strangers if they seek assistance from him. And I say this from my own experience, for merchants live by making deals, and themselves travel around, and they find pleasure in doing unto others what they would have done unto them. And they have the know-how [*ynteligencia*] to send things from one place to another safely, which other sorts of people do not have. And this is why anywhere he must go, the *sumista* must seek the aid of merchants. But I must warn the custodian that when it comes to sending a *sumista* or any other person to purchase books, he should arrange for it to be an Italian, and if not an Italian, a Frenchman or a German who has had frequent contacts out of Germany in Italy or France or Spain, because if he is a native of any of these three nations, he will go more safely abroad from Spain and he will be better regarded than any Spaniard. And this I know by my own experience, for when I traveled outside of these realms I always spoke Italian wherever I went, to avoid being recognized as a Spaniard, and thanks to this I escaped many dangers in which I found myself, in which it would have been death had it been known that I was Spanish.

But going back to the subject of gathering the books, I say that from Naples to Florence they should be gathered in Rome, so that the agent may ship them to Cádiz. And from Florence the *sumista* should [proceed] to Bologna, and there he will perform the same task, searching the bookstores as described above, and from there to Modena, and Arezzo, and Parma, and Piacenza, and Pavia, and Milan, all of them cities which are at a half a day distance from each other, and in all of them there are booksellers, and in each of them he must perform the same task. And from Milan he will go to Lodi, and from Lodi to Cremona, and from Cremona to Mantua, and from Mantua to Venice, and from Venice to Padua, and from Padua to Treviso, and from all of these cities he must bring the books together in Venice, because shipping them is easy using the rivers and canals that go from most of these cities to Venice, from where they will be handed over to the agent or to another Genoese who will then ship them in the galleys or in some other ship bound for Cádiz.

And I leave as my heir don Luis Colón, Admiral of the Indies, my nephew, with the remainder of my goods, with the charge and upon condition that every year, for the augmentation and maintenance of the library, he spends one hundred thousand *maravedís* in perpetuity; and if he will not accept, I leave as my heir the Cathedral Chapter of this city, with the condition that as much rent be bought with my property as will be enough to sustain the library in the form and manner in which I have directed, and if the cathedral will not accept this, then [I leave it to] the Monastery of Saint Paul. And whichever of these accepts the legacy must comply with all the instructions I have formulated regarding the library, and they should buy enough rents with my property to augment and preserve it.

I also name as my executors the *licenciado* Marcos Felipe and Vicencio del Monte, and I direct that when I die he [Marcos Felipe] must be summoned, and together with Desiderius my servant, the said *licenciado* must collect all my documents in a chest, lock them up with the key which is in the custody of the *licenciado,* and he will not open it until the arrival of the said del Monte; and once he arrives he must take custody of all the documents, and he must sort through them, to gather those that pertain to my affairs, since he is familiar with them and responsible for the administration of all my goods wheresoever they are. [All this should be done] by agreement with the said *licenciado,* and always with his consent. The said *licenciado* must always be informed of all decisions, and he will share them with my heir, and while he performs this task the said heir should pay his current wages.

I also order that the *bachiller* Juan Pérez will continue to order and oversee the administration of the library. He is currently in my household and manages [the library], and he must be paid a yearly salary of three ducats per month, plus another twenty-six ducats extra, which makes a total of sixty [*sic*]. And for this he is obliged to attend work every day for five hours, between the morning and the afternoon, and what he falls short one day, he can make up on another day or days within the same week, and if not his salary should be docked pro-rata from the yearly rates for five hours daily. I also leave two gold ducats to the heirs of Diego Méndez, a navigation chart and a marble mortar.

THREE

Hernando's Proposal to King Ferdinand for a Voyage around the World

While he accompanied the court in 1511, Hernando outlined for King Ferdinand a plan to complete his father's design for a circumnavigation of the world, a plan later presented to the king in written form. A copy of this proposal was discovered by Diego Arranz in the New York Public Library in the early 1980s and published by him in 1982. Our translation is based on this transcription.[1] *In his plan Hernando refers several times to a document identified elsewhere as the* Colón de Concordia, *a lost three-part tract that seems to have revisited many of the same materials as the* Libro de las Profecías, *placing the Columbian voyages as part of Christian providential history and providing sources that indicate the universal evangelization and conquest that would result from them. Ferdinand responded by putting Hernando off in vague terms, but the proposal contains important details regarding Hernando's sailing experience and the centrality of universal navigation to his and his father's projects.*

Seville, 19 July 1511

Most Catholic and Excellent Lord

Besides many other reasons that bind me to you, I cannot erase from my thoughts the mercies that I have received from Your Highness, and the desire to increase them, and I fear that I will not, with my feeble abilities, be able to serve your highness in any way. However, I see that, alongside the great prudence and natural excellence with which you administer and expand your kingdoms, you are surrounded by remarkable persons in all arts, and from all estates, who were not present to discuss and weigh what I have to say; consequently, if I deserve reprehension for repeating this, I beseech your highness to judge nothing but my intent.

My impression after I talked to your highness on the road to Guadalupe is that you do have an inclination to support the cause of our highest good, which is knowledge; I shall omit, for the sake of brevity, the many other advantages that could result from this voyage, even if they would cause confusion and jealousy to those opposing this victory, and joy to [your] friends and servants.

As for this, I say that under no circumstance should this voyage be forgotten or delayed: in the first place because of the problems, which I discussed with your highness in person, that would result if other princes undertake this conquest, which I shall not repeat again in writing for the sake of discretion; another inconvenience being that our contemporaries (and also future generations) might attribute this failure to act to pusillanimity and lack of ambition for glory and fame, as it is likely they will. First, because it falls to your highness to take up a project you yourself began; and then, because your highness has people with the skills required for its execution; also, seeing how easily achieved everything has been to present and will likely continue to be; and finally, because there is no other project nor conquest that could possibly stand in the way of this one, since it will require very few ships, not many men, and a small amount of money, so that it stands to reason the cost cannot go beyond five or six hundred [actually, million], which is no more than is spent on provisioning a single town or city overseas. Once invested, the results will be permanent, and this expense will not result from the toil of Spanish vassals [Spanish taxpayers] because the territories themselves will produce it; and besides these, there are other thousand similar arguments in its favor.

And also, we should not fear that the project is impossible, as men should learn from their past experiences: I say this because, for just that reason, the start that the Admiral gave to this endeavor at one time hung in the balance; and it was because of this fear, or reticence, that we failed to take possession of Arabia, Persia, Intra-Gangetic India, and Calcutta, something that the Admiral proposed to your highness well before the Portuguese usurped them. And besides discovering all these territories, my father the Admiral very often proposed to carry out this voyage around the world; and as I expressed (with all due respect) my feelings about the matter, based upon the experience I gained by navigating with my father, what I learned from his own teachings, from the many books and documents that he left me, and what I have culled from other sources.

As for the project, I think it is an excellent and commendable proposition: first because that voyage must result in the swift diffusion all over the world of the doctrine of the Holy Gospel, as I have proved through a compilation [*Colón de Concordia*] that prophesizes this will be put into effect during our time, and by your highness; also, because this voyage will increase the resplendent fame of your numerous achievements, which your highness already enjoys, and I dare say that this voyage will be the cornerstone of your future reputation and fame, because this voyage will bring numerous territories and provinces under your sovereignty, which will redound in a great abundance of valuable products and wealth. With them, and through the intercession of divine grace and thanks to your great prudence, you will then submit the rest of the world to your rule—as many prophecies I have collected say it shall be. And to prove that the great wealth to be obtained in this conquest that God has miraculously bestowed upon Your Grace is no fiction, I attach to this letter a collection of what some authors say about it. And apart from the great mercy and glory the Spanish will receive from your highness thanks to the performance of this voyage, since they will be the executors of this deed, all the generations and people of the world will benefit from it as a whole, because they will finally experience what our predecessors were in ignorance of, the roundness of the world, how it can all be navigated and inhabited, and many other important secrets that will be revealed as a result of this voyage, whose knowledge will result in great advantages to all peoples. No prince, in particular not one of your high power, should give up any project as impossible, being possible by its nature—in particular this one given its holy character. For if those made famous by their great deeds, such as Julius Caesar or Alexander, had focused on the great travails and the enormity of what they would conquer, and the fortitude of their opponents, as things impossible, they certainly would have given up these conquests in which they obtained such great victories. And we need not go to the past in search of examples, since your highness himself has experienced this in the victories that you have so miraculously obtained.

I say that this voyage can be put into effect and brought to a successful conclusion, and that for the following reasons, which learned men have proved, as I have collected in great profusion in a treatise I have collated and edited myself, by reason, authority, and experience. The first of them is that the earth and the water are both part of a sphere or a round body which is situated in the middle of the cosmos; the second one is that this sphere can be inhabited, and is, indeed, inhabited, in all of its regions, although it can be more fertile and temperate in some places than in others; the third one is that this earth is relatively small and that most of it has already been navigated by diverse voyages; the fourth one is that this sphere is navigable with vessels from east to west, so that going westward the waters will finally give way to a return through the east to the same place of origin; the fifth is that the Admiral could have undertaken this voyage thanks to the disciplines and skills he mastered, and the particular information he gathered, without which this project would have been impossible. And I would like to list them briefly, so that your highness can more efficiently appoint the person or persons necessary for the execution of this voyage.

In the first place, the person charged with this expedition must know the size and design of the vessels that he will take with him, for each sea and each region requires different vessels on account of the diversity of currents, channels, and banks, and for the depth of the shores and the harbors, the winds that run through them, and the profile of the land. In the second place he must know which wood should be employed, and in which provinces they should be harvested, and the time when they must be felled. In the third place, he must know the quality, and the quantity, and the regions that will provide the hawsers and ropes, and all the other things which are required for navigation in the regions where he intends to travel, because sailors say, quite rightly, that on account of a single rope an entire vessel can be lost. Fourth, it is necessary to know how to correctly provision an expedition, based on the crew sailing and the region where it is headed, as well as the duration of the voyage, and thus deciding whether to carry more or less, and how, and what keeps best, most importantly so that there is no fraud nor over-expense incurred, as is usually the case. The fifth is that he must know the number of crew required, both at sea and on land, the officers who are necessary, to care for the health of both bodies and souls, for the preservation of the expedition and to best acquire and conquer the territories and the wealth to be obtained from them. Sixth, it is necessary to have experience in sailing and in managing the crew to lead the fleet through the many dangers that there are at sea, in particular for explorers, such as running aground on banks, which is usually due to lack of proper attention in watches or ignorance of the particular coast. Seventh, it is necessary to know the storms that are coming, which can be done by calculating the celestial houses [*casas çelestes*], and through knowledge of the signs, the planets, the fixed stars and the aspects they reveal, and what they mean, and which can also very roughly be estimated from diverse signals that appear in the sun and the moon and in the other stars, as they rise and set, and also at other different times of day, and through thunder and lightning, and fire, and the waters, and the birds and the fish, and the times of year with respect to the different regions where they happen to be at the time. And the knowledge of this helps shun many dangers. Eighth, they need to know the distances from one place to another, both by routing [*singladuras*], as well as by shadows [*sombras*] and astrolabes, and the length of the days and the proportion that a major parallel has with a minor one, to know the place where he is, and situate the lands in their proper distances and places, both on a map and on a globe, which requires expertise in arithmetic, astronomy, cosmography, and mapmaking. Ninth, that they should not always use the ancient cosmographers as their guide, because they say themselves about the diversity and mutation of the landmasses, the islands, and the seas, for they are never continuously the same, as proved by many authorities and also by experience. Tenth, they must not waste time in harbors on account of greed, or gathering information, or finding rest and refreshment, because this endangers the supplies and leads to problems with fog, which requires knowledge about the places where these fogs are frequent, which can be achieved by a number of signs. Finally, it is necessary that the person responsible for this office must come from a good background, with good breeding and reputation, on many counts: in the first place because these individuals are always very zealous to serve God, and in those they command, and those they discover, they always seek to sow good doctrine; also because they are more zealous to serve their king, for their fame and loyalty; then because those who are good are given to command as well, and for this reason they are good at this and those they command prefer being under their service, and they both love and fear them; also because those who are good are also prone to do good and great deeds, again because they are wary of shame, and this is why in danger they are more constant and can undergo deprivation and toil, and they welcome situations that let them exercise their virtue, and, in the end, for a thousand other similar things that pertain to those of good parts.

I humbly apologize to your highness for my prolixity, because in truth, if God would grant me that with these my words, I could form my works so as to obtain the good will of Your Majesty, to proffer my own person—which I do not fail to propose, because I think that with my zeal, and with the collaboration of many people who are here at your service, such as the *Adelantado,* my uncle, and Amerigo, Viçenti Anes, Solis, and others who are experts in these things, they will not fail to do a great service for your highness. And above all, I submit myself to the correction of your highness, since in all of this there is so much at stake. May Our Lord grant Your Excellency and High Majesty long days of life and may the enlargement of many more kingdoms under your service continue to prosper. Amen. In Seville, on 19 July 1511.

FOUR

Hernando's Appointment as the Coordinator for the Elaboration of a New Version of the Padrón Real

*Following the ending of the Elvas-Badajoz conference in stalemate, Hernando was appointed acting head (*piloto mayor*) of the Casa de Contratación, while the official* piloto *(Sebastian Cabot) was absent on a cosmographical reconnoitering expedition.*[1] *This document acts as Hernando's letter patent from the emperor to gather cosmographical data and it bears remarkable similarities to the procedures Hernando developed for the* Descripción.

The King: In so much as I have been informed about the diversity that there is among the *mappaemundi* and navigational charts, both as regards the location of the islands and of land, and in their size and in the routes that lead to them [*derrota*], and about the harm, dangers, and inconveniences that this causes, in particular to those who trade and sail in the seas of our Indies and *terra firme* in the Ocean sea; and meaning to provide a remedy for it, and being also informed about your skills, don Hernando Colón, since you have studied these arts, and your wish to serve me: I hereby command and charge you that you gather information in writing, by report, and in drawings, and in any other manner you may find convenient, from all and any persons who know about these arts, and have skills and experience in navigation. And we command them to meet with you, and you to receive from them whatever they can declare and say about these matters I have just mentioned, and also that they show you all the drawings and the written documents they may have about this, which could be of any use to you for this purpose. And if any of these persons are absent and not able to meet you in person, we command our magistrates in those places where they might be that they press them and take from them, under oath, their declaration, and that they present these drawings and writings to the person designated by you, both in our kingdoms and seignories here as well as in the Indies, the islands, and the *terra firme* of the Ocean sea: for which we give you in this complete power. And once this has been performed, and all the information and declarations have been received, you will take Diego Ribero with you, who is our pilot and master in the elaboration of charts and astrolabes, and any other learned person who has skills in this craft, and we command them to meet with you, and you will craft a navigation chart, and a *mappamundi* or globe [*esfera redonda*], in which all the islands and *terrae firmae* can be found that have so far been discovered, as well as those that will be discovered after this, to be deposited in our Casa de Contratación of the Indies which is in the city of Seville, and they will serve as patterns for all the other charts and *mappaemundi* that will be made, and all pilots must use them in their navigation and in their routes; and neither you nor the rest of them [i.e., the rest of the team] will do anything other under penalty of your mercy and ten thousand *maravedís* to each of those who did otherwise. Signed in Granada, on October sixth 1526. I, the King.

FIVE

Hernando's Memorial al Emperador

Hernando prepared the following petition, likely around 1536, to request that Charles transform his lifetime pension of five hundred gold pesos into a perpetual grant for the running and upkeep of the library. Although the petition seems not to have been sent, and survives only in a transcription of codicils compiled by Hernando's executor Marcos Felipe, it contains some important statements regarding the plan for the library and represents a shorter, firsthand version of the much lengthier treatment given in the Memoria *(appendix 1, above).*[1]

So that the effects and the advantages which the lord don Hernando Colón wished that his library would generate should be known, they are explained here in a petition that he prepared for His Majesty about his library [. . .]

.S.ce.Ca.m.

Don Hernando Colón kisses Your Majesty's royal feet and hands for graciously submitting to the consideration his petition about a perpetual rent for the library. And in order to inform Your Majesty of the benefits that will result from it, he declares that the first one will be the creation of a place in Your Majesty's kingdoms that brings together all the books, in all languages and disciplines, that can be found within Christendom and beyond it too. That is something that no prince has ever ordained to this day, for it is one thing to create a library with the books of one's own day, as some have already done, and another to organize books for perpetuity, including the new ones which are published.

The second [benefit] is to collect all these books in order to preserve the memory of noble men who worked for our good, since the memory of many of them has already been lost. Possessing a copy of all these should lend certainty and balance in matters touching religion and the governance of the republic. They will also serve the common good, as there will be a place of resort where scholars can consult any doubt they may have.

The third one is to provide information everywhere about these authors. To this effect don Hernando, alongside his assistants and scholars, has reduced to an alphabetical order all the authors there are, a task which is still underway and will continue in the future, which records that such an author composed such and such works, putting all the works [i.e., the titles] also in alphabetical order, so that the works of these authors can be more easily found.

The fourth is the elaboration of a book that divides by the general disciplines [*ciencias*], such as theology, canon law, civil law, etc. And under each of these, in alphabetic order, are listed all the subjects, authors, and books written within that particular discipline. And so in law, under the title *de suma trinitate et fide catholica* you will say, such and such authors wrote on this, and on that particular law such an author composed an opinion [*repetición*] and another a treatise, etc. And so for each part of the other disciplines, as for instance, on the books of Aristotle's *De anima* such and such authors have written, and on the book of Job, these other authors, etc.

The fifth is another book whose purpose is to record information about the contents of such books, in which it recounts the summary and substance of each book; which in effect is an epitome or argument of the book in question, so that by just reading the brief epitome or argument the reader can decide whether the book fits his purpose, in which case he can find it and read it in full, or whether this brief summary will suffice. For nobody can read the multitude of books that have been written in each discipline.

The sixth because there are those who lecture or preach in public, and need guidance to compose their orations, on the subjects they would like to speak about, but do not have information about the places where they could find these resources. To this end another book of propositions is under elaboration, with the variety of subjects in alphabetic order, in which it says "this author writes about this subject in this particular place," and so all authors that deal with that particular subject are listed in it, with a symbol showing whether the text is brief or longer and more detailed. This book will be to all knowledge and disciplines what Bertachino is to law.[2]

A considerable part of these four books is already done, and of the first two of them we are already making neat copies. And regarding the other two, containing the epitomes and propositions, we have recorded propositions and subjects out of more than three thousand five hundred books in fifteen years.[3] This is the same task that will be continued by the assistants for whose sustenance, and for the purchase of new books, don Hernando petitions support, so that, in time, this library will not only contain all the books that exist, but also everything in them will be also recorded in other books in alphabetical order, so that each user can be educated in whichever discipline he chooses. This is something that has never been done and it is a project of such a quality that will render excellent service to

Our Lord and Your Majesty, and for the service of the Christian republic. This is why don Hernando beseeches Your Majesty that, in view of the great end that is pursued, and the fact that it is one of your servants who pursues it, who does wish for his service, or from all that his father left him, any other remembrance or entailment [*mayorazgo*], but the putting into effect of this through Your Majesty's mercy and favor. And to this end he begs the perpetuity of the five hundred pesos to fund the aforesaid project, since it pertains to Your Majesty, as prince and emperor, to sustain and promote both arms and letters, following in the example of your illustrious predecessors, as their institution of your laws demonstrate.

There follows the rules that don Hernando had established during his lifetime for those who were employed in the administration of the library, which are as follows . . .

NOTES

Translations are ours unless otherwise indicated.

INTRODUCTION

1. "Considerò che tutta l'acqua e la terra dell'universo costituivano e formavano una sfera, che poteva essere da Oriente in Occidente circondata, camminando gli uomini per quella, fin che venissero a star piedi contra piedi gli uni con gli altri in qual si voglia parte che in opposito si trovasse" (Hernando, *Historie*, 1:41).

2. This proposal is translated in full in appendix 3.

3. Augustine 2010, book 19, chapter 7, pp. 205–6. ("The first misfortune is the lack of communication resulting from language differences.")

4. On Clenardus's plans for universal translation, see Roersch 1940–41; an example of Jacobo de Testera's pictographic gospels can be seen in the Codex Testeriano Bodmer, Cod. Bodmer 905.

5. These genealogies included Noah's, which had for centuries been used to account for the diversity of races in the known world and their continental distribution: according to this narrative, Europe, Asia, and Africa were peopled by three of Noah's sons, Japheth, Shem, and Ham. This interpretation would survive beyond Hernando's lifetime well into the seventeenth century.

6. Schedel's annotated copy of Piccolomini's *Historia rerum ubique gestarum* is preserved

at the Bavarian State Library in Munich and can be consulted online, see ISTC, https://data.cerl.org/istc/ip00730000.

7. For instance, Schedel incorporates an illustration with the fort of Sabatz, where a military encounter between King Matthias of Hungary and the Ottomans had taken place just sixteen years before the publication of the book (fol. ccliiir).

8. "Constituantur bibliothecae publicae in quas omnium librorum copia congeratur, preponanturque viri peritissimi bibliothecis, qui libros diligentissima collatione revideant et omnem varietatum discordiam recte diffinitionis iudicio noverint removere" (Salutati 1985, p. 49; English translation in Celenza 1996, p. 271, note 53).

9. Valla would create a clean copy of his Thucydides that was intended to stand as a textual gold standard for the transmission of the text (what he referred to as *archetypus translationis*), Nebrija curated the second edition of Peter Martyr's pioneering history of the New World, the *Decades de Orbe Novo,* aided by a lexicon of American neologisms to facilitate the understanding of the text; Erasmus produced an influential and controversial *clean copy* of the original Greek text of the New Testament with a Latin translation (two new textual gold standards); and Vives engaged in a redefinition of the public forum of knowledge (and by extension, the public forum of print), which included the regulation of prose style, normative reading lists, and the establishment of different hierarchies among their audiences.

10. Ullman and Stadter 1972, p. 7 passim.

11. Ibid., p. 5; also G. Cecchini 1967.

12. Manfredi 1998, p. 104.

13. Following Trinkaus's account of Italian humanism, Parentucelli's emphasis on the church fathers is notable, as is his inclusion of the canon of Greek authors. See Labowsky 1979, p. 14, and Sforza, ed. 1884; Ullman and Stadter 1972, pp. 15–16.

14. Although Pope Sixtus IV also played an important role in the establishment of the Vatican library, it was Nicholas V who first came up with the idea of a public Vatican library as opposed to a purely papal or private one. See a further account of the history of the library in chapters 1 and 4, and Boyle 1993, pp. xi–xiii.

15. Bisticci 1859, p. 39.

16. For instance, not all the books printed and edited by Aldus Manutius and his associates came from Bessarion's Greek manuscripts and other Venetian libraries. Many of them came from other European collections and from Aldus's own networks, which included contacts in the international republic of letters such as Thomas Linacre, Conrad Celtis, John Reuchlin, and the resident French ambassador in Venice, John Lascaris (whom Lowry calls "the last great manuscript hunter"). As Lowry concludes: "Few of Europe's more celebrated scholars were beyond Aldus's sphere of influence" (Lowry 1974, pp. 140–41). Bessarion's intention was "to acquire the whole of Greek literature, and all that had survived both by pagan and by Christian authors, and to make it accessible 'in some safe place,' in order to preserve the Greek heritage towards the day when the Greeks would once more be a free nation" (Labowsky 1979, p. 13, q.v. also for the early catalogues of the Marciana). On the role of Venice, its collectors, its publishers, and its translators in the dissemination

of Greek texts within the general context of the transition from manuscript to print, see Lowry 1974, in particular pp. 140–46.

17. Unfortunately, the list of works that Bessarion sent to his correspondents with his desiderata for the collection of what he considered the most important or the fundamental works in the classical and Christian Greek canon have not been preserved, for "taken in conjunction with the inventories of Bessarion's library it would have furnished us with a Greek counterpart to Thomas Parentucelli's famous *canon,* drawn up for Cosimo de' Medici, of the works which a representative library should contain" (Labowsky 1979, p. 14).

18. Labowsky 1979, p. 7, pp. 8–9.

19. Further details on Bessarion and Regiomontanus in King and Turner 1994.

20. See the entry on Pere García in the *Diccionario Biográfico Español,* http://dbe.rah.es/biografias/68490/pere-garcia, accessed 10 March 2018.

CHAPTER ONE
Life in the Library

1. Marín Martínez 1970, p. 67. See our appendix 1.

2. "There was a man from the territory of Milan, a merchant in printed books, who traded in this land of Andalusia, mainly in Seville, whom they called Christopher Columbus, a man of elevated wit even if he did not have much education, very cunning in the art of cosmography and the zones of the world" (Bernáldez 1962, pp. 269–70, our translation). Andrés Bernáldez knew the explorer and his family personally, and according to his own account he was his host in 1496 (ibid., p. 308). Bernáldez also had access to original documents that have now been lost (for further details about this, see Manuel Gómez-Moreno's and Juan de M. Carriazo's "Introduction" to Bernáldez 1962, pp. xxxi–xxxii).

3. Aeneas Silvius Piccolomini, *Historia rerum ubique gestarum* (Venice, 1477), Colombina 10-3-1, ISTC ip00730000; Pliny, *Historia naturalis* (Venice, 1489), Colombina 119-7-2; ISTC ip00803000. Juan Gil (1992) provides a critical edition of Columbus's *Marco Polo,* including its manuscript marginalia, as well as those in the Italian edition of Pliny's *Historia naturalis.*

4. Pierre d'Ailly, *Imago Mundi* (Louvain, 1480/3), Colombina 10-3-4, ISTC ia00477000, with 898 annotations by Columbus, his brother Bartholomew, and Hernando. Importantly, the debate about how many leagues lay between the west of Europe and the east of Asia was further complicated by a lack of agreement—often unacknowledged—over the length of a league. While this was to become a central part of Hernando's focus during his later works (central to his arguments at the Juntas de Elvas-Badajoz and his father's biography), Columbus himself usually simply treats the length of a league as a given.

5. Discussed in some detail by Gil and Varela, ed. 1984, pp. 129–41, who also include a transcription of the letter. Rumeu de Armas includes a transcription of the Toscanelli letter, in several versions, as an appendix (Rumeu de Armas 1973, pp. 435–42).

6. Marco Polo, *De consuetudinibus et conditionibus orientalium regionum* (Gouda, 1483), Colombina 10-3-2, ISTC ip00902000. The 1497 letter from John Day to Columbus, dis-

covered in the Archivo de Simancas in 1956 (AGS, Estado de Castilla, leg. 2, fol. 6), is reprinted in Gil and Varela 1984.

7. Although Pané's original manuscript has not survived, Hernando transcribed it in his *Historia del Almirante*, and Bartolomé de las Casas later summarized part of its information about the Taíno Indians in his *Apologética historia de las Indias.* Since it was also used by Peter Martyr in his *First Decade,* the information he provided about the language of the Taínos must have also been employed (albeit indirectly) by Nebrija in the *Vocabula Barbara* he included in his 1516 edition of Peter Martyr's *Decades de Orbe Novo* (fig. 16). For a modern edition (translated from Hernando's *Historia del Almirante*), see Arrom 2004.

8. These documents, many of which are discussed separately in this book, are contained either in the early inventory of possessions, the "Memorial de las cosas que han de hazer y dezir en Castilla," printed in Berwick Alba, ed. 2011, pp. 77–79, or in the (badly damaged) inventory taken after Hernando's death, reproduced in Hernández Díaz and Muro Orejón (1941), document 93, pp. 262–66. The maps inherited from his father-in-law Bartolomeu Perestrello are mentioned in Hernando's *Historie,* 1:38–39.

9. This set can be produced by using the catalogue to isolate those of Hernando's surviving books that contain his characteristic purchase note ("este libro me costó . . .") but which lack a purchase date, information he only began to record after 1509. Martínez (1970, p. 574) suggests that as many as a quarter of the books are lacking a purchase note of any kind and so cannot be placed in his book-buying chronology.

10. Aristotle, *Opera* (Venice: Gregorium de Gregoriis, 1496; Colombina 15-5-35, ISTC ia00966000); Aquinas, *Summa theologica: Prima pars* (Venice: Antonium de strata de Cremona, 1489; Colombina 118-8-13, ISTC it00201000), *Prima Secunde sancti Thome de Aquino* (Venice: Ioannem Rubeum Vercellensem, 1497; Colombina 118-8-14[1], ISTC it00207000), *Summa theologica: Secundae partis* (Venice: Iohannis Colonie & Iohannis Manthen Gheretzen, 1480; Colombina 118-8-14[2], ISTC it00216000); *Summa theologica: Tertia pars* (Venice: Iohannis Colonie & Iohannis Manthen Gheretzen, 1478; Colombina 118-8-15, ISTC it00221000).

11. "Q̧ tuvo mucho poder aristoteles por cabsa de alexandre e sie[m]pre lo exercito e[n] hazer bien" (Colombina 15-5-35), [aaivr].

12. Antonio de Nebrija, *Gramática Castellana* (Salamanca: [Juan de Porras], 1492; Colombina 118-5-33, ISTC ia00902000); *In A. Persium Flaccum . . . interpretatio* (Seville: for Cromberger, 1503; Colombina 15-6-18[1]); *Introductorium in Cosmographiam Pomponii Melae* (Salamanca: [Juan de Porras], ca. 1498; Colombina 4-1-18[1], ISTC ia00908000, purchased in Toledo).

13. *De Orbe Novo Decades* (Alcalá: Brocar, 1516), of which Hernando had a copy (Colombina, 10-3-3[1], USTC 334326). This second printed edition featured *Decades I–III,* a preface by Nebrija, and a five-page appendix, also by Nebrija, with "Vocabula Barbara . . . Ne lectoris ingenium barbara nouarum nationum uocabula confundant," the first ever European lexicon with American neologisms. The first edition (which only featured the first *Decade*) had been published by Cromberger in Seville in 1511.

14. *Horatius cum quattor comentariis* (Venice: Ioannem Alvysium, 1498; Colombina, 6-4-6, ISTC ih00460000); *Opera Luciani* (Venice: Ioa[n]nem Baptista[m] Sessa, 1500; Colombina 118-5-24, ISTC il00331000). The anecdote portraying Peter Martyr in the classroom is in Hieronymus Munzer, *Viaje por España y Portugal: 1494–1495* (Madrid, 1991), p. 275. Hernando may also have absorbed humanist fashions from the circles surrounding his father, as witnessed by the hands of humanist scribes in the *Book of Prophecies;* see Rusconi, ed. 1997, pp. 40–47.

15. In addition to early editions of Aristotle's *De Animalibus* (Venice: Simon Bevilaqua, ca. 1495; Colombina 13-4-14, ISTC ia00975000) and the *De Animalibus* of Albert the Great (Rome: Simon Nicolai Chardella, 1478; Colombina 119-7-1, ISTC ia00223000), this early undated group also contains Alphonsus X's *Tabulae Astronomicae* (Venice: Erhard Ratdolt, 1483; Colombina 12-6-29, ISTC ia00534000), Regiomontanus's *Epitoma in Almagestum Ptolemaei* (Venice: Johannes Hamman for Kaspar Grossch and Stephan Roemer, 1496; Colombina 119-7-7, ISTC ir00111000), and Albumasar's *Flores Astrologiae* (Venice: Johannes Baptista Sessa, ca. 1500; Colombina 4-6-52[1], ISTC ia00358000).

16. The "Institución de Mayorazgo" (AGI, Patronato, 101) is reprinted in Varela 1982, pp. 190–99.

17. See Rusconi's "Introduction" to his critical bilingual edition (Rusconi, ed. 1997, pp. 1–51). On Columbus's use of prophecy, see Kadir 1992.

18. Rusconi, ed. 1997, pp. 290–91. Hernando's note (". . . prophecia . . . per patre[m] . . . cristoforo . . . almirante . . . anno 1492") is in *Tragedie Senece cum duobus commentariis* (Venice: Philippo pincio Mantuano, 1510; Colombina 1-4-19, USTC 855881), fol. xciiv, sig. q.iiv.

19. See Arranz 1982, pp. 97–102, and documents 15 and 16 in his appendix.

20. Guillén 2006, p. 116.

21. The original of this inventory is in the *Archivo de la Fundación Casa de Alba* in Madrid. For a modern edition see Berwick Alba, ed. 2011, p. 78.

22. In 1509 he paid 442 *maravedís* for a folio with Latin works by Pico della Mirandola (Colombina 12-5-9, USTC 667780).

23. In a rare instance of an early purchase that is dated with a day, Hernando paid 51 *maravedís* in Toledo on 8 October 1511 for a quarto with a Latin biography of Thomas Beckett (Colombina 1-1-10, USTC 339093); the addition of specific days to the purchase month and year did not become regular practice until 6 December 1521, during Hernando's stay in Nuremberg.

24. Tissard's *Alphabetum Graecum* (Colombina 12-3-23[1], USTC 142311); Chrysoloras's *Erotemata* (Colombina 12-3-23[4], USTC 180245); Tissard's *Grammatica Hebraica et Graeca* (Colombina 12-3-23[5], USTC 180316); Tissard's edition of Hesiod, *Opera et dies* (Colombina 12-3-23[3], USTC 180246); Tissard's edition of the pseudo-Homeric *Batrachomyomachia* (Colombina 12-3-23[2], USTC 180247); Crastonus's *Lexicon Graeco-Latinum* (Colombina 6-5-19, USTC 760742); Nebrija's *Repetitio sexta de mensuris* (Colombina 6-2-3[5], USTC 334619). There is an example of Hernando's Greek handwriting in the *Loci Communes*

(Colombina 7-2-60, fol. 4r), but the Greek volumes of the library seem noticeably lighter in annotations than volumes in other languages.

25. The newly discovered records of the case are to be found in ASV, S. R. Rota, *Manualia Actorum,* 83, with about 200 pages of relevant entries being found between fols. 150r and 933v. We are grateful to Kirsi Salonen for her help in locating and decoding these records. An excellent guide to the workings of this court can be found in Salonen 2016. On later suggestions that Hernando may have had an ambassadorial role, see Jos 1945, pp. 609–14. On the rumors of the pirate attack and on Hernando's supposed ambassadorial roles while in Rome, see Rumeu de Armas 1973, p. 29; it seems that both of these stories originate in seventeenth-century sources.

26. On the *Pleitos Colombinos* see the recent, four-volume edition with primary documents by Colón de Carvajal and Pérez Prendes (2015).

27. Hernando owned a number of works by members of the Rota Court, whom he may have met in person. Such is the case of Giovanni Mercurio Vipera: Hernando owned two of his orations; one of them was 8-2-31(23) (EDIT16 75046), and the other was 8-2-35(7), in praise of peace, delivered before Pope Hadrian (of the latter, Hernando's copy appears to be the only surviving one). Another one was Giovanni Stafileo, whom Hernando might have met either at the Roman Studium (where he taught canon law) or at the Rota Court—where he delivered an oration (8-2-31[20], EDIT16 23637) on Friday 25 May 1528, which Hernando bought in Rome in September 1530.

28. A list of those lecturing at the Studium Urbis in 1514 is provided in Renazzi 1803, pp. 235–39.

29. See Erasmus's epistle 2987, in which he explains public attendance at Italian lectures to his correspondent; and Colón, ed. Caddeo 1930, 23, for Hernando's claims about Columbus's education, refuted by Fernández-Armesto 1991, p. 5.

30. The note in his copy of Suetonius (Colombina 2-5-11, USTC 857783) reads "A die 23 iulij usq[ue] 2>am<. augusti sequentis año 1515 audivi hu[n]c librum mag>ro< Castrensi cu[m] recitante seu cursim absq[ue] expositione cum perlegenti." For his note on the lectures by Sebastianus that he attended in 1515 (in his copy of Silvestrio di Prierio's *Commentaria in theoricas planetarum Georgii Purbachii* [Colombina 12-6-35]), see chapter 2. Hernando's list of Greek verbs compiled by Bartolomeo de Castro is Colombina 7-1-10, which the *Abcedarium B* notes as being "editum a Roma 1516." The list of logical terms is 5-1-1, "Termini logicales/a magistro Bartholo Castrensi."

31. Hernando's index to Lucretius is in (Colombina 6-4-12), *In Carum Lucretiu[m] poeta[m] Co[m]me[n]tarii a Joa[n]ne Baptista Pio editi* . . . and covers just over 28 pages in an insert after the flyleaf.

32. Suetonius, [*Vitae duodecim Caesarum*] *Svetonius Tranquillus cum Philippi Beroaldi et Marci Antonii Sabellici commentariis. Cum figuris nuper additis* (Venice: Giovanni Rosso, 1506; Colombina 2-5-11, USTC 857783).

33. Hernando bought Flavio Biondo's *De Roma Triumphante* (Brescia: Angelum Brita[n]nicu[m], 1503; Colombina 13-4-7, USTC 814548) in Seville in 1511, and his *De Roma Instau-*

rata: libri tres (Venice: [Gregorius de Gregoriis], 1510; Colombina 13-4-10, USTC 814146) in 1515. His copies of the *Mirabilia Urbis Roma* ([Rome: Johann Besicken, n.d. 1508]; Colombina 14-1-4[2], EDIT16 33255) and Albertini's *Opusculum de mirabilis novae et veteris urbis Romae* (Rome: Jacobus Mazochius, 1510; Colombina 4-2-5[5]) both seem to have been purchased late in 1512.

34. Hernando owned a copy of Arsenios Apostolios, *Praeclara dicta philosophorum, imperatorum, oratorumque, & poetarum* (Rome: Ginnasio Mediceo, ca. 1519, USTC 810066), *Abcedarium B*, col. 153, *Reg. B* 5117, and a "Didimi proverbia in greco" (*Abcedarium B*, col. 475, *Reg. B* 2190) which may have been Didymus Chalcenterus's *Scholia palaia ton pany dokimon eis ten Omerou Iliada. Ypothesis tes A Omerou rapsodias* (Rome: Ginnasio Mediceo, 1517, USTC 826728), though it is hard to be certain about the latter as the registry number provided does not accord with the entry in the *Registrum B*. On the Colocci press see Manfredi 2010, p. 278.

35. *Opera nobilissima composa per lo excellente maistro Agogo mago re. De tute le pasion vien a falconi astori e sparaueri* (Venice, 1508?); Colombina 14-2-9(6); EDIT16 (69402) suggests that this 1508 edition is a single surviving copy. The *obrezillas* by Marco Rosiglia are signatures 14-1-9(2) (*Rispetti Damore di maestro Marco da Fuligno [et] di piu auctori—Nuouamente sta[m]pati*—Impresso in Siena: p[er] Symione di Niccolo & Giouanni di Alixandro . . . , 1512, EDIT16 68662; Hernando paid 8 *quatrines* for it in 1512) and 14-1-9(4) (*Froctola recitata da Vno Giouano, El quale per troppo Amore sifece* [sic] *Heremita: nella q[ua]le co[n]tiene due belli Capitoli & una Epistola Composta p[er] . . . Marco Rosilio da Fuligno; opera nuoua*—Impresso in Siena: per Symione di Niccolo & Giouanni di Alixandro . . . , 1511; EDIT16 68661; Hernando paid 2 *quatrines* for it in Rome on an unspecified date). Of 14-1-10(16) there is another copy at the Biblioteca Nazionale Braidense in Milan (EDIT16 66948).

36. Georgius Merula, *Georgii Alexandrini in librum de Homi[n]e Galeoti Narniensis opus* (Venice, ca. 1474; Colombina 3-6-3; ISTC im00504000); Messahala, *In nomine Domini Incipit Epistola Messehallah* (manuscript, Colombina 12-1-18[7]); Hernando's copy of the Potken/Silber *Psalterium in Lingua Chaldica* does not survive, but it is noted in *Abecedarium B*, col. 1405 and given a *Registrum B* number of 5967.

37. Hobson 1975, p. 48.

38. The first two registers of borrowers have been edited by Bertòla (1942). On Leo Africanus, see Natalie Zemon Davis 2008, p. 56.

39. Manfredi 2010, p. 252.

40. Ibid., pp. 283, 317.

41. Thomeis 1999.

42. Vigli's catalogues are Vat. Lat. 7134–36; the quote is taken from 7135, fol. 49r. A similar project was Jean Matal's *Iter Italicum*, which also provides descriptions of the structure and daily life of the Vatican library; part of Matal's catalogue is preserved as Cambridge University Library Add. MS 565. Matal was, however, largely interested only in the Greek holdings of the libraries; see Hobson (1975).

43. In a letter addressed to the Duchess of Soma, Boscán mentions how he had a long

conversation with Navagero on "cosas de ingenio y de letras, y especialmente en las variedades de muchas lenguas, [le] dixo por qué no provava en lengua castellana sonetos y otras artes de trobas usadas por los buenos authores de Italia, y no solamente [se] lo dixo assí livianamente, más aún [le] rogó que lo hiziese" (Boscán 1957, p. 89, i.e., they conversed on "matters of wit and letters, and especially on the diversity of languages, [and he also suggested] he try his hand in Castilian at sonnets and other verse forms used by good Italian authors, and he did not merely suggest it casually, but begged him to do so"). A well-established tradition in Spanish literary history recounts how Boscán then passed the suggestion on to his friend Garcilaso de la Vega, and both set about composing Spanish poetry in Italian meters—thus triggering the onset of the modern canon in Spanish poetry.

44. Ramusio's *Delle Navigationi et Viaggi* was, like Martyr's *Decades* and, in general, like any other project that relied upon the ceaseless flow of information that was in circulation at the time, a long-term work in progress which he took up with the collaboration of the Giunti of Venice in 1520, but which only saw print posthumously in 1550. Ramusio's work is a monument to the sort of practices involved in the gathering and coordination of information, which involved correspondents, translators, editors, and publishers. For the networks around Ramusio, with whom he engaged in an intense series of textual exchanges and editorial projects, see Horodowich 2005.

45. In a letter dated on 27 March 1531 to the Italian Hebraist Agostino Steuco, who in 1525 was appointed as custodian of part of Grimani's collection when these books were deposited at the Augustinian monastery of Sant' Antonio in Venice. Grimani had one of the best European collections of Hebraica (further details in Delph 2008).

46. "Ditto Cardinal lassa 15 milia volumi di libri, di qual, parte è in ditto monasterio [i.e., Santa Chiara di Murano] et parte ha con lui a Roma; e quì in monasterio *etiam* è quelli bronzi et marmi che lassa a la Signoria: il safil l'è a Roma" (Sanudo, *Diarii,* vol. 34, Venice, 1892, cols. 407–8, entry of 15 September 1523). Grimani left part of his books to a nephew and the rest to the Venetian monastery of San Antonio di Castello, destroyed by fire in the seventeenth century. Unfortunately, Grimani's library did not survive, and Sanudo's testimony is the only source of information we have about its extraordinary dimensions. But if he is correct, Grimani would have been the only serious competitor Hernando would have had during his lifetime, for at the time of Hernando's death in 1539, his shelves in Seville housed over 15,000 titles.

47. Johannes Trithemius, *De Scriptoribus Ecclesiasticis* (Paris: Berthold Rembolt, 1512; USTC 209371, Colombina 3-3-28), aii^{r}: "In seqe[n]ti tabula continetur 1014 nomina auctorum in hoc opere contentoru[m] incipientia a litteris alphabeti pront. seguitur. A. 103. B.60 . . ." Hernando would adapt Trithemius's practice of listing works under each author in his own *Registrum B,* in which he breaks down works into their constituent parts/books.

48. *Pomponius Mela Cosmographus de Situ orbis ab Hermolao Barbaro fideliter eme[n]datus* (Pisauri: per Petrum Capha: In domo Hieronymi Soncini, 1510; Colombina 4-1-18[3], USTC 841936). The terms in the index correspond with their appearance within the main

body of the text, where lines have been numbered in series of ten and each of the terms systematically underlined.

49. *Tragedie Senece cum duobus commentariis* (Venice: Filippo I Pinzi, 1510; Colombina 1-4-19, USTC 855881). The life of Seneca is copied onto the verso of the front flyleaf, while the rear flyleaf contains the following note, which records in revealingly meticulous detail the different phases for Hernando's reading and indexation of the book: he purchased and started to read it in Valladolid on Saturday 6 March 1518, he finished reading it in Brussels, on Sunday 8 July 1520, and the index was not completed until Wednesday, 19 January 1524, between noon and one pm: "Este libro costó quatro reales y dos por encuadernar en Valladolid por marzo de 1518, así que costo seis reales. Está registrado 478. Sábado seis de marzo de 1518 comencé a leer este libro y a pasar las notas dél en el índice en Valladolit y distraído por muchas ocupaciones y caminos no lo pude acabar hasta el domingo ocho de julio de 1520 en Bruselas de Flandes en el qual tiempo las annotaciones que ay desde el numero 1559 en adelante aún no están pasadas en el índice porque quedó en España. Miércoles 19 de enero de 1524 entre las doze y la una lo torné otra vez a pasar y añadí las annotaciones que tienen dos virgulitas y las dicciones sublineados que tienen una al fin de la línea y comenzé a pasar otra vez las notas añadiendo las autoridades." "This book cost four *reales*, and two for the binding, in Valladolid around March 1518, so it cost a total of six *reales*. It is registered as 478. On Saturday 6 March 1518 I started to read this book, and to pass the notes I made about it on to the index, in Valladolid, and because I became distracted by many different tasks and journeys, I could not finish it until Sunday 8 July 1520 in Brussels of Flanders, during which time the annotations that start in number 1559 are not yet passed on to the index, because it [i.e., the index] was left behind in Spain. On Monday 19 January 1524, between twelve and one [pm] I took it up again, and registered those annotations that have two little virgules and the underlined words that have one [virgule] at the end of the line, and I started to pass on the notes again, adding the authorities."

50. Fol. xciiv, sig. q.iiv.

51. Further details in chapter 4; see also appendix 1 for Juan Pérez's description of the project.

52. Toward the end of the fifteenth century, Leon Battista Alberti had also created a description of Rome based on alphanumeric tables and a circular grid (for a modern edition, see Alberti, *Descriptio Urbis Romae,* 2005). For a detailed description of the *Cosmografía de España,* its critical and editorial fortunes, see Marín Martínez 1970, pp. 159–252, and more recently Rodríguez Toro 2018.

53. The text of this royal order is given in Marín Martínez 1970, pp. 163–64; see discussion of it in Rumeu de Armas 1973, p. 25.

54. This process is described in the *Memoria* of Juan Pérez (appendix 1).

55. "The Creation of a European Book Market," in Pettegree 2010, pp. 65–90, and Pettegree 2008.

56. Some of these titles related to the Lutheran controversy include the following:

Libro, fol. 28r, epitome 239 is Ioannes Oecolampadius's *Translatio Gregorii Nazianzeni De Moderandis Disputationibus* (of which there exist two 1521 editions, one published by Cratander in Basel, USTC 630527, and another one published in Augsburg by Grimm and Wirsung, USTC 630526). It is also registered in col. 924 of the *Abecedarium B,* which records a long list of works by Oecolampadius in cols. 922–24.

Libro, fols. 283v–284r, epitome 1080 is a treatise by Melanchthon on Pauline doctrine. The *Abecedarium B* (col. 1324) proves that Hernando had a very long list of titles by Melanchthon.

Libro, fol. 29r, epitome 246 is Philip Melanchthon's *Loci communes rerum theologicarum seu hypotyposes theologicae* (also in the *Abecedarium B,* col. 1324). First published in Wittenberg in 1521, this influential Lutheran treatise went through several different editions, some of them published before Hernando's death in 1539.

Libro, fols. 624v–625r, epitome 1601 is Joannes Briardi's (Jan Briart) *Quaestio quodlibetica contra dispensationes vel magis dissipationes commissariorum in genocio indulgentiarum* (Leipzig, 1519). For further details on Briart and this particular treatise, see Bietenholz, *Contemporaries of Erasmus,* p. 195; see figs. 7 and 8.

Libro, fols. 888r–v, epitome 2163 is Giovanni Antonio Modesti's *Oratio ad Carolum Caesarem contra Martinum Luterum* (Impræssum Romæ: per Iacobum Mazochium, 1520 die II mensis Octobris, EDIT16 53754); a 44-page quarto, i.e., another *obrezilla,* on the Reformation controversy. Also recorded in the *Abecedarium B,* col. 895.

57. Marín Martínez (1970, pp. 253–314) describes the nature and the editorial fortunes of this *Memoria de los Dibujos o Pinturas.*

58. Anonymous Italian after Titian, *The Triumph of Christ,* 2812 in Hernando's inventory; *La triomphante entrée et couronnement de Fernand, roi de Hongrie et de Bohême,* (s.n., d. 7 November 1527), Colombina 4-1-4(6); Robert Peril, *The Genealogical Tree of the House of Habsburg,* 2804 in Hernando's inventory.

59. Colombina 5-3-25(3), an undated fifteenth-century manuscript, *Cronicon usque ad destructionem Hierosolymae* may represent an exception to this rule. It should also be noted that Hernando's bibliographic symbols allowed for tracts of single pages, though as the *Tabla* using these symbols has disappeared it is not clear whether this marking was ever employed; see chapter 4.

60. See Juan Pérez's account in his *Memoria* (appendix 1).

61. Documents 34, 35, and 36 in Hernández Díaz and Muro Orejón (1941, pp. 37–38) testify to some of the reforms implemented in the orchard and gardens; see also their documents 39 (pp. 67–70), 44 (pp. 75–84), 63 (pp. 98–109), 74 (pp. 114–19). See also the description in Juan de Mal Lara's *Recibimiento que hizo la muy noble y muy leal ciudad de Sevilla a la C.R.M. del rey don Felipe N.S.*, Seville, En casa de Alonso Escrivano, 1570. Digital edition available at http://www.cervantesvirtual.com/obra-visor/recibimiento-que-hizo-la-muy-noble-y-muy-leal-ciudad-de-sevilla-a-la-crm-del-rey-don-felipe-ns—0/html/, accessed 20 July 2019.

62. For primary documents related to the construction and decoration of the Casa de

Goles, see Hernández Díaz and Muro Orejón (1941) and their documents 41 (p. 74), 46 (p. 85), and 71 (p. 113). For a recent approach to Hernando's reading of architectural treatises in his collection within the general context of Charles V's imperial project see Plaza 2017.

63. A letter from the Consejo de Indias to Alonso de Chavez in 1528 suggests that the instruction of pilots in the use of the astrolabe, quadrant, and maps was at that time happening in Hernando's house; see AGI, Indiferente, 421, L. 13, fol. 295v.

64. Juan Pérez refers to the catalogues being kept in the "sala de teología" (appendix 1); see also Marín Martínez 1970, p. 47.

65. As chapter 2 demonstrates, the typographic design, the illustrations, and other paratexts employed in Italian *libretti* (i.e., *obrezillas*) with the lives of saints and recreational amatory poetry—both genres also composed in the same meter (*ottava rima*)—were hard to distinguish from each other.

66. On the *Libro de las Materias,* see Marín Martínez 1970, pp. 363–428.

67. Hernández Díaz and Muro Orejón 1941, document 44, pp. 75–84. On the survival of Hernando's trees in Seville, see "El Zapote: Ultima memoria de las casas de don Fernando Colón," in Gestoso Pérez 1910, pp. 31–46.

68. Hernández Díaz and Muro Orejón 1941, document 43, p. 263.

69. Barrera-Osorio 2006, pp. 16–17.

70. Clenardus's letters were published by Plantin in two volumes in 1566 (*Nic. Clenardi epistolarum libri duo,* Antwerp: Plantin, 1566). Alphonse Roersch published a bilingual Latin-French edition in three volumes (Roersch 1940–41)

71. See *Registrum B* entry 3330, *Arte p[ar]a apre[n]der arabigo de mano,* which he bought for a real in Madrid in November 1516; Marín Martínez 1970, p. 63.

72. See *Abcedarium B,* col. 65; the Koran is given epitome number 3488.

73. The letter can be found in Roersch 1940, vol. 3, pp. 164–206, in French translation, and in vol. 1, pp. 206–39, in the original Latin. Clenardus's opinion coincides with Mexía, Pedro de Medina, and other contemporaries about the nature of Hernando's library, and his correspondence is witness to the international reputation it enjoyed.

74. In his *Chronici rerum memorabilium Hispaniae Tomus Prior* Vasaeus includes a reference to Hernando's library in a preface titled "Quo consilio haec scripserim." The gist of what Vasaeus tells his readers is that he left Louvain encouraged by Clenardus and subsequently came under the patronage of Hernando, in whose library he also admits he worked for some time (*Chronici rerum memorabilium Hispaniae Tomus Prior,* Salamanca: Junta, 1552, fol. 1v).

75. See appendix 5.

76. As suggested in chapter 4, the final shelf marks for the library suggest that numbers 5000–5900 were law books.

77. Rumeu de Armas 1973, pp. 71–72.

78. *Secunda pars enneadum Marci Antonii Subellici ab inclinatione romani imperii vsque ad annum MDIII cum epitome omnium librorum et indice litterarum ordine diggesto* (Venice: Bernardino I

Viani, 1504); Colombina 2-7-11, USTC 854024. The evidence for the authenticity of the biography is discussed at length in Wilson-Lee 2018.

CHAPTER TWO
Trade Secrets

1. *Stanze bellissime et ornatissime intitulate Le selue damore composte dal magnifico Lorenzo di Piero di Cosimo de Medici; opera nuoua* (Siena: Symione di Niccolo & Giouanni di Alixandro, 1511). Hernando's copy (Colombina 14-1-9[1]; EDIT16 68092) appears to be the only one available of this 1511 edition.

2. Lorenzo de' Medici, *Stanze,* 1986, pp. 41–42.

3. *Philippi Calandri ad nobilem et studiosum Julianum Laurentii Medicem de aritmethrica opusculum* (Impresso nella excelsa cipta di Firenze per ser Lorenzo de Morgiani et giovanni Thedesco da Maganza. Finito a di primo di Gennaio 1491 [1492]; ISTC ic00034000), a[i]r. Hernando's copy of the *Aritmethrica* was of the 1518 edition; it is now lost, but it appears in an entry in col. 1322 of the *Abecedarium B.*

4. Peter Martyr of Anghiera, *Decades of the New World,* I.2, in Anghiera 1992, pp. 240–41.

5. Fernández-Armesto 1991, 18.

6. For further details of the information that Day shared with Columbus, including a transcription of the letter, see Vigneras 1956 and 1957.

7. Jardine 1996, pp. 299–301.

8. Ibid., pp. 297–98 ff. for further details; see also Maifreda 2012, pp. 32–33.

9. "[The origin of double-entry bookkeeping] was a lengthy and convoluted process which, between the fourteenth and fifteenth centuries, brought arithmetic from simple linear calculation, through the positional number system and Tartaglia's tables to the *Summa de arithmetica, geometria, proportioni e proportionalità* by Franciscan monk Luca Pacioli (ca. 1445—ca. 1517) whose mercantile experience was considerable" (Maifreda 2012, p. 63).

10. This plan with four simultaneous catalogues was so central to Hernando's vision of his library and of his personal mission that he fashioned his own postmortem persona by including them in the coat of arms he designed and recorded in his testament.

11. Blair 2010, p. 3.

12. For a modern, critical edition and English translation of *The Book of Privileges,* see Nader, ed. 1996.

13. *El libro de los privilegios de la nación genovesa* is now deposited in the *Archivo de Simancas;* for a modern edition see González Gallego 1974, which can be consulted online at http://institucional.us.es/revistas/historia/01/10%20gonzalez%20gallego.pdf, accessed 24 August 2018.

14. Further details in Zamora 1993, p. 67. Hernando used similar notarial practices to collect reliable information for his *Cosmografía de España:* he dispatched his agents to every town in Spain to make eyewitness records, which were then notarized "before trustworthy

witnesses." For more details on the emerging series of actuarial and recording practices within the administrative culture of the Hispanic monarchy, and the connection between sovereign rule and knowledge, see Brendecke 2016, pp. 17-21 passim.

15. Vilches 2010, pp. 67–68.

16. One of the couriers to Genoa was Francisco de Riberol, a veteran among the Genoese merchants of Seville, whom Columbus probably met in 1492—when Riberol formed a partnership with the Florentine slave trader and banker Juanoto Berardi for the conquest of the island of La Palma; Nader, ed. 1996, p. 215.

17. On the Casa di San Giorgio and the important role of Genoa in financial history, see Felloni and Laura 2014.

18. Padgett and Powell 2012, p. 116 ff.; Neal 2015, pp. 29–33; Goldthwaite 1972, pp. 213–14.

19. For further details, see de Roover 1963, pp. 108–11, also p. 113.

20. "The use of bills of exchange as pure credit instruments therefore required not one transaction but two. The first was the outgoing bill of exchange. The second was a rechange operation by which the value payable was returned back to the place of origin. The buyer of a bill of exchange's profits (and thus the interest rate) resulted from the differential between the exchange rate at place A when the bill was originated and the exchange rate at place B when the bill was rechanged." (Bell, Brooks and More 2015, p. 5, q.v. for further details on the increasing complexity of the international financial system toward the end of the Middle Ages.) For a more recent account of the nature and function of bills of exchange, see Trivellato 2019, pp. 1-4 and 24-30.

21. "The *luoghi* were not physical securities as they only existed as book entries in the registers of the public debt" (Marsilio 2013, p. 125).

22. "La riqueza ha andado y anda en el aire, en papeles y contratos, censos y letras de cambio, en la moneda, en la plata, en el oro y no en bienes que fructifican y atraen a sí como más dignos las riquezas de afuera, sustentando las de dentro" (*Memorial de la política necesaria y útil restauración a la República de España* [Valladolid, 1600], quoted in Vilches 2010, p. 45). See also Vilches 2010, pp. 6–7. "Wealth has circulated, and still circulates, up in the air, in papers and contracts, registers, and letters of exchange, in currency, silver, and gold, not in more deserving material goods that do bear fruit and by attracting foreign wealth support domestic affluence."

23. Neal 2015, pp. 48–49. An earlier version of this abstract exchange mechanism was developed by the Mallorcan mathematician Joan Ventallol, who in his *Practica Mercantivol* (1521) suggested the use of the Venetian ducat as a standard currency to which to peg exchange rates; Hernando's copy of this bore the *Registrum B* number 14608.

24. Further details at Pelozzo and Tattara 2008, pp. 1100–1106 passim.

25. Doria 1986, pp. 75–78 passim.

26. For instance, Saminiato de' Ricci's 1416 *Manuale di Mercatura* proclaims on its first page that its contents lay out "modi e forme che si deono [*sic*] tenere in merchantie e chambi": it lists different types of currency, includes information on custom duties and

taxes, as well as on fluctuations in the price of money depending on the season, and includes some basic mathematics operations ("raggioni d'abaco") for the use of bankers and those engaged in currency exchange. This version is dated in December of 1416, but de' Ricci acknowledges that its updated information is based on a previous "quaderno fatto 1396 per Saminiato di Ghuciouozzo de' Ricci" in Genoa (Borlandi 1963, p. 69).

27. Its long title runs thus: *Libro de abaco ilquale insegna fare ogni ragione mercantile: et pertegare le terre con larte di la geometria et altre nobilissime ragione straordinarie con la tariffa come respondeno li pesi et monede de molte terre del mondo con la inclita citta di Vinegia. El qual libro se chiama Thesauro Universale.* [Venice]: opus Lucha Antonio de Uberti fe in Vinetia, [1520?] (Colombina 12-1-30, EDIT16 67543). Other *quaderni,* such as the *Prattica della mercatura* of Francesco di Balducci Pegolotti, provide an ekphrastic cosmography of the world at the time, i.e., a textual version of Behaim's globe, listing information that ranges from data about sheep-raising monasteries in England to markets in spices from Egypt to Persia, as well as providing practical information about trading posts in North Africa, in Crimea, and along the silk road all the way down to Cathay.

28. See Raymond and Moxam, eds. 2016, in particular chapter 1, "News Networks in Early Modern Europe" (pp. 1–16), and Pettegree 2014.

29. Note the similarity of this to the list of cities that form the hubs of William van de Lare's early sixteenth-century description of trade networks, the *Regula Transporti* (Plantin-Moretus Museum Archive, Arch 318): Antwerp, Nuremburg, Frankfurt, Lisbon, Lyon, Paris, and Venice; Lucas Rem's *Tagebuch* uses Augsburg, Antwerp, Lyon, Venice, and Lisbon. See "An Education in Commerce: Transmitting Business Information in Early Modern Europe," in Ojala and Müller, eds. 2007.

30. Elvira Vilches points out an equivalent reliance of Columbus upon traditional economic practices, where gold—not abstract financial instruments detached from precious metals and goods—still "provided a symbolic mode of representation" of value (Vilches 2010, p. 63).

31. Maifreda 2012, p. 63; also Mills 1994. Note that although one of the earliest public accounts in double-entry bookkeeping was indeed these Genoese records, its precise origin is far from clear. It can be located, in general, within the economic region dominated by Florence, Venice, and Genoa rather than in a single spot. For a general overview, see "Banking and Finance," in Goldthwaite 1972, pp. 203–62.

32. Lowry 1988, p. 6.

33. Ciocci 2003, pp. 20–23.

34. This *Libro de Mercantie* had circulated in many different copies—at least eight different manuscripts survive, dated between 1444 and 1496. Its first printed edition was produced in Florence in 1481, the result of the systematization of all the data gathered in the preceding notebooks, which had evolved from a sort of impromptu collection of accumulated practical information, into a more formalized handbook (Spufford 2002, p. 53). The colophon to this edition reads thus: "Finito el libro di tvcti I chostvmi : cambi : monete : pesi : misvre: & vsanze di lectere di cambi : & termini di decte lectere che ne paesi si

costvma et in diverse terre. Per me Franesco di Dino di Iacopo Kartolaio Fiorentino A di X di Dicembre MCCCCLXXXI in Firenze Appresso al munistero di Fuligno."

35. These methods were spread in large part through handbooks for merchants (*artes mercatoriae,* as they were generally known), more than a thousand of which were published between 1474 and 1600 (Dittmar 2015, p. 11).

36. Hernando bought a copy of the first edition of Pacioli's *Summa* (Venice: Paganino de Paganini, 1494) in September 1512 (Colombina 15-6-31; ISTC ip00315000).

37. "Prima novembris 1515 incepi hunc librum exponente eum magistro Sebastiano Rome inmediate post 24am horam octoque prima folia tantum in octo lectionibus exposuit" (further details in Wagner 1992, p. 480, and Marín Martínez 1993, p. 195).

38. See documents 21, 22, and 23 in Hernández Díaz and Muro Orejón 1941, pp. 28–29.

39. Documents 24 in Hernández Díaz and Muro Orejón 1941, pp. 30–33, and 29, p. 35—the latter of which demonstrates the significant amount of debt (510,000 *maravedís,* well beyond the Venetian loan) that Hernando owed to Niculoso Grimaldo, the Grimaldi's representative in Seville.

40. See for instance document 65 in Hernández Díaz and Muro Orejón 1941, p. 110: "Protocolización de una cédula del Emperador, a petición de Bautista Justinián, mercader genovés, en nombre de don Hernando Colón, con objeto de enviarla a la isla Española y evitar su extravío."

41. See Hernando's detailed description in his will (our appendix 2). The Feria de Medina del Campo had started early in the fifteenth century and by the early decades of the sixteenth it had developed into one of the most relevant markets in the Iberian Peninsula, connecting the domestic Castilian market with the rest of the world. Held twice a year (May and October), it traded in goods such as wool (a traditional Castilian export); after the invention of print it became a publishing hub as well as an important book fair, and by the early sixteenth century it had developed into a thriving market for all sorts of financial products whose maturity date was scheduled to coincide with the fair. For details on the sort of commercial and financial culture upon which it thrived, see Maravall 1999; on its role as a publishing hub, see Sánchez del Barrio 2011.

42. "Magnum ergo Latini sermonis sacramentum est [. . .] ibi . . . Romanum imperium est, ubicunque Romana lingua dominator" (Valla 1544, p. 8). The preface can also be found in Garin, ed. 1952, pp. 594–96. Hernando bought Fernando de Herrera's commentaries on Valla's *Elegantiae latinae linguae* in Medina del Campo in 1518 (*Expositio laurentij vallensis de elegantia lingue latine,* Salamanca, ca. 1515–16, Colombina 118-7-35[3], USTC 339129), and two years later, in 1520, and in Ghent, he bought Jodocus Badus Ascensius's commentaries on the same work (*Epitome ascensiana in Laurentii vallensis Patricii romani Viriq[ue] clarissimi & de litteris latinis optime meriti linguae latinae grammaticos co[m]mentarios* [s.l.: s.n., a. agosto 1520], Colombina 6-2-5[9]).

43. "Haec enim gentes illas, populosque omnes omnibus artibus, quae liberales vocantur, instituit. Haec optimas leges edocuit: haec viam ad omnem sapientiam muniuit: haec denique praestitit, ne barbari amplius dici possent" (Valla 1544, p. 7). As shown in chapter 3,

Nebrija was also interested in cosmography and lectured on methods for quantification and measurement, not just in astronomical time but also as regards weight and distance.

44. *Memorial al Emperador,* see appendix 5.

45. Maifreda 2012, p. 60.

46. Prodi 2009, pp. 137–38, our emphasis.

47. "Language is the shrine of erudition, and as it were *a storeroom for what should be concealed, and what should be made public.* Since it is *the treasury of culture and the instrument of human society,* it would therefore be to the benefit of the human race that there should be a single language, which all nations should use in common." "Sacrarium est eruditionis lingua, & siue quid recondendum est, siue promendum velut proma quaendam conda. Et quando *aerarium est eruditionis, ac instrumentum societatis hominum,* e re esset generis humani vnam esse linguam, qua omnes nationes communiter vterentur" (*Ioannis Lodouici Viuis Valentini De disciplinis libri XX* [Antwerp, 1532], fol. 97r, English translation by F. Watson in Vives 1971, p. 91). Hernando bought his own copy (Colombina 6-5-1, USTC 667155) in 1532, soon after the book was published.

48. *De sermone* 1.13; for a modern bilingual edition with Florence Bistagne's French translation see Pontano 2008, p. 96. Pontano's *Accademia Pontiniana,* which presided over the intellectual and cultural life of Aragonese Naples, mingled discussions of humanistic literature with the discipline of cosmography. Hernando was far from the only one to make the link between book collecting and measuring; Angelo Colocci, whose famous library Hernando would have known during his time in Rome, also embarked on a project to document and reconcile the weights and measures used throughout the world. See Davis 2008, p. 72.

49. Further examples of early incunabula among Hernando's purchases include a copy of Johannes Annius's *De futuris christianorum triumphis in saracenos* (Genoa, 1480; Colombina 4-2-37[2], ISTC ia00750000), purchased in Rome in November 1515. Another early incunabulum is his *Prognosticon astrologicum anni 1475* (Venice, 1474?; Colombina 12-6-34), which he purchased from Marino Sanudo (see Wagner, "Judicia," 1975a, no. 97).

50. *Registrum A,* fol. 113: "Magnifico micer octaviano de grimaldis priego a la señoria vostra de gratia se diome."

51. Further details on Hernando's itineraries and his purchases in Wagner 1984.

52. Martin Luther, *Tractatulus de his qui ad ecclesias confugiunt. Et de judicibus qui in ecclesia: et eius atrio civiles vel criminales causas tractant: placita tenent: et alia contra imunitates ecclesiarum faciunt* (Oppenheim: Jakob Köbel, 1520, USTC 699004). Johann Pinicianus, *Promptuarium vocabulorum edium partiu locorum artificu instrumentorum. Multarum quoque reru nomina continens, per librorum capita breviter et concinne distributum* (Augsburg: Silvan Otmar, 1516; Colombina 6-2-43, USTC 669219); Ulrich Burchard, *Hortulos Musices* (Leipzig, 1514; Colombina 12-1-24[4]); Hugo Reutlingensis, *Flores Musice* (Strasburg, 1492; Colombina 12-6-9, ISTC is00637400).

53. See Wagner 1981, 450. For further details about Lutheranism and the Reforma-

tion controversy among the titles that Hernando acquired, see Wagner 1981 and Marín Martínez 1975.

54. This is Juan Pérez's description in his *Memoria* (our appendix 1):

> They may also find a cross in the following manner
>
> 
>
> in the margins, which we call *pro vel contra,* and it marks a book where some author defends another, or rebuts [*impugna*] him, so one can identify who wrote against Erasmus and who defended him, and who against Luther, and so on with the rest; therefore, whoever has this symbol is opposing or defending another.

55. For instance, Hernando bought Alain de Lille's *Parabolarum Alani cum commento* (London, 1505; Colombina 2-1-36[4], USTC 500878) in Seville for 10 *maravedís* (possibly before 1509, as he does not record the date), and the *Preclarum op[us] Cyrilli Alexa[n]drini q[uod] Thesaur[us] nuncupat[ur]* (London and Cologne, 1514; Colombina 3-6-6[2], USTC 209535) in November 1515, in Rome, shortly after it was printed. See Rhodes 1958 for a list of Hernando's London purchases.

56. Vives's new program of studies evinces a pragmatically elitist ethos with contractual overtones: it is founded upon knowledge of the past, oratory, and "the celebrated art of living well with their fellow citizens" (*artemque illam civilem esse compertum est*). These are fundamental for the education of a citizen, above all for those in power, and they are all combined with very specific and very practical purposes in mind: "to develop the arguments and strategies for handling public affairs, which must be thought and wrested *from the midst of life, from a fund of practical experience,* and from acquaintance with all of antiquity" (from the preface to the Antwerp 1520 edition, in Vives 1989, p. 103). Hernando's summary of Vives's *Declamationes* survives, in a truncated form, as the very last page in the Copenhagen *Libro de los Epítomes* (no. 2330, fol. 973r, see fig. 11).

57. Further details in Hernando's testament, in Hernández Díaz and Muro Orejón 1941, pp. 153–57.

58. Marín Martínez 1970, pp. 61–62.

59. Infantes 1989.

60. Conrad Gesner, *Pandectarum sive partitionum universalium,* 1548, fol. 95r; see also Zambelli 1960, pp. 159–60.

61. See Colombina 4-2-18(2), *Incipiu[n]t prenosticata Iuliani Pomerii urbis toletane episcopi de futuro seculo* (Alosti: Theodoricus Martens, ca. 1487–1488), mistakenly attributed to Julianus Pomerius, an early church theologian with whom Saint Julian of Toledo was conflated at this period. See Roth 2002, p. 95.

62. See Hillgarth 1957; for a modern critical edition with English translation, see Stancati 2010, who describes him as the first theologian to have compiled a systematic work on

Christian eschatology. Hernando's copy of Julian's *Prognosticon futuri saeculi* (*Abecedarium B*, col. 978) has a surviving epitome (1817) in fols. 694r–v of the *Libro de los Epítomes*.

63. One of them is 12-1-12(18), a Venice edition published by Thomas de Blavis in 1487 (ISTC ip00188100); the other copy (12-1-13[15]) was also published in 1492 by Johannes & Gregorius de Gregoriis, also in Venice (ISTC ip00188200).

64. See Sherman 1995.

65. Rouch, ed. 2006, p. xviii.

66. The surviving shelf mark numbers—explained in chapter 4—allow us to confirm that all of the tracts contained in the modern volume 6-3-29 were bound together during Hernando's life (in vol. 10938 of the library), with the exception of two, which have differing shelf marks and so must have been kept separately at that point and added to 6-3-29 during a later rebinding. The same is true of the modern sammelband 6-3-30, which contained all the same pamphlets during Hernando's lifetime and bore the shelf number 10871.

67. 6-3-30(2).

68. 12-1-15(87), *De la vera Pronosticatione del Diluuio del mille [et] cinquecento [et] vintiquatro Composto per lo excelle[n]tissimo Philosopho Thomado da Rauenna; Intitulato al Christianissimo Imperador* ([Venice: s.n., 1523]; [6] h.; 4° [21 cm], EDIT16 68597).

69. See, for instance, Zambelli 1982.

70. This tract was personally presented to Hernando by the author on 11 January 1530, when both men were in northern Italy to attend the coronation of Charles as Holy Roman Emperor at Bologna.

71. 8-2-33(18), *Exemplar ep[isto]le ad doctorem Hennignum Gode Prepositum . . . Contra fratrem Martinu[m] Luttheri Scismaticum per Theodericum de Eynem* ([s.l.: s.n., ca. 1520]; [4] h.; 4° [22 cm]).

72. The fact that pamphlets and *libretti* are also summarized in the *Libro de los Epítomes*, alongside Plato's works, confirms the importance that Hernando granted to these materials and the sort of public controversies that they recorded. See for instance epitome 904 (fols. 231r–v) with a summary of a collection of *libretti* by Pasquil: "Est in re literaria libellus quidam pasquilli." Epitome 926 (fols. 328r–v), also recorded in the *Abecedarium B* (col. 1268) alongside a long list of Pasquil titles, proves that Hernando had a long list of the almost yearly *Carmina apposita Pasquillo;* these were *libretti*, some in quarto, others in octavo, with just a few pages (ca. 28–48) which collected the controversial satirical poems and texts that were posted in Roman statues. EDIT16 records seven of them: 9609 (1512) 4°; 9610 (1513?) 4°; 9611 (1514?) 4°; 9612 (1515?) 4°; 9613 (1521) 8°; 9614 (1525?) 8°; 56437 (1526) 4°. Hernando's *Abecedarium B* records at least fourteen collections, for the years 1509, 1510, 1512, 1513, 1514, 1515, 1516, 1517, 1518, 1519(?), 1522, 1524, 1525, and 1526. A collection from 1526 survives in the Colombina, the *Carmina apposita Pasquillo M.D.xxvj* (14-2-3[6]), which is bound in a sammelband with the *Carmina apposita Grillo Monoculo ad Pasquill[u]m MDxxvj* (also registered in the *Abecedarium B* 14-2-3[5], and the *Registrum B* 10833). A third collection in the Colombina is *Anno .M.d.xvj. Carmina ad Protheum* (14-2-5[9], *Registrum B* 3756, also registered

in the *Abecedarium B*), which Hernando purchased in Rome in June of the same year of its publication (1516) for 3 *quatrines*.

73. Hernando's *pliegos poéticos* were catalogued by Rodríguez-Moñino (1976), the chief expert in this particular format.

74. *Lamento de Italia: diuiso in capituli septe composito per Iacobo Rossetto Darthonese; al Beatissimo Papa Iulio Secundo*—[Italia?: s.n., a. octubre 1512], EDIT16 68779. *La summa gloria di Venetia: con la su[m]ma de le sue uictorie, nobilita, paesi, e dignita, [et] officii, et altre nobilissime illustre cose di sue laude e glorie come nela presente operetta se contiene: Dicta est gloria cronice noue Venetorum* . . . [Fra[n]ciscus de Alegris]—[Venice: s.n., 1501], EDIT16 1204.

75. The online catalogue of the Colombina yields seven different titles penned by him, whereas EDIT16 records fifteen titles under his authorship. 6-3-24(7), *Lamento de Bartolomeo Dalviano* [a co[m]posto elamento el perosino]—[Italia?: s.n., a. junio 1513], EDIT16 68780. D'Alviano (1455–1515) was a *condottiero* who put his considerable military acumen at the service of the Vatican States, Venice, King Ferdinand the Catholic, and the French monarchy—among others. Perossino is also the author of *El fatto darme fatto ad Rauena nel MDXii Adi xi de apprile*, a remarkable case of news in *ottava rima*. The title itself already records the year and the date of the events which are being reported: the Battle of Ravenna, one of the most important battles in the Italian Wars.

76. 13-2-16(40), *Lassault de Le[m]pereur a barberosse*—[Lyon: Pierre de Sainte-Lucie, 1535], USTC 53625.

77. *La grant armee de Lempereur lequel sen va combatre contre le Turc. Barberousse et tous infidelles*—[Lyon: Pierre de Sainte-Lucie, 1535]; (13-2-16[4], USTC 34834).

78. *La copie dune lettre mandee de Thunes de la prinse de la gollete au Seigneur do[n] Gaspard de Mendoza gentilhomme de Lempereur* [Francoys de Ferrare]—[Lyon: Pierre de Sainte-Lucie, 1535]; 13-2-16(42), USTC 53651.

79. Some of Hernando's sammelbands actually record documents whose publication was prompted by the celebration of this council (e.g., 12-1-22, 12-1-21, and 12-1-20). They include for instance the *Conuocatio generalis Concilii ex parte cardinalium*, bound in a sammelband with numerous bulls and other *obrezillas* related to the policy and the administration of Vatican affairs (13-3-5, "Collectio Bullarum Variarum Tom. 1"; the document in question is 13-3-5[21]).

80. See Carabias Torres 2012, pp. 21, 149. *De correctione kalendarii propositiones XIII. Recollectae ex multis disceptationibus habitis per d. ad hoc specialiter deputatos ex parte s.d.n. papae & sacrae deputationibus fidei in Concilio Lateranensi* (12-1-22[1], USTC 802145). Andreas de Pace's *In nouum modum corrigendi kalendarium* [Rome: Stephanus Guileretus, 1516]; EDIT16 54774. "Este tratado me envió maestre Pedro de Salamanca de Roma a los 29 de mayo de 1517 y recibido en Madrid a 16 de junio del dicho año. Está registrado '2668' y '4256.'"

81. The volume bears a later label, "Opuscul. Mathematica Diversor. Tom. 5."

82. In Genoa, January 1515, and on his way to Rome, Hernando purchased a copy of Silvestre de Piero's *In theoricas planetarum praeclarissima commentaria Georgii Purbachii*. As

his own manuscript note confirms, he used it as a textbook for the lectures by Sebastiano Veterani: "El día primero de noviembre de 1515 comencé este libro que exponía mi maestro Sebastián en Roma; sólo las primeras ocho páginas lo fueron en ocho lecciones y 24 horas." Sebastiano Veterani gave him a copy of his own *Disputatio de eccentricis et epiciclis* several months later ("mihi idem Sebastianus dedit 5 die mensis anni 1516").

83. 6-1-18, *Calendarium romanum magnum: Caesareae maiestati dicatum D. Ioanne Stoeffler iustingensi Mathematico authore,* Oppenheim: Jakob Köbel, 1518 (USTC 617753). Zambelli's roll call of German and Italian astrologers in the early decades of the sixteenth century demonstrates that most, if not all of them, are represented in Hernando's collection (Zambelli 1986b, pp. 239–40).

84. Carabias Torres 2012, pp. 71–72.

85. 5-3-25(3). The same sammelband also includes *Cronicon usque ad destructionem Hierosolymae,* a single-leaf manuscript on the destruction of Jerusalem.

86. 5-3-25(17), *Anno domini 151[cortado] secundum Ecclesiam pronosticho fatto a di 15 frebuario . . . Del 1519 fina nel 1524 o puocho auanto o puocho dapoi.* This manuscript in several different hands has a possessor's note in fol. 1r that reads thus: "n° 3754 Est Marini Sanuti Leonardi filij." For another among Sanudo's books with a prognostication, see 12-6-34, *Prognosticon astrologicum anni 1475*—an incunabulum, apparently not recorded in ISTC. According to Wagner ("Judicia," 1975a, no. 97), this is one of Sanudo's books (something which the online catalogue of the Colombina does not record).

87. *Ioannis Lodouici Viuis Valentini De disciplinis libri XX,* Colombina 6-5-1.

88. "The first thing man has to learn is speech. It flows at once from the rational soul as water from a fountain. As all beasts are bereft from intellect, so they are also lacking in speech. *Discourse is also the instrument of human society.*" (Prima in homine peritia est loquendi. Quae statim ex ratione ac mente tanquam ex fonte profuit. Idcirco bestie omnes sicut mente, ita & sermone carent. *Est etiam sermo societatis humanae instrumentum.* Vives 1532, fol. 96r, English translation by F. Watson in Vives 1971, p. 90, our emphasis.) As we mentioned in the introduction, the idea of a universal language had already been formulated in Augustine's *City of God,* which invokes the problem of human communication caused by the diversity of languages. ("The first misfortune is the lack of communication resulting from language differences.") The entire passage can be consulted in Augustine 2010, book 19, chapter 7, pp. 205–6.

89. Angelo Poliziano, *Panepistemon,* in *Opera,* Basle, 1553, 462. Hernando registered Poliziano's *Panepistemon* in entry no. 1760 of his *Libro de los Epítomes* (fols. 676r–v). The entry on *Astronomia* in the *Loci Communes* (Colombina 7-2-60) is on fol. 5r.

CHAPTER THREE
Cartography

1. "The Soldier and the Carthusian," in Erasmus, *Colloquies* (1997, p. 330).

2. "The Old Men's Chat, or The Carriage," in ibid., p. 453.

3. AGI, Indiferente, 421, vol. 11, fol. 234r; see our appendix 4.

4. Alongside theoretical considerations on cosmography and abstract Ptolemaic principles, the *Espejo* also includes very practical information and instructions not just for navigation, but also for the efficient preparation of expeditions in terms of investment and logistics, such as the amounts of victuals required or the sort of crew to be recruited. It also has a section on how to craft and use ("la fabrica y uso," p. 103) all the different instruments which are necessary not just for navigation itself, but also for the elaboration of sea charts.

5. "Se nos representa la imagen del mundo por ausencia suya de él, y nos da a entender por su *traza, escritura y pintura,* la misma traza, semejanza o posición que el mundo guarda consigo mismo." *Qvatri partitv en cosmographía práctica i por otro nombre llamado Espeio de navegantes. Obra mvi vtilíssima i compendiosa en toda la arte de marear i mvi neccesaria i de grand provecho en todo el cvrso de la navegación, principalmente de España. Agora nueua mente ordenada y compuesta por Alonso de Chaues cosmógrapho dela Magestad Cesárea del emperador y Rei delas Españas Carlo quinto semper augusto* (MS 9/2791 de la Real Academia de la Historia, Madrid, ca. 1537, p. 110). There is a copy of the original manuscript in the digital library of the Real Academia de la Historia, http://bibliotecadigital.rah.es/dgbrah/es/catalogo_imagenes/grupo.cmd?path=1022533&texto_busqueda=&interno=S&posicion=1, accessed 10 August 2019.

6. "Y así, por este instrumento, en breve cantidad o espacio, *comprendemos todo lo que por otras vías no podríamos con muy grandísimos volúmenes de libros y escrituras.* Y tal instrumento hallaron los sabios antiguos ser el más cómodo y provechoso para la navegación, y para *representarnos en breve figura lo que no se puede dar a entender por muchas palabras*" (ibid., our italics).

7. Ibid., p. 251.

8. "Muy asentado tengo en el ánima que *allí donde dije es el Paraíso Terrenal* y descanso *sobre razones y autoridades sobreescritas*" ("El tercer viaje. Carta del Almirante a los Reyes Católicos," in Colón 2006, pp. 206–12).

9. MS 652, Biblioteca del Palacio Real de Madrid. Online copy available at http://fotos.patrimonionacional.es/biblioteca/ibis/pmi/II_00652/index(3).html. Marín Martínez deduces that the manuscript of the *Colón de Concordia* must have been written in Seville around 1510–11, and that at least two copies must have been made, one for Hernando's own library and another one sent to Cardinal Cisneros (Marín Martínez 1993, pp. 189–90).

10. "En el primero de los cuales se mostró que en nuestros días sería todo el mundo de Oriente a Occidente por todas partes navegado, y la forma que en ello se debía tener; en el segundo se dijo que por todo el mundo así mesmo en nuestros días sería la palabra del Evangelio divulgada y recibida; y en el tercero se probó que el universal imperio había de ser a la corona de España concedido."

11. "Demas desto descubrir, espeçialmente a que se diese fin en el viaje de rrodear el mundo que el almirante mi padre muchas veses platico de poner en efecto; y a esto segund dixe con devido acatamiento, die lo que dello siento, asi por la experiençia de lo que alcançe navegando con mi padre, como por lo que del aprendi de palabra y de muchos libros y escripturas que del me quedaron y de otras partes he recojido" (see appendix 3).

12. Portuondo 2009, pp. 20–21.

13. For instance, in February 1514 Hernando bought Nebrija's *Introductiones latinae* in Madrid (*Aelii Antonii Nebrissen[sis] introductiones in latinam grammaticen: cum longioribus glossematis* [. . .] —Logronii [. . .]: Arnaldus guillelmus [. . .], 1513; Colombina 12-5-5); later that year he bought copies of Feliciano de Silva's *El séptimo libro de Amadís* (Seville: Juan Varela de Salamanca, 1514; now lost but recorded in *Registrum B* 4000, USTC 347821) and the *Historia de Melosina* (Valencia: s.n., 1512; *Registrum B* 4146, USTC 347537).

14. "And when we saw so many inhabited cities and villages on the water, and other great populations on terra firma, and that road, so straight and leveled in the direction of Mexico, we stood in admiration, and told each other that they looked like the enchanted things recounted in the book of *Amadís*" ("Y desde que vimos tantas ciudades y villas pobladas en el agua, y en tierra firme otras grandes poblazones, y aquella calzada tan derecha y por nivel cómo iba a México, nos quedamos admirados, y decíamos que parecía a las cosas de encantamiento que cuentan en el libro de *Amadís*," Díaz del Castillo [1632] 1939, chapter 87, p. 308). Díaz del Castillo's *Historia* did not go into print until 1632, but Hernando owned a copy of the Latin translation of Cortés's letters with his report of the conquest of Mexico—which included the first map of Tenochtitlan ever seen in Europe. In contrast with the more literary account of Díaz del Castillo, or Peter Martyr's resort to the well-known myth of the Golden Age, Cortés restricted himself to more mundane comparisons, describing the natives' houses and their garments as *Moorish,* their urban design as similar to Granada—all of these familiar, domestic *others*—and their political systems as resembling those of the republics of Venice, Genoa, or Pisa, "for they have no overlord." *Praeclara Ferdinādi Cortesii de noua maris Oceani Hyspania narratio Sacratissimo ac Inuictissimo Carolo romanorū imperatori* [. . .] [Impresa in [. . .] Norimberga: per Fridericum Peypus], 1524 (Colombina 6-4-28, USTC 686162). For an English translation, see Cortés 2001, pp. 67–68.

15. Randles 1988, p. 115. As we mention below, Jose Vizinho also translated into Portuguese Abraham Zacuto's *Almanach Perpetuum,* from its original Hebrew (*Hajibbur hagadol*). Zacuto's numerical tables were used to calculate latitudes by direct observation of the meridian altitudes of the sun.

16. The quotation by Augustine is the full text of chapter 24, book 17, which stresses the continuity between the prophets of the Old Testament and the prophecies included in the New Testament. This chapter is a prelude to book 18, where Augustine details Christian chronography through the succession of prophets until the birth of Christ. As he does so, he contrasts the chronography of these prophets with pagan documentary records, which are thus incorporated within Augustine's universal repertory of times. Josephus's work is itself also a chronography of Jewish history: book 8 goes from the death of King David to the death of Ahab. The copy of Toscanelli's letter with its description of the geographical features of the globe and the map (the latter of which is now missing) were subsequently used by Bartolomé de las Casas for his *Historia de las Indias*—a practical demonstration of how iconic geographical data could feed back into historical narrative, of how cartography could be transformed into chronography. See Gil and Varela, ed. 1984, pp. 129–41, who

include a transcription of the letter. Rumeu de Armas also includes a transcription of the Toscanelli letter, in several versions, as an appendix (Rumeu de Armas 1973, pp. 435–42).

17. Ptolemy, *Geography,* book 1, chapter 5. Augustine, *Confessions,* 11.28.

18. Soja (1989, p. 120) discusses the "classical debates in the history of science over the absolute versus the relative qualities of physical space," a subject which is related to the coexistence of these two types of patterns in cartography (i.e., rational vs. mythical). Soja describes these debates in terms of the dichotomy between "concrete spatialities" ("the physical space of material nature"), qua substantial forms, and those which are socially produced, i.e., "a set of relations between individuals and groups, an 'embodiment' and medium of social life itself" (i.e., the "mental space of cognition and representation").

19. It includes, for instance, details obtained by the expedition of Bartholomew Diaz, who sailed around the Cape of Good Hope in search of a new route to India.

20. This suggests that the author of the note in Piccolomini's *Historia* must have been Bartholomew. In fact, Martellus's map contributed to cementing the errors Columbus made in his calculation of the distance between Europe and Cipango. The information employed in its creation was similar to the data included in Toscanelli's letter and in Behaim's globe, all of which ignored the existence of an entire new continent between Europe and the Far East. See "Prólogo" in Varela 1982, p. lxii. For further details and the relevant primary sources, see also Gil, ed. 1992, pp. xxxviii–xxxix; Rumeu de Armas 1973, p. 227; and also Gil, ed. 1987, p. xviii.

21. *De optimo reip. statu deque noua insula Utopia libellus [. . .] uiri Thomae Mori [. . .]; Epigrammata clarissimi dissertissimiq[ue] uiri Thomae Mori pleraq[ue] e Graecis uersa. Epigrammata Des. Erasmi Roterodami* (Apud inclytam Basileam: apud Ioannem Frobenium, 1518, Colombina 12-2-39 bis, USTC 630792). Hernando bought the book in Ghent in 1520 and read it in Brussels two years later: "Hu[n]c libru[m] perlegi Bruselis 26 et 27 diebus mensis martij 1522." As is well known, More's work also reproduced the paratexts and iconic conventions of travel narratives, including maps of the island, and even a table with a lexicographic and grammatical description of its language. On Polo, see Gil's edition of the text and the notes (Gil, ed. 1992, p. xxxviii passim). Hernando had three different editions of Marco Polo, including Santaella's Spanish translation, a version that contradicted Columbus's interpretation of the new discoveries (Gil, ed. 1987, p. xviii). This also proves that a translation could be among the battlefields, or the public arenas, where the interpretation of the world, the nature and identity of the new lands, were being discussed and debated.

22. This is how Pliny summarizes his endeavor: "I have included in thirty-six books 20,000 topics, all worthy of attention, (for, as Domitius Piso says, *we ought to make not merely books, but valuable collections*) gained by *the perusal of about 2,000 volumes,* of which a few only are in the hands of the studious, on account of the obscurity of the subjects, procured by the *careful perusal of 100 select authors;* and to these I have made considerable additions of things, which were either not known to my predecessors, or which have been lately discovered." (Pliny the Elder, *The Natural History,* trans. John Bostock. book 1, dedication, "C. Pli-

nius Secundus to His Friend Titus Vespasian," Perseus Digital Library, http://www.perseus.tufts.edu/hopper/text?doc=Perseus%3atext%3a1999.02.0137, accessed 16 April 2016; punctuation slightly modified, our emphasis. For the Latin original, see Pliny the Elder, *Naturalis Historia,* ed. Karl Friedrich Theodor Mayhoff, also available at the Perseus Digital Library, http://www.perseus.tufts.edu/hopper/text?doc=Perseus%3Atext%3A1999.02.0138%3Abook%3Dpreface%3Achapter%3D4, accessed 28 August 2018.) Further details on the links between Pliny and Roman imperialism in Murphy 2004, pp. 49–50 passim.

23. See Casson 2001.

24. On Callimachus's catalogues, the *pinakes,* see Blum 1991.

25. Gómez 2008, pp. 67–68.

26. See Edson 2007, pp. 209–10. Niccoli's collection was first housed in the Convent of San Marco, in Florence. The library was designed by the architect Michelozzo Michelozzi, who had previously built the library of San Giorgio Maggiore in Venice for Cosimo in 1433 and now "succeeded in creating at the same time the architectural model for the renaissance library and its most effective realization" (Ullman and Stadter 1972, p. 5, q.v. for further details). Columbus's copy was published in Rome, 1478 (ISTC ip01083000). Hernando's surviving copy, however, is not the same as that originally owned by Columbus but a different edition purchased in Nuremberg (10 December 1521), which included Johannes Ruysch's *Universalior Cogniti Orbis Tabula*—one of the earliest printed world maps to include the new territories (Colombina 119-5-2, USTC 669005).

27. *Quadratum geometricum* (Nuremberg: Johannes Stuchs, 1516; Colombina 15-5-14[3], VD16 912136); *Epitoma in Almagestum Ptolemaei* (Venice: Johannes Hamman for Kaspar Grossch and Stephan Roemer; Colombina 119-7-7, ISTC ir00111000). The curriculum in Salamanca also included Aristotle's *De coelo et mundo* and *Meteorologica;* Pomponius Mela's *De situ orbis,* and Pliny's *Historia naturalis*. For further details, see Carabias Torres 1995, p. 965.

28. Another important figure in this nexus was Johannes Sacrobosco (Portuondo 2009, pp. 26–28). Sacrobosco shared with Strabo the combination of scientific sources (e.g., Alfargani, Aristotle, Macrobius) with literary sources (Ovid, Virgil, Lucan) in his account of cosmic order—which adds a secular literary dimension to the narratives of Christian teleology that also pervaded cosmography.

29. In 1545 the first professor of cosmography at the Casa de la Contratación, Jerónimo de Chaves, produced an enlarged and profusely annotated Castilian translation of Sacrobosco's *Sphere,* which also featured new astronomical tables. *Tractado de la Sphera qve compvso el doctor Ioannes de Sacrobvsto [sic] con muchas additiones. Agora nueuamente traduzido de Latin en lengua Castellana por el Bachiller Hieronymo de Chaves: el qual añidio muchas figuras tablas, y claras demonstrationes: junctamente con vnos breues Scholios, necessarios a mayor illucidation, ornato y perfection del dicho tractado* (Seville: Juan de León, 1545). For information on the sort of books that were in current use by cosmographers, see Wagner's inventory of the books owned by Jerónimo de Chaves (Wagner 2001).

30. Turnbull 1996, pp. 7–9.

31. For the history of the Casa's accounting practices, see Donoso Arnés 1996, 2016; for its early years, Ladero Quesada 2002.

32. On Mexía's incorporation to the project for the *mappamundi* at the Casa de la Contratación around 1535, see Sandman 2002, pp. 86–87. Mexía was also an organic intellectual of sorts at the service of the Habsburg dynasty. His *Historia Imperial y Cesárea* (Seville, 1545) traced the chronographic map of empire from Augustus through Maximilian, grandfather of Mexía's boss, Charles V. And in the entry on libraries within the encyclopedic *Silva de Varia Lección* (Seville, 1540), which very closely follows the same entry in Saint Isidore's *Etymologies,* he locates Hernando's collection as the most recent episode within the long history of libraries—which naturally included the library of Alexandria ("De la primera librería que hubo en el mundo, dónde fue, y de otras librerías que ha habido muy señaladas. Y cómo se ponían las imágenes y figuras de los excelentes hombres en letras en ella antiguamente," in Mexía 2003, pp. 549–54).

33. "En todo no se an de seguir por los antiguos cosmographos, según dellos lo disen por la diuersidad y mutaçion que hasen las tierras y las yslas y los mares, pues no estan contino en vn ser, como por muchas esperiençias y avtoridades se prueva" (see appendix 3). His own lexicographic projects would also confirm that language was also subject to constant diversity and mutation.

34. See chapter 1 for a discussion of Nebrija's *Vocabula Barbara* in Peter Martyr's *Decades* (*De Orbe Novo Decades* [Alcalá: Brocar, 1516]; USTC 334326, Colombina 10-3-3[1], fols. [65]r–[67]r). In November of 1513 Hernando bought in Madrid Elio Antonio de Nebrija's *Introductiones latinae,* which had just been published in Logroño.

35. *Aelii Antonii nebrissensis gram[m]atici in cosmographiæ libros introductoriu[m] incipitur fœliciter ad lectorem* (Salamanca: Juan de Porras, ca. 1498; ISTC ia00908000).

36. *Lexicon, hoc est, dictionarium ex sermone Latino in Hispaniensem* (Salamanca: Juan de Porras, 1492; ISTC ia00899000); *Dictionarium ex Hispaniensi in Latinum Sermonem* (Salamanca: Juan de Porras, ca. 1494; ISTC ia00897000).

37. On the importance of Zacuto's work in the international context of techniques and methods to calculate longitude, see Randles 1998, pp. 49–50 passim.

38. They were also incorporated in Martín Fernández de Enciso's *Suma de Geographia* (Seville, 1519), and from Enciso's *Suma* these tables were in turn rendered into English by Sebastian Cabot's associate, the merchant adventurer Roger Barlow, in his manuscript *A Brief Summe of Geographie* (ca. 1535–1543).

39. The brothers took with them at least four trunks with 57, 78, 75, and 28 volumes, respectively, which included the ever-present *Book of Prophecies,* some "cartones de Zacuto" (i.e., Zacuto's astronomical tables), and "papeles y figuras de astrologia" (Berwick Alba, ed. 2011, p. 78). Hernando epitomized Zacuto's *Almanach perpetuum* as entry no. 2025 in his *Libro de los Epítomes* (fols. 785r–v).

40. For a modern edition with a Spanish translation, see Costas Rodríguez 1981. Hernando's *Supplementum* confirms that in his library he had copies of *De mensuris* and *De ponderibus* (fol. 3r).

41. Its full title runs *Tabla de la diversidad de los dias y horas y partes de hora en las ciudades, villas, y lugares de España, y otros de Europa, que les responden por sus paralelos* ([Alcalá de Henares]: Arnao Guillén de Brocar, ca. 1516). Hernando's copy has been lost, but he records the book in his *Registrum B*, entry 2725, which reads (inter alia): "Diómela el mismo author en Alcalá de Henares, año 1517."

42. The only method available, between Ptolemy and the early nineteenth century, was the simultaneous observation of lunar eclipses. See Portuondo 2009, pp. 24–25.

43. On Nebrija, see the classic study by Rico 1978, and Carmen Lozano's "Antonio de Nebrija y la *Gramática sobre la Lengua Castellana*," in her critical edition of Nebrija's work (Nebrija 2011, pp. 345–452).

44. Randles actually attributes to Nebrija "the earliest attempt in Europe to measure experimentally the value of the degree of the meridian," which if true would be an important achievement, were it not for the fact that "nothing is known of the circumstances and methods of Nebrija's measurement and the result does not seem to have been taken account of by sailors at the time" (Randles 1998, p. 48).

45. That Hernando was interested in this aspect of Nebrija's work is demonstrated by some of the items listed in the *Supplementum*, which include normative works on punctuation, orthography, grammar, and general language use in Spanish, Latin, Greek, and Hebrew. They include titles such as: *De dictionibus latinis accentus, Relectio nova de accentu latino, De litteris grecis, De litteris hebraicis cum annotationibus in sacram scripturam, De punctis clausularum, Gramatica cum [¿] et introductio ad litteras graecas, Grammatica cum commentariis ipsius et [. . .], Ortographia, Reglas de ortografia en español, Repeticio [¿] de corruptis [. . .] vocibus.*

46. Marín Martínez 1970, p. 48; Marín Martínez 1993, pp. 278–80. See also Laborda Orihuela 2002, who has edited the scattered notes that went into Hernando's *Cosmografía de España.*

47. "Se concluye . . . que ninguna de las partes podrá convencer a la que quisiere tergiversar, y así digo que en este caso no puede haber sentencia por el presente, salvo que será necesario hacer de acuerdo la experiencia de la grandeza de los grados, y esta habida habrán de disputar naos y personas que por algunas de las dichas vías o de otras mejores que hallaran para medir la longitud, vayan a definir e señalar el principio e fin de la dicha demarcación, y las tierras que en cada parte o hemisferio se encierra" (*Parecer que dio D. Hernando Colon en la junta de Badajoz sobre la pertenencia de los Malucos*, 13 April 1524, in Fernández de Navarrete 1835, vol. 4, pp. 334–35).

48. "D. Hernando Colon dice que el primer capítulo contenido en la capitulación asentada entre los Reyes católicos, que en gloria sean, y el Rey D. Juan de Portugal, explica cierta división de mares y tierras, de la cual, como el vulgo no tuviese cierta noticia ni entendimiento, ha provenido que por todas partes se haya sembrado por pública fama que habían dividido entre sí el mundo, y desto asimismo resuelta que infieran otra conclusion general del vulgo que es han dividido, luego siguese que dividieron por iguales partes; por manera que la dicha fama proviene que en las personas que mandó al presente S.M. entender en lo tocante a la propiedad cató una impresión tan arraigada, que se persuaden que en

realidad de verdad ello es asi: y puesto caso que hayan visto e leido diversas veces la dicha capitulacion, no basta para que en la manera de su proceder no tengan aquel presupuesto por verdadero, especialmente viendo que no les fue dicho lo contrario por los señores del Consejo de S.M., allá en la corte." *Memorial de D. Hernando Colón a los diputados letrados de la Junta de Badajoz, para que declaren lo relativo al derecho de S.M. al dominio y pertenencia del Maluco* (27 de abril de 1524), and *Parecer de los astrónomos y pilotos españoles de la Junta de Badajoz sobre la demarcación y propiedad de las islas del Maluco* (Fernández de Navarrete, *Colección de viajes y descubrimientos* . . . , Madrid, 1837, vol. 4, pp. 333–39, 342–55).

49. According to the *Índice general de papeles del Consejo de Indias* (fol. 60v), Hernando had first been given this commission on 20 May 1518; another order was issued on 6 October 1526 (AGI, Indiferente, 421, L. 11, fols. 234r–234v); Hernando was evidently still working on the map in 1535 as the crown wrote to him on 20 May (AGI, Indiferente, 1961, L. 3, fols. 276r–276v) to order him to complete the map. The royal order seems actually to have been issued in March of that year (Rumeu de Armas 1973, p. 81n).

50. "Orden a D. Hernando Colón para convocar los pilotos que le pareciere y hacer con ellos un mapamundi y carta de navegar que quedase por patrón en la Casa de Contratación de Sevilla" (October 1526), quoted in Gil, ed. 1992, pp. xiv–xv. For data on these and related primary sources, see Rumeu de Armas 1973, pp. 81–82. There is another complementary order from March of 1527, the "Real Cédula mandada a los maestres y pilotos que se junten con Don Hernando Colón y hagan una carta general de navegar, a causa de los defectos de las que había y obligándoles a que hiciesen diarios de sus viajes, en que anotasen lo que iban descubriendo, para dar cuenta de ello en la Casa de Contratación" (Fernández de Navarrete 1835, vol. 4, p. 342).

51. Sandman 2002, p. 85. A few years later, Münster would also have a network of correspondents, and he used a standard questionnaire that he sent to each of them, to collect information for his monumental *Cosmographia*—the sort of information he intended to gather reveals the similarity between Münster's plan and Hernando's more modest, and unfinished, *Cosmographía de España*. See Grafton 1992, pp. 106–7.

52. According to some unconfirmed traditions this map was once part of Hernando's library, and some secondary sources even attribute its authorship to Hernando himself—which is somewhat implausible (Köhl 1860, p. 21; quoted in Castañeda Delgado et al. 1983, p. 18 n20). Castañeda Delgado et al. conclude that the author of the Weimar chart was Diego Ribero (see their pp. 16–20), whereas Cerezo attributes it to Chaves, who in his view then inspired Ribero as a model for all his subsequent charts, including his 1529 mappamundi. Cerezo quotes primary sources like Pinelo and Antonio de Herrera, both of whom attribute to Hernando the authorship of these maps—or at least the coordination of the team that produced them. Diego Ribero's 1529 map is now at the Vatican library, and its full title is *Carta universal en que se contiene todo lo que del mondo Se ha descubierto fasta agora: Hizola Diego Ribero Cosmographo de Su Magestad: Año de 1529. La qual se devide en dos partes conforme a la capitulacion que hizieron los catholicos Reyes de españa, y El Rey don Juan de portugal e la Villa de Tordessilas: Año de 1494.*

53. Marín Martínez 1993, p. 276.

54. Cerezo Martínez 1994, pp. 202–3.

55. Wagner 1975b.

56. Jacob 2006, p. xv.

57. There are innumerable examples. The Bodleian was originally designed as a rock to establish the foundations of Protestantism, for instance; as Valla's preface to his Latin translation of Thucydides demonstrates, some collections and manuscripts in fifteenth-century Italy had a decidedly cultural imperialist agenda.

58. For further details, see Soja 1989, pp. 20–21.

CHAPTER FOUR
New World Order

1. Marín Martínez (1970), 81, includes the "Coloquio sobre las dos graduaciones que las cartas de Indias tienen," Real Biblioteca II/652 (7), as potentially Hernandine; see Wilson-Lee 2018, p. 363, for further discussion.

2. Hernández Díaz and Muro Orejón 1941, p. 160; see also our translation in appendix 2.

3. Marín Martínez 1970, pp. 136–38. The document, which covers nineteen closely written folios in BNE MS 652, appears not to be in the hand of Juan Pérez but to be a roughly contemporary copy in another hand. See appendix 1 for our translation of the original.

4. Marín Martínez 1970, pp. 138–39.

5. Ibid., pp. 144–45.

6. See our Appendix I. For a transcription and discussion of the royal mandate withdrawing the letters of authorization, see Marín Martínez 1970, pp. 161–67. Though this mandate does not make clear when the letters had originally been issued, we know it must have been by November 1518, when one of his emissaries is noted in the manuscript of the *Cosmografía* as not having found Hernando at home.

7. "En breve cantidad o espacio, *comprendemos todo lo que por otras vías no podríamos con muy grandísimos volúmenes de libros y escrituras*" (Alonso de Chaves, *Espejo de navegantes,* see chapter 3). See also Alberti, *Descriptio Urbis Romae,* 2005.

8. As mentioned in chapter 2, with these sorts of practices Hernando was following his father's habit of recording information in notarized documents—such as the *Libro de los Privilegios.*

9. Our description of the manuscripts is drawn largely from the extensive study in Marín Martínez 1970, pp. 201-52, as well as consultation of the Colombina manuscripts.

10. See chapter 3 for some of Nebrija's projects, which appeared to have inspired Hernando in their combination of lexicography and cosmography.

11. It seems likely that this is an error of description on the part of Juan Pérez, as the presence of Hernando's hand in these volumes means that it cannot postdate the *Memoria;*

in any case this alphabetical register closely resembles the project described both by Hernando in his *Cosmografía* notes (fol. 20) and by Juan Pérez in the *Memoria.*

12. "Todos los nombres propios se an de sacar en un papel poniendo los que comiençan en *a* en un pliego y los que comiençan asimesmo en otra letra en otro el qual no se ha de escrevir salvo por la una haz y despues todos los nombres que comiençan por una letra se cortan y se dividiran o pornan por orden alfabetico como un vocabulario hasta la quinta letra y aun mas adelante y luego se escrivan en un libro por manera que de un vocablo á otro aya dos dedos de blanco y esto para que como se oviere escrito mas quadernos desta escritura en que avra nombres nuevos se podran poner en aquel blanco que quedo en lugar que la orden alphabetica lo require; despues que desta manera aya escrito tantos lugares y nombres propios que no se crea aver mas en españa por aquella orden en un libro se trasladara no poniendo en cada hoja mas de un nombre y de que ay esten traslados entonces todo lo que está en estos quadernos se escribirá en aquel libro ponyendo lo que toca a avila en avila y lo que toca a qualquier otro lugar en su nombre propio y no todo a rreo mas una parte de la hoja lo que dize del casco del lugar y en otra parte el cuyo es y en otra los lugares que tiene y en otra que ay hasta cada lugar y cada cosa todo con numero de guarismos sea de notar ally sy esta dicho una vez o dos o mas en estos por que quantos mas veces esto viere dicho tanto mas cierto sera y sera tenydo por mas verdadero que lo que pocas veces estuviere dicho."

13. Hernando also used similar methods in his commonplace book, the *Loci Communes.* On the use of slips of paper in compilations, see Blair 2010, pp. 210–13.

14. The idea of iterated information also, of course, applied to Hernando's *obrezillas,* which similarly repeated near-identical information in slightly different forms.

15. Marín Martínez (1970, pp. 861–62) associates the abbreviations found in the margins of the early folios—*Cor.*, *Neb.*, *Eccl.*, *Pal.*—with Niccolò Perotti's *Cornucopia sive comentarii in martialis epigrammata* (Venice: Aldus Manutius, 1513; *Reg. B* 2588, purchased in Rome for 320 *quatrines* in June 1515; copy lost); Elio Antonio de Nebrija's *Dictionum Hispaniarum in latinem sermonem translatio* (Salamanca, 1513; *Reg. B* 2014, purchased in Medina del Campo for 9 *reales* in June 1518; today BCC 15-5-20[2]); the *Grammatica Ecclesiastici;* and the *Grammatice ars* of Palaemon (1503; *Reg. B* 3996, purchased in Seville for 21 *maravedís* in 1511). Ambrosius Calepino's *Diccionarium,* evidently a staple of the library as it springs to Juan Pérez's mind as an example of an author better known by a single name ("Calepino" for Ambrosius Calepinus), appears to have been owned in an earlier copy purchased in July 1519, which was replaced by a second copy in 1530 (see *Reg. B* 1963); the existence of this copy is confirmed by its appearance in the *Abecedarium A*—the Old Alphabetic Register—at number 697, meaning it was one of the books purchased before Hernando's 1521 stay in Venice.

16. Marín Martínez 1970, p. 680.

17. *Proyecto de Hernando Colón en nombre y representación del Almirante, su hermano, para dar la vuelta al mundo* (Seville, 19 July 1511, our appendix 3).

18. McDonald 2004, p. 23.

19. "Como ayuntó gran número de [dibujos pinturas o imágenes] . . . fue neçessario dar

orden para tener memoria de las que se comprasen y para una mesma pintura dos vezes" (see appendix 1). The following description draws on McDonald 2004 (the translation of Hernando's description of the print is on p. 142).

20. The first edition of *Silva de varia lección* was published in Seville by Domenico di Robertis in 1540, just a year after Hernando's death ("De la primera librería que hubo en el mundo, dónde fue, y de otras librerías que ha habido muy señaladas. Y cómo se ponían las imágenes y figuras de los excelentes hombres en letras en ella antiguamente," in Mexía 2003, pp. 549–54); see Isidore, *Etymologiae,* VI.iii.

21. *Contenta in hoc opusculo Vetus editio Ecclesiastae. Olympiodorus in ecclesiasten inserta noua tralatione interprete Zenobio Acciaiolo Florentino. Aristeas De lxxij legis hebraicae interpretatione interprete Matthia Palmerio Vincentino* (Paris: Henri Estienne, 1512; Colombina 2-3-28, USTC 143916). This volume is missing the letter from Aristeas, but Hernando also had a different 1510 edition (*Reg. B* 1637).

22. Thackeray, trans. 1917, p. 23.

23. Strabo's *Geography* 13.1.54 claims that Aristotle was the first one "to have collected books and to have taught the kings in Egypt how to arrange a library."

24. Hernando's copy of the 1498 edition of the *Suda* is listed in *Abecedarium B,* col. 1708.

25. This account follows Vincente Baz 2014. On the origins of the Sevillian Biblioteca Capitular, see Guillén 2006.

26. Manfredi 1998; Smith and O'Connor 2001; Blasio et al. 1984.

27. Manfredi 1998, p. 104.

28. Ibid., p. 106.

29. Hobson 1975. The earliest lending registers of the Vatican library were published by Bertola 1942.

30. BAV Cod. Lat. 3966, fols. 111–17.

31. In this fresco Ptolemy appears bearing a crown, since the Middle Ages tended to mistake him for King Ptolemy; further details on Bonaiuto's fresco in Ciocci 2011.

32. "Aristotle bequeathed his own library to Theophrastus, to whom he also left his school; and he is the first man, so far as I know, to have collected books and to have taught the kings in Egypt how to arrange a library" (*Geography* 13.1.54, http://data.perseus.org/citations/urn:cts:greekLit:tlg0099.tlg001.perseus-eng1:13.1.54, accessed 8 June 2018). For the intricate relations between the foundation of the library of Alexandria and the textual transmission of the Aristotelian corpus, see Canfora 1986. Hernando owned two copies of Strabo's *Geography,* the 1516 Greek edition published by Aldus and Torresano in Venice (Colombina 1-4-16[1], USTC 857595) and a massive Latin translation with commentaries by Guarinus of Verona and others, published in Basel in 1523 by Valentin Curio (Colombina 1-5-12, USTC 700257), a very sophisticated critical edition preceded by a long index to the work. Hernando purchased these two expensive folios on 6 December 1535.

33. "Note que todos los libros contenidos desde el numb 925 hasta aquí son los que yo dexé en uenecia a miser octauiano de grimaldo que me los enuiase y se enegaron en la mar."

34. As the image shows (see fig. 19), Hernando classifies the different entries into sev-

eral subcategories, such as "Historia," "Poesia," "Humanitas, "Ius," "Theologia," but then also "Coplas" (e.g., nos. 954, 956), with subcategories such as "Coplas Toscano" (which include a number of *obrezillas* with "coplas toscanas" on religious and humorous matter), also "Gramaticha" (e.g., no. 1000), "Logica" (e.g., 1039, Tomas Nieto's *Margarita Logice,* 1514), "Astrologia" (e.g., no. 1044, a prognosticon for 1518), and "Cosmographia" (e.g., 1048, *Veridica Terre Sancte* . . . EDIT16 7931).

Marín Martínez 1970, p. 715 (our translation). One of the most remarkable encyclopedic classifications of knowledge in circulation before and during Hernando's lifetime was Gregor Reisch's *Margarita philosophica*—the USTC records twelve different editions between 1496 and 1535, and three more between 1583 and 1599. Hernando did own a copy of the 1504 edition (*Reg. B* 3207, USTC 675101), which he seems to have bought before 1509 in Seville but has now sadly disappeared; he bought a copy of the new (1515 Strasburg) edition in Venice in 1521 (*Reg. A* § 1980, fols. 274–76), which was also lost with the shipwrecked books, but not before he had made an extensive summary of the contents of the book in the *Registrum A*. The *Margarita philosophica* had visual allegorical representations of the hierarchy of disciplines (similar to Andrea di Bonaiuto's fourteenth-century fresco in the Florentine Capellone degli Spagnoli and Raphael's frescoes in the Stanza della Segnatura) as well as branching diagrams like those employed by Hernando in the *Loci Communes* for his summary of Poliziano's *Panepistemon* (see fig. 14).

35. "Y fue éste un exceleente [*sic*] aviso ansí para esto como para el comprar de los libros, por que no puedan engañar los libreros, los cuales muchas vezes maliçiosamente, por vender un libro po obra nueva, quítanle el nombre del auctor y véndenlos [*sic*] sin él o por de otros; pero si miran el prinçipio por estos índiçes, no los podrán engañar; y ansí le acaeçio a mi señor don Hernando Colón que, andando a buscar estos libros, unos libreros le querían vender un libro de Derechos que era de Juan Andrés por de otro, y el miró el prinçipio y vido que era del Juan Andrés y díxoselo al librero el cual dixo que era verdad y aun le suplicó que no lo dixiese porque no lo vendrería si tal se supiese; ansí que en esto fue muy gran aviso" (appendix 1).

36. Chartier 2006.

37. See Hernando's *Memorial al Emperador* (our appendix 5); Marín Martínez 1970, pp. 347–54.

38. Marín Martínez 1970, pp. 318–38, 341–43.

39. The process of checking the scribal copy of the *Epítomes* against the rough quarto version is described in the *Memoria* of Juan Pérez (our appendix 1).

40. The epitome number for Plato's works is 1444; see Marín Martínez 1970, pp. 345–46.

41. The epitome of *Gasparis lact prognosticon an[n]i 1522,* numbered 2321, survives on fol. 969v of AM 377 fol.; the epitome of *La bella mal mariada,* noted on *Abcedarium B*, col. 975 as being epitome 3543, is sadly among those that do not survive.

42. Fols. 19r–22r of the *Compendia Diversorum Librorum* (Colombina 5-3-26[18]) contain a very rough draft for an epitome of Juan Luis Vives's *Introductio ad sapietiam.*

43. Marín Martínez 1970, pp. 347–54.

44. "[Por] él en breve se podrá saber lo sustançial que el libro trata difusamente, y si uno no puede tener muchos libros para llellos, a los menos t[e]rná uno que le dará una muestra de lo que se trata en muchos, y de alli resulta que si le paresçiere bien el libro y la materia de que trata, comprallo ha, y si no, dexallo ha, y no se engañara en compralo, porque hay muchos libros de grandes y hinchados títulos y después no tractan lo que prometen y esto hazen los impresores por engañar" (see appendix 1).

45. Hernando's epitome of Lucretius is in fols. 467v–470r in the Sevillian draft, and fols. 532v–533r in the clean copy of the Libro de los Epítomes in Copenhagen.

46. In Rome, June 1515, Hernando bought a copy of Domenico Nanni Mirabelli's *Polyanthea* (Savona: Simone Bevilaqua; Colombina 3-5-25; EDIT16 33845), which used these branching diagrams with great profusion. This was also common practice in medieval manuscripts (see Blair 2010, pp. 144–52). Hernando's entry on *Astronomia* in his *Loci Communes* (fols. 5r–6v) includes a branching diagram with Poliziano's classification of disciplines, or *doctrines*—as Hernando calls them (*Doctrinarum genera ex Politiani Panepistemon,* see fig. 14).

47. Marín Martínez 1970, p. 55.

48. Ibid., p. 405. These volumes are Colombina 10-1-1, 10-1-2, and 10-1-3.

49. It is not clear whether the discrepancy between the surviving materials and Juan Pérez's description is the result of a mistake by the library assistant or a stage of refining this project which took place after he wrote his account.

50. Marín Martínez 1970, p. 13.

51. On this sort of practice, see Blair 2010, pp. 210–27 ("The Use of Slips in Compiling" and "Cutting and Pasting from Manuscripts and Printed Books").

52. Marín Martínez 1970, pp. 434–46.

53. See the headnote to appendix 1 for a discussion of the important confusion in these documents regarding pages, folios, and printers' sheets.

54. "Es bien advertir que hasta agora estaban los libros todos juntos y las ciencias mezcladas y confusas . . . agora hanse dividido por çiençias de manera que todos los libros de una çiençia están por sí" (see appendix 1).

55. "Quanto a la orden en que an de estar los libros digo que yo tengo esperaza sy nuestro señor fuere seruivo [*sic*] de dar para ello vida e possibilided de labrar vna pieza grande y en ella a rayz de la paredes poner caxones como agora estan e los libros en ellos puestos de canto cada qual con so titulo del nonbre e numero pero an de estar apartadas las facultades conforme a la tabla que de la ciencias se haze" (see appendix 2).

56. These classifications can be confirmed by reference to a fragmentary list of numbers in subject orders (which survives today as Colombina 10-1-3), in which the following subject areas are used: "grammatica, dictionaria, humanitas, historia, poesia, 'mixtur.,' cosmographia, mathematica, musica, astrologia, alchimia, philosophia naturalis, philosophia moralis, philosophia moral, hebreii, arabicum, hispan" (fols. 1r–2r). The numbers given over to the interesting category "mixtur." contain (for instance) Ramon Llul's philosophical romance *Blanquerna* and Nicholas of Cusa's *Opuscula theologica et mathematica.*

57. *Reg. B* 1219 bears the *Tabla* number 9210 and was a copy of Johann Boschenstein's *Precatio ad divam virginem Hebraica* (Augsburg: Sigm Grimm & Marx Wirsung, 1521; USTC 625092), a volume that also contained a Hebrew psalter (*Reg. B* 1436). *Reg. B* 1534 (*Tabla* number 9114) was a copy of a bilingual edition of the *Proverbia Salomonis* with the Hebrew and Latin texts in facing pages, a preface by Konrad Pellikan, and the *Epitome Hebraicae grammaticae* of Sebastian Münster (Basel: Johannes Froben, 1520; USTC 661264).

58. "Si dizen que desta forma no podran estudiar a su plazer los que quisieren digo que esta libreria no se haze tanto para estudio comun como para guarda de todos los libros e para que se hagan dellos las tablas de lo abtores y ciencias e los epitomes e materias e que lo demas para el comun basta para satisfazerse de dubdas o ver una cosa notable que para estudiar *ad longun* no les ha de faltar estudios e libros en que deprendan pies vemos ques ynposible guardarse los libros aunque esten atados con cient cadenas" (see appendix 2).

CHAPTER FIVE
After Hernando

1. "Estaba desechada esta puerta (la que se llamó de Hércules y ahora de Goles) y baja que se le venían a cubrir con la tierra que había crecido casi la mitad, y tenía delante un montón grande de tierra, donde don Fernando Colón, hijo de don Cristóbal Colón, el que halló las Indias Occidentales, comenzó a hacer un edificio y plantar una huerta de más de cinco mil árboles por lo largo del río, haciendo que la ciudad por allí tuviese lustre y la ribera quedase más fresca; juntó en ella copia de casi 20.000 libros, esperábase de hacer allí un verdadero Monte Parnaso, así por la frescura de la huerta como por las casas y multitud de libros, la cual está ahora en la iglesia mayor de Sevilla, en una pieza que corre desde la torre hasta el Sagrario." (*Recibimiento que hizo la muy noble y muy leal ciudad de Sevilla a la C.R.M. del rey don Felipe N.S.*, Seville: En casa de Alonso Escrivano, 1570, p. 93.)

2. The house and gardens were expropriated on 29 January 1549 (Hernández Díaz and Muro Orejón 1941, document 102, p. 287). Hernando's nephew continued for years his litigation at court with the heirs of Leardo for the rights to the house and gardens—document 105 (p. 293) in Hernández Díaz and Muro Orejón proves that he only gave up on 11 February 1563.

3. See Juan Pérez's *Memoria* in our appendix 1: "My lord don Hernando, who is in Heaven, also had a great desire to collect many books, indeed all those he could find . . . *and left rent so that any others that emerged could be purchased.*" ("Tuvo también don Hernando mi señor, que está en la gloria, muy gran deseo de allegar muchos libros y aun todos los que pudiese hallar . . . *y dexó renta para que siempre se comprasen los que demás se hallasen.*" Juan Pérez, "Memoria de las obras y libros de Hernando Colón," in Marín Martínez 1970, p. 50; our italics.) In spite of this, documents 84 to 91 (among others) in Hernández Díaz and Muro Orejón 1941 (pp. 210–25) profusely illustrate the sorry state of Hernando's finances and the enormous amount of debt that had to be paid after his death.

4. Further details in Hernández Díaz and Muro Orejón 1941, pp. xiv–xvi; the original

document was published by Bernal Ulecia 1936; see also Marín Martínez 1993, p. 283, and Guillén 2006, pp. 150–51.

5. See, for instance, document 96 in Hernández Díaz and Muro Orejón 1941, p. 273, by means of which the Cathedral Chapter gives powers to three gentlemen living at La Hispaniola to urge don Luis to accept or give up his uncle's legacy.

6. Hernández Díaz and Muro Orejón 1941, document 98 (pp. 274–80) and 100 (pp. 281–83).

7. "Quienes se obligan en ella a recibir en depósito dicha librería y las demás cosas a ella anexas, que al presente estaban en sus casas a la Puerta de Goles *y ponerlos y conservarlos en el mismo orden*" (our italics). For a transcription of the document, see Hernández Díaz and Muro Orejón, document 98, pp. 274–80. The representatives of the convent officially accepted the deposit in another document dated on 13 June 1544 (ibid., document 100, pp. 281–83).

8. Some original Columbian manuscripts were not at San Pablo but at the Carthusian monastery of Las Cuevas, on the other side of the river just opposite the Casa de Goles, where Columbus had also deposited one of the four notarized copies of his *Libro de los Privilegios*. Marín Martínez suggests Bartolomé de las Casas could have been instrumental in the transfer of the books to San Pablo (Marín Martínez 1993, p. 333; see also Clayton 2012, pp. 397–98). On how las Casas probably used Hernando's manuscript version of his father's biography, see Rumeu de Armas 1973, pp. 238–39.

9. Álvarez Márquez 1992, pp. 61–62, and Guillén 2006, p. 188, who quotes from the official document at the Archivo Catedral de Sevilla, Secretaría, Actas Capitulares 29, 42v that records the dismissal of the librarians.

10. Guillén 2006. This could be attributed to the fact that Guillén (who was the director of the library from 1986 until his death in 2003) was also a cleric, had held a position as a lecturer in the Cathedral Chapter since 1973, and was therefore an insider in the institution. His appointment followed in the well-established tradition of appointing ecclesiastical administrators for the collections. Our survey of the history of the library after Hernando's death, in particular the period between the seventeenth and the nineteenth centuries, relies on Guillén's (2006) authoritative account—which itself relies on his familiarity with the primary sources in the cathedral archives that document its history.

11. Guillén 2006, pp. 191–92.

12. "[Don Hernando] donó su librería a la Iglesia mayor de Sevilla, donde agora estan encarcelados en una sala alta a la nave del Lagarto, no siendo a nadie de provecho lo que se dexó para aprovechamiento y estudio de los ingenios." (*Aparato o apuntamientos que para escribir la historia de Sevilla disponía y dexo principiados de su mano el erudito don Gonzalo Argote de Molina*, ca. 1592, p. 88.) We quote from the digital edition of an 1811 manuscript copy, http://fondosdigitales.us.es/media/books/3657/aparato-o-apuntamientos-que-para-escribir-la-historia-de-sevilla-disponia-y-dexo-principiados-de-su-mano-el-eruditodon-gonzalo-argote-de-molinahmanuscrito.pdf, accessed 21 July 2018.

13. Guillén 2006, pp. 197–98; Gil 1992, pp. xxi–xxiii. The idea of a public library, when

it was first proposed by Salutati, and inspired by Petrarch and Boccaccio, was a novelty that stood in contrast to traditional medieval libraries, many of which were church property, like the Biblioteca Capitular, and thus only available for use by its members, not the general public.

14. In 2015 we inspected a quarto sammelband that was being sold privately, bound in seventeenth-century vellum and labeled on the spine as "Aug. Dathi Orationū et Varia," as well as "SII/11[?].37," which contained the following works in this order: [1] DATI, Agostino. Orationum Prima pars [and] Orationum Secunda pars. [Paris]: Guilaume le Rouge for Dionysii Roce, [1513–14]; [2] CARRANTUS, Petrus Mathaeus. Ludovici Sphortiae captivitas. Bolonia, per Joannem Antonium de Benedictis . . . 1507; [3] MORE, Thomas. Utopia . . . [Louvain]: Thierry Martens, [1516]. The verso of the last leaf of the Carrantus (i.e., no. [2] above) contained an inscription noting, "Este libro costo en Roma 5 quatrines blancos año 1512," which strongly suggested that the book was part of Hernando's collection. This Carrantus purchased in 1512 did not, however, contain the second characteristic formula inscribed in Hernando's books following the note on place/date/cost ("Está registrado . . ."), which provides the serial number given to the title in his master catalogue, the *Registrum B*. The *Registrum B* does contain a copy of this work—number 3658—but that copy survives in the Biblioteca Colombina and bears the following formula: "Este libro costó en Roma 5 quatrines por setie[m]bre de 1519. Está registrado 3658." The likely explanation for the lack of a serial number in the Carrantus purchased in 1512, then, is that the 1512 purchase was a duplicate and so was replaced by the copy in the Colombina before the elaboration of *Registrum B;* although the *Registrum B* was developed to prevent such duplicate purchases, it is not clear when Hernando's use of the *Registrum* became consistent. We have no evidence of how Hernando treated duplicate volumes in the collection, though this volume might provide some clues. There is less evidence to place the other two volumes (i.e., nos. [1] and [3] above) in Hernando's collection at any time.

The Carrantus volume was purchased by Hernando in Rome in 1512 and discovered at some point subsequent to 1519 to be a duplicate of the Carrantus he purchased in Rome in September 1519. The sammelband seems then to have passed from the periphery of Hernando's collection into the library of the Jesuit seminary in Marchena as suggested by manuscript annotations that record its presence in this religious institution—probably at some point before the end of the seventeenth century.

15. The Seville University library has Hernando's copy of Strabo's *Geographia* ([Venice]: Johannes Rubeus Vercellensis, 1494/95, ISTC is00798000, U. of Seville catalogue A 336/109[2]). Hernando's final note reads: "hunc librum perlegi ego don Ferdinandus Colon in oppido Alua de Tormes circa finem anni 1508 a principio usque ad finem eumque anotaui prout tyrocinij litteratura suppeditabat," followed by his characteristic purchase note: "costó este libro .187 mrs. en Medina del Canpo. Está registrado 3076." See also Wagner (1988a, p. 404).

16. "Despojo del tiempo, más olvidada y menos frequentada que la quiso su dueño, difícil de gozar, y fácil de consumirse" (Ortiz de Zúñiga 1795, vol. 3, pp. 377–78).

17. Guillén 2006, pp. 194–96.

18. There are other historians of the library, and some librarians, who mention this—and Harrisse, for instance, says that royal intervention should be held responsible for the loss of at least half of the library, though a thorough and documented study of Hernando's books in the royal collection still remains to be undertaken. The library in El Escorial has at least one manuscript which belonged to Hernando, the *Commentarii in Donatum. Versus ad S. Columbanum,* an Italian eleventh-century codex that bears one of Hernando's purchase notes ("Este libro costo en pauia 44 quatrines a 6 de março de 1521 y el ducado de oro vale 440 quatrines").

19. Before they joined the Cini collection, some of these titles had belonged to Victor Masséna, prince of Essling and duke of Rivoli (1838–1909), a Parisian collector and a historian of Venetian illustrated books published between the invention of print and the early sixteenth century. After Masséna's death his collection was offered for sale in several different auctions, in Zurich and Lucerne, in 1939 and 1942 (of the former there is a catalogue, the *Livres à figures provenant de la bibliothèque du prince d'Essling,* 1939; see also Zorzi 2003, pp. 17–18, and Barbieri 2003, pp. 45–46). Some other of Hernando's titles reached the Cini collection via the bibliophile and bookseller Tammaro de Marinis (Zorzi 2003, p. 18).

Their provenance can be confirmed in some cases by Hernando's own manuscript notes. In other cases these notes are barely visible or have vanished altogether as a result of a rather vigorous process of restoration that involved aggressive whitewashing. Only the records and catalogues of the nineteenth-century collectors and librarians who purchased and classified these works allow their identification as part of Hernando's collection. Among them are:

Regula del patriarcha Ioseph ([Ferrara, ca. 1500], ISTC ij00479500, Harrisse's *Excerpta Colombiniana,* p. 221, no. 382). A manuscript note confirms that this pamphlet was sold in Paris in 1885. There is a loose leaf, with a long manuscript note by Giuseppe Martini (1870–1944), bookseller and collector, who records Hernando's manuscript note before it was whitewashed: "10627.10128. Este libro costo. I. quatrin en Ferrara a . 12 . de mayo . 1521 .y el ducado de oro vale 426 quatrines." The lower left-hand corner of the title page has one of Hernando's registry numbers barely visible under utraviolet light, which appears to be 10128.

Ladichiaratione della chiesa di sancta M. delloreto & come ella uenne tucta intera (ca. 1497, ISTC it00427100). Once part of the collection of Tammaro de Marinis.

Laudiuius eques Hierosolimitanus Ad Franciscum Beltrandum Barohinonensem de vita beati Hieronimi, Rome, 1495 (ISTC il00086000), which bears faint traces of one of Hernando's purchase notes, only perceptible under ultraviolet light: "Este libro costo en Roma 3 quatrines. Año 1512." It is registered in *Registrum B* as 3010.

Predicatio amoris. Incipit tema (ISTC ip00958050, recorded by Harrisse, *Excerpta Colombiniana,* 372 and Tammaro de Marinis's *Catalogue,* 150, pp. 60–61, planche CLXXXI; see also Rhodes 2011, P110, p. 214). Its final page has very faint traces of manuscript annotations, which appear to be one of Hernando's register numbers for the *Registrum B,* but it is extremely hard to read even under ultraviolet light.

Rhodes (2011, C66, p. 65) includes another title (Eustachio Celebrino's *Li Stupendi et marauigliosi miracoli del Glorioso Christo de Sancto Roccho Nouamente Impressa,* EDIT16 2669), also whitewashed but identified as one of Hernando's *obrezillas* by de Marinis (*Il Castello di Monselice,* p. 129, see also Harrisse, *Excerpta,* p. 304). There are no traces of Hernando's manuscript notes, not even under ultraviolet light. The binding has Essling's coat of arms, so it could very likely have gone for sale in Paris in 1885. The last page has a price in pounds.

Another title (*Confessione nuouamente composta brieue et molta [*sic*] diuota & di grande utilita a contritione del peccatore* [Rome? ca. 1520], Rhodes 2011, C170, p. 90; Harrisse, *Excerpta,* p. 199 n287) bears faint traces of Hernando's manuscript notes and registry numbers, but they can hardly be read even under ultraviolet light. It has a price at the end of the book, for 8,000 pounds.

There are some other titles for whose identification as part of Hernando's collection we have to rely on the testimony of de Marinis, who might have used information closer to the nineteenth-century sources before the manuscript notes were eliminated, or who relied on Harrisse's *Excerpta.* They are the following:

Joannes Baptista. *Inomenza [*sic*] la predica che fece. sancto. Ioanne baptista Qui rationeʒ voluptatibus: submiserit humanitatem deserit & in brutalem natura mutatur. C&* (EDIT16 62587, Rhodes 2011, J19, pp. 150–52).

Justinianus, Agustinus. *Precatio pietatis plena ad Deum Omnipotentem composita ex duobus et septuaginta nominibus diuinis Hebraicis et Latinis unà cum interprete commentariolo* (EDIT16 28187, Rhodes 2011, J38, p. 156; de Marinis, *Il Castello di Monselice,* p. 55; Harrisse, *Excerpta,* p. 317).

The *Rappresentatione di Sancta Barbara nuouamente composta* also bears the ex libris of Tammaro de Marinis (Harrisse, *Excerpta,* p. 9 n380; de Marinis's *Catalogue* 172, p. 67). There are traces of Hernando's manuscript notes (detectable only under ultraviolet light), with a registry number within a rectangle that seems to end in 74; at the bottom of the final page there are traces of a longer manuscript note which appears to say "Este libro costó . . . ," but the only really legible word (under ultraviolet light) is "diziembre."

20. *Newe Zeittung. Von dem Lande. Das die Sponier funden haben ym 1521. Iare genant Jucatan.; Newe Zeittung vo[n] Prussla, vo[n] Kay: Ma: Hofe 18 Martze. 1522.; Newe Zceyt von des Turcken halben von Offen geschrieben* (Augsburg, 1522); John Carter Brown Library J522.N543z.

21. Further details in Wagner 1988 and Marín Martínez 1993, p. 341.

22. The lost copy is annotated as no. 2032, in fol. 305v of the *Memorial de Libros Naufragados.* The new copy is *Libri de situ orbis tres, adiectis ioachimi vadiani heluetii in eosdem scholiis. Addita quoque in geographiam catechesis: et epistola vadiani ad agricolam Digna lectu. Cum indice* (Vienna: Johann I Singriener, Lukas Alantsee, 1518), Colombina 1-4-4, USTC 684766.

23. The inquisitor's note at the bottom of the title page reads thus: "In his Ioachimi Vadiani Commentariis satis multa proscribit Expurgatorius Index, quorum illaque inveriri[?] potuerint deleta sunt: alia uero, que post accuratam diligentiam sed hibitam haud

comparuerunt vel quia perpe am[?] designate sunt in Indice, velquia in hac editione, que diversa est apilla, quam. . . . Tu lector tibi consule." Below this one, in a different hand, there is another manuscript note that refers to the index (or the expurgation) of 1640, signed in 1662. Joachim Vadian's collection has now become the *Vadiana,* the cantonal library of St Gallen. Approximately two and a half lines have been expurgated in fol. 95r (with a commentary next to them that mentions Erasmus); also a longer paragraph in fol. 95v, between the end of this sentence: "Id uero laudandum, q Gaecas Latinasq literas eximie colere coepic, magistra Italia, e cuius scholis doctrinaru allatus est splendor" until "vnde avtem Germani dicti sint." The commentary next to this expurgated paragraph (16 lines) reads "Germania Graecas & Latinas literas colit." Then between the end of 96v and the beginning of 97r there are about eleven expurgated lines, next to a commentary that reads "Iacobus Spiegel Caesare us a secretis," between "Illustrare" and "Paludibus. Tacitus."

24. Luciano de Samosata [*Opera. Latín*], Colombina 1-6-12, USTC 673740; pages 137 to 174 are missing and much of the content has also been blotted out by the censors (Segura Morera and Vallejo Orellana 2001, vol. 3, p. 407, entry 821). Another Lucian that belonged to Hernando, now at the Seville University Library, was also expurgated following the Index of 1632, as recorded in its title page ("corregido según el índice de 1632," *Luciani Samosatensis Deorum Dialogi,* Strassbourgh: Iohannes Schottus, 1515). The title page also bears one of Hernando's symbols and the stamp of a Jesuit library. This suggests this bilingual Lucian must have been one of the books borrowed by a *prebendado* which was never returned, remained in the Jesuit library, and then passed on to the Sevillian public libraries during the nineteenth century. It also appears to have a sixteenth-century binding, which means it must have left early enough to have escaped Loaysa's rebinding program, and may be one of the few surviving examples of Hernando's original bindings. Hernando's manuscript note at the end informs readers that he bought it in Maguntia on 26 November 1520, and paid 33 *maravedís* for it. Its number in the *Registrum B* is 1140. For an electronic copy see https://archive.org/embed/ARes10515, accessed 8 March 2020.

25. Guillén 2006, p. 193. According to the *DNB,* Antonio del Corro was the illegitimate son of Antonio del Corro ("doctor of law") and a prostitute.

26. Guillén 2006, pp. 193–94.

27. Wagner 1981, p. 405 passim.

28. Initial findings on the manuscript and its provenance were published on the website of the Arnamagnæan Institute by Dr. N. Kıvılcım Yavuz, to whose research we are indebted here; see https://manuscript.ku.dk/motm/hernando-colons-book-of-books/, accessed 27 May 2019. Evidence that the volume once resided in Olivares' library can be found in Bibliotheca Selecta del Conde-Duque de Olivares, Real Biblioteca, Madrid, II/1781, f. 213r (an eighteenth-century copy of Olivares's original catalogue).

29. Loaysa, *ABCdario borrador y Memoria de todos los libros que oi están en la Librería de esta Santa Iglesia Metropolitana y Patriarchal de Sevilla, el cual se acabó de hacer en 11 de abril de 1684* (Biblioteca Capitular 57-1-19).

30. Marín Martínez 1993, p. 334.

31. This is confirmed by the report from Ignacio de Valencia, prepared for the Cathedral Chapter in 1788 (Informe presentado el 25 de Agosto de 1788, Archivo Catedral de Sevilla, Secretaría, Actas Capitulares 151, tras. fol. 67, quoted by Guillén 2006, p. 243).

32. Loaysa, *ABCdario,* fol. 5v.

33. Ibid., fol. 5r.

34. Gallardo 1866, p. 514; also Guillén 2006, pp. 273–74.

35. Another document dating from 1706 demonstrates that there were several persons in possession of the keys to the library, and that the Cathedral Chapter was not in control of those who had them: "acordó el cabildo que tan solamente tenga la llave de dicha librería el dicho señor canónigo doctor don Ambrosio y que se recojan las demás llaves que hubiere de la dicha librería" (Archivo Catedral de Sevilla, Secretaría, Actas Capitulares, 88, 54v) (Guillén 2006, p. 236).

36. "Cuando muchacho iba él con otros a jugar allí, y se entretenían en hojear los libros de iluminaciones y estampas, especialmente los litúrgicos antiguos, que algunos las tenían primorosas en dibujo y colorido" (Gallardo 1866, p. 514).

37. More details and primary sources in Guillén 2006, pp. 299–300.

38. Gil 1992, p. xxvi.

39. "Visitar e inspeccionar la biblioteca Colombina a uso del derecho que me asiste como sucesor y representante de su instituidor y se me faciliten a este fin cuantos libros, papeles, y documentos para enterarme de su estado" (Guillén 2006, pp. 377–78).

40. Around 1.5 percent of the total funds, according to Guillén (2006, pp. 404–5).

41. Gil 1992, pp. xxvi–xxvii.

42. Harrisse 1885, pp. 27–34.

43. Guillén, 2006, pp. 519–21 suggests that some of the stolen books were returned to the library.

44. Harrisse voiced the unconfirmed news about the project to create an Imperial College of mathematics and navigation for which Hernando supposedly received an approbation from the emperor himself in 1537 (*Fernand Colomb,* 1872, p. 27), something that Harrisse must have read in Eustaquio Fernández de Navarrete (1850, pp. 357–60), and in Loaysa, who also mentions it in the introduction to his catalogue of 1684, where he also confirms that the project never took off (Loaysa 1684, fol. 4r). Harrisse grossly miscalculated the income that Hernando received from his father (ibid., pp. 28–29), since he did not take into consideration the notarial documents which, published several decades later by Hernández Díaz and Muro Orejón (1941), demonstrate the sorry state of Hernando's finances at the time of his death.

45. Rumeu de Armas 1973; see also Arranz 1982 and 1984, pp. 7–37.

46. Serrano y Sanz 1932; Jos 1945; Anglés 1947; Ruffini 1960; Chapman 1968; Rodríguez-Moñino 1976.

47. Marín Martínez 1970. See also Marín Martínez 1973 and 1975.

48. Wagner 1971, 1972, 1975b, 1981b, and 1981a.

49. See for instance *El Pais* 19 January 1986, https://elpais.com/diario/1986/01/19/cul

tura/506473204_850215.html, accessed on 22 July 2018. Further details about the case can be found in the *ABC de Sevilla* of 9 January 1986, the day after the collapse, http://hemeroteca.abcdesevilla.es/nav/Navigate.exe/hemeroteca/sevilla/abc.sevilla/1986/01/09/001.html, accessed 22 July 2018.

50. Guillén, in Wagner and Guillén 1990, pp. 68–69.

51. Sáez Guillén 2002; Segura Morera and Vallejo Orellana 2001; Segura Morera, Vallejo Orellana, and Sáez Guillén 1999.

52. Gil 1992; other interesting publications include the prologue to Gil 1989; Álvarez Márquez 2003; Fernández Vega 1997. Ruiz Asencio, ed. 1995; Dotson, ed. 1998; Severin 2000.

53. Walsby 2013, pp. 4–5. McDonald 2004. Wilson-Lee 2018.

54. Juan de Loaysa, who in 1684 produced the first proper catalogue of the collection after Hernando's death, acknowledged the importance of the contents in Hernando's sammelbands (*miscellaneos*) as the most relevant aspect of his library: "lo mas considerable y de mas estimacion" (Loaysa 1684, fol. 5v).

55. *De bibliothecis syntagma* (Antwerp: ex officina Plantiniana, apud Ioannem Moretum, 1602). Recent scholarship on Lipsius's treatise includes two bilingual critical editions, one in Italian by Diego Baldi (2017) and an English edition by Thomas Hendrickson (2017). Naude's work was published originally in Paris by François Targa; for a modern edition, see Teyssandier 2008.

56. *Somma delle Opere che in tutte le scienze et arti piu nobili, et in varie lingue ha da mandare in luce l'Academia Venetiana, parte nuove, et non piu stampate, parte con fedelissime tradopttioni, giudiciose correttioni, & utilissime annotationi riformate* (Venice: nell'Academia Venetiana, 1558, EDIT16 71).

57. See Bolzoni 1995, in particular her chapters 1 and 2 ("Rendere visibile il sapere: l'esperienza dell'Accademia Veneziana" and "Alberi del sapere e machine retoriche").

58. See Juan Pérez's *Memoria* (our appendix 1):

> In the margins they will also find this symbol
>
> 
>
> which are two long lines and this is to distinguish authors from translators, because the symbol of two lines means that it is a translator who rendered the text from Greek to Latin, or from Latin into Romance, or into any other tongue.

59. "And since, in due time, it could be that many books will not just have duplicates, but triplicates, in these cases there should be a bookseller or a bookbinder who takes an inventory of these books and puts them up for sale, for a price that leaves some profit for him. In this way the triplicates, far from being a problem, in time will become quite useful, since this bookstore will have a large and varied supply of books from many different parts of the world, so that with the growth of business he may end up in a position to import more

books. So that, if right now books for a value of twelve ducats are sent from each city, then it could become a hundred, the profit would grow, and the store could hire its own factor to travel around the said cities, and also some others (as I did myself) and so these occasional trips would be more worthwhile than always relying on what the booksellers decide to send." (Hernando's will, our appendix 2.)

60. "There is no doubt that there is no town where some honest merchant will not be pleased to aid strangers if they seek assistance from him. And I say this from my own experience, for merchants live by making deals, and themselves travel around, and they find pleasure in doing unto others what they would have done unto them. And they have the know-how [*ynteligencia*] to send things from one place to another safely, which other sorts of people do not have. And this is why anywhere he must go, the *sumista* must seek the aid of merchants." (Hernando's will, our appendix 2.)

APPENDIX ONE
Juan Pérez's Memoria

1. We have based our translation on the edition of the *Memoria* by Marín Martínez, and those wishing to investigate the document further can refer to that thorough study. Marín Martínez 1970, pp. 47–76.

2. Juan Pérez clearly does not have a word for the modern category of "print" here, and after introducing the collection as consisting of "debujos pinturas o imagines" usually refers to them as "pinturas," even though the collection consisted entirely of printed images.

3. The original uses the word "pergamino" here and elsewhere below, though it is unclear whether vellum is meant or parchment proper.

4. Juan Pérez variously uses the word "pliego" in both the technical and non-technical senses, i.e., here to refer to a sheet of printer's paper (subsequently cut or folded to make folios, quartos, octavos, etc.), and below to refer simply to a page in a book, regardless of the size. We have differentiated in the translation but left a reminder of the original term in square brackets.

5. We have consistently rendered Juan Pérez's phrases "de mala letra" and "de buena letra," meaning in rough or neat handwriting, using the contemporary equivalents in English, "a good hand" and "a bad hand."

6. We have used the technical term "fair copy" here to translate Juan Pérez's circumlocution "los que se sacaron en limpio" to describe making neat scribal copies of the rough originals.

7. "De cuadernos de pliego de pliego"—literally "of gatherings of sheet pages"; see note 2 above regarding Juan Pérez's loose terminology for page sizes.

8. It seems likely that Juan Pérez here is referring to "Maestro Ortega," one of the *sumistas* employed in the library of whom little is known other than his name. See Marín Martínez 1970, pp. 13, 365–421, where he discusses Ortega's contribution to these catalogues.

9. Juan Pérez probably simply means here that the entries should be alphabetized using the entire word (not just the initial letter); the concept of alphabetization was evidently sufficiently new to require detailed explanation, as in Hernando's instructions to his emissaries in the *Itinerario*.

10. The word "sciences" here is (as in the original, *ciencias*) for want of a better term. This is not science in the modern sense, nor yet "discipline" (since many of the texts fall outside the traditional notion of academic disciplines); rather, the meaning is "areas of knowledge," meant in the broadest sense.

11. In this rather confusing passage Juan Pérez may be differentiating from another, earlier topic index, which gathered the authors and sciences together rather than (as here, in the final forms) treating them separately.

12. We have used "symbol" throughout to refer to Hernando's biblioglyphs, which Juan Pérez designates by the word "señal."

13. Juan Pérez appears to be using "marca real" here to indicate outsized folios, whereas earlier he had been using it to refer to a full printer's sheet (i.e., a bi-folio, unfolded), but as ever his terms are not specific.

14. This section of the *Memoria* is rather confusing, as it is not clear what these further symbols for "alctor" [*sic*, i.e., height/size] refer to; the most likely sense seems that this was a symbolic system to calculate the construction of any given book—so an octavo using half a sheet would form one quire of eight pages, etc. While the symbols for folio, quarto, etc., are regularly used in the *Abcedarium B*, and can be checked, this second set of symbols (for sheet-use and page numbers) seems to have been used only in the *Tabla de Ciencias*, of which nothing remains.

15. The end of this clause is somewhat cryptic, though it seems that the language symbols were double underlined to differentiate them from similar symbols marking out those to be emended.

16. This suggests that there was an eventual intention to include a description of how the catalogues worked at the front of each volume.

APPENDIX TWO
Hernando's Will

1. Our translation is made from Hernández Díaz and Muro Orejón 1941, pp. 123–61.

2. It is not clear whether the word "bancos" used here means "bookcases" or the more literal benches, though a later passage makes clear that the library is to use a wall-system for storage.

3. Hernando uses the word "sumista" for the scholar(s) employed to work on the catalogue entries, though it would be misleading to suppose that abridging was their only task as they were required to work on the other catalogues as well.

APPENDIX THREE
Hernando's Proposal to King Ferdinand for a Voyage around the World

1. *Proyecto de Hernando Colón en nombre y representación del Almirante, su hermano, para dar la vuelta al mundo* (Seville, 19 July 1511), Arranz 1982, pp. 338–43; also Marín Martínez 1993, pp. 180–84.

APPENDIX FOUR
Hernando's Appointment as the Coordinator for the Elaboration of a New Version of the Padrón Real

1. Archivo General de Indias, Indiferente 421, vol. 11, fol. 234r.

APPENDIX FIVE
Hernando's Memorial al Emperador

1. We have taken the text from Hernández Díaz and Muro Orejón 1941, pp. 241–43.

2. Giovanni Bertachino was an author of important law digests and compilations of legal maxims, of whose works Hernando owned several copies (see *Abcedarium B*, col. 901).

3. Around 2,200 of these epitomes survive, largely in the recently discovered scribal copy of the *Libro de los Epítomes*, now part of the Arnamagnæan Collection in Copenhagen (AM 377 fol.), with a smaller number only available through the rough quarto volumes kept at the Biblioteca Colombina in Seville.

BIBLIOGRAPHY

Archives and Libraries

AGI—Archivo General de Indias, Seville

AGS—Archivo Generas de Simancas, Simancas

AM—Arnamagnæan Collection, Copenhagen

ASV—S. R. Rota, Rome

BAV—Biblioteca Apostolica Vaticana, Rome

BCC—Biblioteca Capitular y Colombina, Seville

BNE—Biblioteca Nacional de España, Madrid

Online Databases and Catalogues

Colombina—Catálogo online de las Bibliotecas Capitular y Colombina (https://opac.icolombina.es/opac)

EDIT16—Censimento nazionale delle edizioni italiane del XVI secolo (http://edit16.iccu.sbn.it)

ISTC—Incunabula Short Title Catalogue (https://data.cerl.org/istc/_search)

SDBM—Schoenberg Database of Manuscripts (https://sdbm.library.upenn.edu/)

USTC—Universal Short Title Catalogue (https://www.ustc.ac.uk/)

VD16—Verzeichnis der im deutschen Sprachbereich erschienenen Drucke des 16 (http://www.vd16.de/)

Hernando's Catalogues

Abecedarium A (aka *Índice Alfabético Antiguo;* BCC 10-1-8)
Abecedarium B (aka *Índice General Alfabético;* BCC 10-1-6)
Diccionario for the *Diccionario o Vocabulario Latino* (BCC 10-1-5)
Itinerario o Descripción y Cosmografía de España (BCC 10-1-10, 10-1-11)
Libro de las Materias (BCC 10-1-1, 10-1-2, 10-1-3)
Libro de los Epítomes (AM 377 fol.)
Memoria de los Dibujos o Pinturas or *Registrum C* (BCC 10-1-16)
Registrum A (aka *Registro Antiguo,* aka *Memorial de los Libros Naufragados;* BCC 10-1-15)
Registrum B (aka *Índice Numeral;* BCC 10-1-14)

Catalogues

Arbolí y Faraudo, Servando, et al. 1888–1948. *Biblioteca Colombina. Catálogo de sus libros impresos publicados [. . .] bajo la inmediata dirección de su bibliotecario [. . .] Servando Arbolí y Faraudo, con notas bibliográficas del Dr. D. Simón de la Rosa y López.* 7 vols. Seville.

Babelon, Jean. 1913. *La bibliothèque française de Fernando Colomb.* Paris: Librairie Ancienne Honoré Champion.

Catalogue d'une collection d'anciens livres à figures italiens appartenant à Tammaro de Marinis. 1925. Preface by Seymour de Ricci. Milan: Ulrico Hoepli.

De Marinis, Tammaro. 1941. *Il Castello di Monselice. Raccolta degli Antichi Libri Veneziani Figurati.* Verona: Bodoni.

Fernández Vega, María del Mar. 1997. *Los libros catalanes de la Biblioteca de Fernando Colón.* Berkeley: University of California Press.

Gálvez, Diego Alejandro, and Rafael Tabares. 1878. *Index librorum omnium qui conservantur in bibliotheca Sanctae Ecclesiae Patriarchalis Hispalensis.* [Seville].

Livres à figures provenant de la bibliothèque du prince d'Essling. Zurich: Zunfthaus zur Meise. Exposition: 10–14 Mai; Vente: 15–17 Mai 1939.

Loaysa, Juan de. 1684. *ABCdario Borrador y Memoria de todos los Libros que están en la Librería de esta Santa Iglesia Metropolitana y Patriarchal de Sevilla, el cual se acabó de hacer en 11 de abril de 1684* (BCC 57-1-19).

Marín Martínez, Tomás, José Manuel Ruiz Asencio, and Klaus Wagner. 1993.

Catálogo concordado de la Biblioteca de Hernando Colón. 2 vols. Madrid: Mapfre y Cabildo de la Catedral de Sevilla.

McDonald, Mark P. 2004. *The Print Collection of Ferdinand Columbus.* London: British Museum.

Rhodes, Dennis. 2011. *Catalogo del fondo librario antico della Fondazione Giorgio Cini.* Florence: Leo Olschki Editore.

Rodríguez-Moñino, Antonio R. 1976. *Los pliegos poéticos en la Biblioteca Colombina.* Berkeley: University of California Press.

Sáez Guillén, José Francisco. 2002. *Catálogo de Manuscritos de la Biblioteca Colombina de Sevilla.* Elaboración de índices: Pilar Jiménez de Cisneros Vencelá and José Francisco Sáez Guillén. Seville: Cabildo de la S.M. y P.I. Catedral de Sevilla & Institución Colombina. 2 vols. (vol. 1 catalogue, vol. 2 indexes).

Segura Morera, Antonio, and Pilar Vallejo Orellana. 2001. *Catálogo de los impresos del siglo XVI de la Biblioteca Colombina de Sevilla.* 5 vols. Seville: Cabildo de la S.M. y P.I. Catedral de Sevilla & Institución Colombina.

Segura Morera, A., P. Vallejo Orellana, and J. F. Sáez Guillén. 1999. *Catálogo de incunables de la Biblioteca Capitular y Colombina de Sevilla.* Seville: Cabildo de la S.M. y P.I. Catedral de Sevilla & Institución Colombina.

Wagner, Klaus. 1975b. "Judicia Astrologica Colombiniana. Bibliographisches Verzeichnis einer Sammlung von Praktiken des 15. und 16. Jahrhunderts de Biblioteca Colombina Sevilla," *Archiv für Geschichte des Buchwesens* 15, cols. 1–98.

Wagner, Klaus, and Manuel Carrera. 1991. *Catalogo dei libri a stampa in lingua italiana della Biblioteca Colombina di Siviglia. Catálogo de los impresos en lengua italiana de la Biblioteca Colombina de Sevilla.* Modena: Panini.

Primary Sources

Alberti, Leonis Baptista. 2005. *Descriptio Urbis Romae.* Ed. J.-Y. Boriaud and F. Furlan; introd. M. Carpo and F. Furlan. Florence: Leo S. Olschki.

Anghiera, Pietro Martire d'. 1912. *De Orbe Novo: The Eight Decades of Peter Martyr d'Anghiera.* Trans. F. A. Macnutt, 2 vols. New York: G. P. Putnam's Sons.

Anghiera, Peter Martyr. 1992. *The Discovery of the New World in the Writings of Peter Martyr of Anghiera.* Ed. E. Lunardi, E. Magioncalda, and R. Mazzacane; trans. F. Azzola, rev. L. F. Farina. Rome: Istituto Poligrafico e Zecca dello Stato, Libreria dello Stato.

Arrom, José Juan, ed. 2004. Fray Ramón Pané. *Relación acerca de las antigüedades de los indios,* Madrid: Siglo XXI, 6th ed.

Augustine. 2010. *The City of God*, books 17–22. Trans. Gerald G. Walsh. The Fathers of the Church, vol. 24. Washington: Catholic University of America Press.

Bernáldez, Andrés. 1962. *Memorias del Reinado de los Reyes Católicos que escribía Andrés Bernáldez, Cura de Los Palacios.* Edición y estudio por Manuel Gómez-Moreno and Juan de M. Carriazo. Madrid: Real Academia de la Historia.

Berwick y de Alba, Duquesa de. 2011. *Autógrafos de Cristóbal Colón.* [Madrid, 1892]. Seville: Extramuros.

Bisticci, Vespasiano da. 1859. *Vite di uomini ilustre del secolo XV.* Ed. Adolfo Bartoli. Florence: Barbera, Bianchi e Comp.

Borlandi, Antonia. 1963. *Il manuale di mercatura di Saminiato de' Ricci.* Genoa: Di Stefano.

Boscán, Juan. 1957. *Obras poéticas.* Ed. Martín de Riquer, Antonio Comas, and Joaquín Molas. Barcelona: Servicio de Publicaciones de la Universidad de Barcelona.

Campanella, Tomasso. *La Città del Sole: Dialogo Poetico / The City of the Sun: A Poetical Dialogue.* Trans., introd., and notes by Daniel J. Donno. Berkeley: University of California Press, 1981.

Chaves, Alonso de. 1983. *Quatri partitu en cosmografía práctica, y por otro nombre Espejo de navegantes.* Transcripción, estudio y notas, Paulino Castañeda Delgado, Mariano Cuesta Domingo, y Pilar Hernández Aparicio. Madrid: Instituto de Historia Cultural y Naval.

Cherubini, P. 1988. *Mandati della Reverenda Camera Apostolica (1418–1802)*, inventario a cura di P. Cherubini, Rome (Quaderni della Rassegna degli archivi di Stato, 55), pp. 27–44.

Colón, Cristóbal. 2006. *Los cuatro viajes del Almirante y su testamento,* Madrid: Espasa-Calpe, 2006.

Colón, Hernando. 1930. *Historie della vita e dei fatti di Cristoforo Colombo, per d. Fernando suo figlio.* 2 vols. Ed. Rinaldo Caddeo. Milan: Alpes.

Cortés, Hernán. 1524. *Praeclara Ferdinãdi Cortesii de noua maris Oceani Hyspania narratio Sacratissimo ac Inuictissimo Carolo romanorũ imperatori . . .* [Impresa in . . . Norimberga: per Fridericum Peypus].

———. 2001. *Letters from Mexico.* Trans. and ed. Anthony Pagden, introd. J. H. Elliott. New Haven: Yale University Press.

de las Casas, Bartolomé. 1951. *Historia de las Indias.* 3 vols. Ed. A. M. Carlo and L. Hanke. Mexico City: Fondo de Cultura Económica.

———. 1967. *Apologética Historia Sumaria,* edición preparada por Edmundo O'Gorman, con un estudio preliminar, apéndices y un índice de materias. 2 vols. Mexico City: Universidad Autónoma Nacional de México.

De Mal Lara, Juan. 1570. *Recibimiento que hizo la muy noble y muy leal ciudad de Sevilla a la C.R.M. del rey don Felipe N.S.* Seville: Alonso Escrivano.

Della Francesca, Piero. 2016. *De prospectiva pingendi.* A cura di Chiara Gizzi. Venice: Edizioni Ca' Foscari. Digital edition (DOI 10.14277/978-88-6969-099-0), available at http://edizionicafoscari.unive.it/it/edizioni/libri/978-88-6969-091-4/.

Díaz del Castillo, Bernal. 1939. *Historia verdadera de la conquista de la Nueva España.* [1632]. Ed. Joaquín Ramírez Cabañas. Mexico: Pedro Robredo. Digital edition available at http://www.cervantesvirtual.com/nd/ark:/59851/bmc90213.

Dotson, John, ed. and trans., Aldo Agosto, textual ed. 1998. *Christopher Columbus and His Family: The Genoese and Ligurian Documents.* Turnhout: Brepols.

Erasmus. 1997. *Colloquies.* Trans. and annotated by C. R. Thompson. *The Collected Works of Erasmus,* vol. 39. Toronto: University of Toronto Press.

Fernández de Navarrete, Eustaquio. 1850. *Noticias para la vida de don Hernando.* Colección de Documentos Inéditos para la Historia de España, vol. 16. Madrid: Viuda de Calero.

Fernández de Navarrete, Martín. 1825. *Colección de los viajes y descubrimientos que hicieron por mar los españoles desde fines del siglo XV.* Tomo I, *Viajes de Colón: Almirantazgo de Castilla.* Madrid: Imprenta Nacional.

———. 1835. *Colección de los viajes y descubrimientos que hicieron por mar los españoles desde fines del siglo XV,* tomo IV, Madrid [vuelto a publicar en el tomo I de las *Obras* de Fernández de Navarrete, 75 de BAE].

———. 1880. *Colección de los viajes y descubrimientos que hicieron por mar los españoles desde fines del siglo XV.* Tomo III, *Viajes menores y los de Vespucio; poblaciones en el Darién, suplemento al Tomo II.* Madrid: Imprenta y Libraría de Moya y Plaza.

Foronda y Aguilera, Manuel de. 1914. *Estancias y viajes del Emperador Carlos V desde el día de su nacimiento hasta el de su muerte, comprobados y corroborados con documentos originales.* Madrid: Sucesores de Rivadeneira.

Garin, Eugenio, ed. 1952. *Prosatori Latini del Quattrocento.* Milan & Naples: Ricardo Ricciardi.

Gesner, Conrad. 1548. *Pandectarum sive partitionum universalium.* Zurich: Christoph I. Froschauer.

Gil, Juan, ed. 1992. *El libro de Marco Polo. Las Apostillas a la Historia Natural de Plinio el Viejo.* Madrid: Alianza, Universidad de Sevilla & Sociedad Quinto Centenario.

Guerre in ottava rima. 1988–1989. Modena: Panini. In 4 vols. Vol. 1 *Repertorio bibliographico e indici.* Vol. 2 *Guerre d'Italia (1483–1527),* a cura di Marina Beer, Donatella Diamanti, Cristina Ivaldi. Vol. 3 *Guerre d'Italia (1528–1559),* a cura di Marco

Bardini, Maria Cristina Cabani, Donatella Diamanti. Vol. 4 *Guerre contro i Turchi (1453–1570)*, a cura di Marina Beer e Cristina Ivaldi.

Hendrickson, Thomas. 2017. *Ancient Libraries and Renaissance Humanism: The* De bibliothecis *of Justus Lipsius*. Leiden: Brill.

Hernández Díaz, José, and Antonio Muro Orejón, eds. 1941. *El Testamento de Don Hernando Colón y otros documentos para su historia*. Seville: Publicaciones del Instituto Hispano-Cubano de Historia de América. Fundación Rafael G. Abreu.

Laborda Orihuela, Antonio. 2002. *Descripciones de Don Fernando Colón 1517–1523. Una Visión de la España del Renacimiento*. Madrid: Instituto Nacional de Estadística.

Medici, Lorenzo de'. 1986. *Stanze*. A cura di Raffaella Castagnola. Florence: Olschki.

Munzer, Hieronymus. 1991. *Viaje por España y Portugal, 1494–1495*. Madrid: Polifemo.

Nebrija, Elio Antonio de. 2011. *Gramática sobre la lengua castellana*. Ed. Carmen Lozano. Barcelona: Real Academia Española & Círculo de Lectores.

Ortiz de Zúñiga, Diego. 1795. *Anales eclesiásticos y seculares de la muy noble y muy leal ciudad de Sevilla*. 5 vols. Madrid: Imprenta Real.

Pacioli, Luca. 1494. *Somma di aritmetica, geometria, proporzioni e proporzionalità*. Venice: Paganino de Paganini.

Piccolomini, E. 1874. "Inventario della Libreria Medicea privata compilato nel 1495." *Archivio Storico Italiano* 20, no. 4 (1 January): 51–94.

Poliziano, Angelo. 2010. *Lamia*. Text, translation, and introductory studies. Ed. Christopher S. Celenza. Leiden: Brill.

Pontano, Giovanni Giovano. 2008. *De sermone. De la conversation*. Texte établi et traduit per Florence Bistagne. Paris: Honoré Champion.

Roersch, Alphonse, ed. and trans. 1940–41. *Correspondance de Nicolas Clénard*. 3 vols. in 1. Brussels: Palais des Académies.

Rouch, Monique, ed. 2006. *Giulio Cesare Croce. L'eccellenza e trionfo del porco e altre opere in prosa*. Bologna: Pendragon.

Ruiz Asencio, José Manuel, ed. 1995. *Testamento de Hernando Colón*. Con estudio crítico y transcripción de José Manuel Ruiz Asencio. Madrid: Testimonio.

Rusconi, Roberto, ed. 1997. *The Book of Prophecies Edited by Christopher Columbus*. Trans. Blair Sullivan. Berkeley: University of California Press.

Salutati, Coluccio. 1985. *De fato et fortuna*. A cura di Conceta Bianca. Florence: Olschki.

Sanudo, Marin. 1879–1903. *I diarii di Marino Sanuto (MCCCCXCVI-MDXXXIII) dall' autografo Marciano ital. cl. VII codd. CDXIX-CDLXXVII*. 58 vols. Pubblicati per cura di Rinaldo Fulin, Federico Stefani, Nicolò Barozzi, Guglielmo Berchet, Marco Allegri; auspice la R. Deputazione venta di storia patria. Venice: F. Visentini.

———. 1997. *I diarii (1496–1533): pagine scelte.* A cura di Paolo Margaroli. Vicenza: Neri Pozza Editori.

Stancati, Tomasso, ed. 2010. *Julian of Toledo. Prognosticon Futuri Saeculi.* Paulist Press, 2010.

Teyssandier, Bernard, ed. 2008. *Gabriel Naudé: Avis pour dresser une bibliothèque.* Paris: Klinckcsieck.

Thackeray, Henry St. John, trans. 1917. *The Letter of Aristeas.* London: Macmillan.

Thomeis, Antonio de. 1999. *Rime. Convivium Scientiarium. In Laudem Sixti Quarti Pontificis Maximi.* A cura di Fabio Carboni e Antonio Manfredi. Vatican City: Biblioteca Apostolica Vaticana.

Thompson, Craig R., ed. 1978. *Collected Works of Erasmus,* vol. 23. Literary and Educational Writings 1. *Antibarbari/Parabolae.* Toronto: University of Toronto Press.

Trevisan, Angelo. 1993. *Lettere sul Nuovo Mundo. Granada 1501.* Testo critico, introduzione e note a cura di Angela Caracciolo Aricò. Venice: Albrizzi Editore.

Valla, Lorenzo. 1544. *Elegantiarum Latinae Linguae Libri Sex. Eiusdem De Reciprocatione Sui, & Suus, Libellus.* Lugduni Apud Seb. Gryphium.

Varela, Consuelo, ed. 1982. *Cristóbal Colón. Textos y documentos completos.* Madrid.

Vives, Juan Luis. 1531. *De disciplinis libri XX.* Antwerp: Michael Hillenius Hoochstratanus.

———. 1971. *On Education.* A translation of *De tradendis disciplinis,* with an introduction by Foster Watson and a foreword by Francesco Cordasco. Totowa, NJ: Rowan & Littlefield.

———. 1989. *Declamationes Sullanae.* Part 1. Ed., trans., and introd. Edward V. George. Leiden: Brill.

———. 2012. *Declamationes Sullanae.* Part 2. Ed., trans., and introd. Edward V. George. Leiden: Brill.

Secondary Sources

Alden, John, and Dennis C. Landis, eds. 1980. *European Americana: A Chronological Guide to Works Printed in Europe Related to the Americas, 1493–1776,* vol. 1: 1493–1600. New York: Readex Books & The John Carter Brown Library.

Álvarez Márquez, María del Carmen. 1992. *El mundo del libro en la Iglesia Catedral de Sevilla en el siglo XVI.* Seville: Diputación Provincial.

———. 2003. "El itinerario de adquisiciones de libros de mano de Hernando Colón." *Historia. Instituciones. Documentos* 30: 55–102.

Anglés, Higinio. 1947. "La música en la Biblioteca Colombina y en la Catedral de Sevilla." *Anuario Musical* 2: 3–39.

Armitage, David. 2013. *Foundations of Modern International Thought.* Cambridge: Cambridge University Press.

Arranz, Luis. 1982. *Don Diego Colón, almirante, virrey y gobernador de las Indias.* Madrid: Instituto Gonzalo Fernández de Oviedo & Consejo Superior de Investigaciones Científicas.

———. 1984. "Introducción," to Hernando Colón, *Historia del Almirante.* Madrid: Historia 16, pp. 7–37.

Babelon, Jean. 1913. *La bibliothèque française de Fernando Colomb.* Paris: Librairie Ancienne Honoré Champion.

Baldi, Diego, ed. 2017. De Bibliothecis Syntagma *di Justus Lipsius. L'apice di una tradizione, l'inizio di una disciplina.* Rome: CNR Edizioni.

Balsamo, Luigi. 2001. "How to Doctor a Bibliography: Antonio Possevino's Practice." In *Church, Censorship and Culture in Early Modern Italy,* ed. G. Fragnito. Cambridge: Cambridge University Press, pp. 50–78.

Banfi, Florio. 1952. "The Cosmographic Loggia of the Vatican Palace." *Imago Mundi* 9: 23–34.

Barbieri, Edoardo. 2003. "Collezionismo librario ed editoria religiosa popolare: uno sguardo alla raccolta Cini." In Zorzi, ed., pp. 37–53.

Barrera-Osorio, Antonio. 2006. *Experiencing Nature: The Spanish American Empire and the Early Scientific Revolution.* Austin: University of Texas Press.

Bartosik-Vélez, Elise. 2009. "*Translatio Imperii:* Virgil and Peter Martyr's Columbus." *Comparative Literature Studies* 46, no. 4: 559–88.

Bataillon, Marcel. 1995. *Erasmo y España: Estudios sobre la historia espiritual del siglo XVI.* 2nd ed. [first edition in French, 1937]. Mexico City: Fondo de Cultura Económica.

Bell, Adrian R., Chris Brooks, and Terry K. Moore. 2015. "The 'Buying and Selling of Money for Time': Foreign Exchange and Interest Rates in Medieval Europe." January 6, 2015. Discussion Paper Number ICM-2015-01, Henley Business School, University of Reading. Available at SSRN: https://ssrn.com/abstract=2546003 or http://dx.doi.org/10.2139/ssrn.2546003 and http://citeseerx.ist.psu.edu/viewdoc/download;jsessionid=909F14ED92DD973353AD1FB7A89A2D06?doi=10.1.1.709.4951&rep=rep1&type=pdf (accessed 12 November 2016).

Bernal, Antonio-Miguel. 1992. *La financiación de la Carrera de Indias (1492–1824). Dinero y crédito en el comercio colonial español con América.* Seville: Fundación El Monte.

———. 2011. "Historia de la contabilidad e historia económica." In *Before and after Luca Pacioli: Atti II Incontro Internazionale,* ed. Esteban Hernández-Esteve and Matteo Martelli. Sansepolcro: Centro Studi Mario Pancrazi, pp. 381–90.

Bernal Ulecia, A. 1936. "Hernando Colón y los intereses de los herederos del almirante. Un documento revelador." *Tierra Firme* 2: 305–18.

Bertola, Maria. 1942. *I due primi registri di prestito della Biblioteca Apostolica Vaticana: Codici Vaticani latini 3964, 3966.* Vatican City: Biblioteca Apostolica Vaticana.

Bietenholz, Peter G., ed. 2003. *Contemporaries of Erasmus: A Biographical Register of the Renaissance and Reformation.* Vols. 1–3. Toronto: University of Toronto Press, 2003.

———. 2009. *Encounters with a Radical Erasmus: Erasmus' Work as a Source of Radical Thought in Early Modern Europe.* Toronto: Toronto University Press.

Blair, Ann M. 2010. *Too Much to Know: Managing Scholarly Information before the Modern Age.* New Haven: Yale University Press.

Blasio, Maria Grazia, Cinzia Lelj, and Giuseppina Roselli. 1984. "Un Contributo alla lettura del Canone Bibliografico di Tommaso Parentucelli." In *Le Chiavi della Memoria: Miscellanea in Occasione del i Centenario Della Scuola Vaticana di Paleografia Diplomatica e Archivistica.* Vatican City: Scuola Vaticana Paleografia, pp. 125–65.

Blum, Rudolf. 1991. *Kallimachos: The Alexandrian Library and the Origins of Bibliography.* Trans. H. H. Wellisch. Madison: University of Wisconsin Press.

Bolzoni, Lina. 1995. *La Stanza della Memoria. Modelli Letterari e Iconografici nell'Étà della Stampa.* Turin: Einaudi.

Boyle, Leonard E. 1993. "The Vatican Library." In Grafton, ed., pp. xi–xxvi.

Brendecke, Arndt. 2016. *The Empirical Empire: Spanish Colonial Rule and the Politics of Knowledge.* Berlin: De Gruyter Oldenburg.

Brown, Rawdon. 1837–38. *Ragguagli sulla vita e sulle opere di Marin Sanuto detto il Juniore.* 3 vols. Venice: Dalla tipografia di Alvisopoli.

Canfora, Luciano. 1986. *La biblioteca scomparsa.* Palermo: Sellerio.

Carabias Torres, Ana María. 1995. "Los conocimientos de cosmografía en Castilla en la época del Tratado de Tordesillas." In *El Tratado de Tordesillas y su época,* ed. Luis Antonio Ribot García et al. Madrid: Junta de Castilla y León, pp. 959–76.

———. 2012. *Salamanca y la medición del tiempo.* Salamanca: Ediciones de la Universidad de Salamanca.

Carman, Glen. 2006. *Rhetorical Conquests: Cortés, Gomara and Renaissance Imperialism.* West Lafayette, IN: Purdue University Press.

Casado Alonso, Hilario. 2014. "Circuitos comerciales y flujos financieros en Castilla a fines de la Edad Media e inicios de la Modernidad." In M. A. Ladero Quesada et al. *Estados y mercados financieros en el Occidente Cristiano.* Pamplona: Gobierno de Navarra, pp. 273–307.

Casson, Lionell. 2001. *Libraries in the Ancient World.* New Haven: Yale University Press.

Castañeda Delgado, P., M. Cuesta Domingo, and P. Hernández Aparicio. 1983. "Introducción" to Alonso de Chaves, *Quatri partitu en cosmografía práctica, y por otro nombre Espejo de navegantes.* Madrid: Instituto de Historia Cultural y Naval, pp. 15–65.

Castro Díaz, Antonio. 1997. *Los* Coloquios *de Pedro Mexía: Un Género, Una Obra y un Humanista Sevillano del Siglo XVI.* Seville: Diputación.

Cecchini, G. 1967. "Evoluzione architectonico-strutturale della biblioteca publica in Italia dal secolo XV al XVII." *Accademie e biblioteche d'Italia* 35: 27–47.

Celenza, Christopher S. 1996. "The Will of Cardinal Giordano Orsini (ob. 1438)." *Traditio* 51: 257–86.

———, ed. 2010. "Poliziano's *Lamia* in Context." In Angelo Poliziano, *Lamia.* Text, translation, and introductory studies by Christopher S. Celenza. Leiden: Brill, pp. 1–45.

Cerezo Martínez, Ricardo. *La cartografía náutica Española en los siglos XIV, XV y XVI.* Madrid: CSIC, 1994.

Chapman, Catherine W. 1968. "Printed Collections of Polyphonic Music Owned by Ferdinand Columbus." *Journal of the American Musicological Society* 21, no. 1: 34–84.

Ciocci, Argante. 2003. *Luca Paccioli e la matematizzazione del sapere nel Rinascimento.* Bari: Cacucci Editore.

———. 2009. *Luca Pacioli tra Piero della Francesca e Leonardo.* Sansepolcro: Aboca Museum Edizioni.

———. 2011. "Le matematiche tra Medio Evo e Rinascimento." In *Before and after Luca Pacioli: Atti II Incontro Internazionale,* ed. Esteban Hernández-Esteve and Matteo Martelli. Sansepolcro: Centro Studi Mario Pancrazi, pp. 253–85.

Clayton, Lawrence A. 2012. *Bartolomé de las Casas: A Biography.* Cambridge: Cambridge University Press.

Colón de Carvajal, Anunciada, and José Manuel Pérez-Prendes Muñoz-Arraco, eds. 2015. *La herencia de Cristóbal Colón: estudio y colección documental de los mal llama-*

dos pleitos colombinos. 4 vols. Madrid: Centro Superior de Investigaciones Científicas.

Conley, Tom. 2007. "Early Modern Literature and Cartography: An Overview." In *The History of Cartography*, ed. David Woodward, vol. 3, part 1: *Cartography in the European Renaissance*. Chicago: Chicago University Press, pp. 401–11.

Costas Rodríguez, J. 1981. *Repetición sexta sobre las medidas*. Salamanca: Servicio de Publicaciones de la Universidad de Salamanca.

Crespo Sanz, Antonio. 2012. "El padrón real. Una base de datos cartográfica en continua actualización." *CT / Catastro*, 76 (December): 65–89.

Cuesta Domingo, Mariano. 1983. *Alonso de Santa Cruz y su obra cosmográfica*. Madrid: CSIC.

Dalton, Heather. 2016. *Merchants and Explorers: Roger Barlow, Sebastian Cabot, and Networks of Atlantic Exchange, 1500–1560*. Oxford: Oxford University Press.

Davies, Surekha. 2005. "The Navigational Iconography of Diogo Ribeiro's 1529 Vatican Planisphere." *Imago Mundi* 55: 103–12.

Davis, Natalie Zemon. 2008. *Trickster Travels: The Search for Leo Africanus*. London: Faber and Faber.

De la Torre y del Cerro, Antonio. 1956. *Maestros de los hijos de los Reyes Católicos*. Madrid: Instituto Jerónimo Zurita. [Separata de: Hispania. N. LXIII.]

De Roover, Raymond. 1963. *The Rise and Decline of the Medici Bank, 1397–1494*. Cambridge: Harvard University Press.

Delph, Ronald K. 2008. "Emending and Defending the *Vulgate* Old Testament: Agostino Steuco's Quarrel with Erasmus." In *A Companion to Biblical Humanism and Scholasticism in the Age of Erasmus*, ed. E. Rummel. Leiden: Brill, pp. 297–318.

Di Sante, Assunta. 2010. "La biblioteca rinascimentale attraverso i suoi inventari." In Manfredi, ed., pp. 309–50.

Dittmar, Jeremiah. 2015. "New Media, Competition and Growth: European Cities after Gutenberg." https://pdfs.semanticscholar.org/d736/2a3f03dd803c177e54e97cfd76777183112f.pdf?_ga=2.32830908.341285134.1596720003-794714586.1596720003, accessed on 6 August 2020.

Donoso Anes, Rafael. 1996. *Una contribución a la historia de la contabilidad: análisis de las prácticas contables desarrolladas por la tesorería de la Casa de la Contratación de las Indias de Sevilla (1503–1717)*. Seville: Universidad de Sevilla.

———. 2012. "La documentación contable de la Tesorería de la Casa de la Contratación de las Indias de Sevilla (1503–1717)." *Comptabilités: Revue d'histoire des comptabilités* 3, http://comptabilites.revues.org/754, accessed on 30 September 2016.

Doria, Giorgio. 1986. "Conoscenza del mercato e sistema informativo: il know-how dei mercanti-finanzieri genovesi nei secoli XVI e XVII." In *La repubblica internazionale del denaro tra XV e XVII secolo*, ed. Aldo de Maddalena and Hermann Kellebenz. Bologna: Il Mulino, pp. 57–115.

Edson, Evelyn. 2007. *The World Map, 1300–1492: The Persistence of Tradition and Transformation.* Baltimore: Johns Hopkins University Press.

Eisenstein, Elizabeth. 1979. *The Printing Press as an Agent of Change.* Cambridge: Cambridge University Press.

Esteban Piñeiro, Mariano. 1995. "Elio Antonio de Nebrija y la búsqueda de patrones universales de medida." In *El Tratado de Tordesillas y su época*, ed. Luis Antonio Ribot García. Madrid: Junta de Castilla y León, pp. 569–82.

Felloni, Giuseppe, and Guido Laura. 2014. *Genova e la storia della finanza: una serie di primati? / Genoa and the History of Finance: A Series of Firsts?* Genoa. Available at http://www.giuseppefelloni.it/rassegnastampa/GenovaFinanza12primati.pdf, accessed on 1 July 2018.

Fernández-Armesto, Felipe. 1991. *Columbus.* Oxford: Oxford University Press.

Foucault, Michel. 1980. "Questions of Geography." In *Power / Knowledge: Selected Interviews and Other Writings, 1972–1977*, ed. C. Gordon. New York: Pantheon, pp. 63–77.

Gallardo, Bartolomé José. 1866. *Ensayo de una biblioteca española de libros raros y curiosos*, vol. 2. Madrid: Rivadeneyra.

Gentile, Sebastiano, curator. 1992. *Firenze e la scoperta dell'America. Umanesimo e Geografia nel '400 Fiorentino.* Catalogo a cura di Sebastiano Gentile. Florence: Leo S. Olschki.

Gestoso Pérez, José. 1910. *Curiosidades Antiguas Sevillanas.* Seville: El Correo de Andalucía.

Gil, Juan, prol. 1989. *Las joyas de la Colombina. Las lecturas de Hernando Colón.* Seville: Consejería de Cultura de la Junta de Andalucía, Biblioteca Nacional de España & Cabildo de la Catedral.

Gil, Juan, and Consuelo Varela, eds. 1984. *Cartas de particulares a Colón y Relaciones coetáneas.* Madrid: Alianza.

Gil Fernández, Luis. 1997. "Las bibliotecas." In *Panorama social del humanismo español.* [1981]. 2nd ed. Madrid: Tecnos, pp. 648–66.

Goldthwaite, Richard A. 1972. "Schools and Teachers of Commercial Arithmetic in Renaissance Florence." *Journal of European Economic History* 1, no. 2: 418–33.

Gómez, Nicolás W. 2008. *The Tropics of Empire: Why Columbus Sailed South to the Indies.* Cambridge: MIT Press.

González Gallego, Ignacio, ed. 1974. "El *Libro de los privilegios de la nación genovesa.*"

Historia. Instituciones. Documentos 1: 275–358. Available online at http://institucional.us.es/revistas/historia/01/10%20gonzalez%20gallego.pdf.

Grafton, Anthony. 1992. *New Worlds, Ancient Texts: The Power of Tradition and the Shock of Discovery*. Cambridge: Harvard University Press.

———, ed. 1993. *Rome Reborn: The Vatican Library and Renaissance Culture*. Washington, DC, and Vatican City: Library of Congress and Biblioteca Apostolica Vaticana.

Guillén, Juan. 2004. *Hernando Colón. Humanismo y bibliofilia*. Seville: Fundación José Manuel Lara.

———. 2006. *Historia de las bibliotecas Capitular y Colombina*. Seville: Fundación José Manuel Lara.

Hanke, Lewis. 1974. *All Mankind Is One: A Study of the Disputation between Bartolomé de las Casas and Juan Ginés de Sepúlveda in 1550 on the Intellectual and Religious Capacity of the American Indians*. DeKalb: Northern Illinois University Press.

Harrisse, Henry. 1866. *Bibliotheca Americana Vetustissima: A Description of Works Relating to America Published between the Years 1492 and 1551*. New York: G. P. Philes.

———. 1871. *Don Fernando Colón, historiador de su padre*. Seville: Sociedad de Bibliófilos Andaluces.

———. 1872. *Fernand Colomb: sa vie, ses oeuvres*. Paris: Librairie Tross.

———. 1885. *Grandeur et décadence de la Colombine*. Paris.

———. 1887. *Excerpta Colombiniana*. Paris: H. Welter.

———. 1890. *Cristoforo Colombo e Il Banco di S. Giorgio, studio di Henry Harrisse, eseminato da Cornelio Desimoni*. Edizione italiana su testo corretto ed ampliato dall'autore. Genoa: A Spese del Municipio.

Helgerson, Richard. 2007. *A Sonnet from Carthage: Garcilaso de la Vega and the New Poetry of Sixteenth-Century Europe*. Philadelphia: University of Pennsylvania Press.

Hernández, Bernat. 2015. *Bartolomé de las Casas*. Madrid: Taurus.

Herrán Alonso, Emma. 2010. "Una de esas 'Otras cosillas que también se han de tener en la librería': *La Historia de Amic y Meliz*, Seville, Juan Comberger, 1531." *Criticón* 108: 143–55.

Hillgarth, J. N. 1957. "El *Prognosticon futuri saeculi* de San Julián de Toledo." *Analecta Sacra Tarraconensia* 30: 5–61.

Hobson, Anthony. 1975. "The *Iter italicum* of Jean Matal." In *Studies in the Book Trade in Honour of Graham Pollard*. Oxford Bibliographical Society Publications n.s. 18: 33–61.

Horodowich, Liz. 2005. "Armchair Travellers and the Venetian Discovery of the New World." *Sixteenth Century Journal* 36, no. 4: 1039–62.

Hyma, Albert. 1930. *The Youth of Erasmus.* Ann Arbor: University of Michigan Press.

Infantes, Víctor. 1989. "La prosa de ficción renacentista: Entre los géneros literarios y el género editorial." *Journal of Hispanic Philology* 13: 115–23.

Irving, Washington. 1828. *A History of the Life and Voyages of Christopher Columbus.* 3 vols. New York: G. and C. Carvill.

Jacob, Christian. 2006. *The Sovereign Map: Theoretical Approaches in Cartography throughout History.* Trans. T. Conley, ed. E. H. Dahl. Chicago: University of Chicago Press.

Jardine, Lisa. 1996. *Worldly Goods: A New History of the Renaissance.* London: Macmillan.

Jarrott, C. A. L. 1964. "Erasmus '*In Principio Erat Sermo*': A Controversial Translation." *Studies in Philology* 61, no. 1 (1 Jan.): 35–40.

Joost-Gaugier, Christiane L. 1998. "Ptolemy and Strabo and Their Conversation with Appeles and Protogenes: Cosmography and Painting in Raphael's 'School of Athens.'" *Renaissance Quarterly* 51, no. 3 (Autumn): 761–87.

———. 2002. *Raphael's* Stanza della Segnatura: *Meaning and Invention.* Cambridge: Cambridge University Press.

Jos, Emiliano. 1945. *Investigaciones sobre la vida y obras iniciales de don Fernando Colón.* Seville: Escuela de Estudios Hispano-Americanos de la Universidad de Sevilla.

Kadir, Djelal. 1992. *Columbus and the Ends of the Earth: Europe's Prophetic Rhetoric as Conquering Ideology.* Berkeley: University of California Press.

Kellenbenz, Hermann. 1986. "Lo Stato, la società e il denaro." In *La repubblica internazionale del denaro tra XV e XVII secolo,* ed. Aldo de Maddalena and Hermann Kellebenz. Bologna: Il Mulino, pp. 333–83.

Kelley, Donald R., ed. 1997. *History and the Disciplines: The Reclassification of Knowledge in Early Modern Europe.* Rochester: University of Rochester Press.

Kimmel, Seth R. 2010. "Interpreting Inaccuracy: The Fiction of Longitude in Early Modern Spain." *Journal of Medieval and Early Modern Studies* 40, no. 2: 299–323.

King, David A., and Gerard L'E. Turner. 1994. "The Astrolabe Dedicated to Cardinal Bessarion by Regiomontanus in 1462." In *Bessarione e l'Umanesimo. Catalogo della mostra,* a cura di Gianfranco Fiaccadori. Naples: Vivarium, pp. 341–67.

Kohl, Erläutert Von J. G. 1860. *Die beiden altesten general-karten von Amerika ausgeführt in den Jahren 1527 und 1529 auf Befehl Kaiser Karl's V, in Besitz der Grossherzoglichen Bibliothek zu Weimar.* Weimar: Geographisches Institut.

Labowsky, Lotte. 1979. *Bessarion's Library and the Biblioteca Marciana: Six Early Inventories.* Rome: Edizioni di Storia e Letteratura.

Ladero Quesada, Miguel Ángel. 2002. *El primer oro de América. Los comienzos de la Casa de la Contratación de las Yndias (1503-1511)*. Madrid: Real Academia de la Historia.

Lefebvre, H. 1976. "Reflections on the Politics of Space." Trans. M. Enders. *Antipode* 8: 30–37.

Leporace, Tullia Gasparrini, and Elpidio Mioni, eds. 1968. *Cento Codici Bessarionei. Catalogo di Mostra,* a cura di . . . Venice: Centro Arti e Mestieri Fondazione Giorgio Cini.

Lestringant, Frank. 1991. "The Crisis of Cosmography at the End of the Renaissance." In *Humanism in Crisis: The Decline of the French Renaissance,* ed. P. Desan. Ann Arbor: University of Michigan Press, pp. 153–79.

López-Vidriero, María Luisa, and Pedro M. Cátedra, eds. 1992. *El libro antiguo español: actas del segundo coloquio internacional* (Madrid). Salamanca: Universidad de Salamanca.

Lorenzetti, Giulio. 1929. *Itinerario Sansoviniano a Venezia.* Venice: Comitato per le Onoranze Sansoviniane.

Lowry, M. 1974. "Two Great Venetian Libraries in the Age of Aldus Manutius." *Bulletin of the John Rylands University Library of Manchester* 57, no. 1: 128–66.

———. 1988. "Venetian Capital, German Technology and Renaissance Culture in the Later Fifteenth Century." *Renaissance Studies* 2, no. 1: 1–13.

MacPhail, Eric. 2008. "The Elegance of the Ecolier Limousin: The European Context of Rabelais' Linguistic Parody." *Modern Language Notes* 123, no. 4 (September; French issue): 873–94.

Maddalena, Aldo De. 1986. "La repubblica internazionale del denaro: un'ipotesi infondata o una tesi sostenibile?" In *La repubblica internazionale del denaro tra XV e XVII secolo,* ed. Aldo de Maddalena and Hermann Kellebenz. Bologna: Il Mulino, pp. 7–16.

Madoz, Pascual. 1849. *Diccionario geográfico-estadístico-histórico de España y sus posesiones de Ultramar,* 16 vols. Vol 14. Madrid.

Maifreda, Germano. 2012. *From* Oikonomia *to Political Economy: Constructing Economic Knowledge from the Renaissance to the Scientific Revolution.* Trans. L.V. Mannucci. London: Ashgate.

Manfredi, Antonio. 1998. "The Vatican Library of Pope Nicholas V: The Project of a Universal Library in the Age of Humanism." *Library and Information History* 14, no. 22: 103–10.

———. 2010. "La nascita della Vaticana in età umanistica da Niccolò V a Sisto IV." In Manfredi, ed., pp. 147–236.

———, ed. 2010. *Le Origini della Biblioteca Vaticana tra Umanesimo e Rinascimento.*

Storia della Biblioteca Apostolica Vaticana. Vatican City: Biblioteca Apostolica Vaticana.

Manzano Manzano, Juan. 1989. *Cristóbal Colón. Siete años decisivos de su vida, 1485–1492*. Madrid.

Maravall, José Antonio. 1999. "La imagen de la sociedad expansiva en la conciencia castellana del siglo XVI." In *Estudios de historia del pensamiento español*. Vol. 2. *La época del Renacimiento*. Madrid: Centro de Estudios Políticos y Constitucionales, pp. 267–310.

Marín Martínez, Tomás. 1970. *Obras y Libros de Hernando Colón*. Seville: Consejo Superior de Investigaciones Científicas.

———. 1973. "La participación de Hernando Colón en las Juntas de Badajoz-Elvas de 1524." In *El Tratado de Tordesillas y su proyección*. Valladolid: Universidad de Valladolid, vol. 1, pp. 171–78.

———. 1975. "Presencia de Erasmo en la Biblioteca Colombina de Sevilla." In *Homenaje a Don Agustín Millares Carlo*. Madrid: Caja de Ahorros de Gran Canaria, vol. 1, pp. 685–708.

———. 1993. "Estudio introductorio." In Tomás Marín Martínez, José Manuel Ruiz Asencio, and Klaus Wagner, *Catálogo concordado de la Biblioteca de Hernando Colón*. Madrid: Mapfre y Cabildo de la Catedral de Sevilla, vol. 1, pp. 19–352.

Marsilio, C. 2013. "Genoese Finance, 1348–1700." In *Handbook of Key Global Financial Markets, Institutions and Infrastructure*, ed. in chief Gerard Caprio, Jr. Boston: Elsevier, pp. 123–32.

Martínez Millán, José. 2001. "Del humanismo carolino al proceso de confesionalización Filipino." In *Andrés Laguna. Humanismo, ciencia y política en la Europa renacentista*. Valladolid: Junta de Castilla y León, pp. 123–59.

Mexía, Pedro de. 2003. *Silva de Varia Lección* [Domenico de Robertis, Sevilla, 1540]. Ed. Isaías Lerner. Madrid: Castalia.

Mills, Geoffrey T. 1994. "Early Accounting in Northern Italy: The Role of Commercial Development and the Printing Press in the Expansion of Double-Entry from Genoa, Florence and Venice." *Accounting Historians Journal* 21, no. 1: 81.

Muro Orejón, Antonio, et al. 1964. *Pleitos Colombinos*. Vol. 8. Seville.

Murphy, Trevor. 2004. *Pliny the Elder's* Natural History: *The Empire in the Encyclopedia*. Oxford: Oxford University Press.

Nader, Helen, ed. and trans. 1996. *The Book of Privileges Issued to Christopher Columbus by King Fernando and Queen Isabel, 1492–1502*. Luciano Formisano, philologist. Berkeley: University of California Press.

Nardi, Bruno. 1963. "La scuola di Rialto e l'umanesimo veneziano." In *Umanesimo europeo e umanesimo veneziano*, ed. V. Branca. Florence: Sansoni, pp. 116–36.

Neal, Larry. 2015. "The Italians Invent Modern Finance." In *A Concise History of International Finance: From Babylon to Bernanke*. Cambridge: Cambridge University Press, pp. 28–51.

Nelles, Paul. 1997. "The Library as an Instrument of Discovery: Gabriel Naudé and the Uses of History." In Donald R. Kelly, ed. *History and the Disciplines: The Reclassification of Knowledge in Early Modern Europe*. Rochester: University of Rochester Press, pp. 41–57.

Niccoli, Ottavia. 1982. "Il diluvio del 1524 fra panico collettivo e irrisione carnevalesca." In *Scienze credenze occulte livelli di cultura. Convegno Internazionale di Studi (Firenze, 26–30 giugno 1980)*. Florence: Olschki, pp. 369–92.

Nuovo, Angela. 2013. *The Book Trade in the Italian Renaissance*. Trans. Lydia G. Cochrane. Leiden: Brill.

Ojala, Jari, and Leos Müller, eds. 2007. *Information Flows: New Approaches in the Historical Study of Business Information*. Helsinki: Suomalaisen Kirjallisuuden Seura.

Padgett, John F., and Walter W. Powell. 2012. *The Emergence of Organizations and Markets*. Princeton: Princeton University Press.

Padrón, Ricardo. 2002. "Charting Empire, Charting Difference: Gómara's *Historia general de las Indias* and Spanish Maritime Cartography." *Colonial Latin American Review* 11, no. 1: 47–69.

Pantin, Isabelle. 2012. "The First Phases of the *Theoricae Planetarum* Printed Tradition (1474–1535): The Evolution of a Genre Observed through Its Images." *Journal for the History of Astronomy* 43, no. 1: 3–26.

Pettegree, Andrew. 2008. "Centre and Periphery in the European Book World." In *Transactions of the Royal Historical Society*, 6th ser., 18: 101–128.

———. 2010. *The Book in the Renaissance*. New Haven: Yale University Press.

———. 2014. *The Invention of News*. New Haven: Yale University Press.

Pezzolo, Luciano, and Giuseppe Tattara. 2008. "'Una fiera senza luogo': Was Bisenzone an International Capital Market in Sixteenth-Century Italy?" *Journal of Economic History* 68, no. 4: 1098–1122.

Piacentini, Paola. 2009. *La Biblioteca Vaticana e i registri di* Introitus *ed* Exitus. *Da una ricerca di Giuseppe Lombardi*. Rome: Roma nel Rinascimento.

Plaza, Carlos. 2017. "Buscando Roma. Hernando Colón, Carlos V y la Arquitectura entre Antiguos y Modernos." In *El Patio Circular en la Arquitectura del Renacimiento. De la Casa de Mantegna al Palacio de Carlos V*, ed. Pedro A. Galera and Sabine Frommel. Seville: Universidad Internacional de Andalucía, pp. 227–64.

Portuondo, María M. 2009. *Secret Science: Spanish Cosmography and the New World*. Chicago: Chicago University Press.

Prodi, Paolo. 2009. *Settimo non rubare. Furto e mercato nella storia dell'Occidente*. Bologna: Il Mulino.

Randles, W. G. L. 1988. "From the Mediterranean Portulan Chart to the Marine World Chart of the Great Discoveries: The Crisis in Cartography in the Sixteenth Century." *Imago Mundi* 40, no. 1 (1 January): 115–18.

———. 1998. "The Emergence of Nautical Astronomy in Portugal in the XVth Century." *Journal of Navigation* 51, no. 1: 46–57.

Raymond, Joad, and Noah Moxam, eds. 2016. *News Networks in Early Modern Europe*. Leiden: Brill.

Renazzi, Filippo Maria. 1803. *Storia dell'Università degli Studii di Roma*. Rome: Stamparia Pagliarini.

Rey Pastor, J. 1970. *La ciencia y la técnica en el descubrimiento de América*. Buenos Aires: Espasa-Calpe.

Rico, Francisco. 1978. *Nebrija frente a los bárbaros: El canon de gramáticos nefastos en las polémicas del humanismo*. Salamanca: Servicio de Publicaciones de la Universidad de Salamanca.

Rita, Andreina. 2010. "Per la storia della Vaticana nel primo Rinascimento." In Manfredi, ed., pp. 236–307.

Rodríguez Toro, José Javier. 2018. "Nuevos datos sobre la extraña edición de un manuscrito geográfico de Hernando Colón." *Bulletin Hispanique* 1: 163–84.

Roersch, Alphonse. 1933. "Le maitre de Salamanque Johannes Vasaeus." In *L'humanisme belge a lépoque de la Renaissance. Études et Portraits. Deuxième série*. Louvain: Librairie Universitaire, pp. 79–96.

Rosen, Mark. 2015. *The Mapping of Power in Renaissance Italy: Painted Cartographical Cycles in Social and Intellectual Context*. New York: Cambridge University Press.

Roth, Julian. 2002. *Conversos, Inquisition, and the Expulsion of the Jews from Spain*. Madison: University of Wisconsin Press.

Ruffini, Mario. 1960. *Fernando Colombo e i libri italiani della Biblioteca Colombina di Siviglia*. Turin: Erasmo.

Rumeu de Armas, Antonio. 1973. *Hernando Colón, historiador del descubrimiento de América*. Madrid: Instituto de Cultura Hispánica.

Salonen, Kirsi. 2016. *Papal Justice in the Late Middle Ages: The Sacra Romana Rota*. Abingdon: Routledge.

Sánchez del Barrio, Antonio, dir. 2011. *Libros y Ferias. El Primer Comercio del Libro Impreso. V Centenario de la Imprenta de Medina del Campo (1511–2011)*. Medina del Campo: Fundación Museo de las Ferias.

Sandman, Alison. 2002. "Sea Charts, Navigation, and Territorial Claims in Sixteenth-Century Spain." In Smith and Findlen, eds., pp. 83–108.

———. 2004. "An Apologia for the Pilots' Charts: Politics, Projections and Pilots' Reports in Early Modern Spain." *Imago Mundi* 56, no. 1 (1 January): 7–22.

Sandman, Alison, and Eric H. Ash. 2004. "Trading Expertise: Sebastian Cabot between Spain and England." *Renaissance Quarterly* 57, no. 3: 813–46.

Schoeck, R. J. 1990. *Erasmus of Europe: The Making of a Humanist 1467–1500*. Edinburgh: Edinburgh University Press.

Serrano y Sanz, Manuel. 1932. "Vida y escritos de don Hernando Colón." Proemio de la *Historia del Almirante don Cristóbal Colón por su hijo don Fernando*. Madrid: Librería General de Victoriano Suárez, vol. 1, pp. i–clxi.

Severin, Dorothy Sherman, ed. 2000. *Two Spanish Songbooks: Cancionero Capitular de la Colombina (SVA) and Cancionero de Egerton (LB3)*. Hispanic Studies Textual Research and Criticism. Liverpool: Liverpool University Press.

Sforza, G. 1884. "La patria, la famiglia, e la giovinezza di Papa Niccolò V" [Canone bibliographico di Papa Parentucelli]. *Atti della Reale Accademia Lucchese di Scienze, Lettere ed Arti* 23, Lucca, Appendix A, pp. 359–81.

Sherman, William. 1995. *John Dee: The Politics of Reading and Writing in the English Renaissance*. Amherst: University of Massachusetts Press.

Smith, Christine, and Joseph F. O'Connor. 2001. "What Do Athens and Jerusalem Have to Do with Rome? Gianozzo Manetti on the Library of Nicholas V." In *Perspectives on Early Modern and Modern Intellectual History: Essays in Honour of Nancy S. Struever*, ed. J. Marino and M. W. Schlitt. Rochester: University of Rochester Press, pp. 88–115.

Smith, Pamela H., and Paula Findlen, eds. 2002. *Merchants and Marvels: Commerce, Science and Art in Early Modern Europe*. New York: Routledge.

Soja, Edward W. 1989. *Postmodern Geographies: The Reassertion of Space in Critical Social Theory*. London: Verso.

Spufford, Peter. 2002. *Power and Profit: The Merchant in Medieval Europe*. London: Thames & Hudson.

Summers, David. 1981. *Michelangelo and the Language of Art*. Princeton: Princeton University Press.

Swerdlow, N. M. 1993. "The Recovery of the Exact Sciences of Antiquity: Mathematics, Astronomy, Geography." In Grafton, ed., pp. 125–68.

Tracy, James D. 1972. *Erasmus: The Growth of a Mind*. Geneva: Librairie Droz.

Trinkaus, Charles. 1995. *In Our Image and Likeness: Humanity and Divinity in Italian Humanist Thought*. 2 vols. Notre Dame, IN: University of Notre Dame Press.

Trivellato, Francesca. 2007. "A Republic of Merchants?" In *Finding Europe: Discourses on Margins, Communities, Images ca. 13th–ca. 18th Centuries*, ed. A. Molho, D. R. Curto, and N. Koniordos. New York: Berghahn Books, pp. 133–49.

Trivellato, Francesca. 2019. *The Promise and Peril of Credit*. Princeton: Princeton University Press.

Turnbull, David. 1996. "Cartography and Science in Early Modern Europe: Mapping the Construction of Knowledge Spaces." *Imago Mundi* 48, no. 1 (January): 5–24.

Ullman, Berthold L., and Phillip A. Stadter. 1972. *The Public Library of Renaissance Florence: Niccolò Nicoli, Cosimo de' Medici, and the Library of San Marco*. Padova: Editrice Antenore.

Vicente Baz, Raúl. 2014. "Evolución Histórica de la Biblioteca de la Catedral de Salamanca." In *La Catedral de Salamanca: De fortis a magna*, ed. Mariano Casas Hernández. Salamanca: Diputación de Salamanca, pp. 1283–1351.

Vigneras, L. A. 1956. "New Light on the 1497 Cabot Voyage to America." *Hispanic Historical Review* 36: 503–9.

———. 1957. "The Cape Breton Landfall." *Canadian Historical Review* 38: 219–28.

Vilches, Elvira. 2010. *New World Gold: Cultural Anxiety and Monetary Disorder in Early Modern Spain*. Chicago: University of Chicago Press.

Von Ostenfeld-Suske, Kira. 2012. "A New History for a 'New World': The First One Hundred Years of Hispanic New World Historical Writing." In *The Oxford History of Historical Writing*, vol. 3: 1400–1800, ed. José Rabasa, Masayuki Sato, Edoardo Tortarolo, and Daniel Woolf. Oxford University Press, pp. 556–74.

Wagner, Klaus. 1966. "Un hijo de Colón en Alemania." *Anales de la Universidad Hispalense* 26: 101–9.

———. 1967/69. "Ein sohn des Kolumbus in Worms zur Zeit des Reichtages 1521." *Der Wormsgau* 8: 34–37.

———. 1971. "Sulla sorte di alcuni codici manoscritti appartenuti a Marin Sanudo." *La Bibliofilia* 73: 247–62.

———. 1972. "Altre notizie sulla sorte dei libri di Marin Sanudo." *La Bibliofilia* 74: 185–90.

———. 1975a. "Aldo Manuzio e i prezzi di suoi libri." *La Bibliofilia* 77, no. 1: 77–82.

———. 1981a. "Nuove notizie a proposito dei libri di Marin Sanudo." *La Bibliofilia* 83: 129–31.

———. 1981b. "La reforma protestante en los fondos bibliográficos de la Biblioteca Colombina." *Revista Española de Teología* 41: 393–463.

———. 1984. "El itinerario de Hernando Colón según sus anotaciones. Datos para la biografía del bibliófilo sevillano." *Archivo Hispalense* 203: 81–99.

———. 1986. "Libros obsequiados a Hernando Colón y otras curiosidades de su biblioteca." in *Homenaje a Pedro Sáinz Rodríguez,* vol. 3. Madrid: Fundación Universitaria Española, pp. 713–24.

———. 1988a. "Bibliotecas antiguas en la Biblioteca Universitaria de Sevilla." In *El libro antiguo español. Actas del primer coloquio internacional,* ed. María Luisa López-Vidriero and Pedro M. Cátedra. Salamanca: Universidad de Salamanca, Biblioteca Nacional de Madrid, Sociedad Española de Historia del Libro, pp. 403–8.

———. 1988b. "Libros de la Biblioteca Colombina perdidos y hallados." *Journal of Hispanic Philology* 13: 7–11.

———. 1991. "Hernando Colón en Italia." *Archivo Hispalense* 74, no. 225: 51–62.

———. 1992. "Hernando Colón: semblanza de un bibliófilo y de su biblioteca en el quinientos aniversario de su nacimiento." In *El libro antiguo español. Actas del segundo Coloquio internacional,* ed. María Luisa López-Vidriero and Pedro M. Cátedra. Salamanca: Ediciones de la U. de Salamanca, Biblioteca Nacional de Madrid, Sociedad Española de Historia del Libro, pp. 475–92.

———. 2001. "A propósito de la biblioteca de Jerónimo de Chaves, catedrático de cosmografía de la *Casa de Contratación,* y el paradero de algunos de sus libros." In *La cultura del libro en la Edad Moderna: Andalucía y América,* coord. Manuel Peña Díaz, Pedro Ruiz Pérez, and Julián Solana Pujalte. Córdoba: Servicio de Publicaciones de la Universidad, pp. 187–231.

Wagner, Klaus, and Juan Guillén. 1990. "Pasado, presente y futuro de la Biblioteca Colombina." *Boletín de la Real Academia Sevillana de Buenas Letras* 18: 61–77.

Walsby, Malcolm. 2018. "Book Lists and Their Meaning." In *Documenting the Early Modern Book World: Inventories and Catalogues in Manuscript and Print,* ed. Malcolm Walsby and Natasha Constantinidou. Boston: Brill, pp. 1–24.

Watts, Pauline Moffitt. 2007. "The European Religious Worldview and Its Influence on Mapping." In *The History of Cartography,* vol. 3, part 1: *Cartography in the European Renaissance,* ed. David Woodward. Chicago: Chicago University Press, pp. 382–400.

Wesseling, A. 2009. "How to Explore the World while Staying at Home: Erasmus on Maps." In *Syntagmatia: Essays on Neo-Latin literature in Honour of Monique Mund-Dopchie and Gilbert Tournoy.* Leiden: Leiden University Press. Supplementa Humanistica Lovaniensia, pp. 301–5.

Wilson-Lee, Edward. 2018. *The Catalogue of Shipwrecked Books: Young Columbus and the Quest for a Universal Library.* London: William Collins.

Woodward, David. 1991. "Maps and the Rationalization of Geographic Space." In *Circa 1492: Art in the Age of Exploration,* ed. J. A. Levenson. New Haven: Yale University Press, pp. 83–88.

Zambelli, Paola. 1960. "Umanesimo magico-astrologico e raggruppamenti segreti nei platonici della preriforma." In *Umanesimo e Esoterismo*. Padua: Antonio Milani, pp. 141–74.

———. 1982. "Fine del mondo o inizio della propaganda? Astrologia, filosofia della storia e propaganda politico-religiosa nel dibattito sulla congiunzione del 1524." In *Scienze credenze occulte livelli di cultura. Convegno Internazionale di Studi (Firenze, 26–30 giugno 1980)*. Florence: Olschki, pp. 291–368.

———. 1986a. "Introduction: Astrologers' Theory of History." In *"Astrologi hallucinati": Stars and the End of the World in Luther's Time*. Berlin: Walter de Gruyter, pp. 1–28.

———. 1986b. "Many Ends for the World: Luca Gaurico Instigator of the Debate in Italy and in Germany." In *"Astrologi hallucinati": Stars and the End of the World in Luther's Time*. Berlin: Walter de Gruyter, pp. 239–63.

———. 2001. "Profezie, Intolleranze e Incoerenze nell 'Astrologia di Terra e di Cielo' alla Vigilia della Congiunzione del 1524." In *La Formazione Storica della Alterità. Studi nella storia della tolleranza nell'età moderna offerti a Antonio Rotondò*, promossi da Henry Mèchoulan, Richard H. Popkin, Giuseppe Ricuperati, Luisa Simonutti. 3 vols. Vol. 1: Secolo XVI. Florence: Leo Olschki, pp. 25–50.

Zamora, Margarita. 1993. *Reading Columbus*. Chicago: University of Chicago Press.

Zorzi, Marino. 1990. "La circolazione del libro a Venezia nel Cinquecento: biblioteche private e publiche." *Ateneo Veneto* 28: 117–89.

———, ed. 2003. *La vita nei libri. Edizioni illustrate a stampa del quattro e cinquecento dalla Fondazione Giorgio Cini*. Venice: Edizioni della Laguna.

INDEX

Page numbers in *italics* indicate illustrations. Titles of works by authors other than Hernando or Columbus generally are listed under the author's name.

Abecedarium A (Índice *Alfabético Antiguo)*, 49, 53, *127*, 146, 149, 226, 276–77n11, 277n15
Abecedarium B (Índice *General Alfabético)*, *127*, 147–48, 218–22, 266–67n72
Adagia, 173
"Agogo Mago," falconry book by, 31, 255n35
Ailly, Pierre d', 107, 193; *Imago Mundi*, 16, *17*, *18*, 84–85, 99, 105, 251n4
Alain de Lille, 265n55
Alberti, Leon Battista, 129; *Descriptio Urbis Romae*, 257n52
Albertini, *Opusculum de mirabilis novae et veteris urbis Romae*, 255n33
Albert the Great, *De Animalibus*, 253n15
Albumasar, *Flores Astrologiae*, 253n15
Aldus Manutius, 250n16
Alexander V (pope), 107
Alexander VI (pope), 31
Alexander the Great, 22, 141, 240
Alexandria, library of, 5, 107, 137–38, 141, 273n32
Alfargani, 272n28
alphabetization, alphabetical order, 36, 290n9
Alphonsus X of Castile, *Tabula Astronomicae*, 253n15
Alviano, Bartolomeo d', 89, 267n75
Amadeo de Saboya (king of Spain), 185
Ambrose of Milan, 100
Andrés, Juan, 147, 219
Andrés de León, 173
Anes, Viçenti, 242

Annius, Johannes, 264n49
Annotaciones or *Tabla de Autores y Ciencias, 127,* 136, 158–60, 210–18
Antoine, Jean (Johannes Hammonius), 50
Antonio de Toledo, 169
Apelles, 142, 143
Apostolios, Arsenios, 255n34
Aquinas. *See* Thomas Aquinas, Saint
Arabic texts in Hernando's library, 48–49
Araoz, Antonio María, 182
Arbolí, Servando, 186
Arias Montano, Benito, *Antiquitatum iudaicarum libri ix,* 193–94
Aristotle, 141, 161, 272n28, 278nn23,32; *De Animalibus,* 253n15; *De coelo et mundo,* 272n27; *Ethics,* 93; *Meteorologica,* 272n27; *Opera,* 22; *Physics,* 102
Arranz, Diego, 238
Assault de L'Empereur a Barberosse, 90
astronomical time and calendar reform, 91–92, 268n83
Augustine of Hippo, Saint 104; *City of God,* 3, 104, 268n88, 270n16
Autores y Ciencias, 127, 224

Babelon, Jean, 188, 189
Bacon, Sir Francis, *New Atlantis,* 109
Badius Ascensius, Jodocus, 78, 263n42
Balducci Pegolotti, Francesco de, *Prattica della mercatura,* 262n27
banking system and exchange rates, 63–66, 261n23
Barlow, Roger, 273n38
Barlowe, Arthur, 194
Barlowe, Samuel L., 188
Basiniana, Pero Benito de, 168
Bayezid III (sultan), 90
Beckett, Thomas, Saint, biography of, 253n23
Bede, the Venerable, 100
Behaim, Martin, and globe, 58–59, 108, 262n27
Bembo, Pietro, 49
Berardi, Juanoto, 261n16
Bernáldez, Andrés, 251n2; *Cronica,* 56
Bertachino, Giovanni, 156, 246, 291n2
Bessarion, Cardinal, 6, 34, 108, 250–51nn16,17
Bianco, Andrea, atlas of, 105
biblioglyphs, markings, or symbols, 81, 82, 136, 158, 159–60, *200,* 210–18, 219–21, 265n54, 288n58, 290n12, 290nn14,15
Biblioteca Ambrosiana, Milan, 195–96
Biblioteca Capitular, Seville, 138, 171, 172, 180, 190
Biblioteca Colombina, Seville, 28, 86, 129, 148, 170, 180, 182, 186, 188, 190
Biblioteca Corviniana, Hungary, 6–7, 108
Biblioteca di San Marco, Florence, 5, 7, 16, 29
Biblioteca Laurenziana, Florence, 45, 139
Biblioteca Malatestina, Cesena, 139
Biblioteca Marciana, Venice, 5, 6, 34, 250–51nn16,17
Biblioteca Palatina (Vatican Library), 5, 25, 31–34, 139–43, 161, 250n14, 255n42
bills of exchange, 63, 65, 67, 72, 261nn20,22
Biondo, Flavio, 129, 254–55n33
Bisticii, Vespasiano da, 5, 140
Blair, Ann, 62
Boccaccio, Giovanni, 5, 283n13; *Nimphale Fiesolamo,* 89
Bodleian Library, Oxford, 276n57
Bonaiuto, Andrea di, *The Triumph*

of Thomas Aquinas (Santa Maria Novella, Florence), 141, 142, 277n31
Book of Privileges (*Libro de los Privilegios*), 62–63, 65, 73, 282n8
Book of Privileges of the Genoese Nation, 62
Book of Prophecies (*Libro de las Profecías*), 23–24, 62, 100, 154–55, 238, 253n14, 273n39
booksellers and printers: acquisition of additional books, Hernando's will and testament on, 232–37; Columbus, as bookseller, 16, 56, 251n2; *géneros editoriales* or "publishing genres," 82–84; in Germany, Low Countries, Switzerland, and Venice (1520–21), 38, 77–81; in Rome, 29, 31; Vatican library lending books to, 32. *See also specific individuals and firms*
Borges, Jorge Luis, 198
Borromeo, Federico, 195–96
Boscán, Juan, 34, 255–56n43
botanical garden, Casa de Colón/Casa de Goles, Seville, 45–47, 167–68, 258n61
Bracciolini, Poggio, 5
branching diagrams, *94*, 196, 279n34, 280n46
Brant, Sebastian, 78
Briart, Jan, *Quaestio quodlibetica contra dispensationes*, 39, *40–41*, 258n56
Brigit of Sweden, Saint, *Revelations*, 77
Bruni, Leonardo, 5, 107

cabinet de curiosité, differentiation of Hernando's library from, 134
Cabot, John, 57, 187
Cabot, Sebastian, 120, 187, 243, 273n38
Calandri, Filippo, *De aritmethrica opusculum*, 55–56, 260n3
calendar reform and astronomical time, 91–92, 268n83
calendars and prognostications, as printed material, 84–89, *86*, *87*, 91–93
Calepino, Ambrosius, *Dictionarium*, 132, 217, 277n15
Calixtus III (pope), 140
Callimachus, 107
Calvo, Vicente, 169
Camillo, Giullio, *Trattato delle materie*, 196
Capitulaciones de Santa Fe (1492), 28, 51, 62–63
Carona, Antonio Maria de, 44
Carrantus, Petrus Mathaeus, 283n14
Carta General de Navegar, 120–21
cartography, 13, 97–124: absolute versus relative qualities of physical space in, 271n18; cataloguing and, 124; chronography and, 101, 103–5, 192–94, 270n16, 273n32; ekphrastic or discursive modes of description versus, 97–99, 103–4; in ephemeral works or *obrezillas*, 123; heterogeneous streams of information, reconciling, 98–99, 102, 110–18; imagination, as mediator of, 97; Imperial College of mathematics and navigation, proposal for, 287n44; intellectual traditions underpinning, 102–6; Las Juntas de Elvas-Badajoz and, 108, 118–20, 243; library of Hernando and, 101–2, 106–10, 123–24; linear representations, moving beyond, 58–62; mariners and cosmographers, conflict between, 110–11; navigator, Hernando's experience as, 99–101; portolan maps, 58–60, 99, 102, 103, 105, 123. *See also* Casa de Contratación, Hernando's cartographical project at
Cartuja de las Cuevas, 44, 46, 63, 190

Casa da Mina (Portugal), 108, 120
Casa de Colón/Casa de Goles, Seville, 43–45, 158, 167–68
Casa de Contratación, Hernando's cartographical project at, 13, 120–24; appointment letter, 243–44; *Carta General de Navegar,* 120–21; cataloguing practices of Hernando and, 14; circumnavigation of globe, findings and consequences of, 2; Bartolomeo Columbus in Portugal and, 105–6; ephemera/*obrezillas* and, 92; library and, 13–14, 46, 53, 106, 109; purpose of, 108–9; *real cédula,* 122; Weimar chart and Diego Ribera map, 121–22, 275n52
Casa di San Giorgio, Genoa, 63–65
Castañeda Delgado, P., 122, 275n52
Castellanos, Pedro de, 169
Castro, Bartolomeo de, 28, 254n30
Catalina de Ayahibex, 47
Catálogo concordado, 191
catalogues and cataloguing, 13–14, 125–66; accidental versus essential qualities, use of, 136; after Hernando, 178–80, 182, *183, 184,* 186, 188, 189, 191; book titles, unreliability of, 147–48, 154–55, 218–19; branching diagrams, *94,* 196, 279n34, 280n46; cartography and, 124; categories and hierarchies in, 136; duplication, as means of preventing, 39, 134, 139, 147–48, 230; early modern world, as reflection of, 96; existing models for library organization, 33–34, 137–43; Hernando's *reportorios,* 126, *127;* of indices and other paratexts, 196; inventory of possessions (1509), 25–26, 42; Juan Pérez's *Memoria* on, 15, 53, 125–29, 136, 195, 198, *200,* 201–26, 276–77n11, 276n3; linear systems, moving beyond, 60–62, *61;* markings, symbols, or biblioglyphs, use of, 81, 82, 136, 158, 159–60, *200,* 210–18, 219–21, 265n54, 288n58, 290nn12,14,15; *Memorial al Emperador* on, 245–46; mercantile/financial culture and, 165; order and life, relationship between, 15, 38–39, 54; physical format of books, describing, 135, 158, 159, 196, 290n14; physical layout of library and subject classification, 158–63, 280n56; purpose and use of, 164–65; tombstone design by Hernando and, *61,* 260n10; Vives on, 93; in will and testament of Hernando, 230. *See also specific catalogues*
Celtis, Conrad, 250n16
census or *vocabulario* of Spanish towns, 36, 37, 38, 130, 131, 158
Centurione family, 56, 57
Cerezo Martínez, Ricardo, 122, 275n52
Chalcenterus, Didymus, 255n34
Charlemagne, 69
Charles V (king of Spain and Holy Roman emperor): arms and letters, responsibility for joint progress of, 75; Casa de Contratación and, 106, 121–22; cataloguing practices of Hernando and, 148, 156; financial arrangements of Hernando with, 72–73; Imperial College of mathematics and navigation, proposal for, 287n44; investiture of, and travels of Hernando, 38, 77, 168; *Jornada de Túnez* (1535), 90; library of Hernando and, 34, 35, 37–38, 48, 49, 50, 52; *Memorial al Emperador* requesting funds to support library, 52–53, 75, 149, 188, 245–47; Mexía's genealogy of, 192; pamphlets ap-

pealing to, collected by Hernando, 88–89; Spanish Lutheranism, concerns about, 178
Chaves, Jerónimo de, 96, 193, 272n29; *Chronographia o reportorio de los tiempos,* 193
Chavez, Alonso de, 110, 116, 120, 121, 123, 129, 193, 259n63; *Espejo de navegantes,* 98–99, 109, 193, 269n4
chests, books stored in, 25
chronography, 3, 4, 96, 101, 103–5, 192–94, 270n16, 273n32
Chrysoloras, Manuel, 27, 48, 107, 108
Ciocci, Argante, 71
circumnavigation of globe, 2, 101, 110, 238–43
Clenardus (Cleynaerts), Nicolas, 48–49, 249n4, 259n73; *Letter to Christians,* 49
Codex Testeriano Bodmer 905, 249n4
Colet, John, 81
Collegium Trilingue, Louvain, 47–48
Colloquio on longitude, 125
Colocci, Angelo, 29, 264n48
Colón, Diego (older, legitimate brother), 23, 25, 27, 35, 168, 188
Colón, Hernando. *See* Hernando Colón, universalizing projects of
Colón, Luis (nephew and heir of Hernando), 168–69, 227, 236, 281n1, 282n5
Colón de Concordia, 100, 238, 239, 269n9
Colonis, Ferdinand, 92
Columbus, Bartholomew, 16, 57, 58, 99, 103–4, 105–6, 243, 251n4, 271n20
Columbus, Christopher: biography of, by Hernando, 1, 2, 15, 50–52, 99, 188–89, 251n4; bond with Hernando, 23; as bookseller, 16, 56, 251n2; cartography and voyages of, 99–100, 103–6, 114; circumnavigation of globe first proposed by, 101; creation of myth of, 1–2; ephemera of Hernando including poetic version of first letter on New World, 90, 123; intentional underaccounting of distances by, 59; Irving's biography of, 187; Jerusalem, plan to reconquer, 56, 63; library of Hernando, archives forming original nucleus of, 15–21, 103–4; mercantile culture and voyages of, 9, 56–57, 58, 62–63, 262n30; "narrow earth" theories and, 7, 16; Pavia, attendance at lectures at, 28; Piccolomini's *Historia* influencing, 3–4, 103–4; Portuguese influences on, 103; tomb at Cartuja de las Cuevas, 44, 46; Tordesillas treaty, interpretation of, 119. *See also specific works*
commonplace book *(Loci communes)* kept by Hernando, 93, *94,* 156, 160, 161, 196, 277n13, 279n34, 280n46
Compagnia del Mantellaccio co laggiunta, 86
Compendia diversorum librorum, 92, 149
Consejo de Indias, 259n63
contractual life of marketplace, 75–76
conversion/evangelization projects, universal, 3, 6, 49, 70, 238
Copernicus, Nicolas, *De revolutionibus orbium coelestium,* 194
Córdoba, Umayyad library at, 138
Corro, Antonio del (senior and junior), 173–78, 286n25
Cortés, Hernán, 25, 270n14
Cosmografía, Itinerario, or *Descripción de España,* 54, 110, 117, 126, *127,* 128–31, 132, 160–61, 202–3, 243, 260–61n14, 275n51
cosmography: cartography and, 97, 98, 100, 102–7, 109–11, 114, 116–18,

cosmography (continued)
120–22; cataloguing and, 13, 14; Columbus and, 16; library and, 6, 7, 22, 23, 26; mercantile/financial culture and, 62, 67, 85
Counter-Reformation, 172
Crastonus, 27, 48, 253n24
Cronicon usque ad destructionem Hierosolymae, 258n59, 268n85
Crusades, funding, 64, 70
Cusa, Nicolas de, 91
custodians: of Hernando's library, 229–31, 234, 236; Vatican library, *custodes* of, 31, 33, 140
Cyril of Alexandria, 265n55

Dante, 142; *Commedia,* 33, 140
Dati, Giuliano, 90, 123
Day, John, 16, 57, 251–52n6
Declaración del derecho que la Real Corona de Castilla tiene a la conquista de Persia, Arabia, e India, e de Calicut e Malaca, 100, 125
Declaraciones de Marcos Felipe, 188
De correctione kalendarii propositiones XIII, 91
del Monte, Vicenzio, 237
Demetrius of Phalerum, 138
de Pace, Andreas, *In nouum modum corrigendi kalendarium,* 91
de Roover, Raymond, 64
desamortizaciones, 182
Descripción, Itinerario, or *Cosmografía de España,* 54, 110, 117, 126, *127,* 128–31, 132, 160–61, 202–3, 243, 260–61n14, 275n51
Desiderius (servant of Hernando), 237
Deza, Fray Diego, 11, 21–22
Diaz, Bartholomew, 271n19
Díaz del Castillo, Bernal, *Historia,* 103, 270n14
Diccionario or *Vocabulario Latino,* 36–37, *112, 113, 127,* 128, 131–32, 224–25
Diego Colón (older, legitimate brother), 23, 25, 27, 35, 168, 188
Diluio di Roma, 86–88
Doria, Giorgio, 66
double-entry bookkeeping, 70–72, 260n9, 262n31
Duns Scotus, John, 100
duplication, catalogues as means of preventing, 39, 134
Dürer, Albrecht, *Bath House,* 135–36

Eguía, Miguel de, 114
Eisenstein, Elizabeth, *The Printing Press as an Agent of Change,* 9–10
Elcano, Juan Sebastián, 118
Encisco, Martín Fernández de, 273n38
Enlightenment: Columbus's "discovery" of New World and, 1; print, emergence of, 10
ephemeral works, or *obrezillas,* 81–96; *cabinet de curiosité,* differentiation of library from, 134; calendars and prognostications, 84–89, *86, 87,* 91–93; cartographic elements in, 123–24; distinct catalogue markings for, 82; erosion of collection after Hernando, 172, 186; as iterated information, 277n14; knowledge organization and distillation, as objects of experiments in, 92–96, *94, 95; libretti* as, 89, 266n72; Loaysa's appreciation for, 288n55; news network, as part of, 80, 86, 88, 89–92; as part of Hernando's library collecting, 31, 34, 42–43, 58; public opinion, influence on, 120; recreational tracts (ballads and poetry), 89–90; shelf marks, 161, 266n66; significance of, in Hernando's

library, 80, 81–84, 85, 266–67n72; technical expertise and knowledge, transmission of, 91–92
Erasmus, Desiderius, 4, 34–35, 48, 78, 99; *Antibarbari,* 48, 74, 78, 173, 178; *Ciceronianus,* 29; *Colloquies,* 97; Er. Epist. 3043, 254n29; Greek New Testament of, 8, 250n9; *Lengua,* 157, 208; Lucian, Basel edition of, 173, *176, 177*
Eratosthenes, 107, 137
Escorial, El, 172, 193–94, 284n18
Ethiopian language of Ge'ez, books in, 31
Euclid, 99, 102, 142; *Elements,* 70–71
Eugenius IV (pope), 140
evangelization/conversion projects, universal, 3, 6, 49, 70, 238
exchange rates and banking system, 63–66, 261n23

falconry book by "Agogo Mago," 31, 255n35
Felipe, Marcos, 53, 169, 210, 226, 237, 245
Ferdinand I of Hungary, coronation of, 42
Ferdinand II of Aragon (king of Spain), 2, 27, 35, 37, 63, 101, 106, 119, 180, 238–42
Ferdinand III (saint and king of Castile), 180
Feria de Medina del Campo, 69, 73, 232–33, 263nn41,42
Fernández de Navarrete, Eustaquio, 187, 287n44
Fernández de Navarrete, Martín, *Colección de los viages y descubrimientos que hicieron por mar los españoles desde fines del siglo XV,* 187, 188
Fernández de Oviedo, Gonzalo, 50
Fernández y Velasco, José María, 182
Ferrara, Francesco de, *La grant armee de L'Empereur lequel sen va combatre contre le Turc,* 90
Field of the Cloth of Gold, 77
Fifth Lateran Council (1512–16), 91, 267n79
financial culture. *See* mercantile and financial culture
First Voyage of Columbus (1492), 8, 11, 51, 190
Flaubert, Gustave, 188
Florence: acquisition of additional books, Hernando's will and testament on, 236; Biblioteca di San Marco, 5, 7, 16, 29; Biblioteca Laurenziana, 45, 139; books acquired by Hernando in, 35; Santa Maria Novella fresco of *The Triumph of Thomas Aquinas* (Bonaiuto), 141, 142, 277n31
Fondaco de Tedeschi, Venice, 70
Foucault, Michel, 124
Fourth Voyage of Columbus (1502–4), 11, 21, 24–25, 62, 99
Fragmenta librorum ex nota Ferdinandi Colonis, 92
Francis I (king of France), 35
Froben/Frobenius, Johannes, 78
Fugger, Georg and Jacob, 70

Galeottus, Martius, 31
Galileo, 193, 194
Gallardo, Bartolomé José, 181
Gálvez, Diego Alejandro, 181–82
García, Pere (cardinal-archbishop of Barcelona), 7, 31
Garcilaso de la Vega, 256n43
garden, Casa de Colón/Casa de Goles, Seville, 45–47, 167–68, 258n61
Garrido, Jerónimo, 169

Ge'ez (Ethiopian language), books in, 31
géneros editoriales, or "publishing genres," 82–84
Genoa: *Book of Privileges of the Genoese Nation,* 62; Casa di San Giorgio, 63–65; mercantile and financial culture of, 62–66, 78
Germany, Hernando traveling to, 38, 47–48
Gerson, Jean, *De Contractibus,* 75–76
Gesner, Conrad: *Biblotheca universalis,* 195; *Pandectae,* 84, 85
Gil, Juan, 171, 251n3
Ginnasio Mediceo, 29
Giunti, Venice, 256n44
golden ratio, 71
González de Cellórigo, Martín, 65
Gorricio, Gaspar de, 23
Great Schism, 85
Greek, Hernando's struggles with, 27, 48, 253–54n23
Grimaldo, Francisco de, 73
Grimaldo, Nicolas, 73
Grimaldo, Niculoso, 263n40
Grimaldo, Octaviano da, 38, 73, 78, 79, 143
Grimani, Cardinal Domenico, 34–35, 256nn45,46
Grotius, Hugo, *De origine gentium Americanum,* 194
Guillén, Juan, 170, 171, 178, 180, 191, 282n10; *Historia de las Bibliotecas Capitular y Colombina,* 191
guyacam plant used to treat syphilis, 47

Habsburg, genealogy of House of, 42
Hadrian (pope), 254n27
Hammonius, Johannes (Jean Antoine), 50
Harriot, Thomas, 194
Harrisse, Henry, 169, 170, 172, 186–89, 284n18, 287n44; *Bibliotheca Americana Vetustissima,* 188; *Don Fernando Colón, historiador de su padre,* 188; *Grandeur et Decadence de la Colombine,* 186
Hebrew works and Hebraica, 5, 27, 48–49, 114, 161, 178, 195, 215, 256n45, 274n45, 280–81nn56,57
Henry VIII (king of England), 77
Hernández Díaz, José, 187, 189
Hernando Colón, universalizing projects of, 1–14; bond between Columbus and Hernando, 23; brother and brother's family, relationship with, 168–69; circumnavigation of globe proposed by, 2, 101, 110, 238–43; Columbus, creation of myth of, 1–2; contextualization of, 9; cultural fascination with the universal, 2–3; death of Hernando, 53; family lawsuits, involvement in, 27–28, 35, 50–51, 52, 254n25; Imperial College of mathematics and navigation, proposal for, 287n44; institutionalization of projects, 37–38; knowledge organization, interest in tools of, 10, 29, 37, 47, 53–54, 85, 92, 143, 161; millenarian outlook and, 3, 4, 6, 9, 11, 23, 49, 62–63, 70, 85, 102, 105, 117, 192; print, significance of emergence of, 7, 8, 9–11, 29; Rome, sojourn in, 27–35; significance of, 192–98; Spanish court, childhood and education at, 7–8, 11, 21–23; tombstone, design for, *61,* 231, 260n10; will and testament of Hernando, 53, *61,* 69, 188, 227–37. *See also* cartography; catalogues and cataloguing; Columbus, Christopher; ephemeral works, or *obrezillas;* library of Hernando Colón;

library of Hernando Colón after Hernando; mercantile and financial culture; travels of Hernando Colón; *and specific works*
Herrera, Antonio de, 275n52
Herrera, Fernando de, 263n42
Hesiod, 27
Historia del Almirante, 188, 252n7
"Historias Toscanas," 86
Homer, 27, 32, 107, 142
Horace, 22
humanists and humanism, 3–8, 11, 22, 24, 29, 34, 44, 74, 75, 78, 81, 253n14
Huntington, Archer M., 147

images, printed, collection of, 39–42
imperial ambitions and Hernando's universalizing projects, 27, 74–75, 118–24
incunabula, 3, 31, 78, 264n49, 268n86
Índice *Alfabético Antiguo (Abecedarium A),* 49, 53, *127,* 146, 149, 226, 276–77n11, 277n15
Índice *de Autores y Obras, 127,* 223–24
Índice *de impresos y manuscritos,* 182, *183, 184*
Índice de libros prohibidos, 178
Índice *General Alfabético (Abecedarium B), 127,* 147–48, 218–22, 266–67n72
Índice *muy generales, 127,* 225–26
Índice *Numeral (Registrum B),* 85, *87, 127,* 146–47, *154,* 160, 161, *162,* 206, 207, 222–23, 266–67n72, 281n57, 283n14
indices and other paratexts: catalogues recording presence of, 196; Hernando's interest in, 29, *30,* 35–37, 43, 156; *Libro de las Materias* and, 156; Lucretius, index to, 254n31; "Memoria de plantas y ortelanos" (for garden at Casa de Colón), 46; to Pomponius Mela, *Cosmographia,* 35, 256–57n48; for sammelbands, 88; Suetonius, Hernando's "indice completissimo" to, 29, *30;* in Tagliente's *Libro d'abaco,* 67. *See also* catalogues and cataloguing; *and specific indices*
Infantes, Victor, 82
Inghirami, Tommaso, 141
Inquisition and Hernando's library, 170, 173–79, *174–77*
Interpretatione di Daniel Propheta, 86
Ipolito et Dianora, 86
Irving, Washington, *A History of the Life and Voyages of Christopher Columbus,* 187
Isabel I of Castile (queen of Spain), 23, 62, 119
Isabel II (queen of Spain), 182, 185
Isabella of Portugal, 34
Isidore of Seville, 172; *Etymologies,* 137, 138, 194, 273n32
Italian, Hernando's use of, when traveling, 236
Itinerario, Cosmografía, or *Descripción de España,* 54, 110, 117, 126, *127,* 128–31, 132, 160–61, 202–3, 243, 260–61n14, 275n51
Iuditium ab anno 1515 ad annum 1524, 92

Jacob, Christian, 123–24, 197
Jacobo de Testera, 3, 249n4
Jacopo di Angelo da Scarperia, 6, 107, 121
Jardine, Lisa, 58
Jerusalem: Columbus's plan to reconquer, 56, 63; *Cronicon usque ad destructionem Hierosolymae,* 268n85
Jewish chronology of the world, 16, *19*
John II (Juan) of Portugal, 58, 119
John Carter Brown library, Rhode Island, Hernandine materials at, 172

Joost-Gaugier, Christiane L., 141, 142
Jornada de Túnez (1535), 90
Josephus, 16; *De antiquitate,* 104, 270n16
Juan (infante), 21, 22
Juan Pérez: on cartography, 117; on catalogues and cataloguing, 132, 133–34, 147, 148, 149–57, 160, 162; on furniture of library, 162; library of Hernando and, 43, 45, 48, 50, 259n64; *Memoria,* 15, 53, 125–29, 136, 195, 198, *200,* 201–26, 276n3, 276–77n11; mercantile/financial culture and, 265n54; in will and testament of Hernando, 201, 237
Julian of Toledo, Saint, *Prognosticon futuri saeculi,* 84, 265–66nn61,62
Julius II (pope), 89, 91, 141
Julius Caesar, 137, 240
Juntas de Elvas-Badajoz, 59, 108, 118–20, 243, 251n4
Juvenal, 22; *Satires,* 28

Knights Templar, 64
knowledge organization, Hernando's interest in tools of, 10, 29, 37, 47, 53–54, 85, 92, 143, 161. *See also* catalogues and cataloguing

labeling of books in library, 42–43, 126, 231
Landino, Cristoforo, 16, 22
language: empire and, 27; Ge'ez, books in, 31; Greek, Hernando's struggles with, 27, 48, 253–54n23; Italian, Hernando's use of, when traveling, 236; Latin dictionary project (*Vocabulario* or *Diccionario Latino*), 36–37, *112, 113, 127,* 128, 131–32, 224–25; universal, 71, 93, 268n88
Lanzio, Antonio, 44
Lascaris, John, 250n16
las Casas, Bartolomé de, 25, 51, 169, 282n6; *Apologética historia de las Indias,* 169, 252n7, 270n16
Latin dictionary project (*Vocabulario* or *Diccionario Latino*), 36–37, *112, 113, 127,* 128, 131–32, 224–25
Leardo, Franco and Pedro Juan, 168, 281n2
legal texts in Hernando's library, 50
Leo X (pope), 32
Leo Africanus, 32
Leonardo da Vinci, 71
Lerche, Cornelius, 179
lettere di compagnia, 67
lettere merchantesche, 66–67
letters of credit, 64, 65
libraries other than Hernando's: Alexandria, library of, 5, 107, 137–38, 141, 273n32; Biblioteca Ambrosiana, Milan, 195–96; Biblioteca Capitular, Seville, 138, 171, 172, 180, 190; Biblioteca Corviniana, Hungary, 6–7, 108; Biblioteca di San Marco, Florence, 5, 7, 16, 29; Biblioteca Laurenziana, Florence, 45, 139; Biblioteca Malatestina, Cesena, 139; Biblioteca Marciana, Venice, 5, 6, 34, 250–51nn16,17; Bodleian Library, Oxford, 276n57; Córdoba, Umayyad library at, 138; John Carter Brown library, Rhode Island, Hernandine materials at, 172; Pierpont Morgan Library, New York, Hernandine materials at, 172–73; Pisistratus, library of, Athens, 137; public library, concept of, 4–6, 138, 282–83n13; Salamanca cathedral library, 138–39; Seville University Library, 171, 173; University of Salamanca library, 25; Vatican

Library (Biblioteca Palatina), 5, 25, 31–34, 139–43, 161, 250n14, 255n42; Venice, state library at, 49; Würzburg, library of Trithemius at, 49
library of Hernando Colón, 2–8, 15–54; administrative archives, early modern decoupling of libraries from, 106, 108–9; articulation of vision and purpose for, 52–54; biography of Columbus and, 15, 50–52; botanical garden, Casa de Colón/ Casa de Goles, Seville, 45–47, 167–68, 258n61; *cabinet de curiosité*, differentiation from, 134; cartographic interests and, 101–2, 106–10, 123–24; Casa de Contratación and, 13–14, 46, 53, 106, 109; childhood and youth, books collected during, 21–24, 252n9; Columbus's archive forming original nucleus of, 15–21; date of acquisition, earliest books recording, 26–27; Florence, books acquired while in, 35; Germany, Low Countries, Switzerland, and Venice (1521), purchasing books in, 38–39, 47–48; inclusive accession model for, 139; indices and other paratexts, interest in, 29, *30*, 35–37, 43; institutionalization of projects, 37–38; knowledge organization, interest in tools of, 29, 37, 47, 53–54; librarians recruited for, 43, 45, 48–50; *Memorial al Emperador* requesting funds to support, 52–53, 75, 149, 188, 245–47; mercantile/ financial culture and, 72–77, 197–98, 289n60; modern wall-system bookshelves, development of, 42; order and life, relationship between, 15, 38–39, 54; other library projects as patterns for, 3–8, 29–35, 49; permanent home (Casa de Colón/ Casa de Goles, Seville) for, 43–45; physical layout of, 158–63, 229–30; printed images, collection of, 39–42; Reformist/Lutheran texts in, 38–39, *40–41*, 80–81, 89, 172, 178, 189, 257–58n56; Rome, books acquired while in, 27–35; sales of extra copies from library, plan for, 197, 288–89n59; second voyage of Hernando to New World (1509), books from, 24–26; shelf marks and shelf order, 161, 180, 266n66; shipwrecked books, 38–39, 73, 78. *See also* catalogues and cataloguing; ephemeral works, or *obrezillas;* indices and other paratexts
library of Hernando Colón after Hernando, 167–98; acquisition of additional books, Hernando's directives for, 232–37; catalogues, 178–80, 182, *183, 184*, 186, 188, 189, 191; collapse of Cathedral library ceiling (1986) and aftermath, 189–92; early studies of (before 1986), 187–89; in eighteenth and nineteenth centuries, 181–86, *183, 184;* El Escorial, movement of some materials to, 172, 193–94, 284n18; erosion and scattering of collection, 169–73, 178, 181, 182; family and descendants of Hernando's brother and, 168–69, 182–85, 227, 236, 281n2, 282n5; financial situation at Hernando's death, 168, 281n3; Inquisition and, 170, 173–79, *174–77;* Las Cuevas, manuscripts at monastery of, 282n8; Loaysa, rescue and recataloguing of books by, 178, 179–80; memorial of founder directed for, 231; rebinding and cutting down volumes, 179–80; sale

library of Hernando Colón after Hernando (continued)
and demolition of house and garden, 168; San Pablo, moved to convent of, 169–70, 237, 282n7; Seville Cathedral, in custody of, 168–73, 179–86, 189–91, 236–37, 287n35; significance of, 192–98; will and testament of Hernando, plans for library in, 227–37
Libro de las Ciencias, 53
Libro de las Materias, 45, 50, 53, *127,* 148, 155–57, 206, 207–10
Libro de las Profecías (*Book of Prophecies*), 23–24, 62, 100, 154–55, 238, 253n14, 273n39
Libro de los Epítomes, 127, 148–55; Copenhagen manuscript (scribal copy), 148–49, *152–53,* 155, 178–79, 291n3; dating of, 148, 149, 157; ephemera/*obrezillas* in, 92, 266n72; Juan Pérez's *Memoria* on, 205–7; Lutheran/Reformist texts in, 38–39, *40–41;* rediscovery of scribal copy, 9, *10,* 178–79, 192; Seville manuscript (draft copy), 148, *150–51,* 155, 291n3; use and purpose of, 43, 53, 149–55, 204–5, 245–47; on Vives's *Declamationes Sullanae, 83,* 265n56
Libro de los Privilegios (*Book of Privileges*), 62–63, 65, 73, 282n8
Libro de Mercantie, 71, 262–63n34
Lichtenberger, Johannes, 84
life and order, relationship between, 15, 38–39, 54
Linacre, John, 250n16
linear accounting and representations, moving beyond, 58–62
Lipsius, Justus, *De bibiothecis syntagma,* 195–96, 288n55
literatura de cordel, 89
Loaysa, Juan de, 178, 179–80, 287n44, 288n54
Loci communes (commonplace book kept by Hernando), 93, *94,* 156, 160, 161, 196, 277n13, 279n34, 280n46
Longolio, Christoforo, 29
Lotharingian Axis, 69–70
Louis XII (king of France), 91
Louvain, Collegium Trilingue, 47–48
Low Countries, Hernando traveling to, 38, 47–48
Lowry, M., 250n16
Lucan, 272n28
Lucian of Samosata, 22, 173, *176, 177,* 286n24
Lucretius, 155; *De rerum natura,* 28, *150–54,* 254n31
Luis Colón (nephew and heir of Hernando), 168–69, 227, 236, 281n1, 282n5
luoghi, 63, 65, 261n21
Luther, Martin, and Lutheranism, 38–39, *40–41,* 80–81, 89, 172, 178, 189, 257–58n56; *De captivitate babylonica ecclesiae,* 80; *Explanatio dominicae orationis,* 80; *Tractatus De his qui ad ecclesias co[n]fugiunt,* 80, 264n52

Macrobius, 272n28
Madrid, Hernandine materials at libraries of, 173
Magellan, Ferdinand, 2, 103, 118
Magnússon, Árni, 178
Maifreda, Germano, 75–76, 260n9
Malaga, siege of (1487), 57
Mandeville, Bernard, 103
Manuel II Palaeologus (Byzantine emperor), 107
maps. *See* cartography
Marco Polo, 16, 57, 99, 106, 191, 251n3, 271n21

María Álvarez de Toledo, 169
Marignano, Battle of, 35
Marín Martínez, Tomás, 9, 128, 132, 179, 189, 252n9, 258n57, 276n1, 277n15
markings, symbols, or biblioglyphs, 81, 82, 136, 158, 159–60, *200,* 210–18, 219–21, 265n54, 288n58, 290n12, 290nn14,15
Martellus, Henricus, 105, 271n20
Martins, Fernan, 104
Marucelli, Francesco, 60; *Mare Magnum Omnium Materiarum,* 195
Masséna, Victor, 284n19
Matal, Jean, *Iter Italicum,* 255n42
Matthias Corvinus (king of Hungary), 7, 250n7
Maximilian (Holy Roman emperor), 84, 88
Mazzolini, Silvestro da Prierio, 28, 254n30
McDonald, Mark P., 9, 133, 136, 192
Medici, as bankers, 64, 67
Medici, Cosimo de', 5, 7, 139, 251n17, 272n26
Medici, Giovanni de' (Cardinal), 139
Medici, Lorenzo de', 8, 76; *Le selue damore,* 55
Medici, Lorenzo di Pierfrancesco de', 123
Medina, Pedro de, 259n73
Medina del Campo, Feria de, 69, 73, 232–33, 263nn41–],42
Melanchthon, Philip, 258n56
Memoria de los Dibujos o Pinturas (Registrum C), 72, *127,* 133–36, 203–4
"Memoria de plantas y ortelanos" (for garden at Casa de Colón), 46
Memorial al Emperador, 52–53, 75, 149, 188, 245–47
Memorial de la política necesaria y útil *restauración a la República de España,* 261n22
Memorial de los Libros Naufragados (Registrum A), 38–39, 72, 78, *127,* 143–46, *144–45,* 160–61, 225, 278–79n34
Méndez, Diego, 237
Mendoza, Gaspard de, *La copie dune lettre mandee de Thunes,* 90
mercantile and financial culture, 8–9, 12–13, 55–96; banking system and exchange rates, 63–66, 261n23; book-buying travels of Hernando in Europe and, 73, 77–81; cartography and trade rights with Moluccas, 118, 119, 120; catalogues/cataloguing and, 165; Columbus Day exchange and, 16, 57; contractual life of, 75–76; double-entry bookkeeping, 70–72, 260n9, 262n31; ephemeral works, or *obrezillas,* and, 80, 81–96 (*see also* ephemeral works, or *obrezillas*); importance to universalizing/exploratory projects, 55–58; information-sharing tools developed by, 66–67; library of Hernando and, 72–77, 197–98, 289n60; linear accounting and representations, moving beyond, 58–62, *61;* network used by Hernando, 69–70; purchase notes of Hernando and, 77; sales of extra copies from library, plan for, 197, 288–89n59; Tagliente's *Libro d'abaco* and other practical handbooks, 67, *68, 69,* 262n27; tools for conceptualizing, rationalizing, and coordinating, 57–58; voyages of Columbus and, 9, 56–57, 58, 62–63
Messahalla, 31
Mexía, Pedro, 109, 259n73, 273n32; *Historia Imperial y Cesárea,* 192,

Mexía, Pedro (continued) 273n32; *Silva de Varia Lección*, 137, 138
Michelangelo, 45, 139
Michelozzi, Michelozzo, 272n26
Milan: acquisition of additional books, Hernando's will and testament on, 233, 236; Biblioteca Ambrosiana, 195–96
millenarian outlook, 3, 4, 6, 9, 11, 23, 49, 62–63, 70, 85, 102, 105, 117, 192
Mirabelli, Domenico Nanni, *Polyanthea*, 280n46
Mirabilis Urbis Roma, 255n33
modernity: catalogues of Hernando as reflection of, 96; Columbus's "discovery" of New World and, 1–2; combination of early financial capitalism/politico-religious *Universitas Christiana* and, 13; language and empire, links between, 27; print, emergence of, 10
Modesti, Giovanni Antonio, 258n56
Molina, Argote de, 171
Moluccas, trade rights with, 118, 119, 120
Monardes, Nicolas, 47
More, Thomas: Lucian, Basel edition of, 173, *176*; *Utopia*, 106, 271n21, 283n14
Müller von Königsberg, Johannes. *See* Regiomontanus
Münster, Sebastian, *Cosmographia*, 275n51
Munzer, Hieronymus, 253n14
Murillo, Bartolomé Estaban, 180
Muro Orejón, Antonio, 187, 189

"narrow earth" theories, 7, 16
Naude, Gabriel, *Advis pour dresser une bibliotheque*, 196
Navagero, Andrea, 34, 256n43
navigator, Hernando's experience as, 99–101
Nebrija, Elio Antonio de, 4, 7, 11, 99, 250n9, 274nn44,45; *De mensuris, De ponderibus*, and *De numeris*, 27, 116, 264n43; *Dictionarium Hispaniarum in latinem sermonem translatio*, 277n15; *Dictionarium sive vocabularium*, 132; *Gramática de la Lengua Castellana*, 74, 263–64n43; *In A. Persium Flaccum . . . interpretatio*, 22; *In cosmographiae libros introductorium multo quam antea castigatius (Cosmography)*, 111–17; *Introduction to the Cosmography of Pomponius Mela*, 22; *Introductiones Latinae*, 22, 270n13; *Tabla de la diversidad de los días y las horas*, 116, 117; *Vocabula Barbara*, 80, *95*, 96, 252nn7,13
Nemopuceno González de León, Juan, 181
Newton, Isaac, 193
Niccoli, Niccolò, 5, 7, 272n26
Nicolas V (pope; formerly Tomasso Parentucelli), 5, 7, 25, 29, 31, 139–40, 250nn13,14, 251n17
Nicolas de Cusa, 91
Noah, genealogy of, 193, 194, 249n5
North Passage, Cabot's search for, 57

obrezillas. *See* ephemeral works, or *obrezillas*
Oderigo, Nicolò, 63
Oecolampadius, Ioannes, 258n56
Olivares, Gaspar de Guzmán, Count-Duke of, 179, 286n28
ombú plant, Cartuja de las Cuevas, 46
order and life, relationship between, 15, 38–39, 54

Ortega, Maestro *(sumista)*, 157, 289n8
Orthodox and western Christianity, efforts to reconcile, 6
Ottoman Empire, 4, 6, 9, 56, 90, 104, 138, 250n7
Ovid, 116, 272n28; *Metamorphoses*, *19*, 104

Pace, Richard, 81
Pacioli, Luca: *Divina Proportione*, 71; *Summa de arithmetica, geometria, proportiani e proportionalità*, 70–71, 260n9, 262n36; *Tractatus de computis et scripturis*, 71
Padrón Real, 98, 109, 132, 197, 243–44
Palaemon, *Grammatice ars*, 132, 277n15
Palmerio, Mattia, *Letter of Aristeas*, 137–38
Palomba, Giovanni Battista, 136
Pané, Fray Ramón, 21, 51, 252n7
Panonius, Janus, 78
paratexts. *See* indices and other paratexts
Parentucelli, Tomasso (later Pope Nicholas V), 5, 7, 25, 29, 31, 139–40, 250nn13,14, 251n17
Paris: acquisition of books by Hernando from, 27, 77, 81; National Library, Hernandine materials at, 172, 186; will and testament of Hernando on acquisition of additional books from, 69, 73, 232–37
Pasamonte, Miguel de, 73
Pasquil, *libretti* by, 266n72
Paul of Middelburg, 84
Pedro de Salamanca, 91
Perestrello, Bartolomeu, 252n8
Pérez, Juan. *See* Juan Pérez
Peril, Robert, 258n58
Perossino della Rotonda, *Lamento de Bartolomeo Dalviano*, 89, 267n75
Perotti, Niccolò, *Cornucopia*, 132, 217, 277n15
Peter Martyr d'Anghiera, 7–8, 11, 56, 76, 197, 253n14, 270n14; *Decades de Orbe Novo*, 22, 80, 96, 197, 250n9, 252nn7,13, 256n44
Petrarch, 5, 34, 283n13
Pettegree, Andrew, 38
Peuerbach, Georg von, 91
Pezzolo, Luciano, 66
Philip II (king of Spain), 172, 178
Philip IV (king of Spain), 179
Piccolomini, Aeneas Silvius (later Pope Pius II), *Historia rerum ubique gestarum*, 3–4, 7, 16, *19*, *20*, 49, 99, 103–4, 169, 193, 249–50n6, 271n20
Pico della Mirandola, Giovanni, 253n22
Piero della Francesca, *De prospectiva pingendi*, 142
Pierpont Morgan Library, New York, Hernandine materials at, 172–73
Pinakes, 138
Pinelo, Antonio de León, 275n52
Pinicianus, Johannes, 80, 96, 264n52
Pisa, Council of (1511), 91
Pisistratus, library of, Athens, 137
Pius II (pope). *See* Piccolomini, Aeneas Silvius
planispheres, *20*, 59, 104
Plato, 22, 107, 122, 141, 142, 149, 266n72
Pleitos Colombinos, 28, 50
Pliny the Elder, *Natural History*, 3, 16, 22, 99, 102, 103, 106, 116, 251n3, 271–72n22, 272n27
Pliny the Younger, *Letters*, 28
Poliziano, Angelo, 31, 280n46; *Panepistemon*, 93, 196, 268n89
Polyglot Bible, 8
Pomerius, Julianus, 265n61

Pomponius Laeto, 29
Pomponius Mela: *Cosmographia,* 22, 35, 102, 114, 256–57n48; *De situ orbis,* 173, *174–76,* 272n27
Pontano, Giovanni, *De sermone,* 76, 264n48
portolan maps, 58–60, 99, 102, 103, 105, 123
Portuondo, María M., 123
Potken, Johannes, 31
Prierio, Silvestrio di, *Commentaria in theoricas planetarum Georgii Purbachii,* 71
print: "fertile crescent" of, 38–39, 47–48; significance of emergence of, 7, 8, 9–11, 29
printers. *See* booksellers and printers
Prodi, Paolo, 76
prognostications and calendars, as printed material, 84–89, *86, 87,* 91–93
Protogenes, 142
pro vel contra marking, 81, 265n54
Psalterium Hebraeum, Graecum, Arabicum, & Chaldaeum, 48
Ptolemy, 3, 22, 67, *68,* 99, 100, 104–5, 110, 114, 119, 121, 123, 138, 142, 277n31; *Almagest,* 108; *Cosmographia,* 107, 108; *Geography,* 6, 121
Ptolemy I Soter (pharaoh), 141
public library, concept of, 4–6, 138, 282–83n13
publishing. *See* booksellers and printers; print
Purbachius, Giorgius, 71, 108, 254n30, 267–68n82; *Quadratum geometricum,* 108
Pythagoras, 67, *68*

Qaitbay (Egyptian sultan), 90
quaderna di mercatura, 66–67, 262n27

Raleigh, Sir Walter, *History of the World,* 194
Ramusio, Giovanni Baptista, 34; *Delle Navigationi et Viaggi,* 34, 256n44
Randles, W. G. L., 274n44
Rangoni, Tomasso Gianotti, 88
Raphael, *The School of Athens,* Stanza della Segnatura, Vatican, 141–43
real cédula, 122
Reformist/Lutheran texts, 38–39, *40–41,* 80–81, 89, 172, 178, 189, 257–58n56
Regiomontanus (Johannes Müller von Königsberg), 6–7, 58, 59, 91, 108, 121; *Epitoma in Almagestum Ptolemaei,* 108, 253n15; *Epytoma Ioannis de monte regio in almagestum ptolemei,* 108
Registrum A (Memorial de los Libros Naufragados), 38–39, 72, 78, *127,* 143–46, *144–45,* 160–61, 225, 278–79n34
Registrum B (Índice *Numeral),* 85, *87, 127,* 146–47, *154,* 160, 161, *162,* 206, 207, 222–23, 266–67n72, 281n57, 283n14
Registrum C (Memoria de los Dibujos o Pinturas), 72, *127,* 133–36, 203–4
Reisch, Gregor, *Margarita philosophica,* 279n34, 280n46
Renan, Ernest, 188
Reuchlin, John, 250n16
Ribero, Diego, 120, 121, 243, 275n52
Riberol, Francisco de, 261n16
Ricci, Saminiato de', *Manuale di Mercatura,* 261–62n26
Rodriguez, Maria, 46, 47
Romanticism, and Columbus's "discovery" of New World, 1
Rome: acquisition of additional books, Hernando's will and testament on, 232–37; Hernando's sojourn in, 27–35, 71, 141, 254n25; libraries of,

139–43; *obrezillas* on flood forecast for (1524), 86–88; sack of, 140
Rosenkrantz, Jens, 179
Rosiglia, Marco, 31, 255n35
Ruiz Asencio, José Manuel, 191
Rumeu de Armas, Antonio, 51; *Hernando Colon, historiador del descubrimiento de America,* 189
Rusconi, Roberto, 23
Ruysch, Johannes, *Universalior Cogniti Orbis Tabula,* 272n26

Sabellicus, *Enneads,* 51
Sacrobosco, Johannes, 110, 272nn28,29
Salamanca: cathedral library at, 138–39; library at University of, 25
Salutati, Coluccio, 107, 283n13; *De fato et fortuna,* 4–5
Sand, George, 188
Sanudo, Marín, 34–35, 92, 189, 256n46, 268n86
Savonarola, 91
Scaliger, Joseph Justus, *De emendatione temporum,* 193
Schedel, Hartmann: annotated copy of Piccolomini's *Historia* belonging to, 249–50n6; *Liber Chronicarum,* 3–4, 80, 250n7
Scholasticism, 3, 11, 21
science, concept of, 290n10
scudo di marco, 65–66
Scuola di Rialto, Venice, 71
Second Voyage of Columbus (1493–96), 21
Seneca the Younger: manuscript copy of life of, 36, 257n49; *Medea,* 24, 36, 187; *Tragedies,* 35, 257n49
Sentencia de las Dueñas, 50, 52
Septuagint, 138
Sepúlveda, Juan Ginés de, 89, 266n70
Seville: Biblioteca Capitular, 138, 171, 172, 180, 190; Biblioteca Colombina, 28, 86, 129, 148, 170, 180, 182, 186, 188, 190; botanical garden, Casa de Colón/Casa de Goles, 45–47, 167–68, 258n61; Casa de Colón/Casa de Goles, 43–45, 158, 167–68; Cathedral, Hernando's collection in custody of, 168–73, 179–86, 189–91, 236–37, 287n35; University Library, 171, 173. *See also* Casa de Contratación, Hernando's cartographical project at; library of Hernando Colón
shelf marks and shelf order, 161, 180, 266n66
shipwrecked books, 38–39, 73, 78, 143, 278–79n34. See also *Memorial de los Libros Naufragados*
Silber, Eucharius and Marcellus, 31
Silva de Varia Lección, 273n32, 278n20
Silvia, Feliciano de, *El séptimo libro de Amadís* and *Historia de Melosina,* 103, 270nn13,14
Sixtus IV (pope), 31, 140, 250n14
Soja, Edward W., 271n18
Solis, 242
Stafileo, Giovanni, 254n27
Stancati, Tomasso, 265–66n62
Steuco, Agostino, 256n45
Stoeffler, Johannes, *Calendarium romanum magnum,* 91
Strabo, 3, 6, 100, 103, 114, 142, 155, 272n28; *Geography,* 278nn23,32, 283n15
Strozzi, Palla, 107
Studium Urbis, Rome, 28, 29
Suda, 138, 278n24
Suetonius: Hernando's "indice completissimo" to, 29, 30; *Lives of the Twelve Caesars,* 28, 173, 254n30

Sumaria plurium iuditiorum anni MDXV, 92
sumistas, 163–64, 165–66, 228–29, 234–36, 289n60, 290n3
Supplementum, 274n45
Swift, Jonathan, *Academy of Lagado,* 109
Switzerland, Hernando traveling to, 38, 47–48
symbols, markings, or biblioglyphs, 81, 82, 136, 158, 159–60, *200,* 210–18, 219–21, 265n54, 288n58, 290n12, 290nn14,15
syphilis, *guyacam* plant used to treat, 47

Tabares, Rafael, 181–92
Tabla de Autores y Ciencias or *Annotaciones, 127,* 136, 158–60, 210–18
Tafur, Pero, 138
Tagliente, Girolamo, *Libro d'abaco,* 67, *68, 69,* 262n27
Taíno, 21, 47, 51, 252n7
Tartaglia, Niccolò Fontana, 260n9
Tattara, Giuseppe, 66
Theophrastus, 278n32
Third Voyage of Columbus (1498–1500), 21, 23, 100
Thomas Aquinas, Saint: Bonaiuto's *Triumph of Thomas Aquinas* (Santa Maria Novella, Florence), 141, 142, 277n31; *Summa Theologica,* 22
Thomas Beckett, Saint, biography of, 253n23
Thucydides, Valla's edition of, 5, 8, 250n9, 276n57
Tissard, François, 27, 48, 253n24
Titian, 258n58
tombstone, Hernando's design for, *61,* 231, 260n10
Tomeis, Antonio de, *Convivium Scientarum,* 32–33, 140
Tordesillas, Treaty of (1494), 118, 119, 122
Torres, Dr., medical recipes of, 25
Toscanelli, Paolo dal Pozzo, 7, 16, 104, 107, 108, 169, 270–71n16
Tous de Monsalve, Nicolas Maestre, 182
trade. *See* mercantile and financial culture
translatio studii and *translatio imperii,* 74
travels of Hernando Colón: in Germany, England, Low Countries, Switzerland, and Venice (1520–21 and 1529), 38, 47–48, 73, 77–81, 168; Italian, use of, 236; to New World, 11–12, 24–26, 62, 100; Rome, sojourn in, 27–35, 71, 254n25
Traversari, Ambrogio, 6
Trinkaus, Charles, 250n13
Trithemius, Johannes, 35, 49, 256n47
Triumph of Christ, 39, 258n58
Tunisia, Charles V's expedition against (1535), 90

universalizing projects. *See* Hernando Colón, universalizing projects of
Universitas Christiana, 13, 56, 74

Vadian, Joachim, 173, 284–85n23
Valdés, Fernando de, 173
Valencia, Ignacio de, 181,286–87n31
Valla, Lorenzo, 4, 5, 8, 74–75, 78, 99, 250n9, 263n42, 276n57
van de Lare, William, *Regula Transporti,* 262n29
Varro, 116
Vaseus, Johannes (Jan Waes), 49, 259n74
Vatican Library (Biblioteca Palatina), 5, 25, 31–34, 139–43, 161, 250n14, 255n42

Vatican Palace, Stanza della Segnatura, Raphael's *The School of Athens*, 141–43
Venerable Bede, 100
Venetian Academy, *Somma delle Opere*, 196
Venetian method, 71
Venice: acquisition of additional books, Hernando's will and testament on, 232–37; Biblioteca Marciana, 5, 6, 34, 250–51nn16,17; Fondaco de Tedeschi, 70; Giorgio Cini Foundation, Hernandine materials at, 172, 284–85n19; Hernando purchasing books in, 38, 47–48, 73; state library at, 49
Ventallol, Joan, *Practica Mercantivol*, 261n23
Veragua, Duke of, 182
Verrazano, Giovanni da, 187
Vesalius, *De humani corporis fabrica*, 194
Vespucci, Amerigo, 107, 109, 187, 242; *De ora antartica per regem Portugalliae pridem inventa*, 123; *Mundus Novus*, 123
Vespucci, Antonio, 107
Veteranis, Sebastianus, 28, 71, 108, 254n30, 268n82; *Disputatio de eccentricis et epiciclis*, 91
Vigli, Fabio, 33–34, 140
Vilches, Elvira, 62–63, 263n30
Villasante, Antonio de, 47
Viñola, paintings by, 133
Vipera, Giovanni Mercurio, 254n27
Virgil, 142, 272n28
Visigoths, 84
Vivero, Gonzalo de, 138
Vives, Juan Luis, 4, 74, 78, 89, 99, 250n9, 265n56, 268n88; *Declamationes Sullanae*, 74, 81–82, *83*, 265n56; *De disciplinis*, 76, 93, 264n47; *Introductio ad Sapientiam*, 92–93
Vizinho, Jose, 103, 114, 270n15
vocabulario or census of Spanish towns, 36, 37, 38, 130, 131, 158
Vocabulario or *Diccionario Latino*, 36–37, *112*, *113*, *127*, 128, 131–32, 224–25

Waes, Jan (Johannes Vaseus), 49, 259n74
Wagner, Klaus, 80–81, 171, 178, 189, 191, 268n86
Weimar chart, 121–22, 275n52
Wilson-Lee, Edward, 191
Wittgenstein, Ludwig, 54
women, formalization of botanical knowledge of, 47

Zacuto, Abraham, 21, 105, 114, 116, 273nn37,39; *Almanach Perpetuum*, 114, *115*, 270n15
Zambelli, Paola, 88, 268n83
Zamora, Alonso de, 46
Zamora, Margarita, 62
Zúñiga, Diego Ortiz de, 171–72
Zúñiga, Don Juan de, 114